FLORIDA FIASCO

FLORIDA FIASCO

Rampant Rebels on the Georgia-Florida Border
1810-1815

REMBERT W. PATRICK

UNIVERSITY OF GEORGIA PRESS
ATHENS

Paperback edition, 2010
© 1954 by the University of Georgia Press
Athens, Georgia 30602
www.ugapress.org
All rights reserved
Printed digitally in the United States of America

The Library of Congress has cataloged the hardcover
edition of this book as follows:
Library of Congress Cataloging-in-Publication Data
LCCN Permalink: http://lccn.loc.gov/53013265

Patrick, Rembert Wallace, 1909–
    Florida fiasco; rampant rebels on the Georgia-Florida
    border, 1810–1815.
    x, 359 p. 24 cm.
    Bibliography: p. 337–344.
    1. Florida—History—Spanish colony, 1784–1821. 2.
United States—Foreign relations—1809–1817. I. Title.
F314 .P25
975.953-13265

Paperback ISBN-13: 978-0-8203-3549-0
ISBN-10: 0-8203-3549-5

TO
JULIEN C. YONGE
SCHOLAR, EDITOR, AND FRIEND

Contents

	Preface	ix
1	George Mathews, Special Agent	1
2	Retrospective Journey	16
3	Failure in the West	32
4	Below the St. Marys	40
5	Organizing the Revolution	55
6	That Damn Frenchman Laval	70
7	The Capture of Fernandina	83
8	On to St. Augustine	99
9	Revolution Denied	114
10	Revolution Revived	128
11	War and the Floridas	144
12	Life in the Occupied Land	158
13	The General Retires	174
14	The Black and Reds	179
15	Newnan Meets Defeat	195
16	Plan of Conquest	211
17	The Tennessee Volunteers	225
18	Jackson's Volunteers	237
19	Recalcitrant Senators	248
20	Retreat of the Invader	254
21	Rampaging Rebels	268
22	Tommies and Tars	284
23	The Revival of Anarchy—and Peace	295
	Notes	305
	Bibliography	337
	Index	345

Preface

IN 1945 THE EDITOR OF THE *Florida Historical Quarterly* handed me two letters with a request to edit and prepare them for publication. "You can do it over the weekend," he said; and after glancing at the letters, I nodded agreement. How naive we were.

For almost five years I have followed the lead given by those letters which were written by General John McIntosh just before the War of 1812. The trail has led from the University of Florida to libraries in Washington, New York, Atlanta, Athens, Savannah, St. Augustine, Jacksonville, and Tallahassee. From the site of former Coleraine, Georgia, I have followed the St. Marys River east as it winds between Georgia and Florida to Cumberland Sound, and the Amelia River south to the Atlantic Ocean. I have sailed between the Florida mainland and Fort George and Talbot islands to the St. Johns and up that river to Picolata. Isaac Flood Arnow of St. Marys, Georgia, directed me as we explored the country where John Houstoun McIntosh lived and where General George Mathews enlisted volunteers for the conquest of Florida. I have covered the northern tip of Amelia Island, walked on the banks of the St. Johns, stood among the ruins of Moosa Old Fort, and climbed the parapets of the Castillo de San Marcos in St. Augustine.

All of this stemmed from those brief letters which aroused my curiosity. In historical lore General John McIntosh led a revolutionary movement in East Florida before the War of 1812 and with the support of American military forces almost conquered the Spanish province. Yet when the sources were assembled for editing the McIntosh letters, it was evident that General McIntosh could not have been the leader of the "Patriot Revolution" of East Florida.

Who then headed that revolution? What were the causes, the course, and the results of those disturbances which kept East Florida in turmoil from 1810 to 1815? The answers to these questions were found in the diplomatic affairs of the United States, Great Britain, Spain, France, and Russia, and in the plotting and double-dealing by men of political stature as well as little known politicos. Washington, Jefferson, Madison, Monroe, and Jackson, the Congress of the United States, governors and the legislatures of Southern states, frontiersmen and aristocrats, Indians and Negroes, smugglers and robbers, Spanish militiamen and British seamen, and land-hungry American farmers, all were involved in the story of intrigue and war. Above all others there was a lovable old Irishman and former governor of Georgia, General George Mathews, who lived the happiest and saddest hours of his life while serving the United States in East Florida.

The story of American aggression in Spanish-Florida could not have been pieced together without the resources and the intelligent help of the staffs of the P. K. Yonge Memorial Library of Florida History at the University of Florida, the National Archives, the Library of Congress, the New York Public Library, the Georgia Department of Archives and History, the Georgia State Library, the Georgia Historical Society Library, the University of Georgia Library, the Florida Historical Society Library, and the Florida State Library. The author is indebted to numbers of librarians, and especially to Elizabeth Drewry of the War Records Office of the National Archives, Mary G. Bryan of the Georgia Department of Archives and History, Alberta Johnson of the Florida Historical Society, and Harriet Skofield of the Yonge Library. Anne Goldsborough Fisher of the Georgia Department of Archives and History graciously investigated and supplied many of the first names of men who had minor roles in the Patriot Revolution.

Not only did Julien C. Yonge suggest this study, but he also searched for material, read the completed manuscript, and offered many valuable criticisms. In this as in all things, my wife has given a sympathetic understanding in addition to constructive criticisms and critical readings of the manuscript and the galley and page proofs. Junius E. Dovell read the text and made a number of helpful suggestions. The patience and care of Donna J. Barrow and Jeannette Belcher in typing the manuscript contributed much to the completed volume.

REMBERT W. PATRICK

Gainesville, Florida.

1

George Mathews, Special Agent

IN LATE JANUARY OF 1811 THE young and unkempt town of Washington was covered by the mantle of winter. Coatings of ice magnified limbs and branches of the Lombardy poplars that lined Pennsylvania Avenue from Capitol Hill to the White House. The street, usually a slough of mud, was now frozen solid, and in ditches on either side stagnant water had become slimy, greenish ice.

On the avenue's footpath General George Mathews walked briskly toward the executive mansion. Around him provincial Washington was throbbing with life, for Congress was in session and the United States was the most important neutral in a world at war. On the Hill and in the White House decisions faced the leaders of the young republic — momentous decisions, which at best might result in territorial additions to an already extensive domain or, at worst, war with Great Britain and her allies.

Most pressing of all questions confronting President James Madison was whether to maintain neutrality or yield to popular clamor and occupy the Floridas. General Mathews believed the president was yielding and in his eagerness to be the agent, was convinced that he had been chosen to seize the Floridas. Belief and conviction were soon to be confirmed in the conference with Madison to which Mathews was hastening, for the president was as anxious as the general to annex these Spanish provinces to the United States. So strong was Madison's desire that it may have warped his sense of right and wrong and blinded him to international justice and morality.

For almost twenty years Europe had been torn by war, and during those years presidents Washington, Adams, and Jefferson had maintained neutrality even at the cost of national insult. Although President Madison made conscientious efforts to follow the diplomatic policy of his predecessors, he soon found himself advocating an increasingly unpopular course. A wave of nationalism was sweeping the United States, and except for those who feared for their substantial fortunes, the people demanded action to protect American sailors, to secure neutral rights, and to uphold the honor of the flag.

More fundamental than national honor as well as more impelling to the administration was national opportunity. Even the political amateur saw the advantage which England had acquired in recent decades. Astute Britons had seen in the Spanish rebellion against Napoleonic domination, and in the wars of independence in Latin America, not only the chance to defeat France but also an opportunity to pick the breast meat from the Spanish colonial empire. With money, supplies, and men, Great Britain supported and befriended the Spanish patriots in the Iberian peninsula while acquiring economic leadership, and even territory, in the Spanish empire of the new world.

These sharp English practices impressed the nationalists of the United States and suggested emulation rather than condemnation of Great Britain. If distant England could gain so much, surely the favorable geographic position of the United States and the critical world war which occupied the full energies of Great Britain and Spain would be utilized to American advantage. Since both England and Spain were tied down by war, the nationalists asserted that the United States should grab Canada and the Floridas, thereby adding territory which God in his wisdom surely intended to be American.

Allies of these ardent nationalists were Southern and Western farmers — land-hungry farmers who resented the foreigner on their border, hated the Indian, and coveted all land contiguous to their own. In the congressional elections of 1810, these farmers moved to the polls to elect John C. Calhoun, Henry Clay, Felix Grundy, William Lowndes, and more than sixty other new congressmen, most of whom were declared opponents of a "peace at any price" policy. Although these "War Hawks" must await the convening of the twelfth Congress on November 4, 1811, the influence of their election was immediately apparent. Even before the election, the force of public opinion encouraged President Madison to aggressive action on the Florida problem; and soon after the election he moved toward strengthening the armed forces and other preparations for war. Thus by January, 1811, the United States, like a fledgling vulture, hovered outside the vortex of world conflict, hoping to snatch tempting morsels in North America from England and her weak and dependent ally, Spain.

Of these tantalizing prizes, Canada and the Floridas, West Florida was most immediately available, for in that province the authority of Spain was almost extinct, the quondam American population large, and rebellion in progress. On October 27, 1810, Madison issued a proclamation in which he stated that the territory of West Florida, as far east as the Perdido River, by right and requisite of the title acquired in the Louisiana Purchase, should be occupied for and on behalf of the United States.[1] The territory, he declared, would be held for future fair and friendly adjustment. Acting on instructions from Madison, William C. C. Claiborne, governor of the Orleans Territory, occupied West Florida to the Pearl River and began negotiations with the Spanish governor, Vincente Folch. The latter had only the weapons of diplomacy to save the rest of Florida for Spain. Broadly hinting the necessity of surrendering all the Floridas to the safe-keeping of the United States, Folch artfully convinced his correspondents that an immediate transfer of both East and West Florida would be made to authorized representatives of the United States.

By this time Madison's desire for the Floridas flamed high. Successful accomplishment of his objective required a confidential agent and authorization by Congress. Secrecy was essential, for even an intimation of the plan would stir the British minister in Washington to vigorous protest and his government to action. For the selection of an agent, Madison turned to his friend Senator William Harris Crawford of Georgia. Without hesitation Crawford suggested General George Mathews, who had been investigating the situation along the Florida border for the administration[2] and who would be eager for an appointment adding to his existing authority in confidential affairs of state.

With this problem on the way to solution, Madison threw the full force of his administration to securing congressional approval for the occupation of East Florida. A letter from Governor Folch, dated December 2, 1810, aided the president, for the governor had stated: "I have decided on delivering this province to the United States under an equitable capitulation, provided I do not receive succor from the Havana or Vera Cruz during the present month. . . ."[3] On January 3, 1811, Madison sent a confidential request to Congress for legislation which would enable the United States to take advantage of its opportunity.[4] By the secret act and resolution of January 15, 1811, Congress sanctioned occupation of the Floridas east of the Perdido River, if willingly delivered by the local authorities or if necessary to prevent seizure by a foreign power. President Madison was further empowered to use the army and navy and up to one hundred thousand dollars to secure the area.[5]

Thus it was on a cold morning in January, 1811, that George Mathews walked the streets of Washington. Heedless of the weather, his tanned and wrinkled face glowed with warmth at the thought of once more serving his country. In his old age he believed he was to act as the agent of President Madison, just as he had in his youth served General George Washington.

George Mathews was a curious, almost unbelievable character. In the backwoods and on a dangerous frontier he could hold his own with any man, and in spite of his rough appearance and near illiteracy, his mind was keen and alert. He had crammed into his seventy-odd years more vivid experiences and dangerous living than was usual in the lifetimes of a score of ordinary men.

His father, John Mathews, was an Irish immigrant who had settled in western Virginia shortly after 1735. For years after his birth on August 30, 1739, George played and explored in the woods surrounding his home. While still a youth he took over his father's farm, and before the American Revolution, he claimed to have amassed a sizable fortune.[6]

Mathews first received public notice soon after the opening of the First Continental Congress when he distinguished himself in the bloody Battle of Point Pleasant. On October 10, 1774, Cornstalk, the able leader of the Shawnee Indians, with nearly a thousand braves attacked the colonial forces of General Andrew Lewis which were ensconced on the promontory between the Kanawha and Ohio rivers. Among the motley colonial army of raw recruits and woodsmen, dressed in hunting shirts and wearing moccasins, was George Mathews. It was a typical Indian battle where every man found a tree, and military discipline in the English sense was unknown. In the battle ensuing Mathews shot nine Indians, and escaped with no more than scratches made by the protecting branches.

This first pleasant taste of victory and his inherited Irish hatred of Great Britain led him into the Revolutionary War. He recruited a company, and later as colonel of the Ninth Regiment of the Virginia line, joined Washington's army. He was wounded in the Battle of Germantown, and his men, retreating before the advancing British, failed to see him as he lay on the field. An English soldier lifted his bayonet to stab him, but his commander caught the weapon and angrily demanded, "Would you murder a wounded officer?"

Turning painfully on his back, Mathews asked, "To whom, sar, do I owe my life?"

"If you call it an obligation, sir, to me," replied the British officer as he bent over the wounded American.

Mathews eyed the British uniform above him and muttered, "Well, sar, I'll have you know I scorn a life saved by a damn Briton."

Fortunately his wounds were not fatal. After his recovery, he experienced almost two years of living hell as a captive on board a prison ship in New York harbor; but he was exchanged in time to participate in the Southern campaigns under General Nathanael Greene and to glory in the surrender of Lord Cornwallis at Yorktown.

Mathews was a natural storyteller and the war was the source of some of his tallest tales. His own part in it grew with the years. During his lifetime he was known to acknowledge but two superiors: General George Washington and the Lord Almighty. And as time passed he questioned the high standing of Washington. Mathews never forgot that he "blead from five wounds in his Country's service and sustained a loss in his private interest, of twenty thousand pounds by depreciation of our money" during the war.

While fighting in the South he bought a large tract of land on the Broad River in Georgia and established himself and family there in 1785. On his plantation at Goose Pond he built a one room log cabin in which he and his wife slept. Their daughters used the attic as a boudoir and their sons occupied another but smaller loghouse in the yard. Despite his later affluence and his high place in Georgia politics, he steadfastly refused to waste money for a more suitable house. It remained for his son, after the father's death, to build a magnificent plantation home.

Undoubtedly Mathews' frontier frugality caused some of his domestic troubles. Although he had three wives, except for one, probably his second, history is silent. After some years in Georgia, his Virginia born wife wished to visit her relatives and friends. But Mathews would not have it. Evidently she had a will and temper of her own for she took her hoarded money and departed. When in time the joys of her Virginia sojourn palled, she wrote him to come for her, since she had experienced one journey alone and did not want another. Mathews quickly replied, "I didn't take you to Virginia, and I'm not going to trouble myself to go there to bring you back." After remaining separated for a few years the state legislature granted them a final divorce, whereupon each remarried.

Family disagreements did not prevent a meteoric rise in politics. His experience in the Revolutionary War gained him the rank of brigadier-general in the Georgia State Militia and forever after the title of "general." In 1787 he became governor and on the completion of his term was elected along with Abraham Baldwin and James Jackson as the Georgia representatives to the first Congress of the United States. In 1793 he was again inaugurated as governor, but his second term was his political nemesis. He unwisely signed the infamous Yazoo land grab act, and although he made no personal profits from this notorious fraud, he never recovered from the odium attached to it. So the following years in his political career were lean ones.

In or out of politics, anecdotes which became a part of the folklore of Georgia clung to Mathews. According to one, President Madison appointed him as governor of the Mississippi Territory, but withdrew the nomination in the face of senatorial opposition. When Mathews heard of it, he hurried to Washington on horseback, tethered his horse on the White House grounds, and gave a thundering knock on the door. A responding servant reported the president busy, but Mathews stormed at him and demanded an audience.

The frightened servant ran to Madison, "There's a fellow dressed in a mighty funny suit. Calls himself Governor Mathews, and demands to see you."

"Show him in at once," ordered Madison.

Heedless of all social courtesies, Mathews immediately exploded: "Sar, if you had known me, you wouldn't have taken the nomination back; if you didn't know me, you should not have nominated me to such an important office. Now, sar, unless you can satisfy me, even though you are president of the United States, you won't be free from my ravange."

Madison appeased the angry general by making his son John supervisor of revenues for Georgia, and his second son, George, chief justice of Mississippi. Thus overwhelmed by Madison's generosity, Mathews calmed down and departed a warm friend of the president.[7]

The story is apocryphal, but with an element of truth in it. In 1798 President John Adams appointed Mathews governor of the newly created territory of Mississippi. Secretary of War James McHenry objected because Mathews was interested in the New England Mississippi Land Company, the claimant of extensive acreage in the territory. After Adams withdrew the nomination, Mathews expressed his disappointment in a letter to the secretary of state,[8] but it was 1805 before he received an appointment. In that year, under orders of Jefferson, Secretary of State Madison commissioned him judge of the Mississippi Territory. It was only a recess appointment, but in the following year he assumed the judgeship of the Orleans Territory.[9]

Mathews' long residence in Georgia, his experience in Mississippi and New Orleans, and his frequent trips along the Florida border, qualified him as an authority on the Southeast. Thus Senator Crawford recommended Mathews in the summer of 1810 when Madison was seeking a confidential agent to investigate and report on conditions in the Floridas, and again in January of 1811 for a more important mission.[10]

Mathews happened to arrive in Washington at the moment when the administration had everything in readiness to speed a special agent to West Florida. His reception by the great and near great was enthusiastic. Senator Crawford and Representative George Troup of Georgia sponsored him, and the Southern representatives and senators saw in his agency the realization of a fond dream—the acquisition of the Floridas. Even Western legislators lionized the happy general, for if Florida should be annexed Canada could not be long ignored. Conferences with Secretary of War William Eustis, Secretary of the Navy Paul Hamilton, and Secretary of State Robert Smith gave Mathews information and assurance of cooperation. Only Secretary of the Treasury Albert Gallatin cast doubt on the mission.

The final important conference with President Madison was held late in January. Although Mathews was in his seventy-second year his stride was quick and firm. He was dressed as usual without regard for fashion—only his boots were more polished and his clothes brushed more carefully. These amenities were the extent of his concessions. In one hand he held his old three-cornered cocked hat; he had on worn knee breeches, high-topped boots, and a shirt with little ruffles at the bosom and wrists. A sword, the symbol of his military valor, dangled at his side. He was short, thick-set, with stout muscular legs; he stood straight with his head thrown back, his red hair wind-blown, and his dark-blue eyes framed by a weathered face.

Mathews' eyes were on a level with those of the five-foot six-inch president. Other than in height there was no similarity in the men. One had the flavor of the outdoors, the other the pallor of the drawing room; one was open and frank in countenance, the other reserved and deceptive.[11] But the mind of the frontiersman and that of the president joined in eager desire for the Floridas. Other than this unity of desire the course and details of this conference are unknown. What Mathews thought was agreed upon is recorded, but Madison's official and private correspondence contradicts by implication the recollections of Mathews. A record of what passed between these two principal actors in the subsequent important and dramatic happenings on the Southern frontier might have prevented the interminable discussions or resolved the fierce controversies which followed. At least, the historian could place the blame where it belongs for the stain left on United States diplomacy. But such a record, if it ever existed, has not been found.

From other records, much that was said by Madison and Mathews can be reasonably surmised. Without a doubt they discussed international affairs and the local situation in West Florida. The 1808 revolt of Spanish nationalists against the regime of Napoleon and his brother Joseph had repercussions in Spain's American colonies. At this time Spain had two colonial possessions on the southern border of the United States. East Florida comprised the peninsula with a northern boundary which followed the St. Marys River to the source of its north branch and ran west to a point where the confluence of the Flint and Chattahoochee rivers formed the Apalachicola. West Florida was a narrow strip of land stretching 400 miles from the Apalachicola to the Mississippi and lying between the thirty-first parallel and the Gulf of Mexico. Other than St. Augustine and Fernandina, East Florida had no towns of note; but in West Florida there were Pensacola, Mobile, Baton Rouge, and the important rivers, Perdido, Mobile, Pascagoula, and Pearl along with many small streams which drained the rich agricultural lands of the Mississippi Territory.[12]

In contrast to the other Spanish-American colonies, the population of the Floridas was largely Anglo-Saxon. West Florida in particular had been settled by former citizens of Great Britain and the United States. Among honest farmers and merchants was a notable assortment of "land speculators, army deserters, fleeing debtors, fugitives from justice, filibusters, pirates, and other of like ilk."[13] In the district of New Feliciana, lying below the thirty-first parallel and between the Mississippi and Amite rivers, nine-tenths of the immigrants were from the United States. The district of Baton Rouge, just below Feliciana, was overwhelmingly American in composition.

On June 20, 1810, Governor David Holmes of the Mississippi Territory described the condition of these districts as one of complete anarchy. The regular authorities, who had always been open to bribery, no longer exercised their dishonest functions, and voluntary police were utterly powerless. The people were divided into three factions, the largest of which desired ultimate annexation to the United States, but shunned immediate action for fear of involving themselves in a premature revolt.[14]

Upon receipt of Holmes' letter, Robert Smith, the American secretary of state, dispatched a hasty reply. The "interesting situation in West Florida," he wrote, "has very properly engaged your attention, and I hope you will continue to observe and to detail to this Department the events which take place there. It was apprehended that the present state of the Spanish Monarchy would necessarily lead to something like what you describe . . . and therefore this government has caused enquiries to be set on foot to ascertain what were the intentions and wishes of the people of that country. If you have it in your power to aid in making these enquiries . . . do so, and . . . communicate the results to me without the loss of time."[15]

The secretary of state thought time so important, he forwarded the letter without consulting President Madison, who was vacationing at Montpelier. Madison not only concurred but also stated that Holmes should have his militia in readiness in the event of foreign interference or internal disturbance in West Florida. In either event, the president concluded, it would be proper to take care of the rights and interests of the United States.[16] Smith ordered Holmes to place his forces in readiness for any eventuality. A copy of recent instructions of the state department and an extract from a letter of Governor Claiborne of the Orleans Territory to Colonel William Wykoff were also enclosed to Holmes for his confidential perusal.[17]

While in Washington during June, 1810, Governor Claiborne had persuaded Madison to sanction a plan for the acquisition of West Florida which he had unfolded to Colonel Wykoff, a member of the executive council of the Orleans Territory. Assuming that revolutions in South America would lead West Florida to revolt and the United States to intervene in an area claimed by right of the Louisiana Purchase, Claiborne believed it essential to have the inhabitants invite such intervention. Wykoff was instructed to visit West Florida as an agent of the United States, encourage rebellion against Spain, and suggest the advisability of requesting American intervention.[18]

Undoubtedly, as Madison and Mathews reviewed American policy in West Florida, its subtle implications did not escape the old Georgia general. Secretly the administration had authorized an agent to foment revolution in the territory of a friendly nation. When that hoped-for revolution became reality the militia of governors Holmes and Claiborne would be ready to intervene, restore order, and thereby add West Florida to the United States. Was Madison indicating a possible course of action in East Florida? Mathews thought so.

Certainly the West Florida enterprise paid rich dividends. On July 25, 1810, sixteen delegates from the four districts west of the Pearl River assembled in convention at St. John's Plains near Baton Rouge. There they organized themselves as a legislature with John Rhea as chairman, and proceeded to reorganize the government. The convention and the local Spanish governor, Carlos Dehault de Lassus, worked in harmony, though De Lassus saw his power swept from him, and the assembly adjourned with an expression of loyalty to the legitimate king of Spain.

But this synthetic accord did not last long. At four o'clock on the morning of September 23, approximately eighty men afoot and on horseback attacked the fort at Baton Rouge.[19] Although the long neglected fort was indefensible, its courageous commander rejected the summons: "Ground your arms and you shall not be hurt";[20] "and when the Americans swarmed over the ruinous bastions they found Louis Grandpré almost alone defending his flag. He was killed."[21]

After capturing Baton Rouge the Americans in convention stated their past grievances and, for their own security, declared West Florida free and independent.[22] A few weeks later John Rhea urged immediate annexation of the new territory and its protection as a part of the United States. Additional requests included a loan of $100,000 and reservation of all public lands of the province for those who risked their lives and fortunes to wrest the country from Spain.[23]

Rhea and his fellow hopefuls who envisioned large land grants for themselves were doomed to disappointment. President Madison never recognized the revolutionists, their convention, nor the independence of West Florida. In his proclamation of October 27, 1810, he reiterated the American title to West Florida from the Perdido to the Mississippi which had been secured by the Louisiana Purchase. Although the United States had allowed this territory to remain under Spanish control, the American government had done so not because of any question of its claim but solely in the expectation of an amicable settlement through negotiations with a just and friendly power. Under the present circumstances, Madison concluded, failure to occupy and guard the province might be construed as a dereliction of title.

On the same date as that of the proclamation, the secretary of state issued instructions to Governor Claiborne to guide him in his occupation of West Florida and his governing it as a part of the Orleans Territory.[24] If, contrary to expectations, the occupation should be opposed by the forces of the revolutionists, Claiborne was to call on the regular army troops for help; but should any place, however small, remain in possession of a Spanish force, he was not to take it by assault.[25]

Meanwhile the revolutionary activities in West Florida had thrown Governor Folch on the mercy of the United States. On November 25 he expressed the conviction that the Floridas would speedily be placed in possession of the United States, and immediately suspended collection of all duties in the Mobile and Pascagoula districts on any vessel, goods, or merchandise belonging to citizens of the United States.[26] In consequence of this friendly act, Folch expected the American government to end the anarchy fomented and perpetuated by its citizens. When no immediate action resulted and the revolutionary movement in West Florida continued to gain momentum, Spain faced the loss of the entire province. Folch then played his final card—the offer to deliver the Floridas unless support reached him before January 1, 1811.

His tentative promise and Madison's orders quickly restored order. Governor Claiborne occupied the area west of the Pearl River on December 7, and shortly thereafter American forces were in control to the Perdido with the exception of Mobile and its environs.

The American occupation of Spanish territory brought international protest. Louis de Onís, the unrecognized Spanish minister to the United States, tried to persuade himself that the action indicated no hostility to Spain.[27] To the French minister, L. M. Turreau de Garambouville, Secretary Smith stated: "As for the Floridas, I swear, General, on my honor as a gentleman not only that we are strangers to everything that has happened, but even that the Americans who have appeared there either as agents or leaders are enemies of the Executive . . . these men and some others have been led into these measures by the hope of obtaining from a new government considerable concessions of land."[28] Smith declared the occupation of West Florida was a measure to forestall English seizure and hoped France would "not take it ill that we should defend the part of Florida in dispute between Spain and us . . . [for] your interest, like ours, requires us to oppose the enterprises of England in that country." John Philip Morier, the British chargé d'affaires at Washington, sharply asked: "Would it not have been more worthy and more in keeping with existing ties of friendship between the United States and Spain for your government to have simply offered its assistance to crush the common enemy of both, rather than to have made such interference the pretext for wresting a province from a friendly Power, and that in time of her adversity?"[29]

After concluding his résumé of the West Florida affair during this memorable meeting of January, 1811, Madison surely asked General Mathews for his opinions.

"Sar," replied Mathews, "last fall I covered the border from the St. Marys to Mobile. Florida is ready for rebellion. The fever epidemic prevented my entering Pensacola, but west of Pensacola our citizens outnumbered the Spaniards, and in East Florida only St. Augustine is really Spanish. At Mobile I saw Governor Folch, a sensible man if there ever was one. He agrees that Great Britain should not have the Floridas or any part of them. But Folch and his lieutenants don't want to lose their offices and salaries. If some provision was made to care for them, they'd have no objection to a union with us."[30]

"The recent secret act of Congress provided $100,000 for expenses in acquiring the Floridas. Could some of that sum be used to satisfy them?" Madison inquired.

"Certainly," Mathews replied, "but other inducements should be made."

"Guarantee their jobs then," Madison stated. "Pay the arrears of their salaries, and promise them pensions."

"That will turn the trick in West Florida, but as you know, sar, I'm more interested in East Florida."

Madison smiled. "You and Mr. Jefferson are of one mind. He believes our seizure of West Florida will be a signal to England to take Pensacola and St. Augustine and after that we can get them only by war. He thinks we should forestall England by anticipation since there never was a case where the adage was more true, 'in for a penny, in for a pound,' for no more offense will be taken by France and Spain by our seizure of both parts of Florida than by one."[31]

"Mr. Jefferson is right, sar. But East Florida will be a harder nut to crack than West. Henry White, the governor at St. Augustine, is a Tartar. Governor Folch has no power to deliver East Florida and White will pay no heed to anything he says or does."

"I know the limits to Folch's powers," Madison stated. "Is there anything to be done in East Florida? I desire it as badly as you, or Mr. Jefferson."

"There certainly is, for along the St. Marys and St. Johns rivers the Americans despise the Spaniards. But our citizens have few guns, little money, and not enough men to capture St. Augustine unaided. They fear a revolution would be suppressed by Spanish regulars or English troops sent to aid Spain. If they were certain of American support they would lose all fear of Spain and England. And if there were possibilities of rewards in office and land even the doubtful would be convinced."

"English occupation of East Florida must be prevented, General Mathews, whatever the cost. For a weak and decadent power such as Spain to control so lengthy an area on our southern border is embarrassing; to have Great Britain in possession would be impossible. The United States must have the Floridas."

"I'll do my best, sar."

"A revolution," continued the president, "would create possibilities. As my special agent our army and navy will be at your command. But hide your hand and mine, general."

"Sar," Mathews promised, "you can count on my discreetness."

"Remember that this is not West Florida," Madison cautioned. "There the revolution gave excuse for intervention, but our reiterated claim to the province was justification for the occupation. Except for geography and the indebtedness of bankrupt Spain to our citizens, we have no claim on East Florida."

Whether Madison went this far or even further in his private instructions to Mathews is problematical. Mathews left the president, believing he had been given almost unlimited powers—that his secret instructions were far more inclusive than his official powers.

The official instructions were issued to Mathews and McKee on January 26, 1811. The Indian agent John McKee had received Governor Folch's letter of December 2, 1810, at Mobile and hastened to Washington. Since he was already involved, McKee was chosen to accompany Mathews and was given authority to act in the event of the old general's illness.

They were appointed by the president (ran the instructions) to carry into effect the act of Congress relating to the territory east of the Perdido River. Should Governor Folch or the local authorities existing there be willing to surrender the remaining portions of West Florida, they were to accept them for the United States. And should the authorities insist on a stipulation for redelivery at a future date, they must agree. All debts of the Spanish government to the people were to be assumed by the United States. All land titles should be guaranteed, all civil officials kept in their offices, and all Spanish laws recognized; but religious freedom should be granted. On the first undoubted manifestation of the approach of a foreign force – England was understood but not named – they were to preoccupy by force the territory to the entire exclusion of the advancing enemy.[32]

Those parts of the instructions which specifically applied to East Florida were of most interest to Mathews. "The conduct you are to pursue in regard to East Florida must be regulated by the dictates of your own judgments on a close view and accurate knowledge of the precise state of things there and the real disposition of the Spanish Governor always recurring to the present instructions as the paramount rule of your Proceedings."[33] If in the exercise of any part of their duties the commissioners should require aid from the military, it would be given on application to nearby military and naval officers to whom general orders had been issued by the secretaries of war and navy.

Each commissioner was allowed eight dollars per day and expenses. Immediate authorization to draw on the collector of customs at New Orleans for $8,000 and the collector at Savannah for $2,000 completed the instructions.

The frugal Mathews used only a small portion of these funds. For once, money held little interest. Now that he was a special agent of the United States on a confidential mission, he regained much of the confidence and enthusiasm of his youth.

Retrospective Journey

FROM WASHINGTON TO FORT Stoddert in the Mississippi Territory, by way of St. Marys, Georgia, was more than a thousand miles. Much of the route ran through uninhabited forests, where little more than footpaths guided the traveler, and through Indian lands with the ever-present danger of encountering maverick braves bent on robbery and murder. Through Virginia and the Carolinas to Augusta, Georgia, stage coaches and inns afforded the wayfarer rough accommodations. From Augusta the Federal Road, often called the "Three Chopped Way" from the triple blaze on trees along the route, wound through Georgia and the Mississippi Territory. The road passed through Milledgeville, Fort Hawkins, and the Creek Agency in Georgia, crossed the Chattahoochee River near the present site of Columbus, and continued through Fort Mitchell and Fort Mims to Fort Stoddert. It could scarcely be honored with the name road, and although wagons did bump a part of its way, the wiser traveler chose the horse.

McKee, Mathews, and Ralph Isaacs, the general's secretary, were together for a part of the trip. At some point en route, the two commissioners turned left to Charleston, South Carolina, while Isaacs hurried on to Fort Stoddert and Pensacola, reaching the latter at four on the afternoon of February 25.[1] There he began preliminary negotiations with Folch in preparation for the arrival of Mathews.

The commissioners traveled from Charleston to Savannah and through coastal Georgia where freshets had made the roads almost impassable and the streams unfordable.[2] At Brown's Ferry the Savannah post road reached the banks of the Satilla River, and from there for almost twenty miles the road curved southeast through the lowlands to the small village of St. Marys. When the weary agents arrived in town on February 23,[3] Mathews sought his friends and fellow conspirators made during the previous year's visit. But he was disheartened by their reports. "On my arivil hear," he wrote to Secretary of State Smith, "I found the Gentlemin hows names I give you well disposed to sarve our Government but thare has not one Solder arived. or one armed vesil or a gun Boat in this rivar, from this cause its thought not propar to attempt Eny thing at present . . . from the prospects hear," Mathews continued, "E. F. is growing of more importins to the U. S. evarey day there is now in the Spanish watars hear twenty larg vesils Loding with Lumber for the Bretesh government and Eighty loded the last year on the Same account. You will plase to asare the President evarey thin in my power will be made to Carey his wishes in to afact Give my complaments to Doctr. Eusts and Col. Hamilton."[4]

Promising to return by April 20, Mathews left for Coleraine on the morning of February 26. He and McKee probably skirted the great Okefenokee Swamp on their left as they moved by wilderness trails northwest to reach the Federal Road. The main road from Coleraine to Darien, Savannah, and Augusta would have been less arduous, but comfort was sacrificed for speed. On the night of March 9, 1811, they reached the little settlement known as the Creek Agency, where Benjamin Hawkins entertained them and noted their good health and excellent equipment for travel.[5] After resting for two nights they departed for Fort Stoddert on the eleventh, and reached their destination on the twenty-first.[6]

On this exhausting journey the forty-year-old McKee came to know the man who was his senior by more than thirty years. His first impressions were unfavorable. To hear Mathews speak on his personal affairs, his talented children, his "bastardly" detractors, and his past services brought to mind the inevitable comparison to a puff of wind attempting to blow itself into a cyclone. The remnants of an Irish brogue, a unique pronunciation of the simplest words, and the accenting of the "ed" in words such as drowned, learned, named, and returned, as well as his laborious writing and spelling of coffee as "Kaughphy," sack as "sac," and knock as "nok," and laugh as "laf"[7] caused the more literate McKee to question Mathews' ability. But not for long. His adroit handling of innkeepers and tradesmen along the way (it was said of Mathews that he never made an unprofitable deal or a poor investment), his woodslore, his information about the frontier, and his understanding of men soon drew the respect of McKee.[8] For all his eccentricities of habit and speech Mathews was an informed man and a natural narrator. Avid reading of political literature and conversations with men who knew the secrets of American history gave him a knowledge which was not to be available to historians for generations. Actual contact with Spanish governors of Florida, during his terms as governor of Georgia, added to his store of information. Along with this knowledge went an amazingly retentive memory.[9] Mathews, in spite of his verbosity, held McKee's attention as he traced the historical background of Florida.

Down below the St. Marys lay a land of blood. Christened "Florida" by the gold-hungry, Indian-slaver Juan Ponce de Leon in 1513, inhumanity traduced the implied beauty in the name; for murder, massacre, and revolt colored its sand and swamp and fertile soil. In the beginning the Spaniard fell upon the Indian, and the Indian killed the Spaniard. Later fanatic Spanish nationalists captured hundreds of intruding French Lutherans, bound their hands behind them, and slaughtered them with pikes and swords[10] — and so ever after that spot was called Matanzas, or "Slaughters." Enraged by this butchery, the French replied in kind. In 1568 on the banks of the St. Johns River captured Spaniards were hanged from the trees and over them was inscribed on a pine tablet: *"I do this not as to Spaniards, nor as to Marranos,*[11] *but as to traitors, robbers and murderers."*[12]

Decades of strife extended into centuries. Before the close of the sixteenth century English sea raiders looted the Florida settlements, and within the next hundred years the Carolina colonists were pressing down from the north. In 1702 Governor James Moore of Carolina captured and sacked St. Augustine but not its protecting fort; frustrated by the moated coquina fortress, Castillo de San Marcos, which stood on the northern limit of the ancient city, the Carolinians later turned on the thriving Spanish missions of north central Florida to torture, burn, and kill their priests and devastate the missions. The Spaniards wreaked vengeance by supporting the Indians in the Yamassee War and the Carolinians answered with raids below the St.

Marys and along the St. Johns. Shortly after the colonization of Georgia, James Oglethorpe laid waste the interior coastal region of Florida and occupied the city of St. Augustine, but he too failed to take the Castillo. During this invasion John Mohr McIntosh, whose grandsons were to be leaders in the East Florida Revolution of 1812, was captured and sent to Spain for imprisonment.[13] Although eventually released, he returned to Georgia to die a broken man, willing his children and grandchildren an undying hatred of Spaniards.

Even the transfer of Spanish Florida to England in 1763 brought only temporary peace to a harassed land. When the thirteen American colonies rebelled against Great Britain, they invited East and West Florida to join them; but instead of uniting in rebellion, the Floridians clung more closely to England and offered haven to dispossessed Loyalists of Georgia and the Carolinas. By 1777 Georgians were calling for a punitive expedition to destroy the lawless bands below the St. Marys and exterminate the Loyalists who supported England. Forgetting an unsuccessful 1776 attempted invasion of Florida and heedless of the spring floods, an expedition crossed the St. Marys in May, 1777, and reached Sawpit Bluff at the mouth of Sawpit Creek above the St. Johns River, only to meet defeat on May 17 when most of the Georgia militia precipitately fled on hearing the enemy fire.

Even though the Americans won their independence, Great Britain succeeded in clouding the title of the United States to a large part of West Florida. A secret clause in the Treaty of 1783 provided that if in the general peace Great Britain should retain West Florida, its northern boundary would be on a line 32 degrees and 28 minutes between the Chattahoochee and Mississippi rivers; but should Great Britain return West Florida to Spain, the boundary would be set at the 31st parallel. After Spain reacquired the Floridas, she claimed the northernmost limit of West Florida on the ground of partial conquest during the recent war and unquestioned boundary of the province as a British colony. Thus Spain and the United States disputed the rights of each other to what is today a large part of Alabama and Mississippi. Negotiation failed to settle the controversy, for the Americans demanded the free navigation of the Mississippi River and the right of deposit, or the right to unload and reship goods without payment of a tariff at New Orleans. When Spain offered the territory in question in exchange for complete control of the Mississippi waterway, the United States refused to cripple the growth of her western territories by such an agreement.

Time and the chaotic affairs of Europe favored the United States. In 1789 a strong central government was inaugurated under the Constitution of 1787 and for the first time the United States could threaten unyielding foreign nations with commercial reprisals. The French Revolution brought war in Europe, where Spain soon found herself allied with France[14] and fearful of a possible commercial agreement between England and America. Consequently Spain gave way in 1795, accepted the 31st parallel as the northern boundary of West Florida, and granted United States citizens the right of deposit at New Orleans.

This diplomatic victory whetted the American appetite for additional Florida areas. Since Spain was allied with France and the relations between the latter and the United States were rapidly nearing a state of war, many Americans anticipated the conquest and annexation of the Spanish provinces of Louisiana and the Floridas. In May, 1798, Robert Liston, the British minister to the United States, believed the Adams administration ready to conquer the Floridas and Louisiana and willing to sanction British acquisition of Santo Domingo and other French islands in the Caribbean.[15] This division of Spanish and French colonies appealed to William Grenville, the English foreign minister, but almost at the same moment Liston was penning a dispatch which stated the United States was unwilling to see Santo Domingo and the other large West Indies islands in English hands.[16] Without prospect of territorial concessions for herself, Great Britain saw no advantage in supporting the United States, and the Louisiana-Florida scheme came to a quick death.

The United States, however, did not escape conflict with France; and although war was never declared, French and American privateers and warships fought numerous engagements until the differences between the two nations were resolved by a treaty in 1800. During this quasi-naval war, Spain overstepped the bounds of neutrality. Not only did she allow French privateers to bring 168 captured American ships into the neutral ports of Spain but her own over-zealous privateers seized 104 American merchantmen.[17] The United States government held that Spain "alone was answerable" for all these illegally taken or condemned prizes[18] and estimated the loss to American citizens at from five to fifteen million dollars.

After concluding a peace with France, the United States lost no time in demanding a settlement from Spain for these spoliation claims. Charles Pinckney, the American minister at Madrid, engaged Don Pedro Cevallos, the Spanish foreign minister, in long and apparently fruitless negotiations. Compromise by both parties, however, resulted in the Claims Convention of August 11, 1802, whereby the claims of the United States against Spain were to be adjudicated by a joint commission which was to meet in Madrid and conclude its work within eighteen months after ratification of the agreement.[19] When Jefferson submitted the treaty to the United States Senate, in January, 1803, it was rejected, but was later reconsidered and ratified in the following year. The Spanish Cortes never accepted the agreement. Since the foreign minister of Spain had signed the convention, the United States held her claims substantiated and looked to the Spanish colonies for territorial compensation. The unreliable and bankrupt Spanish government's refusal to pay her just obligations centered American attention on East Florida. Spain lost sovereignty over East Florida, for the United States held a lien or mortgage on the province: Spain could neither give nor sell it to a foreign power until the American mortgage of five or more million dollars was paid in full and the collateral released. This argument, however spurious in international law, was to be reiterated by American expansionists to justify their action in East Florida.

Before the unsatisfactory negotiations for the spoliation claims reached their indefinite conclusions, Spain, by the secret treaty of San Ildefonso of October, 1800, retroceded Louisiana to France. It was May of the following year before Jefferson heard of it and even then the boundaries of Louisiana were not known to him. Without hesitation President Jefferson, who in the past had favored France rather than England, changed his ideas on foreign policy, for the possibility of the United States being contained on the south and west by a powerful country could not be tolerated. "The day that France takes possession of New Orleans . . .," he wrote, "we must marry ourselves to the British fleet and nation. . . . This is not a state of things we seek or desire. It is one which this measure, if adopted by France, forces on us. . . ."[20]

The United States had hardly realized the full implication of the retrocession when on October 16, 1802, Juan Ventura Morales, the Spanish intendant of Louisiana, suspended the American right of deposit at New Orleans. Although Carlos Martinez de Casa Yrujo, the Spanish minister at Washington, assured Jefferson that the suspension was unauthorized by his king and warned Morales that in consequence of his act American citizens would have ground for claiming an indemnity for their commercial losses, crafty Eastern politicians encouraged the aroused trans-Appalachian residents to march in force on New Orleans. Such action and the possibility of a resulting war frightened Jefferson, for he believed:

> Nothing but the failure of every peaceable mode of redress, nothing but dire necessity should force us from the path of peace which would be our wisest pursuit, to embark in the broils and contentions of Europe and become a satellite to any power there. Yet this must be the consequence if we fail in all possible means of re-establishing our rights were we to enter into this war alone. The Mississippi would be blockaded at least during the continuance of that war by a superior naval power, and all our Western States be deprived of their commerce unless they would surrender themselves to the blockading power.[21]

Jefferson's speedy means of restoring American rights was the securing of the Island of Orleans and West Florida, which he believed had been included in the retrocession of Louisiana to France.[22] The Congress hastily appropriated an initial $2,000,000 and the Senate confirmed James Monroe as a minister extraordinary to join Robert Livingston in Paris to negotiate for the desired provinces. By their instructions they could offer France as much as $10,000,000, generous commercial privileges, and even guarantee the west bank of the Mississippi in exchange for New Orleans and West Florida.[23]

When Monroe reached Paris he was keenly disappointed on learning that West Florida had not been ceded to France. Even Napoleon's unexpected offer to sell Louisiana, and the treaty of April 30, 1803, by which the United States acquired that vast area, failed to satisfy the American ministers. But there remained two rays of hope: the promise of French assistance in securing the Floridas from Spain, and the undefined boundaries of Louisiana. Although Napoleon knew the eastern boundary of the province as ceded to France did not include West Florida, he refused to state it, and the language of his treaty with the United States was ambiguous.

"What are the eastern boundaries of Louisiana?" Livingston asked Talleyrand.

"I don't know," replied Talleyrand, "but you must take it as we received it from Spain."

"Just what do you mean by 'take'?" urged Livingston.

"I can't say," repeated Talleyrand.

"Then you mean that we shall construe it our own way?"

"I can give you no direction. You have made a noble bargain for yourselves, and I suppose you will make the most of it," was Talleyrand's final reply.[24]

At first both Livingston and Monroe concluded the United States had no claim to West Florida or any part of it.[25] On May 12, 1803, Livingston was satisfied that France had not received West Florida from Spain, but eight days later he urged Secretary Madison to claim it as a part of the Louisiana territory and declared himself convinced of the legality of such an interpretation of the treaty.[26] When France owned Louisiana it included West Florida, and in 1763 France ceded Canada to England along with all French territory east of the Mississippi except the Island of Orleans, which together with the French lands west of the Mississippi went to Spain. At the close of the American Revolutionary War Spain acquired the Floridas from Great Britain and attached that part of West Florida between the Perdido and the Mississippi to Louisiana. Therefore, Livingston felt Spain had retroceded most of West Florida to France. Since the American treaty with France in 1803 defined "Louisiana with the same extent that it now has in the hands of Spain, and that it had when France possessed it, and such as it should be according to treaties subsequently entered into between Spain and other states," the United States thereby obtained West Florida to the Perdido River through the Louisiana Purchase. Monroe concurred in this view and thought it "too clear to admit of a doubt."[27]

Monroe claimed that he had not hastily reached his decision. From the moment of the Louisiana Purchase he conceived his duty lay in ascertaining correctly the extent of the acquisition by a study of all authentic documents.[28] In his opinion the United States should not take possession of West Florida until such action could be demonstrated to an impartial world, and to Spain herself, as well-founded on principles of justice and equity.

Jefferson also turned his attention to the problem at hand. He recognized in Livingston's ingenious plan as good a ground for a war of conquest as some of the claims which Napoleon had made the world respect: as a diplomatic weapon, backed by sufficient armed force, it would be as effective an instrument as though it had every attribute of morality and good faith.[29] But Jefferson feared war. In August and September, 1803, the West Florida question consumed much of his time as he read maps and documents and wrote to key men for information.[30] He rejected Livingston's master plan of claiming West Florida by purchase and negotiating with Spain after first seizing East Florida. Rather he decided to claim but not occupy West Florida to the Perdido, demand the western boundary of Louisiana be set at the Bravo River, and make these boundaries a "subject of negotiation with Spain, and if, as soon as she is at war, we push them strongly with one hand, holding out a price in the other, we shall certainly obtain the Floridas, and all in good time."[31] For those impatient souls who were willing to exchange a part of Louisiana for Florida, Jefferson confidently predicted: "We shall get the Floridas." He avowed his unwillingness to give up an inch of the Mississippi, for it should be as American as the Potomac or Delaware rivers.[32]

Thus Jefferson accepted in principle Livingston's plan for claiming West Florida and Madison went along with him; Livingston never believed Spain intended to retrocede West Florida, or France to claim it, by the treaty of San Ildefonso. He had been forced to maintain, and Jefferson now accepted, "that Spain retroceded West Florida to France without knowing it, that France had sold it to the United States without suspecting it, that the United States had bought it without paying for it, and that neither France nor Spain, although the original contracting parties, were competent to decide the meaning of their own contract."[33]

Before the United States officially claimed West Florida to the Perdido, Yrujo told Jefferson he had bought stolen goods. Since France had agreed never to alienate Louisiana and in addition had not fulfilled certain provisions of the Treaty of San Ildefonso, she could not give a valid title for Louisiana. Yrujo's protest did not frighten Jefferson for he knew Napoleon would bring Spain to heel; he ordered reinforcements to Natchez and accused Spain of false faith. In the House of Representatives, John Randolph made a blistering attack on Spain while disclosing the American scheme to take West Florida.

Driven by the brilliant but erratic Randolph, the House passed the Mobile Act which authorized the president to create a separate customs direct for Mobile, and extend the revenue and navigation laws to "all navigable waters, rivers, creeks, bays, and islets lying within the United States," and emptying into that part of the Gulf of Mexico lying east of the Mississippi.[34] When the Senate concurred and the Mobile Act became law on February 24, 1804, Yrujo burst into Madison's office to protest violently and intemperately. Later in a more calm and thoughtful mood he penned "a note so severe as to require punishment, and so able to admit of none."[35] Madison wished to ask for his recall but Jefferson advised sending a full account of Yrujo's conduct to the Spanish authorities and leaving action to them.

In May, 1805, on orders from Spain, Yrujo informed Madison of the withdrawal of the Spanish objection to the transfer of Louisiana. Spain's hand had been forced by Napoleon. When France refused to sanction the American claim to West Florida, Madison vainly attempted to explain away the Mobile Act. Jefferson finally came to the rescue with a proclamation establishing Fort Stoddert, north of Mobile and within American territory, as a port of entry for all land within the United States between the Mississippi and Perdido rivers. His proclamation negated the Mobile Act. Notwithstanding Jefferson's explanation that the intention of the act had always been misunderstood, his executive order was a withdrawal from an untenable predicament. Yrujo had won, but it was his only victory: by 1806 he was *persona non grata* to the American government and in the following year left the United States.[36]

While Jefferson acted with aggressiveness at Washington he did not neglect the diplomatic possibility of negotiating with Spain for the Floridas. Shortly after winning Louisiana, Monroe had written: "But the extent of that acquisition does not destroy the motive which existed before of acquiring the Floridas, nor essentially diminish it."[37] With this sentiment Jefferson and Madison were in perfect agreement. Monroe was ordered to Madrid but French opposition to a diplomatic assault on Spain and the urgent need of Monroe's services in London postponed his mission for more than a year.

At Madrid the United States minister, Charles Pinckney, in July,

1803, began pushing Spain for the Floridas and in the following year demanded immediate ratification of the 1802 claims convention. The Spanish minister Cevallos countered by urging the repeal of the Mobile Act, and Pinckney threatened to warn all American consuls of the critical relations between Spain and his country and to direct them to give notice of an impending state of war. Even a dramatic request for his passport was in vain, for Spain supported by France would not yield an inch.[38]

Tired and defeated Pinckney awaited Monroe's arrival in Madrid. In April, 1804, Madison ordered Monroe to Paris where he was to ferret the views of France and then proceed to Pinckney's assistance. At Madrid Monroe was expected to win an acknowledgment of the Perdido as the southeastern boundary of Louisiana, gain the remainder of the Floridas, and settle the spoliation claims; in return he was to promise Spain concessions on the southwestern boundary of Louisiana, a maximum of $2,000,000, and withdrawal of the American claims for damage as a result of the loss of the right of deposit at New Orleans.[39] Even Monroe realized he had much to demand from Spain and little to offer in return.

Late in the fall of 1804 Monroe reached Paris, where Barbe-Marbois, the minister of finance, told him that Spain's critical need for money would force a cession of the Floridas and intimated that payments to certain French officials would speed negotiations. Talleyrand, however, was not so encouraging and warned the American minister of the difficulties ahead. At the moment Napoleon had in hand an exhaustive report from Talleyrand enumerating the United States' threats against Spain for the past three years and denying the American claims one by one.[40]

Both the Spanish ministers, Godoy and Cevallos, received copies of Talleyrand's report before Monroe reached Madrid. For months after January 28, 1805, Monroe made fruitless overtures for the Floridas. At every turn Cevallos forced him to follow the Spanish lead and used French reasoning to trump his every claim. Finally Monroe made his final offer: if Spain would cede the Floridas, ratify the claims convention of 1802, and accept the Colorado River as the southwestern boundary of Louisiana, the United States would maintain a neutral zone 100 miles east of the Colorado, assume the French spoliation claims, ask no damages as a result of the suspension of the right of deposit at New Orleans, and accept West Florida to the Perdido as a cession from Spain, thereby abandoning the claim that it was a part of Louisiana. Cevallos replied that these terms required Spain to concede everything and receive nothing. On May 18, Monroe demanded his passport and after an audience with the king on the following day, he left Madrid.[41]

Emboldened by her defiance of the United States, and at war with England, Spain began to plunder American commerce and reinforce her garrisons in West Florida. When in December, 1805, George W. Erving, who had replaced Pinckney in Madrid, went to protest against the seizures he found Godoy courteous but defiant.

"How goes our affairs?" he asked. "Are we to have peace or war?"

"Spanish seizures of American ships," Erving gravely replied, "are a breach of the treaty of 1795 and may lead to serious consequences."

"The national safety of Spain will not allow American vessels to carry English goods," Godoy stated.

"But we have a treaty which secures us that right."

"I know you have a treaty," Godoy said, "for I made it myself, but the free goods provision of that treaty will no longer be respected. You may choose either peace or war. 'Tis the same thing to me. I will tell you candidly, that if you will go to war this certainly is the moment, and you may take our possessions from us. I advise you to go to war now, if you think that is best for you; and then the peace which will be made in Europe will leave us two at war."[42]

Jefferson agreed with his Secretary of the Treasury Albert Gallatin that war would never do "even for the country between the Mississippi and Perdido."[43] But Jefferson also had determined that "however we may compromise on our Western limits, we never shall on the Eastern" boundary of Louisiana.[44]

In the fall of 1805 the American minister John Armstrong wrote from Paris that he had been approached with a suggestion of seven million dollars as a price for Florida. On November 12 and 19 Jefferson and his cabinet determined on a plan: as a final effort toward an amicable settlement with Spain, France would be the intermediary, and five million would be offered for the Floridas, conditioned by accords with Spain on the spoliation claims and the southwestern boundary of Louisiana.[45] In his message to Congress Jefferson followed Armstrong's suggested use of vigorous, war-like language to alarm the fears of Spain in the hope that she would appeal to Napoleon and set the stage for negotiations in France.

Jefferson requested John Randolph, the chairman of the House Ways and Means Committee, to secure an appropriation of two million dollars for the purchase of the Floridas. Since the president had not called for this sum in his message and all previous negotiations with Spain had failed, Randolph opposed the request, but submitted the proposition to his committee, which promptly voted it down. When Madison then told him the money was needed for France — "France wants money, and we must give it to her or have a Spanish and a French war" — Randolph was more adamant, for he considered "it a base prostration of the national character to excite one nation by money to bully another nation out of its property."[46] In spite of Randolph, Jefferson won a secret appropriation of two million dollars. On March 29, 1806, Fulwar Shipworth, a former American consul at Paris, sailed from New York with remittances for two million dollars to be used discreetly by Armstrong in persuading France to force a Spanish cession of the Floridas; if successful, Spain would later be paid in a separate transaction.[47]

Even though the scheme seemed promising, nothing resulted from it, for Napoleon had turned to more pressing matters. He had tired of the Florida question and met Armstrong's repeated overtures with cold indifference.

Meanwhile the operation of Napoleon's continental system and England's counter blockade of France were injuring American shipping and drawing the United States nearer and nearer to war. In the summer of 1807 relations with Great Britain were so critical that Jefferson thought war probable and feared England would seize the Floridas.[48] To save the peace he persuaded Congress to authorize an embargo on all American shipping.

When in the following year the Spanish patriots unloosed their fury against Napoleon and moved into the camp of England, the American fear of English occupation of the Floridas grew with every passing month. Even the reluctant Albert Gallatin played with the idea of at least occupying West Florida to the Perdido.[49] But Jefferson saw a faint hope for the seizure of the Floridas, without the danger of war with either England or France, under the pretext of enforcing the embargo along the Florida border.[50]

Yet Jefferson's term expired in March, 1809, with the Floridas still Spanish. Although he had failed to secure them, he did buy Louisiana, thereby laying the foundation for a claim to West Florida to the Perdido, and made it possible for his successor to use the spoliation claims as a lien or mortgage against East Florida. Jefferson was hardly out of the White House, however, before he suggested Napoleon might acquiesce in American occupation of the Floridas and even Cuba, but he warned President Madison of Napoleon's queer reasoning and of his policy "so crooked that it eludes conjecture."[51]

Madison followed the plan of his predecessor—aggressiveness short of war—and like him believed United States citizens residing south of the border would eventually bring the Floridas into the American fold. Madison's secretary of state, Robert Smith, assured the British that "we have no views or intentions whatever, that can or ought to give the slightest umbrage to the Spaniards."[52] At the same time he refused to recognize Louis de Onís, the recently appointed minister of the Spanish Regency and hopefully watched the brewing storm in West Florida. Both Smith and Madison stood ready to foster rebellions in the Floridas, and they were prepared to act when American-incited anarchy resulted in the capture of Baton Rouge.

The mission of Mathews and McKee was looked on as the culmination of a decade of overtures, negotiations, and threats to Spain. While the commissioners reviewed past American policy as they rode through the forests toward Fort Stoddert, the import of their mission grew stronger with each fading mile. They knew the reasons why the United States so avidly sought the Floridas.

Even in the eighteenth century the irascible John Randolph swore to his unwillingness to "exchange an eligible place in Hell for all the Floridas": and the ardent Jefferson described Florida as:

A barren sand 600 miles from east to west, and from 30 to 40 to 50 miles from north to south, formed by deposition of the sands by the Gulf Stream in its circular course round the Mexican Gulf, and which being spent after performing a semicircle, has made from its last depositions the sand bank of East Florida. In West Florida, indeed, there are on the borders of the rivers some rich bottoms, formed by the mud brought from the upper country.... But the spaces between river and river are mere banks of sand; and in East Florida there are neither rivers, nor consequently any bottoms.[53]

Jefferson's sciolism of Florida was characteristic of his generation.

In truth more than ninety per cent of the Spanish province was sand and even underneath much of the rich loam of its fertile soil lay yellow-tinted sand. But the clay soil of northern Florida, the black dirt of the great Alachua savanna, the thousands of hammocks, and the river bottoms along the St. Marys, St. Johns, Suwannee, and tens of other rivers held almost unbelievable natural wealth. Extensive forests of virgin long and short leaf pine, oak, and cedar, and the swamps filled with cypress waited the woodsman's axe and the lumberman's mill. Nature's grasses and nuts could feed thousands upon thousands of cattle and hogs; forests and waters abounded with game and fish. While a sub-tropical climate favored the romantic orange and sugar cane, ocean breezes tempered both the winter's cold and the summer's heat. Planters of the South with their slaves and visions of barns filled with cotton, corn, and rice, small farmers yearning for a few free acres and independence, and indolent wanderers seeking the most food for the least effort looked with envy on the Spanish and Indian possessors of Florida.

To those who had no thought of leaving Georgia or the Mississippi Territory, possession of the Floridas was none the less essential. Their arteries of transportation flowed south to the Gulf. Control of the Apalachicola, Mobile, Pascagoula, and other rivers guaranteed peace as against war, prosperity as against poverty. The entire United States west of the Appalachian mountains was tied to the Mississippi waterway, and, as Jefferson stated, "the use of the Mississippi [is] so indispensable, that we cannot hesitate one moment to hazard our existence for its maintenance."[54] Even the American Congress, composed as it was of a majority of Northern men many of whom already looked askance at expansion southward and questioned the institution of slavery, declared: "But if we look forward to the free use of the Mississippi, the Mobile, the Apalachicola, and the other rivers of the West, by ourselves and our posterity, New Orleans, and the Floridas must become a part of the United States, either by purchase or by conquest."[55] Why? Since European powers held the West Indian islands, the jutting Florida peninsula was essential to a free flowing commerce from New Orleans to the Atlantic.

Furthermore, there was a two-fold Indian problem. Between the American settlements in the Mississippi territory and the southern border of Tennessee lay the potent Creek Confederation and below the Georgia line roamed the intractable Seminoles. The Spanish had used both in attacks against the Georgians, and repeated rumors of similar raids in the future shook the frontier with fear. This was sufficient to condemn them in American eyes; the expulsion of the Spanish from Florida and the removal of the Indians to some point beyond the Mississippi came to be viewed as parts of the same inevitable movement.[56]

In one respect the Seminoles were more of a nuisance to wealthy Southern planters than the Creeks. Since Spain held only nominal control in the interior of Florida, the Seminoles prowled at will south of the American border and often swept north to loot and kill. Fugitive slaves from the Southern states found a haven and virtual freedom with the Indians. More than anything else this loss of slaves infuriated the Southerners. Their raids on the elusive Indians often became slave-stealing forays on white planters of Florida, and they in turn plundered north of the border. Under cover of this near-anarchy white robbers and murderers preyed indiscriminately upon Indian, Georgian, and Spaniard. For all this lawlessness the Americans blamed Spain.

In broader perspective, possession of the Floridas became a security measure and a national opportunity. Foreign control along the extensive southern border was an ever-present danger. Because of the chaos which reigned in Spain, she offered no immediate threat; but in the hands of a puissant European state, particularly England, Florida could become a base for invasion. In addition the presence of any foreign nation in Florida could effectively prevent United States expansion, territorial or economic, in the Caribbean. Hegemony in the Gulf, economic penetration of Latin America, and the acquisition of Cuba, already eyed by the Americans, would be impossible without Florida.[57] That province would round out the southeastern border of the American states; by geographic design it was obviously within the destiny of the United States.

Such was the Floridas' importance in the American picture of the early eighteenth century. Many intelligent citizens preferred West Florida and the Island of Orleans to the vast stretches of unknown Louisiana. The keenness of their disappointment in not having secured the desired land in 1803 whetted their appetite for eventual acquisition. With these views Mathews and McKee fully concurred.

Failure in the West

THE BUDS OF THE SPREADING oaks were bursting into tender leaves when Mathews and McKee arrived at Fort Stoddert. Below the fort the languid Mobile River flowed placidly south, its usually crystal clear water, though appearing black from a distance, was cluttered by the dirt and trash of spring freshets. Just above the fort the Alabama and Tombigbee rivers joined to form the Mobile; and a few miles below it, where the terrain flattened, the river divided with an east branch, the Tensaw River, gliding in a sluggish arch to Mobile Bay. The Mobile River flowed more directly to the bay and along its west bank the higher, firmer ground, in contrast to the swamps and lowlands of the east bank, gave access to the town of Mobile.

The fort had been constructed in 1799 and named for the then Acting Secretary of War, Benjamin Stoddert.[1] Just south of it was the Florida border and almost fifty miles farther on lay Mobile. The trail from Natchez on the Mississippi entered Fort Stoddert from the west and continued northeast and east through the Mississippi Territory to the Chattahoochee River and Georgia. Another crude road skirted the west bank of the Tombigbee to a point nearly forty miles north of the fort where it turned west to connect the main trails to Tennessee and western Mississippi. As an official port of entry and the center of converging trade routes, Fort Stoddert was the most important post in southern Mississippi; the presence of agents, land speculators, revolutionists, merchants, and some 500 regular and militia troops overcrowded this army frontier post.

FAILURE IN THE WEST

When Mathews and McKee reached Fort Stoddert on the evening of March 21, 1811, they found Lieutenant Joshua Hamilton on his way to Pensacola with a dispatch from Brigadier General Wade Hampton to Governor Folch. Although the lieutenant refused to divulge the contents of his message, the commissioners persuaded him that his mission might conflict with theirs and he agreed to return to New Orleans with a letter from the commissioners to General Hampton.[2] The general became incensed by their interference with his command and tartly informed the commissioners that he would see them when he found it convenient. Hampton's reply inflamed Mathews and McKee, and the latter complained to the secretary of state of their humiliating position in working with anyone so uncooperative.[3] In this inauspicious way President Madison's agents began their task.

Long before their arrival the preliminary steps had been taken to hasten negotiations with Governor Folch. When Mathews' secretary, Ralph Isaacs, left Washington for Fort Stoddert he held a personal letter from McKee to Folch. In it McKee offered to accept East Florida and West Florida, from the Perdido to the Apalachicola, in the name of the United States, to guarantee adequate protection within the area, and to restore the territory east óf the Perdido to its rightful sovereign upon demand. He further promised to assume a reasonable amount of current local debts of the Spaniards, pay the cost of moving the troops from the province, confirm all land titles, grant religious toleration, and continue local officials in their offices. But if the governor refused to surrender the provinces and there was reason to fear a foreign power intended to land troops therein, the military forces of the United States would preoccupy the Floridas.[4]

Immediately after his arrival in Pensacola on February 25, Isaacs delivered McKee's proposition to Folch. In the following days Isaacs had three interviews with the governor, who was friendly and talkative, but unwilling to deliver the Floridas peaceably. When Isaacs reminded him of his offer of December 2, 1810, to cede the provinces unless aid arrived before the first of January, Folch explained his position.

"When I wrote that letter," he said, "I was confronted by apparently insurmountable difficulties. I was threatened by rebellious forces and had no means of repelling them. Reuben Kempler's army was bearing down on Mobile from the Tensaw River, Sterling Duprée's

33

rebels were on the Pascagoula River to my west, and Phileman Thomas with a reported 1,500 men was approaching Mobile from the northwest. I had no money and no reinforcements for my miserably equipped handful of men. Under these circumstances I believed my honor as a soldier could best be maintained by presenting my sword to the United States."

"And rightly so," Isaacs agreed.

"But now conditions are entirely different," Folch said with a smile. "My government has supplied me with funds and men and the rebels have been quieted, if not destroyed, by the United States. At least they are no longer a threat to me."

At this point Isaacs saw the strategy of Folch. His proposition of December, with its enticing idea of American occupation of all the Floridas, had succeeded in its purpose. United States troops had secured the peace of the frontier and, at the expense of American occupation of a small part of the Floridas, Folch saved Mobile, Pensacola, and East Florida. But the governor had not finished.

"The October 27, 1810, proclamation of your president and the seizing of Spanish territory have tied my hands. I have letters from the Cortes in Spain and my superiors in the colonies. These letters warn me that the proclamation caused decided hostility toward the United States. The Spanish people are inflamed by your president's proclamation and by the capture of Baton Rouge, and I am ordered to hold the Floridas at all costs."

"I'm sorry to hear this," Isaacs stated. "Napoleon's boundless ambition has so weakened Spain that she can no longer protect her colonies. I hoped those colonies would unite with the United States and thus defy the continental powers of Europe."

"That, too, was my wish," replied Folch. "But I am only a subordinate who must obey orders. Your president's proclamation will prevent any united action."

Before concluding his last interview with Folch, Isaacs was determined to have an accurate report for Mathews and McKee.

"I have written a full account of your position, Governor Folch. Would you read it before I send it to the American commissioners?"

Folch accepted the brief manuscript, read it carefully, and returned it to Isaacs. "It contains what I have said without addition or omission."

Isaacs extended his hand in farewell. "As the secretary of General Mathews, I appreciate your courtesy and frankness."

Folch gave him a warm handclasp. "I am sure this is not the last time we shall meet. I shall have the pleasure of seeing you again."[5]

Whatever may have been Folch's secret yearning to sell his country's territory for a price, he had conquered the temptation and remained a loyal Spaniard. Even at the time of his conversations with Isaacs he penned a refusal to McKee's proposal. Rather than approving his offer to surrender the Floridas, Folch's superiors had sent him fifty thousand dollars, with strict orders to retain the provinces. Since he was in no immediate danger of invasion and the occupation of Baton Rouge by the Americans was an act of hostility toward a friendly neighbor, he would have no part in alienating Spanish territory. Furthermore a national Cortes, representing the people, was now assembled in Spain and the United States government should negotiate directly with that body.[6] In explaining his conduct to his superiors Folch assured them that his only purpose throughout the period had been to prevent the capture of defenseless Mobile and Pensacola.[7]

Mathews was shaken but not defeated by this unexpected turn of events. His plans for a hasty return to St. Marys were cancelled and, on the excuse of searching for some of his fugitive slaves, he entered Pensacola as a private citizen. There he called on Folch who received him with "distinguished attention." The governor reiterated his former statements: Madison's proclamation, the occupation of Baton Rouge, and the dispersion of the insurgents had completely altered the situation. Mathews' insistent urging brought additional comments.

"A new government in Spain," Folch said, "has been organized since I offered the Floridas to the safekeeping of your government. The national Cortez has replaced the old authority under which I formerly acted. I wrote the Cortez, and not even an agent of the United States could have used stronger language than I did in pointing out the inconvenience to Spain in retaining the Floridas or the advantages in ceding them upon equitable terms."

"I suggested," Folch continued, "the exchange of the Floridas for lands on the Texas border along the southwestern boundary of Louisiana. This proposal is so reasonable and fair to both countries, I daily expect an order to negotiate with you."

"But suppose France should try to occupy the Floridas?" Mathews drawled. "Or England. Though an ally of your government the English would use Spain's weakness to get valuable territory."

"I will never surrender to France or England," Folch asserted.

"Governor, thousands of miles of water isolate the North American continent from the old world. In this new world we should build a new order free from the politics and wars of the old, and from class distinctions."

"I agree with you, general," Folch quickly replied. "The day will yet come when the continent of North America will lead the world and give law to Europe."[8]

After more than a week in Pensacola and two more equally futile conversations with Folch, Mathews returned to Fort Stoddert on April 23. The general's recuperative powers both physical and mental were extraordinary. By the following day he had matured a scheme for the effective control of Mobile Bay, a plan which would leave the Spaniards undisturbed but completely surrounded in Mobile.

For almost two weeks Mathews explored the east bank of the river and the bay. He found an area of more than forty square miles between the Perdido River and Mobile Bay, inhabited by fifty families, and not occupied by a single Spanish soldier. On the eastern shore of the bay were excellent sites for military posts and good locations for commercial enterprises. Since President Madison had claimed all of West Florida to the Perdido, Mathews thought the area east of Mobile Bay should be seized at once and forts erected along the bay and river. The United States would thus obtain all the commercial advantages expected from the contemplated surrender of Mobile and could cut communications between that town and Pensacola.[9] West Florida to the Perdido, except for the isolated Spanish community at Mobile, would be American without firing a shot.

This scheme called for immediate military occupation before Folch could move troops into the area. Mathews and McKee approached Colonel Leonard Covington, commandant of Fort Stoddert. In view of their commission and his orders from the secretary of war, would the colonel supply a military force at their bidding?[10] Covington quickly dashed their hopes; there was an evident misunderstanding. He was authorized to obey the commissioners only in the certainty of an attempt to preoccupy the Floridas by a foreign power. In every other instance their requisitions were to be transmitted to Brigadier General Hampton for his instruction and orders.[11] Recalling their unsatisfactory exchanges with that officer, Mathews and McKee kept their peace.

Already the American press had sensed the failure of the negotiations. The first published reports in the *Louisiana Gazette* were copied by the newspapers of the South.[12] "Our government, we fear, has been outwitted by the wily Spaniard," wrote one editor; and he concluded that Folch, finding himself pressed by rebellious West Floridians, had called on the United States, not for the purpose of ceding the Floridas, but to gain time; and having succeeded, he retained the Floridas for his royal master.[13] Another editor asked why the United States did not take the provinces by force, since American farmers, merchants, and seamen were suffering indiscriminately as the result of European wars and it was only justice to them to occupy the Floridas.[14]

Mathews' disappointment with the failure of his mission in the west was eased by the thoroughness of his efforts. On May 14, as his thoughts centered more and more on East Florida, news of the dismissal of Robert Smith and the confirmation of James Monroe as secretary of state reached Fort Stoddert. Mathews hastily dispatched a congratulatory letter to his friend Monroe. "I will not recite all the motives I have for joy on this occasion," he wrote. "I find enough in the character and harmony it will give to our national councils and the advantage that will be thereby derived to the Nation."[15] Mathews was later to have cause to regret this letter.

In Washington the newly appointed secretary of state took a dismal view of affairs in West Florida. Although he desired the Floridas as much as Madison, he saw no reason for continued fruitless overtures to Folch. On June 29 he dictated a letter to Mathews and McKee in which he complimented them for their services and terminated their mission; a copy of this letter together with an authorization transmitting their powers in West Florida to Governor Claiborne was prepared; and a brief letter assured Mathews of his continued power to act in East Florida. These letters were never signed or dispatched.[16] For some reason Monroe decided to withhold them and the powers of McKee and Mathews were continued until terminated at a much later date.

Long before this indecisive wrestling of Monroe, Mathews voluntarily retired from West Florida. On May 18 McKee accompanied the general to Tensaw some twenty miles northeast of Fort Stoddert and the following day Mathews and his secretary began the long journey to St. Marys, Georgia.[17]

On his return to the fort, McKee heard reports of the arrival in Pensacola of a vessel from Vera Cruz with from fifty to seventy thousand dollars for Folch. McKee hastened to Mobile to authenticate the rumor and sound out the Spanish officials. His findings were most discouraging: Mobile was reinforced and Folch talked of an expeditionary force to reconquer Baton Rouge.

I ought to observe [wrote McKee] that from my imperfect knowledge of Governor Folch's character it is impossible to form any probable conjecture of what he intends to do from what he has done or said, his mind seems to be a composition not easily analyzed – constantly vacillating betwixt avarice and ambition with a puerile fondness for parade – one day calculating the net proceeds of a pine log at his saw mills and the next soaring almost to a throne, and I would be as little surprised to receive from him tomorrow a proposition for the surrender of the province as I would be to hear that he had demanded the restoration of Baton Rouge. He is very unpopular with his officers and the inhabitants and not less so with the Captain General of Cuba.[18]

McKee's characterization of Folch may be the unknown factor which influenced Monroe to withhold his letters of June 29 – even the faintest possibility of a peaceful surrender of the Floridas would not be neglected by the overanxious secretary. But Folch neither reconquered Baton Rouge nor ceded the Floridas. By the fall of 1811 he was in Havana to answer charges about his custodianship of West Florida and was rewarded with a full exoneration.[19]

During the remaining months of 1811 and to mid-May of the following year McKee continued his futile activities on the border. He reported regularly and fully to Monroe whose interest in the western sector of Florida waned as the United States, with the consent of local Spanish officials, gradually won the area west of the Perdido. On January 2, 1812, the secretary of state assured McKee that the president, who attributed the failure of the mission to circumstances beyond McKee's control, entirely approved his conduct in handling a difficult assignment. Monroe instructed McKee to inform Governor Claiborne and the commandant at Fort Stoddert of the termination of his powers and to transmit his final accounts to the department. These orders were executed on May 14 and shortly thereafter McKee returned to Washington where his unsuccessful mission ended at the place of its beginning.[20]

Notwithstanding the failure of Mathews and McKee, most of West Florida was organized as American territory. In the fall of 1811 a bill to admit the Orleans Territory into the Union as the state of Louisiana with an eastern boundary extending to the Perdido brewed a hot debate in the House of Representatives. Troup and George M. Bibb of Georgia found reason to protest: the former could not consent to include within Louisiana a territory still in dispute and subject to negotiations with Spain; the latter thought West Florida from the Iberville River to the Perdido should be annexed to the Mississippi Territory. By the administration's interpretation of the Louisiana Purchase, West Florida to the Perdido was a part of the Orleans Territory, and Representative Rhea of Tennessee could not agree to Bibb's proposal. The frail reasoning by which the United States had claimed and occupied the Spanish land gave way to a more immediately necessary appraisal: the eastern boundary of Louisiana was fixed at the Iberville. No boundary sat well with Josiah Quincy of Boston, who voiced his protest to the relative decline of New England in the ever-increasing number of American states. In a sentence which was to be mulled over, questioned, and uttered again, he said:

If this bill passes, it is my deliberate opinion that it is virtually a dissolution of this Union; that it will free the States from their moral obligation; and, as it will be the right of all, so it will be the duty of some, definitely to prepare for a separation, – amicably if they can, violently if they must.[21]

Neither his own state of Massachusetts nor any other New England state upheld the stand of the querulous Quincy. Louisiana became a state in 1812 and in the summer of that same year Governor Holmes organized the territory between the Iberville and the Perdido as a county of the Mississippi Territory. The governor, however, made no attempt to enforce his rule in Spanish-held Mobile and its environs. Less than a year later by the Act of February 12, 1813, Congress authorized the occupation of the last Spanish areas west of the Perdido, and on April 15 the American flag replaced the Spanish over Fort Charlotte at Mobile. After ten years of bloodless but far from amicable diplomatic warfare, Florida west of the Perdido was American.

Below the St. Marys

On JUNE 9, 1811, TWENTY-three days after their departure from Fort Stoddert, Mathews and Isaacs reached the little village of St. Marys, Georgia. Fast riding and long hours in the saddle had cut one day from the record time made by Mathews and McKee in their outward journey the previous winter. In those last days of travel Mathews clung feebly to his saddle: only his iron will brought him through. Yet after reaching St. Marys, exhausted and burning with fever, he refused to give up; in the afternoon and evening of the ninth he conferred with old friends and associates; by the morning of the following day he was confined to his bed. For fifteen days malaria racked his weakened body. After the fever abated he rested impatiently for time to restore his vitality.[1]

Illness and the consequent inactivity infuriated Mathews, who had left Fort Stoddert immediately after hearing of the death of Enrique White.[2] Since 1796 Governor White had resided in St. Augustine, from which point he ruled the Spanish province of East Florida. The extensive and relatively unimportant province of East Florida was never adequately manned or provisioned by the mother country. Outside of St. Augustine, a few key ports along the Atlantic coast and on the St. Johns River were guarded by a handful of officials whose meager pay was often in arrears and whose only road to wealth lay in accepting bribes and winking at frequent infractions of law. Governor White himself took advantage of any money he could pocket, but in spite of this a suggestion to cede East Florida to the United States enraged this patriotic Spaniard.

In the fall of 1810, on his first assignment for President Madison, Mathews had stubbornly refused to heed the advice of friends in St. Marys and had set out for St. Augustine. He crossed the channel from Georgia into Florida, but at Fernandina he was again urged not to mention the cession of Florida to Governor White. Despite the unanimity of adverse opinion Mathews determined to follow his own course until George Atkinson, one of the leading merchants of Fernandina, bluntly warned him: "As sure as you open your mouth to White on the subject, you will die in Moro Castle, and all the devils in hell can't save you."[3] On the following day Mathews prudently returned to St. Marys to await the passing of the intractable governor of St. Augustine.

White was a dying man. He lasted through the winter but on March 13, 1811, Juan de Estrada took direction of the government, and shortly thereafter, White died.[4] Unfortunately for the plans of the United States, Estrada was as unalterably opposed to a cession of Florida as had been his predecessor. Mathews soon discovered this fact and wasted no time in useless appeals to Estrada. During the summer and fall of 1811 he consulted the important residents below the St. Marys River and planned a new method of obtaining Florida.

General Mathews' headquarters was a room in Major Jacint Laval's summer cottage in the gardens near the United States military post of Point Petre, situated on the north bank of the St. Marys River. Although he had built the cottage for use as his summer quarters, Acting Commandant Laval found it more to his liking than his official quarters at Point Petre.[5] Mathews and Laval shared the cottage for almost a year, and with the services of a woman cook and housekeeper, lived in reasonable comfort.

It was not a happy association. Thin walls gave Laval no peace from the loud voices or guarded whispers of Mathews' numerous visitors. Far into many nights their conversations and argumentative debates kept Laval tossing in his bed, an unwilling listener to every detail of the scheme they plotted. The more he heard the less he thought of their plan to snatch Florida from the loyal Spanish governor at St. Augustine. At some early date Laval reached a decision: if ever the opportunity came, he would use his power to defeat them. For his part, Mathews disliked the French-born major who covered his effeminacy with the brass trappings of his military rank. The old general longed for the arrival of Lieutenant Colonel Thomas A. Smith who had been assigned to command at Point Petre, but whose coming had been indefinitely delayed by the chaotic situation in West Florida. Eventually Smith came, but too late for the purposes of the general.

By July, 1811, Mathews was sufficiently recovered in health to roam the country north and south of the border, observing, questioning, and interviewing the residents. West along the St. Marys River he found the lumber mills of Archibald Clark and the trading centers of Coleraine, Centerville, and Traders Hill. In the fall and winter great caravans came from the interior of Georgia to these villages; farmers in oxcarts, horsecarts, and two and four horse teams brought cotton, beeswax, honey, jerked beef, and cowhides to exchange for flour, sugar, coffee, powder, and shot. From south of the border erstwhile American farmers sent corn, beef, and potatoes, and the sly Seminole Indians traded beef, venison, and furs for guns and ammunition. At many points along the St. Marys farmers, Indians, and merchants evaded the Spanish and American custom laws and swelled the clandestine trade of the villages.

The trade of the river settlements flowed to the town of St. Marys near the mouth of the river. Into its harbor sailed ships from Savannah, Charleston, Baltimore, and more northerly ports with cotton, flour, and rum. From its docks the cotton and flour disappeared into the channels of world trade; and masts, lumber, and naval stores were exchanged for the manufactured goods of England and the sugar of the West Indies. The harbor admitted vessels of seventeen foot draught, and a fairly good road ran from the town through coastal Georgia for 135 miles to the city of Savannah.[6]

With a population of only 585, St. Marys was the fifth largest town in Georgia and fast overtaking Washington, the fourth town of the state.[7] The American embargo of 1807 and the Napoleonic wars of Europe had transformed St. Marys from a somnolent little village into a boisterous town. It was founded in 1788 when settlers from nearby Cumberland Island, who in the previous year had paid thirty-eight dollars for 1672 acres on Buttermilk Bluff, occupied the town site.[8] For a few years the settlement was called St. Patricks, but after 1792 that name gave way to the more geographically appropriate St. Marys. Almost from the first the village became a mecca for fugitives from justice, debtors, and deserters, and soon attracted smugglers, slave traders, rustlers, robbers, and prowlers of every description. Together with these men of illicit ways came planters, merchants, lumbermen, and farmers. In the back country along the St. Marys, Marianna, and Satilla rivers, rice plantations supported an increasing slave and white population, and on the pine lands, cattle and hogs supplied meat for workers and owners. Early in the eighteenth century the Savannah post road was continued from Mrs. Peck's tavern in Glynn County to Brown's Ferry on the Satilla and on to St. Marys. The prominence of the back country plantation owners brought the county seat of Camden County from St. Marys to the little settlement of Jefferson on the south bank of the Satilla River, and the pioneer society aped the activities of Refugee Plantation, the property of George McIntosh, whose land grant dated to an age when Georgia had been a royal province of Great Britain.

For a time the destiny of St. Marys hung in the balance. Proximity to Florida, the lush profits from raiding below the border, from lumbering, and after 1807, from smuggling and the slave trade threw the scales to St. Marys. Some of the original settlers, James Seagrove, William Ashley, Lodowick Ashley, and Richard Cole, acquired wealth; and others achieved frontier comfort. In 1802 William Bellinger Clark of Savannah settled in St. Marys and accumulated a fortune. His two-story white clapboard house amid the moss covered oaks on Main Street, his lumber mills up the river, and his large legal and illegal fees as collector of the port made him the envy of less astute men. But he was not alone. William Cone of North Carolina, in the lumber trade, and Buckner Harris, a turbulent escapee from judgment in his former Georgia home, in the slave trade, found the way to frontier profits.

George Clarke was the first Methodist minister to arrive in St. Marys, and he was shocked by the number of adult men and women who had never heard a prayer or listened to a sermon. But it was the Presbyterians who erected the first church, a rectangular wooden building topped with a square belfry. For many years after its completion in 1808 it served not only as a meeting place for various religious denominations but also as a rendezvous for smugglers. The basement or boarded up space between the elevated floor and ground was convenient for storing smuggled cigars and rum. And when

Archibald Clark adamantly refused to allow one sea captain to load his ship with cotton, the shrewd smuggler bided his time. On the morning following a dark foggy night the townspeople were awakened by the clanging church bell. There in the belfry, cramped and frightened, stood the minister's horse. Throughout the day Clarke and his customs officers aided in rescuing the animal; before they got it down, the cotton had been loaded and the smuggler was off to sea.[9]

If St. Mary's with her money-mad citizens and pleasure-seeking sailors had a soul it was hard to find – harder to save. From the ships at anchor in her harbor came hundreds of reckless seamen on leave from the discipline of an arduous voyage; Point Petre supplied the soldiers; and the United States marines on Cumberland Island, and navy men from the American war vessels could not resist the enticements of the town. There was wine aplenty; and the stronger drink too, rum and the potent whiskey of the Scotch-Irish farmers of the Appalachian region. Tavern keepers and grogshop proprietors kept their casks open weekdays and Sundays, and in so doing defied the laws of Georgia and the authority of the Camden County commissioners.[10] Revellers filled with wine rendered the song, but women, the third part of a notorious trio, were scarce.

Only 349 of St. Marys 585 residents were white, and within the sixteen to forty-five age group 117 men vied for the affections of 65 women.[11] Few single women could long withstand the glittering promises of ardent suitors, but some who saw the drudgery of the kitchen and the annual appearance of a new member in the family, chose the way of easy virtue. Respectable married women put out a protecting hand to shield their children as these harlots swished by, dressed in finery from Paris and smelling of the Rue de la Paix. The white prostitutes could not supply the demand; and since only a few of the thirty free persons of color went into the Negro houses, comely slave girls paid their masters ten dollars per month and, for a fee, serviced the seamen. Their expenses were heavy, $120 for rental and an estimated $320 annually for housing and clothing and doctoring; but their incomes so far outran expenses that within a few years an ambitious girl could buy her freedom.[12]

This was St. Marys in 1811 – a lusty frontier town where smugglers and raiders, pimps and prostitutes, robbers and adventurers, soldiers and seamen, though disliked, associated with and were catered to by the more respectable element of the town. Yet beneath its imposing edifice of evil lay the seeds of normal life. More than 130 children played in the yards of St. Marys' homes and for their offspring, parents had zealous aspirations. In planning the future, Georgians thought of land and looked south of the border to the fertile lowlands for rice, rich hammocks for cotton and corn, and grass and overflowed lands for hogs and cattle. American conquest and settlement of Florida would open new land for exploration, pack the Spaniards off to Cuba, and rid the frontier of marauding Indians.

It was from these respectable men of St. Marys and Camden County that General George Mathews expected support. Lodowick Ashley, William Ashley, William Clark, James Seagrove, John Houstoun McIntosh, John Floyd, Thomas King, and William Johnston were men of wealth and position and influence. Some of them owned large plantations south of the St. Marys River; all of them desired Florida, and their opinions were respected by the quondam American citizens residing south of the border.

Mathews' friends in St. Marys hoped for the success of his mission but predicted failure. The Spanish, they knew, would not willingly cede Florida, and the American farmers below the St. Marys were too prosperous to endanger their incomes by rebellion. Long staple or sea island cotton could be sold for seventy-five cents per pound, corn brought $1.25 per bushel in St. Augustine, timber for lumber was freely cut on the public domain, and meat commanded a high price both in St. Augustine and Fernandina.[13] The prosperity of Florida affected the economy of St. Marys: no longer could one secure fish for ten cents per dozen, two fat hens for twenty-five cents, and beef for three cents per pound.[14] A high ranking naval officer complained of his lodgings in the corner of a very common room for which he paid fifty dollars per month and received the fare of an "independent ordinary" with brandy and water as his beverage.[15]

Mathews brushed aside the pessimism of his friends and set out on a personal tour of the nearby Florida settlements. At St. Marys he boarded a boat for Florida, sailed down the river past Point Petre into Cumberland Sound and southeast to the Amelia River which divided Amelia Island from the mainland of Florida. Approximately one mile below the river's mouth, and just below Clark's Creek on the west side of the island, lay the Spanish town of Fernandina.[16] It was Spanish in little more than name. The rusty guns of Fort San Carlos and the nearby sand-blown battery symbolized both the authority and debility of Spain. The marsh along Clark's Creek on the north and northeast gave the town some natural protection, but the highlands from Morriss Bluff on the south afforded easy access to the settlement.

Amelia Island was discovered early in the history of Florida; and successive waves of French, Spanish, and English nationals explored its surrounding waters and colonized its strategic harbor and fertile land. The island's principal settlement, called Egmont by the British, blossomed into a disordered town during the late years of the American Revolution. Renamed Fernandina by the Spaniards in 1785, it became the focal settlement for an ever-growing American population. Planters and farmers from Georgia and South Carolina, English merchants, Irish adventurers, German refugees, and Spanish officials built houses in the town and occupied the land of the island; while on the mainland waterways to the west and south, farming and lumbering drew numbers of enterprising American colonists. As the back country filled up and trading ships anchored in the harbor to load the products of East Florida, Fernandina grew into an unplanned town with streets a maze of confusion and houses set in hodge-podge.

The seventeen-eighties and nineties and the early years of eighteen hundred passed violently in Fernandina. Indian traders came to swap skins and meat for the white man's rum. The townspeople hid away when drunken Indians roamed the town, but as soon as the savages fell in drunken stupor they were laid in their canoes and towed to the mainland[17] – their furs and meat exchanged for memories and headsplitting hangovers. At times, Georgians rushed down from the north to rob, recapture slaves, or enslave free Negroes; and Floridians voiced their protests to the commandant at Fort San Carlos and penned letters to the governor at St. Augustine.

Just as the American embargo of 1807 and the prohibition of the foreign slave trade had made St. Marys, Georgia, they also transformed Fernandina into a thriving port. By 1811 as many as thirty-eight vessels could be seen anchored in its harbor. Bales of cotton, clandestinely shipped in from the United States, disappeared into the holds of waiting ships; lumber, masts, and naval stores lay on the wharfs ready for loading; and sea captains bargained with provision merchants for meat and flour for their crews. Often the stench from an incoming ship heralded the arrival of a slaver. On the shores of inlets, or even in the port of Fernandina, the Negroes were landed and then herded northwest to the south bank of the St. Marys River. There they rested while the slave runners created a disturbance at some distant point on the Georgia line; when the frontier guards rushed to protect the settlers, the Negroes were moved across the St. Marys and sold into a slavery from which there was no graduation. The tremendous profits from slave trading and smuggling attracted hijackers and robbers who worked out from Fernandina.

The trade of Fernandina developed the settlement so rapidly that in 1811 Governor White ordered Surveyor General George I. F. Clarke to replat the town. Clarke laid out broad streets running from west to east and north to south – Calle de la Marina, Estrada, Amelia, Commandant, White, Fernando – all were streets except one, Paseo de las Damos or Ladies Avenue, at the north of the town.

In the summer and fall of 1811 the sound of hammers and saws resounded in the morning and late afternoon air. Houses were moved to new locations or shifted slightly on old lots, new buildings were erected, and yards were leveled and beautified with shrubs and trees. On Marine Street stood the warehouses and stores of Forbes and Company and George Clarke, while the other large trading firms of Hibberson and Yonge, and Sibbald and Bethune occupied choice lots in the center of town. Jose Garcia operated a provisions business for ships; James Cashen sold ship supplies at public auction; Antonio Martinez, Jose Alvarez, Daniel Donahue, and Francisco de Salas catered to thirsty, hungry patrons. On Estrada Street facing the Plaza de la Constitucion, De Salas could accommodate twenty guests in his hotel. The German doctor Karl Santage's hospital was conveniently located on Commandant Street within one hundred feet of Ladies Avenue. Elsewhere were the carpenter shop of Ezra Patch and the smithy of Mateo Gonzales, the homes of merchants and planters; and sandwiched here and there with no pattern of segregation were the houses and lots of seventeen free Negroes, where "Felipa the Witch" and "Felicia the Fortune Teller" lived. And also there were the houses, the unmentionable houses of whites and Negroes, Casas de Puntas, frequented by town blades and errant husbands, but made prosperous by visiting seamen.[18]

The wealthy planters Joseph Fenwick, Zephaniah Kingsley, and John Rushing had town houses in Fernandina; but most of the rich and moderately well-to-do farmers resided on their Amelia Island farms or within a sixty by twenty mile area between the St. Marys and the St. Johns rivers. Below this quasi-American sector of Florida lay the district of St. Augustine, inhabited mostly by Spaniards and Minorcans; and west of the Spanish and American sectors the Seminole Indians roamed the forests. For the Indian, transplanted United States citizens had utter hatred combined with fear. "The Indians," a correspondent reported to *Niles Register*, "are incorrigible in their cruelties. They are natural enemies to a civilized state of society, as it destroys their independence. They resemble wolves, who would rather be exterminated than domesticated."[19]

George Mathews centered his attention on the American areas of Florida where almost all the residents were of United States extraction and the few Spaniards, Swiss, Irish, and Germans were married to American wives or moved in American society. Plantations of the wealthy overlooked the rivers and lagoons. John Houstoun McIntosh with more than $28,000 invested in land worked hundreds of slaves in Florida and on Refugee Plantation in Georgia.[20] Lodowick Ashley employed his slaves and hired laborers in cutting trees and sawing lumber on the south bank of the St. Marys. William Craig, Kingsley, Fatio, Hogan, Yonge, Hartly, Hendrix, Fenwick, and many others planted the land and grazed cattle. Numbers of less wealthy men such as Francis Pass, whose total wealth in corn, cattle, hogs, horses, buildings, and personal property amounted to over $9,000, imitated the great planters.[21] And there were also the poor farmers who spaded a bare living from the ground and shot their meat supply in the woods.

These enterprising men occupied a potentially rich part of Florida. The coasts, sounds, and inlets abounded with a variety of marine life – bass, drum, mullet, sheepshead, whiting, grouper, and flounder; the bays and lagoons were stored with oysters, shrimp, and large white-meated, tender clams. On land stood the forests of pine, oak, ash, magnolia, and cypress. The dark hammock soil produced 200 pounds of sea-island cotton per acre, twenty-five bushels of corn, 300 bushels of potatoes; and hogs and cattle which foraged in the fields sold for three and ten dollars per head. The demand for labor pushed the price of slaves to $600 for a good field hand and to $800 for a trained lumber man; hired laborers or masters who rented slaves received from eight to thirty dollars per month.²²

The prosperity of Florida was detrimental to the cause of General Mathews: few rich men were willing to break with the Spanish government. Many Spanish Floridians honored the traditions of their native land and clung to the established Catholic church. The strength of their patriotism eliminated them as possible revolutionists. Other less loyal Spaniards and also Americans prospered by the sale of grain, vegetables, and meat in St. Augustine. Economics kept them loyal. Slave runners and smugglers favored Spain, for annexation of Florida by the United States would stop their profitable activities, and even the patriotic American residents of Florida shied away from any action which might interfere with their economic well-being.

Conditions in Florida were unfavorable to revolt but not hopeless. Mathews' eyes were on wealthy, influential men whose leadership would impress President Madison with the respectability of the rebellion. At heart the planters of Florida desired annexation. If they could be assured of United States support, a quick non-destructive revolution, and economic gain in land, they would readily follow the lead of Mathews.

The key to revolution lay in St. Marys. More and more Mathews realized that as he reconnoitered in Florida, and therefore he hastened back to the border town. Here were the poor men who would fight for the promise of land in Florida, and the wealthy men, who, once convinced of presidential backing, would give leadership to the common man and supply the immediate needs of an invading army. After that army invaded Florida, hundreds of quondam Americans would flock to its standard: St. Augustine and Florida would be conquered before the slow-moving Spaniard could act.

Mathews had finally worked out a scheme. Unable to secure peaceful delivery of Florida from the existing local authority, he would foment rebellion, and when Georgia volunteers and American armed forces installed a new authority in Florida, he would accept cession of the province from that new local authority. Though a bold and daring plan, it was not an original one, for in 1810 Governor Claiborne had received President Madison's approval of a similar scheme in West Florida. The fact that his plan closely followed the outline of a scheme once sanctioned by the president pleased Mathews. He and his fellow Georgians would keep to the shadows while residents of Florida grabbed the spotlight and presented to the world a picture of a rebelling people praying for the annexation and protection of the United States. Thus would Mathews execute the will of Madison and heed the president's admonition, "But hide your hand and mine, general."

Notwithstanding the unfavorable signs in Florida, Mathews had reason for optimism. Within the past decade a steady stream of Americans had crossed the St. Marys to take land in Florida, and they had retained their love of the United States. As early as 1790 Spain, having failed to settle Florida with her nationals, opened wide the border to American citizens, offering them 1000 acres of land, exemption from taxes and military duty, subsidies for agricultural products, and religious freedom.[23] This free immigration had been as much opposed by Governor Cespedes of St. Augustine as it later was welcomed by Secretary of State Thomas Jefferson. In 1786 Cespedes had advised opening Florida to Europeans but not to Americans who, he believed, would anglicize Florida;[24] and four years later after Cespedes had been replaced at St. Augustine, Jefferson happily informed President Washington: "Governor Quesada, by order of his court, is inviting foreigners to go and settle in Florida. This is meant for our people.... It will be the means of delivering to us peaceably, what may otherwise cost us a war. In the meantime we may complain of this seduction of our inhabitants just enough to make [the Spaniards] believe we think it very wise policy for them, and confirm them in it. This is my idea of it."[25]

Both Cespedes and Jefferson were wrong. For a year Americans crossed the St. Marys in numbers, but many of them soon returned to the United States.[26] The celebrated case of John McIntosh, the grandson of John Mohr McIntosh, caused many of the Spanish citizens of St. Augustine to protest to their king.[27] Of the three sons of John Mohr, Lachlan and John M. were the fighting McIntoshes, ever ready to serve their country or fight a duel, while the third son, George, was a peaceful McIntosh, who acquired wealth in trade and plantations. Although criticized for their killings and illegal trade,[28] all were highly successful in their chosen way of life. Soon after the outbreak of the Revolutionary War John, a lieutenant, was stationed at Charleston, where he met Sara Swinton and fell in love with her.

When Lieutenant McIntosh heard of the ill-treatment of good Charleston families by Captain Elholm, an excellent swordsman and Polish volunteer in the American cause, he publicly upbraided the captain for his high-handed actions. A duel was the result. In a vain hope of preventing the duel, Sara requested John to visit her in the early morning of the appointed day, and his friends, fearing the power of woman, urged him not to see her. But John came of the fighting McIntoshes, to whom love was important but honor more so, and all the reasoning and womanly guile of Sara could not move him.

The duelists met near a large oak not far from Sara's home. A lucky blow almost severed the right arm of Elholm, but he continued the battle, using his good left arm so effectively that McIntosh was soon bleeding from a number of wounds. The seconds ended the conflict after both men were wounded in many places. Charleston belles lionized John McIntosh, but Sara bound his wounds and nursed him back to health and became his bride.[29]

In later years men recounted the duel, but McIntosh's real fame came from his spirited defense of Sunbury, Georgia. In November, 1788, McIntosh (now a colonel) faced an invading British force of 500 men. Although he had less than 200 men, McIntosh replied to a summons to surrender his post with a terse "Come and take it." For this answer and his successful defense of Sunbury, the Georgia assembly gave him a sword with his defiant words engraved upon it.[30]

After the Revolutionary War McIntosh was granted land by the Spanish Government and developed a plantation by the St. Johns River near the Spanish customs post of San Nicholas. There, boat loads of cotton from the south moving down the river to the sea were stopped for payment of the export duty on cotton. Whenever McIntosh had his cotton ready for export, he went to the commander at San Nicholas to await the approach of his cotton boats. As they appeared in the distance the Spaniard raised his spyglass, intently inspected them, and shrugged his shoulders.

Lowering his spyglass he turned to McIntosh: "There's too much cotton to pass without duty."

Silently McIntosh handed him a Spanish gold doubloon.

The commander put the doubloon to one eye, his spyglass to the other, and remarked, "I still see cotton."

McIntosh gave him another doubloon.

The Spaniard placed a doubloon over each eye and said contentedly, "I see no cotton, now."[31]

But there came a time when bribery did not solve the problems of McIntosh. In 1793 Citizen Genêt of France began his intrigues in the United States, and a phase of his far-flung scheme caught McIntosh. An army of Georgians under Samuel Hammond invaded East Florida, and in conjunction with local men, formed a government under France with the promise of eventual independence, generous salaries, large bounties, and extensive lands for their work.[32] Whether John McIntosh had a hand in the plot or not made no difference: Governor Quesada at St. Augustine thought him a likely suspect.

In January, 1794, when McIntosh had retired after a busy day of trade in St. Augustine, officers of the governor arrested him. Without a definite accusation or formal trial he was shipped off to prison in Moro Castle in Havana. Meanwhile Spanish soldiers ransacked his St. Johns plantation and frightened Sara McIntosh and her boys with threats to execute her husband and their father. For months Sara, who was almost blind, had her hand guided as she penned pathetic letters to Governor Quesada and the captain general of Cuba.[33] Officials high in the administration of George Washington, and even the president himself, interposed in McIntosh's behalf.[34] In less than a year he had gained his freedom, sent his family and property back to Georgia, and with a handful of friends destroyed the post of San Nicholas, burned Cow Ford, and sunk the Spanish ships anchored in the St. Johns. Hastily he shook the sand of Florida from his shoes and retired to his plantation in Georgia. Blind, broken Sara passed away in 1799, but her husband lived to become a brigadier general of Georgia militia and to fight the Spaniards of Florida again.

Hot-headed Georgians would have settled their score against the Spaniards; but George Mathews, who was governor of the state, issued a proclamation forbidding the assembly of troops and any hostile acts against a friendly neighbor.[35] Since Georgia was unprepared for battle and Mathews feared the Spaniards might retaliate by inciting the Indians to war, he exerted his power to quiet the boisterous border citizens. When the men of Camden County continued in their hostile ways he ordered a company of dragoons to patrol the border,[36] but even the troops failed to prevent William Ashley and William Downs from slipping into Florida to rob Daniel Plumer of three slaves. Mathews welcomed Sebastian Kindelan as an emissary from the captain general of Cuba, and together the men worked to solve the immediate frontier problems.[37]

Unfortunately any agreement between Georgia and Florida for peace on the border was hardly worth the pen used in writing it. In 1807 the mayor of Newton, Georgia, led a slave raid; and in the following year Archibald Clark, the United States Collector at St. Marys, headed a party which broke into the home of David Garvin, pulled his wife out of bed, smashed the china in the kitchen, chopped down closet doors, and stole a "slave wench" from him.[38] In defense of his act Clark claimed he had bought the slave girl from the creditors of Garvin who later enticed her to Florida. Almost immediately after the raid Clark sailed from St. Marys for a visit with relatives in Savannah and took the girl with him.[39]

These border raids discouraged many Americans who contemplated migration to Florida, and Spain's closing of the border in 1804 placed an additional handicap on would-be immigrants. Yet in spite of these draw-backs American families began to move in numbers to Spanish Florida where they made homes, and for the first time, refused to fly back to Georgia in troublous times. Southeastern Georgia was filling up; migrating families from more northerly areas found the best acres under cultivation, and so they pushed on into Florida. Many poor farmers who owned but one wife, twelve children, six acres of pine land, four dogs, a rifle, a raccoon-skin pouch, and a powder horn; whose whole "crop" seldom gave more than a near starvation diet to their brood; and whose rifle added an occasional turkey or haunch of venison to their meager bill of fare — these poor piney-woods people looked to Florida for land and plenty. Shifty-eyed "white trash," more eager to father tow-headed moppets than to raise corn; second and third sons of wealthy planters, who had funds or could borrow money; rough adventurers, who knew the race went to the swift and the battle to the strong — all moved into Florida. Population pressure was accomplishing that which Spanish inducements had failed to do, the settlement of Florida.

The nineteenth century migrants found Spanish authority all but a cipher. No border patrols hindered their crossing the St. Marys and squatting on the fertile land below that river; Spanish customs, taxes, and laws were evaded or ignored with impunity. The few Spanish soldiers stationed at Fernandina, Cow Ford, and Picolata preferred their indolent existence to controversy with the recently arrived inhabitants. Former Americans, such men as John Houstoun McIntosh and William Craig, who held the vital positions of the civil government, transacted their business in English and left the governor in St. Augustine the problem of translating their records and reports into Spanish for submission to officials in Cuba and Spain. Just as Jefferson had predicted they would, American citizens were conquering Florida without firing a shot.

Nevertheless conquest was slow — too slow for the impatient transplanted Americans and their Georgia kinsmen north of the St. Marys. Mathews had no doubts as to the popular response to his plan for taking Florida. Neither did he foresee any lack of enthusiasm in Washington where Madison and Monroe were as anxious as he to push Spain out of the southeast. If they should waver he could renew their determination by playing on their fear of British occupation of Florida. American military activity on the border could be justified, to watching European diplomats, as necessary to stop the illegal foreign slave trade and enforce the customs laws of the United States. To execute those laws Commodore Hugh Campbell of the navy and Major General John Floyd of the Georgia militia had been ordered to St. Marys.[40] Under cover of legitimate national activities a revolutionary force would be secretly organized on the Georgia border, and sweeping south, enlarged by recruit after recruit, would force every resisting Spaniard into surrender or into the sea. An improvised revolutionary government would then offer Florida to the United States.

There were fallacies in his reasoning and his plans but Mathews either ignored them or could not see them. With an ample number of potential Georgia volunteers, support from American military forces, and sanction of the Madison administration Mathews eliminated from his thoughts the possibility of failure. His only unsupplied need was able, respectable leadership, men to do his bidding in their own names and cover his actions in fomenting a rebellion in Spanish Florida. Mathews set himself to the task of finding such men and organizing the revolution.

Organizing the Revolution

MATHEWS GAVE MANY HOURS OF thought to the critical problem of leadership for the contemplated revolution. To give a semblance of reality to the movement the leader would have to be a resident of Spanish Florida – a man who could legitimately claim disaffection and act under the natural right of an abused subject to break his compact with an unjust sovereign. Furthermore the right man should be aggressive, an inspiring leader who could attract a large following, and even lead his men in battle, if battle became necessary. Essential, too, was financial support, for volunteers would require guns, powder, food, horses, camp equipment, and the various accouterments of war. Some of these needs Mathews could supply by requisition on army and navy commanders of the United States forces, but he could not furnish every necessity. The leader, then, should be a resident of Spanish Florida and a military man, who had wealth and was willing to use it in a speculative venture on the promise of rewards in money and power. Finding such a man was no easy task.

Two established citizens of St. Marys required no prodding to join forces with Mathews. His confidant, James Seagrove, former Indian agent and collector at St. Marys, was eager to help, but his advanced age and physical feebleness relegated him to the position of an advisor whose name would attract volunteers. Although Archibald Clark had wealth and aggressive youth (he was just over thirty) his official position in the American government and his lack of the Florida residence requirement disqualified him. And Clark held closely to his money; Mathews never pried much from the shrewd frontier wizard. Other men such as Buckner Harris and William Cone, lacked the reputation for respectability which Mathews thought essential to the cause. At least their names are conspicuously absent from the list of revolutionists and they rose to prominence only after Mathews passed from the scene.

In his search for a leader Mathews roamed both sides of the border, but he never found a man who embodied all the ideals prerequisite to leadership. Out from St. Marys he discovered a willing partner in the owner of Refuge Plantation, John Houstoun McIntosh,* who had inherited the plantation and many slaves from his father, George, the son of old John Mohr McIntosh. At the age of nineteen he augmented his already considerable inheritance by marriage to Eliza Bayard of New York, whose wealth compensated for her advanced age of twenty-three. As the highly respected owner of Refuge Plantation, John Houstoun McIntosh served in the Georgia constitutional convention of 1798 and later as justice of the inferior court of Camden County. In 1803 he bought the Florida lands of John McQueen, and although he continued to reside mostly in Georgia, he took the oath of allegiance to Spain and was recognized as a colonial subject of Spanish Florida.[1]

McIntosh had the requirements: residence, respectability, wealth, and a willingness to gamble his money in the revolutionary cause. He also had deficiencies: he came from the trading, peaceable branch of the McIntosh family and his name inspired no "hurrahs" on either side of the border.[2] What Mathews promised him for his participation and advances are known only in part. All loans of McIntosh would be repaid in full by the United States government, and land, acres of rich land, would be his. Perhaps Mathews dangled the territorial governorship before him – at least the old general suggested it in a letter to President Madison.[3]

Mathews and McIntosh met at some time during the summer of 1811. Undoubtedly they used the advice of Seagrove and Clark as step by step they outlined the plan to revolutionize Florida and create a local authority willing to cede the province to the United States.

---

*John Houstoun McIntosh has been confused with his more famous cousin Colonel, and later General, John McIntosh (see pp. 50-52). John Houstoun was born on May 1, 1773, and he was a boy of ten when the American Revolutionary War, in which most historians state he served as a colonel, came to its conclusion.

ORGANIZING THE REVOLUTION

One thing is certain (in spite of later claims to the contrary by antiquarians and historians): they never contemplated an independent republic or state of East Florida. From the inception of their plans the revolutionary government of Florida was to be the creature of a moment. Its only purpose was to transfer title from Spain to the United States. When the United States had possession and had resolved her differences with Spain, a territory of Florida would be sufficient, with the American government paying the salary of local officials, building roads, dredging harbors, and rewarding with land and office those who motivated the transfer from Spain to the United States.

In reality, the government which McIntosh was to head would not be a government but only the provisional forces or "Patriots of East Florida." When those forces had occupied Florida, or any part of it, it would be immediately tendered to the United States. Then Mathews, having received an offer of peaceful cession from the "existing local authorities of Florida" and acting under his authority from President Madison, could order the commander at Point Petre to accept, occupy, and hold the province for the United States. Full authority over Florida would then be vested in the United States and the "Patriots" would cease to function except at the command of agents of the American government. The elapsed time between occupation by the "Patriots" and acceptance in the name of the United States might be a day or even less. In this transaction Mathews would be the agent to receive Florida for the president while McIntosh acted as the commissioner of the "Patriots" to offer the province.

Thus the two men neatly bound into a simple package the cession of Florida. Should the local Spanish officials resist the Patriot occupation, an armed force equipped to give battle was essential. An urgent problem was the recruiting of volunteers for the revolutionary army, and since the conquest of Florida depended largely on surprise, open recruiting of men below the St. Marys was impossible, for it would warn the governor in St. Augustine and give him time to prepare his defenses. A few key men, known to favor the scheme, would be advised of the plan, but the main body of volunteers would come from Camden County, the militia of General John Floyd, and if necessary from the troops at Point Petre.

The most troublesome question for Mathews and McIntosh was the attitude of President Madison and Secretary of State Monroe. This plotted revolution of the royal subjects of Spanish Florida was a barefaced fraud — Mathews and McIntosh knew it. Indeed McIntosh, who was to risk his money and, in the event of failure, to face certain confiscation of his valuable Florida property, repeatedly asked for assurance as to the opinion of the administration. In vain did Mathews read his instructions from the president, retell the interview he had had with Madison, and speak of the orders sent to army and navy commanders to obey his commands. McIntosh remained unconvinced. Mathews himself was not too certain of the reception his bold measures would receive in Washington.

In his characteristic manner he acted to clarify the situation. His first letter from Point Petre after his return from Fort Stoddert described conditions as unsatisfactory; for the Spaniards, flushed with pride by reports of victories of their patriotic armies in Spain and Portugal, were indifferent to all suggestions of delivering Florida to the United States. Mathews warned the secretary of state of a rumor that a regiment of Africans from Jamaica were on their way to St. Augustine. In the face of British aid to the Spanish, the American forces at Point Petre could not preoccupy and hold Florida, or prevent the rampant smuggling along the border. "I am," he concluded, "daily more and more confirmed in a belief of the vast importance of Florida to the U. States in a commercial view."[4]

During the summer and fall of 1811 Mathews kept Monroe informed of his plans and movements. On August 3 he reported the definite refusal of the "powers that exist" in Florida to cede the province. The inhabitants, however, were ripe for revolt but unable to throw off the yoke of Spain without external aid. If 200 guns and 50 swords were supplied them they would rebel with a fair chance of success. These arms could be put into their hands by assignment to the commandant at Point Petre subject to the order of Mathews, and "I would use the most discreet management to prevent the U. States being committed and altho I cannot vouch for the event, I think there would be but little danger."[5] Mathews also restated his opinion of the importance of Florida, for in addition to the impossibility of preventing smuggling under existing conditions, Spanish Florida offered haven for runaway Negroes and asylum for army and navy deserters.

The key sentence in Mathews' letter suggested the method by which he and the potential revolutionists could be assured of American sup-

ORGANIZING THE REVOLUTION

port. He knew full well that Monroe or Madison could not send him direct instructions to foment a revolution in Florida, as that would compromise and embarrass the United States, for there was always the possibility of foreign agents securing the information from an imprudent or dishonest clerk. But Mathews' letters could be acknowledged and the administration's policy be made clear through its answer to the protests which Great Britain was making on American action in Florida. Mathews warned the discontented Spanish-Floridians not to expect prompt and efficient aid from the United States unless American negotiations with the British minister terminated with the two countries still at odds.[6]

Mathews was not content with a mere outline of his plans, restricted by the limitation of prudent, non-compromising words. To clarify his project beyond all shadow of doubt, he left St. Marys for Oglethorpe County on September 30, 1811, to visit Senator Crawford of Georgia and give the senator, who would soon be leaving for Washington, a complete account of plans and operations. Mathews gave the senator "a faithful detail of my operations" in East Florida and requested Monroe to call on Crawford for any information which may have been omitted in written reports.[7] Immediately after his arrival in Washington Senator Crawford sent Madison a note, enclosed a copy of Mathews' letter of August 3, and stated: "As soon as the Senate is organized, I will do myself the honor of communicating the substance of the oral communication made by that gentleman to me."[8]

Mathews continued to report directly to Monroe. According to rumor a Marylander, Richard Reid Keene, a former resident of Cuba, had secured from the Spanish Cortes a grant of all the vacant lands in East Florida.[9] The rumor stirred the residents of Florida to protest. It also reduced their little remaining confidence in the tottering regime in St. Augustine, and engendered sentiments highly favorable for the United States. However, Mathews had disquieting news from Colonel McKee of an unconfirmed report of the revocation of his and McKee's powers as agents of the government. He had, however, given no credit to the rumor, being confident that an act of such importance would have been immediately communicated to him. "Should the information prove well founded I must intreat you to give me the earliest notice, for altho I ever am ready to devote my best abilities to my country, yet I do not wish to remain in its employ any longer than I can render it useful and acceptable services."[10]

In January of 1812, Mathews made one more progress report. Affairs in East Florida, he wrote, remained as before with the people discontented and anxious for American aid; a British sloop was ready to sail from Fernandina to St. Augustine with dispatches; and Colonel Sebastian Kindelan had been appointed governor of East Florida. "I am well acquainted with him," Mathews stated; "he is a gentleman of handsome talents and military experience, and I am fearful on his arrival at St. Augustine he will have the drawbridge repaired, which will render the fort difficult to be taken — at present it is not in condition fit to use."[11] Since Kindelan was not expected for some months, Mathews thought it advisable to plan for the immediate conquest of St. Augustine. In a letter of an earlier date to Senator Crawford he had suggested the need for a company of artillery and one of infantry to reinforce Point Petre: he reiterated this counsel and added a request for more definite orders to be forwarded to Commodore Hugh Campbell, commander of the naval force on Cumberland Sound.[12]

Mathews had now done everything in his power to inform the administration of his plans and to secure approval of his scheme. Final action depended on Madison and Monroe, for without their concurrence McIntosh and the other conspirators would not risk their persons and property in a cause doomed to failure unless aided by the United States. For months Mathews waited expectantly every Friday as the weekly mail came in from Savannah.[13] No word came from either Madison or Monroe. No news, however, was in one sense good news, for at least his acts were not disavowed. Since the administration in Washington had to be circumspect, Mathews and his friends awaited Madison's answer to foreign, and particularly British, protests to the American policy in Florida: to the men at St. Marys the president's reply to the representatives of European countries would either confirm or deny the acts of his agent, George Mathews.

In Washington the American State Department had countered the protests of Spain and England on West Florida by contending the province an American possession by right of purchase in the Louisiana Treaty. Although Luis de Onís had not been recognized as the minister from Spain, he communicated with the State Department through Juan Bautista Bernaben, the Spanish consul at Baltimore.[14] The consul had characterized the seizure of West Florida as a "positive act of hostility" contrary to the friendship and harmony which the Spanish nation tried so assiduously to cultivate with the United States.[15] Bernaben's forceful protest on West Florida had been a mild forerunner of his angry expostulations on East Florida; but the State Department had already determined to disregard feeble Spain. It was no secret that Spain had been prevented from declaring war on the United States by the fear of England's unwillingness or inability to supply Florida with men and war material; and Spain, therefore, had agreed to refer the Florida questions to England and to abide by the decisions made in London.[16]

Great Britain quickly assumed responsibility for the diplomatic battle over Florida. Augustus J. Foster, the British minister at Washington, was instructed to present a solemn protest on the occupation of West Florida; and if any attempt was made to take East Florida, he should "instantly remonstrate against Such a Proceeding, for which It will not be possible to allege Even the slight pretexts, which have been attempted in justification of the Aggression on West Florida." Foster was cautioned not to use hostile or menacing language but to confine his representations to friendly and candid expositions of the unjust and ungenerous nature of the American proceedings, for although Great Britain could not view the acts against her ally without regret and pain, "It is not a necessary Consequence of those Sentiments That This Government should proceed to vindicate the Rights of Spain by force of Arms."[17] England stood ready to support Spain with words but not munitions.

In July, 1811, confining his protest entirely to West Florida, Foster sent his first note to Monroe. He requested an explanation of "the motives which led to this unjust aggression by the United States on the territories" of Spain; and pointed to the reasons heretofore advanced by the American government as so flimsy that the United States could not "avoid the reproach which must attend the ungenerous and unprovoked seizure of a foreign colony, while the parent State is engaged in a noble contest for independence, against a most unjustifiable and violent invasion of the rights both of the monarch and people of Spain."[18]

Within less than a week Monroe replied with a lengthy exposition on American policy in West Florida, at the same time disclaiming the right of Great Britain to interfere in the controversy, but expressing a willingness to explain in a friendly manner the act which Foster had been ordered to protest. It was evident from the minister's letter, Monroe wrote, that Great Britain was laboring under a misapprehension: the United States had not seized a moment of national embarrassment in Spain to occupy a province which Spain could not defend. Although examples of such unworthy conduct were unfortunately too frequent in history, the United States had avoided them; and in all transactions with foreign nations, particularly with Spain, the American government had always given unequivocal proof of an upright policy which would shield it from unmerited suspicion. A long list of injuries which the United States had received from Spain could be enumerated, any one of which most probably would be considered a just cause of war by a nation less committed to peace than the United States. Monroe mentioned only two, the spoliation claims and the suppression of the right of deposit at New Orleans; but unjust as these acts were, the United States did not occupy West Florida as reparation for them. Rather, the American government had bought Louisiana from France in 1803 and, in paying for the territory, the United States understood and believed West Florida as far as the Perdido River to be a part of the Louisiana Purchase. In occupying West Florida the United States acquired no new title to it, for complete and unquestioned title had been secured from the legal owner in return for equitable payment.[19]

After doing his duty by faithfully following his instructions, Foster, except for one personal interview with Monroe, wasted no more time on West Florida. In September Foster penned a second protest in which West Florida received only a passing reference: its subject was the activity of Mathews in East Florida. On August 14 Governor Estrada of St. Augustine sent Luis de Onís a detailed account of Mathews' plan to annex East Florida to the United States by alienating loyal subjects of Spain with promises of fifty acres of land, payment of debts, pensions, and freedom of religion to those who joined in rebellion against Spanish Florida.[20]

Foster's sentences to Monroe were unbelievably gentle at times and embarrassingly sharp at others. He was protesting, stated Foster, at the urgent request of Luis de Onís and because of the intimate alliance between Great Britain and Spain. After the American assurances of friendly intentions toward Spain, he was "wholly unable to suppose that Governor Matthews [sic] can have had orders from the President for the conduct which he is stated to be pursuing; but the measures he is said to be taking in corresponding with traitors, and in endeavoring, by bribery and every art of seduction, to infuse a spirit of rebellion into the subjects of the King of Spain in those quarters, are such as to create the liveliest inquietude, and to call for the most early interference on the part of the Government of the United States."[21] Foster could see not even the slightest pretext, such as was brought forward in the endeavor to justify the aggression on West Florida, to warrant the annexation of East Florida. In concluding his letter Foster called for an explanation of the action of Mathews in subverting Spanish authority in East Florida and requested information as to the source of his authority and the measures already taken by the United States to put a stop to his proceedings.

Monroe waited almost two months before he answered the British minister and in the opening sentence of his reply there was an intimation of the delay being caused in part by a consultation to obtain the views of President Madison. West Florida and East Florida, Monroe stated, were altogether unconnected, for the United States had acquired one by the Louisiana Purchase and had a lien on the other as the result of claims for spoliation and the suppression of the right of deposit at New Orleans. He gave the history of these claims and concluded: "The United States have considered the Government of Spain indebted to them a greater sum for the injuries above stated, than the province of East Florida can, by any fair standard between the parties, be estimated at."[22] The United States looked to the Spanish province for indemnity, and although the American government had suffered its just claims to remain so long unsatisfied, there was a point beyond which patience became strained and the United States could not properly forget what rightfully belonged to injured American citizens.

Under these circumstances, Monroe concluded, it would be both unjust and dishonorable for the United States to allow East Florida to pass into the possession of any other power; unjust, because the United States would thereby lose the only indemnity within reach, for injuries which ought long since to have been redressed; dishonorable, because in permitting another state to take that indemnity, American inactivity and acquiescence could only be imputed to unworthy motives. Since the United States government was not ignorant of what had been suggested in Europe as to disposing of the Spanish colonies, the American Congress, to protect the just claims of its citizens and to preserve friendship with other nations, had authorized the president to accept possession of East Florida from the local authorities, or to take it against any attempt of a foreign state to occupy it, and to hold the province in either case subject to future friendly negotiations.

At no place in his letter did Monroe mention Mathews, or answer the pointed question of Foster as to what the United States was doing, or intended doing, to stop the illegal activities of the general. There was no recognition and also no condemnation of an agent accredited by and operating under President Madison.

When the newspapers published the Foster-Monroe letters, General Mathews read and studied them with avid interest; he broke into a joyous smile and Monroe's pleasing sentences dissipated the fog of haunting fear which had dampened his spirits. Heretofore the vague possibilities that his letters had gone astray, that Senator Crawford had forgotten to give Madison a report, that the administration disapproved of his scheming plot – all those disturbing thoughts had worried the old general. But no more. Foster had put down in black and white a clear outline of the plan to seize East Florida; Monroe had read it and conferred with Madison; Mathews no longer doubted the administration's knowledge and sanction. If either the secretary of state or the president had desired to stop his work, there had been ample time for them to send a letter of dismissal to their agent. Mathews realized that the president, checked by the proprieties of diplomacy from giving official sanction to revolutionizing the subjects of a friendly nation, had by diplomatic repartee told his agent, "Go ahead."

With renewed energy and a happy heart Mathews flung himself into the recruiting of volunteers; and McIntosh, convinced of the administration's intent by the Monroe-Foster letters, aided him.[23] Since the instructions of General Mathews antedated the diplomatic exchange between Monroe and Foster, McIntosh and his fellow doubtfuls immediately concluded that the United States would accept East Florida from some such revolutionary body as the general had in mind.[24] Exactly how many men Mathews persuaded to join with him is difficult, if not impossible, to ascertain. From St. Marys he recruited Archibald Clark, James Seagrove, John Boog, and the overseer of McIntosh's Refuge Plantation; in the area west of Amelia Island and south of the St. Marys he found George Cook, William Kelly, Benjamin Sands, and Francis Young; and from the Florida coast he secured his chief aide, John Houstoun McIntosh, who, in reality, was more of a resident of Georgia than of Spanish Florida. Mathews' most persuasive entreaties failed to move the influential William Craig, a wealthy planter and Spanish civil officer; but Lodowick Ashley finally threw his lot with the conspirators. Just how long it took to convince Ashley or exactly when he agreed to unite with the revolutionists remains hidden. Perhaps the final offer of military command, in addition to promises of land, won the man whose military leadership would inspire the rank and file of the volunteers.[25] Even then, had Mathews known that Ashley once served as an overseer of a South Carolina plantation,[26] the general might not have given him such a high place, for overseers fell far short of the élite in the South.

Notwithstanding the supposedly secret nature of their enterprise, Mathews and his men now openly recruited volunteers. The most lowly Georgia volunteers were promised a minimum of fifty acres of land and more important men believed they would receive large land grants and offices in the future territorial government of Florida. Mathews displayed his commission from the president, spoke of his authority to call on the American military forces for assistance, and flaunted copies of his letters to Monroe and the Monroe-Foster letters in the faces of doubting men. He successfully conveyed the impression, not only that he was the accredited agent of the United States government, and as such, authorized to take possession of East Florida, but that the Madison administration was determined to obtain possession of the province, even by subverting Spanish authority and creating a local government amenable to American orders.[27] Recruiting was not limited to Georgians or American residents below the St. Marys. Men of Spanish extraction were promised the free exercise of their religion, security for their real and personal property, and payment of all Spanish governmental indebtedness to them; civil officials were guaranteed their jobs and salaries; and soldiers were offered the choice of service in the American army and all their arrears of pay, or free transportation to a place of their selection.[28]

Although Mathews expected these liberal inducements to bring in the necessary number of volunteers, the error of his thinking soon became apparent. Only a small per cent of the men in Camden County had a stomach for fighting and many of them were stopped by the insistence of domineering wives or the tears of pleading mothers. Not a single Spanish soldier sold his patriotism for American gold and most of the American and Spanish civilians decided to wait and watch rather than to risk their persons and property in an abortive revolution.

Failure to win a sufficient number of volunteers to assure a successful revolution sent Mathews scurrying to Georgia officials. In February, 1812, he conferred with Governor David Mitchell at Jefferson, the county seat of Camden County, and evidently suggested the use of Georgia militia, for in the following month Brigadier General Floyd was ordered to hold his volunteers in readiness to march on request from the United States authority.[29] In February either Mathews or one of his men conferred with General Floyd, who resided at Fairfield Plantation in Camden County, and on March 9 the general requested advice from Governor Mitchell as to the propriety of allowing the volunteer militia of Georgia to aid in revolutionizing East Florida.[30] As late as February 17 or 18, the plan to conquer the province was still in a nebulous state, for no definite time for action had been fixed.

To Mathews the acquisition of East Florida alone was not enough: nothing less than the ousting of Spain from the Atlantic to Mobile Bay would do. St. Augustine with its protecting fort was the first objective, for loss of that key city would make all other Spanish posts along the Atlantic waterways untenable; but after the capture of St. Augustine, Pensacola and Mobile were to be taken. In furtherance of these plans he received a promise from the Indian agent, Benjamin Hawkins, of free and unmolested passage for the Patriots through the powerful Creek Confederation, if, after reducing St. Augustine, they decided to move against the western towns.[31] On February 28 Mathews called on Commodore Hugh Campbell to ascertain that officer's orders from the navy department. When Campbell informed the general that he had had no orders requiring the naval flotilla to cooperate with the army in East Florida, Mathews brought out his commission as agent of the president, gave Campbell a summary of his experiences in Washington, produced a copy of the War Department's orders to Major Laval, and disclosed the plans for the capture of St. Augustine. Although Campbell regretted that he did not have definite orders from the Navy Department, he was convinced of Mathews' authority and promised to aid him.[32] The cooperation of Major Laval was never questioned; since the major had orders from the War Department,[33] Mathews saw no need to confer with him. With assistance from the army, navy, and Georgia militia and a month or two in which to coordinate their efforts and plan every detail of the march on St. Augustine, success was a certainty.

An unexpected letter, however, precipitated immediate action. For months a man known only as Wyllys, passing as a half-pay English officer, had flitted between St. Marys and St. Augustine, and acting to perfection the self-claimed role of a disgruntled and traitorous Britisher, had met Mathews and McIntosh in the furtive meeting places of conspirators and whispered the secrets of Spain and England. Although Wyllys played a triple part – spying for Spain, reporting to Foster, and conferring with McIntosh[34] – he apparently won the complete confidence of the revolutionists. On March 10 he addressed a letter to McIntosh: by the feelings of a gentleman, by the ties of friendship, Wyllys advised McIntosh "not to delay, *not for one day, the accomplishment of your object.*"[35] He also told Mathews that British troops and supplies were on their way to St. Augustine; unless the revolutionists marched at once the Castillo de San Marcos would be impregnable.[36]

Although the organizational phase of the revolution was not completed, Mathews dared not endanger the success of his mission by waiting.[37] "The business," he wrote Campbell, "upon which we have conversed relative to E. Florida being now ripe for Execution. I have to request you to furnish fifty Muskets and Bayonets fifty Pistols and an Equal number of swords, For the whole of which. I will by my receipt make myself accountable." McIntosh was to select the swords and pistols, giving a receipt for them, and Mathews would later ask of Campbell "farther Cooperation agreeably to my Instructions."[38] Some of the weapons which Campbell readily delivered would go to the unarmed civilians from St. Marys and the remainder would be kept for residents of East Florida who were expected to flock to the revolutionary standard as the march on St. Augustine progressed through Spanish territory. Although Brigadier General Floyd could not order men of the Georgia militia to cross the St. Marys, he would make no objection to armed volunteers from his command joining the revolutionists.

Civilians, militia, and the anticipated East Florida volunteers, under the leadership of Colonel Lodowick Ashley, were to attack St. Augustine quickly and secretly. While the Spaniards knew of the activities north of the St. Marys, and had met in juntas to discuss defense, they had actually done nothing. Not more than 100 effective men of the regular army guarded the Castillo de San Marcos. The continued scarcity of ammunition precluded effective resistance by civilian volunteers in St. Augustine, and the drawbridge to the Castillo remained down and could not be raised.

With all of these favorable factors, Mathews and McIntosh were doubtful of success unless considerable assistance came from Point Petre. A hasty count numbered less than 125 Georgia civilian and militia volunteers[39] and the hoped-for volunteers from East Florida were a gamble. The capture of St. Augustine, especially the reduction of the Castillo de San Marcos which had never fallen to any invader by siege, assault, or trickery, could not be predicated on question-mark volunteers. Success, it was decided, could only be assured with 140 regulars from Point Petre. The soldiers would join the revolutionists, not as a United States detachment but as volunteers, with full equipment of course — rifles, pistols, powder horns, cartridges, swords, and camping accouterments.

Decision fathered action. Mathews hastened to arrange with Major Jacint Laval for the 140 regulars and McIntosh rode to his family for a last farewell. The date was March 11, 1812; on the following morning the revolutionists were to cross the St. Marys and be on their way to St. Augustine.

In St. Marys on the morning of March 12, Eliza and her children hovered tearfully around John Houstoun McIntosh as he made his final preparations. It was a new role for the wealthy, peaceable planter — a dangerous one, should the Spaniards resist. History passed prophetically before him; in his mind's eye he became a historic figure, and to record his feelings for posterity he must write. "Before you receive this," he was writing to Representative George Troup, "the Province of East Florida will have undergone a Revolution and probably [be] in the quiet possession of the officers of the Government of the U. States. Our Plan is all arranged to take the Fort of St. Augustine and the governor on Monday night by surprise and in half an hour I set off to head a few chosen Friends to execute this commission. The thing has been for some months in agitation between General Mathews and myself, but I am afraid never would have been accomplished had not the General been governed by the Spirit of his Instructions and declared wishes of his country."[40]

McIntosh paused for a moment. He could hear the soft sobs of his daughters, the reassuring whispers of his wife Eliza, as she, her cheeks wet with silent tears, comforted the girls. Women must weep, he thought, and men must fight — not the exact wording of the adage but somehow more appropriate. He swelled with pride, and there was a little fear, too, as he continued: "My Horses are at the Door and my wife and children are all around me in tears. Advise my Dear Sir, and let me assure you that my last breath would declare, that I have ever valued the rights and privileges of a citizen of the U. States as the greatest blessing on Earth and that I would rather leave my children in the enjoyment of them than of the mines of Peru."

While McIntosh was composing his letter, Mathews conferred with the French-born Major Jacint Laval. In a few sentences Mathews outlined the scheme for the capture of St. Augustine and demanded of Laval the 140 regulars from Point Petre. The major threw himself into a rigid military stance and answered: "No!"

And with that word the structure which Mathews and McIntosh had built with so much care fell like a house of cards.

That Damn Frenchman Laval

MATHEWS AND LAVAL SHARED THE little cottage near Point Petre for seven months,[1] but each man avoided the other whenever possible; Mathews closeted himself with fellow conspirators and Laval puttered in the gardens, or what he hoped one day would be the gardens of Point Petre. Not once did Mathews invite the major to join the evening-long discussions on East Florida. For this Laval was thankful, but the thin walls of the compact cottage guarded no secrets and when in the evening twilight the major was driven from the gardens and into the house by mosquitoes and other insects, he could not avoid the drone of voices from the living room or from Mathews' bedroom.

With considerable justification Major Laval held himself in high esteem. Like General Lafayette, though not as honored as that famous man, he left his native France to fight and be wounded in the cause of the American colonists. After the Revolutionary War he settled down in South Carolina to a life of comparative ease and honor. When, in that first troubled decade of the nineteenth century, war appeared more and more the only honorable course for the United States, he volunteered in the regular army and rose to the rank of major in the light dragoons. Laval had come to America bursting with ideals of right and justice, the natural God-given rights of man to liberty and freedom, and in his heart still lingered the enthusiasms of youthful rebellion against autocracy and injustice and intrigue.

As he unwillingly listened to plotting against Spain, a country whose patriotic people were dying to leave their sons and daughters a homeland freed from the dictatorship of Napoleon, Laval grew more concerned and disturbed. The friends of Mathews wanted land, fertile land which belonged to Spain and to the Indians. Their talk was of economic gain and personal power, not of justice and honor and brotherhood. To secure their aims they would create discontent and revolutionize a people who in good faith gave their oaths of allegiance to Spain. Could the leaders of young America have forgotten so quickly? Laval asked himself. Were the thoughts of Mathews and his land-hungry friends representative of the best leadership in Washington? Laval could not bring himself to believe it. He decided that blustering, uncouth Mathews, who by accident of birth could claim American nativity, represented the antithesis of everything that Laval had left France to fight for and sustain.

On his part Mathews' basic antipathy toward Laval stemmed from the major's French mannerisms and a close association with more kindred spirits at Point Petre who disliked the pompous little Frenchman. Mathews could not understand how a man, a real American man, could be so concerned with military discipline (fighting was the product of desire and a good musket). How could an army officer even look at flowers when the possibility existed of securing East Florida? Why should a man, unless there was something wrong with him, dawdle over dinner; and why should the major insist on such extraneous things as napkins, table cloths, and clean linen? Mathews frowned at these foibles; but not wanting to arouse the hostility of Laval, kept his peace. Characteristic of his French blood (at least Mathews ascribed it to a Latin heritage) was the major's interest in women. With a son old enough to be in the United States army, Laval, muttered Mathews in disgust, was nothing but a damned Frenchman; and blinded by his own all-consuming passion for East Florida, Mathews forgot that sex was not the monopoly of any age or any nationality.

Mathews erred seriously in not cultivating the friendship of Laval, but from the general's point of view no reason existed which necessitated friendly overtures to the major. Lieutenant Colonel Thomas A. Smith, not Laval, was commandant of Point Petre and the colonel would undoubtedly assume command at the Point before the East Florida revolution broke. Since the Virginia born Smith came from a different mold from that of Laval, his desire for the Spanish province and his eagerness to serve President Madison would make him a partner in Mathews' scheme. If the possibility that Smith would not arrive in time entered the general's head, he gave it only a passing fearful thought. Mathews' confidence was not the product of fatuous reasoning: he had seen and read the orders from Washington to military commanders. Although Commodore Campbell had received no authorization to follow Mathews, this was an oversight or negligence on the part of the commodore's immediate superior, for such an order had been issued by the secretary of the navy. Shortly after the arrival of Campbell at St. Marys on December 25, 1811,[2] Mathews concluded that the commodore, even without definite orders, could be counted on for assistance. The orders of Captain John Williams, commander of the Marine Corps detachment on Cumberland Island, were: "If required by the officer commanding a detachment of the army [at Point Petre, Williams was to join him], and obey the orders of his superior in the army."[3] The orders to Major Laval were prefaced by the information that President Madison had appointed Mathews and McKee to receive the Spanish territory lying east of the Perdido River and south of Georgia in the event of an agreement concluded with the local authorities. The president having directed the use of United States troops, Laval was "authorized and directed on the request of those gentlemen, or either of them, stating that an arrangement has been made as aforesaid to march with the troops under your command to take possession of such parts within the territory aforesaid as may be agreed to be surrendered and to hold and defend the same."[4] Though this order lacked a provision for the preoccupation of East Florida to prevent occupation by a foreign power, it was sufficiently inclusive and definite to Mathews, and he never conceived of any trouble from Major Laval.

Thus it was not until March 10 that Mathews broached the subject of the army's role in the East Florida revolution. Even then he approached it by indirection rather than by an official letter.[5]

On the morning of the tenth as Mathews was on the point of leaving the cottage, he turned to Laval. "Major," he said, "there's a bag of buckshot on my mantle. I'll need it made into cartridges."

The remark caught Laval off guard and he made no comment.

"I expect we'll have a scrap soon," Mathews stated.

No other words passed between the men until the following morning when Mathews remarked, "Major, I want a ball put in each of the cartridges along with the buckshot."

"Who is to account for these balls?" asked Laval who was now prepared to object. "Are they to be used on Point Petre or elsewhere?"

"Never mind about that," the general replied. "If they go out of your hands a receipt will be given you and that's all you need."

"Very well, then," said Laval.

The more the major thought about the probable use of these cartridges, the more he rebelled. Finally he eased his troubled conscience by countermanding the order which he had given for the making of the cartridges. When Mathews learned of this action, he decided the time for candor had arrived. Accompanied by General Floyd, he found Laval in the quarters of Captain Abraham Massias.

"Major Laval," he inquired, "will you order a detachment of 140 men from your command to cross the St. Marys?"

"No!" replied Laval furiously.

Mathews' face turned red. It required will to keep his voice calm. "Major, you have orders to occupy, hold, and defend East Florida, or any part of it, which may be offered to the United States. Your orders are to obey my requisitions for men and materials. Do you dare to defy the orders of the president?"

"I have unbounded respect for the president and his wishes," replied Laval, "but I have no orders to obey an unauthorized command. My orders are, as you say, to hold and defend East Florida when offered by the local authorities of that province. Those orders, however, do no bind me to use troops to create a revolution in East Florida."

"Major Laval," said Mathews, changing to a more intimate tone, "you fought for our freedoms in the Revolution. I did too, and so did Major James Seagrove of St. Marys. We are all men of Seventy-Six. The United States now has a chance to acquire East Florida, and West Florida, too, from the Apalachicola River to Mobile Bay. The opportunity may not come again in our lifetime. Major Seagrove believes in what I'm doing. I talked with President Madison, with Robert Smith and the secretaries of war and navy. I know James Monroe is anxious for my success and so are the other important officials in Washington. You've seen my commission, you have your orders, and know that Commodore Campbell, even without direct authorization, is willing to follow my lead."

"Yes, General Mathews, I fought for your American freedoms and my American ideals. But I did not leave my native land to die in battle so that avaricious men could grab land by debasing the ideals of Seventy-Six."

"Are you inferring, sar, that I, who lost twenty thousand dollars in fighting for liberty, that I who never illegally took a penny from my country, am . . ."

"No, not you, general," interrupted Laval, "but there are many associated with you who lack your patriotism. I, too, see the advantages in acquiring the Floridas, but by negotiation, not by intrigue and theft."

"Then you refuse to obey my order. You defy the wishes of the secretary of war and the president."

"I refuse, general," replied Laval, "to do that which is unauthorized and illegal."

The argument continued until Laval finally ordered the general to leave and never again set foot on Point Petre.

General Mathews stamped off in a huff to find his friends in St. Marys. If the Frenchman would give no aid, some other means must be found. His mission could not fail and East Florida be lost when it was almost within his grasp.

In the town Seagrove, Clark and others bolstered his determination and his anger mounted as he recalled the encounter of the morning. Why those muddle-headed army officials could entrust so important a post to that damn Frenchman, Mathews could not understand. The general was in a discussion with Commodore Campbell and John Houstoun McIntosh when he saw Major Laval walking up the street.

This time there was no note of appeasement in Mathews' voice, no recalling of the days of Seventy-Six, only anger and vicious thrusts with threats of reprisals, dire and quick, for the major. Under this barrage of verbal blows Laval weakened. Reluctantly, dejectedly, he agreed to allow Mathews fifty soldiers.[6] For Mathews it was only a partial victory, but with luck in securing recruits in Spanish Florida, the capture of St. Augustine was yet possible. In the end, however, it was a defeat. When Commodore Campbell heard the abuse heaped on the major, disturbing thoughts entered his mind, and questions arose to plague him and influence him at a later date. Nor had Mathews received the final word from Laval.

THAT DAMN FRENCHMAN LAVAL

When the Major gave in to the insistent demands of Mathews, he did so not from conviction but in a desire to escape the terror of Mathews' anger. Back in the peace of his gardens Laval regained his equilibrium. Although he regretted his promise of fifty men, he would fulfill it. He issued orders to allow the men, soldiers and officers, to volunteer as a regular detachment of the United States army. This was not what Mathews had in mind. To have a force recognized and acting as a part of the American army participate in the rebellion would directly involve the United States government. According to Mathews' plan the fifty men, with their arms and equipment, were to slip away from Point Petre, and disguised as volunteers, join the revolutionists.

When Laval heard of this plan he breathed a sigh of relief. Now he was no longer bound by his promise of the afternoon; now he was sure of his ground. Nothing in his orders or in the commission of Mathews obligated a commander to give his men leave to abandon their posts surreptitiously and join a rebel force which planned to destroy the authority of a state at peace with the United States. Laval confidently countermanded his order.

Mathews could make no personal answer to this final blow. While his anger that afternoon temporarily overawed Laval, it had exhausted Mathews, and unable to face Laval with any hope of again browbeating him, the old general remained with friends in St. Marys.

Before he retired to the comfort of a feather bed, he penned a letter to Laval. The local authorities of East Florida, he wrote, wished to surrender a part of their province, specifically Rose's Bluff, a point on the Florida side of the river and about four miles above St. Marys. In his official capacity as a commissioner of the American government, he ordered Laval to march a detachment of fifty men to the bluff at ten o'clock the following morning to take peaceful possession and to hold and defend the land for the United States.[7]

Ralph Isaacs took the message from St. Marys to Point Petre. There he asked Lieutenant Daniel Appling to accompany him to the major's quarters – Laval had remained on the post grounds that night. It was past midnight when Appling and Isaacs knocked on Laval's door.

They found the major dressed, his sword buckled to his side. From what Laval had seen of Ralph Isaacs, he cared no more for him than for another Jew, Captain Abraham Massias, the second in command at Point Petre. Neither did Laval welcome Lieutenant Appling who was one of the confidants of Mathews.

"Major Laval," said Isaacs as he handed over the letter, "I have come from General Mathews with a requisition for a detachment of troops."

Laval quickly scanned the letter. "Where is Rose's Bluff? Is it a military post?"

"Yes, it is, sir," replied Isaacs, "a military post of the Patriots of East Florida."

For a moment Laval seemed to be studying the hilt of his sword. Raising his head, he said: "I will not march any detachment from Point Petre. If ever I order a force into East Florida, it will be my entire command, and then only after giving the contractor timely notice, so he can furnish provisions."

"You refuse then, sir, either to allow volunteers to leave the Point or to order a detachment to take that part of East Florida which is to be offered the United States?"

"I most certainly do," replied Laval.

"Will you give me a written answer to General Mathews' letter?"

"No," stated Laval. "At least not now. It's late and I need time to prepare an answer."

"I shall be at your service, sir, till morning," said Isaacs, "and take your reply to the general."

"Can't answer by that time," Laval said; "I must take my time to write. The general knows my stand."

The conversation continued, but Laval could not be moved. He spoke with considerable excitement, waving his hands and moving his head to and fro to punctuate his statements.

"There's no need, sir, to work yourself into a passion," said Isaacs with a contemptuous smile on his face.

"I'm not angry," shouted the major. "I'll consider writing to General Mathews later."[8]

General Mathews had slept through the night undisturbed, and he arose at an early hour, refreshed and ready to continue the argument. Laval had defeated him, but there was one possibility of securing men and also revenge. If the officers and soldiers at Point Petre could be induced to rebel against Laval, St. Augustine might still be conquered.

Under the direction of Isaacs, Captain Massias and lieutenants

Appling and Elias Stallings drew up an imposing indictment of Major Laval.[9] Their statement of offenses became the basis of formal charges which Appling later officially submitted to Colonel Smith. In these Major Laval was cited on two charges: conduct unbecoming to an officer and a gentleman, and neglect of duty. Listed under the first charge were sixteen specifications and under the second only three.

Many of the specifications bore no relation to the argument between Mathews and Laval. The major was accused of encouraging soldiers to throw away beef supplied by the contractor, of using abusive language to Captain Massias and the contractor, of issuing orders through non-commissioned officers and soldiers, of treating commissioned officers with disrespect and contempt, of discharging prisoners illegally from the guardhouse, of giving his son William leave to fight a duel in Charleston, of borrowing money from soldiers and not repaying it, and of wasting the public powder in firing salutes.

More serious were the accusations of negligence and immorality. According to specification eleven of charge one, Laval allowed to pass "unnoticed and without investigation the complaint of Mrs. Gaddy the wife of a soldier against a soldier under his command for an attempt to commit rape upon an infant female aged between five and six years which attempt was attended with aggravated circumstances." In specification five of charge one, the major was condemned for "granting a general permission during the months of Nov. and Dec. 1811 at Point Petre to a Sergt. under his command to sleep out of camp with the wife of a soldier . . . provided he would send the woman to him occasionally, and that they might mutually enjoy the said soldier's wife which was duly complied with and which woman has lived in his kitchen from the 27th of Jany to this day 27th Mch. 1812."[10]

Specifications six through nine of the first charge bore directly on the controversy with Mathews. According to Appling, Laval acted in an ungentlemanly manner on March 11, while in the quarters of Captain Massias, by treating generals Mathews and Floyd with rudeness; and on the following day ordered a non-commissioned officer, in the presence of Massias, to double the guard, stating the regular officers could not be trusted. Finally Laval was charged with ordering General Mathews, an agent of the president, off the Point on March 11 in a "most rude and ungentlemanly manner" and doing so "with marked contempt and disrespect without any cause or provocation whatever, knowing at the same time that the Genl. had powers and was treating with the Authorities of East Florida, which powers, he Major Laval had a copy of and knew the necessity of the General's presence at the post at that critical moment." The charges against Laval were signed by thirteen witnesses; Mathews, Floyd, Isaacs, and Massias being among the signers.[11]

Although the formal charges against Laval were not presented until March 27, the Massias-Isaacs-Appling-Stallings statements of March 12 destroyed the little remaining confidence of the commissioned officers in their acting commandant. Captains Massias and Joseph Woodruff were ready to do anything required of them, and other officers offered to resign their commissions and volunteer in the service of Mathews.[12] Some enlisted men talked of absenting themselves without leave and joining the revolutionists. To prevent this Laval doubled the guard at Point Petre. Eventually fifty men, one fourth of his command, stood on guard and he remained on the post during the four critical days from March 12 through 16, foregoing the pleasure of his garden and the privacy of his cottage.

When Mathews received no answer to his letter requesting a detachment of fifty men, he again wrote Laval, demanding an immediate answer to three questions. Upon receiving information that the local authorities of East Florida wished to become a part of the United States, would Laval march with his troops to take possession of any part or portion of that province and defend it for the United States; upon receiving information of a contemplated occupation of East Florida by a foreign power, would he preoccupy the Spanish province; and would he, in conformity with his solemn pledge and engagement made in the presence of McIntosh and Campbell, permit fifty volunteers to proceed and execute the duty allotted to them?[13]

Without hesitation Laval answered the questions. He would occupy the country east of the Perdido River and south of Georgia whenever the local authorities offered it to the United States. Since, however, he had no instructions to accept East Florida from rebellious local authorities, created by intrigue and deception, he would not move a step in response to their offers. He quickly disposed of the second question: his instructions made no mention of preoccupying East Florida and he would not honor a requisition for that purpose.

The third question, Laval stated, was strange and surprising, and it was fortunate the promise had been made in the presence of a reliable witness, namely Commodore Campbell. The promise, continued Laval, had been given only after Mathews exhausted, by every means of cajolery and threats, all hope of securing a greater number of men; and it had been agreed to with the thought of marching the men as a regular detachment of the United States army. As soon as it became apparent that the fifty men were to be employed as volunteers and disguised American soldiers, Laval had refused them permission to leave Point Petre; and now, he concluded, he again emphatically refused to sanction or allow them to leave the post, and he would account to his superiors for his conduct.[14]

With bitterness in his heart Mathews sat down to tell Monroe of Laval's perfidy. The cause of the Patriots was just, he wrote; the friends of liberty, justice, and humanity would support the revolutionists. Had it not been for Laval, their independence would now be completely established. Mathews had no confidence in the major, who exhibited a compound of error and folly and who was "so confident of his own abilities and military knowledge that it is not possible to make him believe he can do any wrong." For the good of the United States, Mathews concluded, Laval must be removed from his command.[15] He also asked for definite orders for military officers to obey him without question, and shipment of 250 muskets with bayonets and the same number of horsemen's swords.[16]

During the night of March 14 and throughout the following day Laval stood guard with fifty of his trusted men to see that no officer or soldier slipped away to join the revolutionists. By March 16 tempers were hot and rebellion against the major's authority seemed imminent. Just after the evening meal, Captain Massias could contain his pent-up emotions no longer. On seeing Laval walk across the parade grounds, the captain forgot discipline and army regulations.

"Stop!" he shouted, "I want to see you!"

He ran to face the astonished major and said, "You've acted contrary to the wishes of our government. All the officers disapprove of your arbitrary conduct. Why don't you leave the post?"

Major Laval made an ineffectual attempt to control his temper, but his voice quivered as he said: "Captain Massias! Report to your quarters and hold yourself for further orders."

"You bastard! You damn Frenchman!" shouted Massias, doubling his fist and shaking it under Laval's nose. "If you leave this camp for fifteen minutes, I'll march the troops to East Florida and use the military stores and ammunition to . . ."

Laval did not allow him to finish. "You are under arrest!" he yelled; and at his command soldiers took the captain away.

Shaking with anger, Laval retired to his quarters and hastily composed charges against Massias.[17] Then buckling on his sword, and with a pistol in each hand, he returned to guard duty. Until almost midnight he marched up and down the camp, checking the guards, and daring anyone to leave. Unexpectedly Colonel Smith arrived at Point Petre and Laval's days of trial were over.[18] He hurried to his little cottage just off the post grounds and calmed his emotions by writing a detailed account of the recent events.

"Tell the President or the Congress," he wrote the adjutant general, "of the danger the United States are in of being involved in a war with Spain if the agent Gen. Mathews is suffered to proceed. The Americans are taking possession of E. Fla. by force through his advice. They expect to cover themselves with the names of Patriots there being 8 or 10 of them mixed with a force of 60 or 70 'deluded' militia." In the opinion of Laval the odium of Mathews' acts would fall on the American government. The "terror," he reported, had been there and in Amelia Island all week, and Point Petre was still in confusion, even with Colonel Smith in command. "I cannot commit any more on paper but believe me Sir," stated Laval, "my bedd being close to the Petition which Separate the Genl. Rooms and mine, I think it highly important to communicate with you."[19]

There was no permanent peace for Major Laval. By order of Colonel Smith he was placed under technical arrest to answer for his conduct and was restricted to his cottage and the grounds of Point Petre. For months Laval remained in solitude except when under the scrutiny of a corporal and three privates. As the postmaster in St. Marys was friendly to the Patriots, the major forwarded his letters to the post office at Darien, Georgia, and, as a precaution, requested the secretary of war to address him in care of a friend at Savannah so that the Washington postmark would not appear on letters.[20]

On May 2 Laval appealed to the secretary of war.[21] The subject of his communication, he wrote, was the plot against East Florida by

General Mathews and his "confidential Jew Col. Isaacs, in which they almost tortured me to death to get me to cooperate with the troops of the United States then under my command to execute their infamous scheme...." Laval appealed as an old soldier, who had never failed to follow principles of honor and duty, against the acts of Colonel Smith, a young officer without experience, who suffered himself to be deluded by Mathews and his satellite, Isaacs. "Is it possible," he asked, "that the government cannot be better furnished with officers [than with] Jews, rogues, traitors, conspirators? Good God! What age is this? What Prospect has an officer who would die at his post Sooner than seeing his honour and that of his flag tarnished?"[22]

In concluding his letter to the secretary of war, Laval requested a transfer from Point Petre and plaintively asked not to be left anywhere near Mathews. His wishes were granted. On June 13, 1812, Colonel Smith authorized him to resume the wearing of his sword and to go to Charleston where he was to await further orders.[23] At Charleston Laval was ordered to a command near Sackett's Harbor on the eastern tip of Lake Ontario and in June, 1813, gained a promotion in rank.[24] But Laval's troubles were not yet over. Before he received news of his promotion, he was charged with improper conduct, and also with having borrowed twenty-five dollars, and not repaying it, from Sergeant John Cooper in March of 1812 and with taking twenty dollars from a private while in command of Point Petre.[25]

Laval was never brought to trial. In the opinion of his superior officer, the charges against him, with the exception of the accusation of taking the twenty dollars, did not justify Laval's arrest.[26] Although his accuser, Captain George Haig, appealed to the adjutant and inspector general of the army, nothing was done. In August of 1813 Laval attained the rank of colonel and in the following year received an honorable discharge. In 1816 he returned to active duty in Washington and one year later, after appealing to the president, became the military storekeeper at Harper's Ferry,[27] where for almost five years, until his death in 1822, he found peace and quiet with his wife and daughters.

What effect Laval had upon the course of history is difficult to fathom. By preventing a single soldier or officer from joining Mathews, he killed any possibility of capturing St. Augustine. And had he not acted with such guarding zeal, St. Augustine would have been attacked. The consequences of fighting the forces of Spain in 1812 are problematical. St. Augustine might have fallen and the Floridas might have been annexed by the United States years before 1821; but on the other hand, such an attack might have stiffened the backbone of Spain and delayed American acquisition of the Floridas. One conclusion, however, is certain: neither Major Laval nor any other man could have put off the inevitable – the Floridas were bound by ties of geography and political economy to become a part of the United States.

The Capture of Fernandina

NEVER AGAIN DID THE RESILIENT brain of Mathews manifest itself more clearly than in those difficult days at Point Petre. Even before the complete fruitlessness of his dealings with Laval became apparent, the general had turned to another scheme which did not depend on assistance from the United States army. With this purpose in mind Mathews directed the Patriots in their declaration of independence and outlined to them a new plan for the subjugation of East Florida.

As originally devised, McIntosh and the volunteers from Georgia were to cross the St. Marys on March 12, and in union with residents of Spanish Florida were to declare their independence. From the south bank of the St. Marys the Patriots were to proceed secretly toward St. Augustine, reaching a point near the city on Sunday night. Since Sunday was more of a day for riotous drinking than for religious observance, the attack on the Castillo de San Marcos was planned for the pre-dawn of Monday, March 16, with the hope of finding guards napping and soldiers deep in sleep.[1] In this contemplated movement into East Florida the town of Fernandina was to be by-passed, but all posts along the St. Johns River were to be quickly surrounded by land and cut off from escape by water. The gunboats of Commodore Campbell were to accomplish the latter, after which they were to be anchored at strategic points in the river to keep open supply lines to Georgia.

Laval's refusal to allow regular soldiers in the guise of volunteers to aid the revolutionists delayed scheduled proceedings. On March 13 a force of less than seventy Georgians watched while McIntosh and not more than nine other residents of Florida issued a manifesto which enumerated their grievances, declared their independence, and invited all freedom-loving men of the Spanish province to join their cause.[2] The Patriot flag, designed by Ralph Isaacs, portrayed a soldier in blue against a white background; the soldier, with his bayonet mounted, musket thrust forward in the act of charging the unseen foe, appeared to be running along the motto, *salus populi, lex suprema*. Amid the hurrahs of the men assembled at Rose's Bluff, the standard was raised on an improvised flagpole.

Among the rough frontiersmen were gentlemen with classical training who pointed a derisive finger at the word *salus*. Revolution, they laughed, promised little safety, health, or welfare to the people of East Florida. Quickly the motto was changed to *vox populi, lex suprema*. But to the common man the flag remained only "a white flag with a man in it, with some writing on it, the substance of which was, the voice of the people the law of the land."[3]

With the ideological preliminaries of the revolution concluded, the Patriots turned to more concrete acts. Lodowick Ashley was elected colonel commandant of the Patriots of East Florida. McIntosh accepted the position of commissioner, and was charged with the duty of offering the occupied land to the United States. This was the extent of the paper government, the purposes of which were to secure parts of East Florida and immediately give them to General Mathews. In a formal letter the general was offered Rose's Bluff to occupy, hold, and defend for the United States.

When Major Laval refused to move a detachment to the bluff, the Patriots were thrown on their own resources. Some of the leaders still thought it possible to take St. Augustine, and Mathews, though questioning their optimism, went along with them. While recruiting parties spread through the country between the St. Marys and the St. Johns to drum volunteers into camp, Mathews requested Commodore Campbell to send one gunboat to Cow Ford on the St. Johns and to anchor another near the mouth of the river.[4] Although Mathews justified his demand on the basis of his orders to preoccupy East Florida to prevent its seizure by a foreign power, Campbell recalled the scene between the general and Laval and refused to comply since the military force would not cooperate.[5]

On Sunday, March 15, John Houstoun McIntosh wrote Don Justo

THE CAPTURE OF FERNANDINA

Lopez, military commandant of Amelia Island, and summoned him either to surrender the town or unite his forces with those of the Patriots.

> The determination of the United States to take possession of our Province by conquest caused us to agree. . . . [Therefore] we have already secured all the country between the rivers St. Johns and St. Marys, and had it not been for an unexpected circumstance we would have had possession of St. Augustine and the Fort on tomorrow-night. . . .
>
> Two gun boats which is all we have required, will enter St. Johns today, and we are encamped, increasing like a snow ball, and we have already sufficient forces to conquer all the Province: we intend laying siege to Amelia Island or, more properly to invite you to unite with us as in one glorious cause. And I assure you that if our proposition is admitted by you without objections none of our soldiers shall place their foot upon it, but otherwise, if you do not admit it, no one can answer for the consequences. The first condition which we have secured, is, that Fernandina shall not be subjected in her commerce, to the restrictions to which the United States are at present, during the term of twelve months, calculated from the first of March next ensuing – and that it shall be a free port until the expiration of the same time, although the United States and Great Britain should declare war. If you Surrender, or agree to unite with us, the gun boats will be immediately ordered there [Fernandina], to preserve good order and to prevent any difficulties, which is my greatest wish.[6]

McIntosh's letter was written before Mathews received the refusal of Campbell to honor the general's request for gunboats. This decision of Campbell ended all hope of an immediate advance on St. Augustine. Volunteers, however, were coming into the Patriot camp. Now that a definite break had been made with the Spanish authorities, dissatisfied East Floridians and land-seekers from Georgia threw their lot with those of the revolutionists. The little band of Patriots soon numbered over 150, and men continued to come in by night and day. Mathews, McIntosh, and the other leaders canvassed the possibilities for action. Thoughts of abandoning the revolution received no serious consideration: at this late date, even if the leaders desired, there could be no holding back of men keyed to strike blows against Spain.

The town of Fernandina was the obvious and easy goal. Its defending garrison numbered only ten, the commanding officer and nine men; its blockhouses and fort were fortifications in name only, and many of the cannon lay half-buried in the sand. Some of the 600 or more inhabitants of Fernandina were loyal Spaniards; there were others even more ready to support a government which allowed unrestricted and profitable free enterprise; but almost two-thirds of the population was Negro, and colored people could be discounted completely as possible defenders, for white men would not arm Negroes. If the town's leaders decided to resist, they could not match in defenders the number of invading Patriots.

On Sunday, March 15, the revolutionists moved down the river to Lower Bluff, almost opposite St. Marys, and only seven miles from Fernandina. To protect life, liberty, and property from unjust violation and to prevent interference by the sailors of British ships anchored in Amelia River, Mathews now asked Campbell to place one gunboat on the St. Marys near Rose's Bluff, to anchor two in Bell's River, and to sail all other available ships to stations opposite the town of Fernandina. These naval vessels, Mathews stated, should be used to cooperate with the Patriots and give general service to them.[7]

During the night on March 15 and the following Monday morning a camp was established at Rose's Bluff on Bell's River. Under the direction of "Colonel" Ashley, officers were elected and the Patriots organized into a semblance of a military force. Rifles and cartridges, muskets and powder-horns, swords and bayonets were issued to officers and men. Boat tenders were assigned their posts and supplies were gathered for the invasion.

While Ashley superintended these activities McIntosh penned a second letter to Lopez. The Spanish commandant was again invited to join the Patriots, to place his soldiers and the people of Fernandina under the protection of the United States with guarantees to every man of his religion, his liberty, his property, and to the soldiers, all arrears of pay, and to widows of soldiers the continuation of their pensions. If Lopez could not accept this invitation, McIntosh called him to surrender Fernandina, and promised him liberal terms for his men and for the people of the town.[8] Ashley signed the letter in a faltering hand: "Lodok Ashley, Col. Commandant," and sent it by "Major" George Cook to Lopez.[9] The promises made in this letter, as in McIntosh's letter of March 15, were based on a signed "treaty" made by Mathews as the agent of the United States with McIntosh as the commissioner of the Patriots.[10]

Residents of Fernandina knew of the activities of Mathews and, in a general way, of the plan to occupy East Florida. As early as March 10, Lopez requested the magistrates of Camden County to explain the American government's position in regard to Mathews, but he received only a vague, noncommittal reply.[11] Although the Spanish officials heard rumors of a contemplated attack by the military and naval forces of the United States, they shrugged them away – during the past decade many such rumors had come from Georgia but time had proved them false. When the people of Fernandina learned of the manifesto of the Patriots and knew for certain of the revolutionary force at Rose's Bluff, they remained doubtful and inactive. Such extensive preparations were unnecessary to capture the inoffensive and unprotected town of Fernandina.[12]

After Campbell refused to send gunboats to the St. Johns, the path of the revolution was replatted and Fernandina was marked for conquest. Charles Witter Clarke heard of the danger to his town while in St. Marys on Saturday, March 14, and hastened back to warn the commandant of Fernandina.[13] On the following day the letter from McIntosh came, and although he wrote before receipt of Campbell's refusal to order the naval vessels to the St. Johns, Fernandina was clearly in the path of march to St. Augustine.

Colonel Lopez called the leaders of the town into council. The colonel's loyalty to Spain was firm and he was no coward; but with a force of only nine soldiers, resistance was impossible without assistance from the townspeople.

For advice he relied on Spaniards, English-born naturalized subjects of Spain, and former citizens of the United States. Joseph de la Maza Arredondo, George Atkinson, Philip Yonge, Joseph Hibberson, and George J. F. Clarke met with the commandant. Of these men the Spaniard Arredondo was best known to Spanish officials of the mother country, but Clarke held the esteem of the colonial authorities. Not only was he the officially appointed surveyor general of East Florida but he was also connected with the influential commercial house of Forbes and Company, a firm in some respects more powerful in Spanish Florida than the colonial government itself.

George John Frederic Clarke, a native Floridian, was the youngest son of Thomas Clarke, an Englishman who arrived in St. Augustine with his Irish born wife, Honoria, during the British occupation of East Florida. When Spain regained the province in 1783 the Clarke family remained in St. Augustine, and three years later Honoria apprenticed her twelve-year-old son to Panton, Leslie, and Company (the predecessor of Forbes and Company). The mother bound her son to keep inviolate the secrets of the company, work for its interest, and obey its legitimate commands; in return George was to receive instruction in business and commerce, "food, drink, and clothing, a house, bed, and clean clothes." His religiously inclined mother demanded and received a promise of the "free exercise of the Apostolic Roman Catholic religion" for her son.

Young George Clarke became a proficient worker but his interests were not confined to the counting house. Among the slaves in the household of John Leslie, where Clarke lived, was Flora, a comely slave girl of fifteen. By a deed of May 5, 1794, "John Leslie sold to George Clarke for 60 pesos in cash a mullatto slave named Philis, age 18 months, who was born in Leslie's home of a slave named Flora."[14] Three years later Clarke paid for and received a deed to Flora and in the same year he emancipated her "because of the fidelity and love with which she served him. . . ."[15] With Flora he established a home in St. Augustine and in the years which followed they reared eight children. In his will, dated August 28, 1834, Clarke describes his family life with honest simplicity, beginning with the statement: "I never have been married, but I have eight children by a free black woman named Flora, now dead. These children, all of adult age . . . all of whom I always acknowledged, freed, raised and educated as my children; and bestowed on them my sirname [sic], Clarke."[16] After Flora's death, Clarke took into his house another slave, Hannah or Anna (he was never certain of her name), and they had four children. In his will he provided for Hannah and requested his executors to invest the money left for her "in healthy, grown negroes, and convey them to the said Hannah or Anna and her children aforesaid – I consider the hire of negroes in these southern countries the most lucrative sane and simple investment of property that can be found."[17]

But George Clarke's second love came long after the demise of the Patriots, while his first lived in their time. In 1808 Clarke and Flora came to Fernandina, where he prospered in trade, acquired landed estates, and became an official in the local government. His advice was sought, his influence recognized, and his power established.

George Clarke advised resistance. Fifty or more able-bodied white men could be counted for defense; more than fifty Negroes could be armed — Clarke did not have the Georgian's fear of the Negro — and some sailors from the ships in the harbor would certainly join in a good fight.

The decision to defend Fernandina against invasion by "rag-a-muffins from the fag-end of Georgia" won the approval of the townspeople. Half buried cannon were dug up, cleaned, charged with powder, and loaded with nails and scrap iron; additional cannon were borrowed from the ships in port. Breastworks of cotton bales were placed around the fort and battery facing the Amelia River. As the most likely route for an invading army was on the ridge of land on the southeastern edge of town, laborers dug entrenchments there and crowned the embankments with bales of cotton. Hibberson and Clarke assumed command of these make-shift fortifications. Altogether the defenders found about fifty muskets, a number of pistols, some swords, and nine cannon of various types. In the magazine of the fort was powder to augment that given by ship captains. The deficiency in shot was remedied by distributing spike nails and langrage shot, long cylindrical missiles filled with nails, bolts, screws, and scraps of iron. Almost all the weapons and ammunition came from the ships anchored in the harbor.[18]

With the two easy approaches to Fernandina, the river and the highland ridge, protected by fortifications, the people rightly believed they could defeat an invading force of Patriots. In total number the regular soldiers, united with the white and Negro volunteers and sailors from the ships in port, nearly equaled the estimated rebel army. A few people of Fernandina deserted, taking their guns with them, but most of the citizens remained steadfast in their determination to fight.

Preparation for battle was one part of the planned defense; the other was negotiation. On March 16 Lopez directed an inquiry to Commodore Campbell asking whether he had orders to aid the rebels.[19] At three in the afternoon George Atkinson and George Clarke, the emissaries of Lopez, found the commodore on a gunboat which was anchored in the mouth of the Amelia River.

The day before, Atkinson had conferred with Campbell at the commodore's lodgings in St. Marys.[20] While Atkinson was there,

Mathews and Isaacs returned from a visit to the Patriot camp at Rose's Bluff, where they had seen almost 200 men in arms. When he was introduced to Atkinson, Mathews made no attempt to disguise his part in the revolution.

"The Patriots will move down Bell's River in the morning," Mathews told Atkinson, "and demand the surrender of Amelia Island. I've ordered Commodore Campbell to aid and assist the Patriots. If Colonel Lopez refuses to surrender Fernandina, the United States gunboats have orders to knock the town down around his ears."[21]

On the following day, March 16, Campbell questioned the manner in which Mathews was involving the United States.

"General Mathews," he said, "the public way in which the Patriots are to be assisted by our gunboats will be cause for England to join her ally, Spain, in a declaration of war on the United States."

"If that happens," Mathews replied, "it will serve a good purpose. We need a war with England. But don't worry about using the gunboats. I'll hold myself accountable for your acts."

Campbell wondered about this open action of Mathews, and thought the general must be invested with extraordinary powers. Otherwise he would not have dared act with so little reserve in his declaration to Atkinson.[22] Campbell frankly did not know what to do. He refused to answer the question of Lopez, stating he must await an answer to a letter he had sent to Mathews. Atkinson and Clarke remained on board the ship until Campbell promised to forward an answer as soon as he received a reply from Mathews.[23]

On March 16 Lopez also ordered Arredondo and Hibberson to inquire of Major Laval whether the United States was a principal or an auxiliary in the contemplated invasion of Amelia Island.[24] At the same time the commissioners were to confer with Lodowick Ashley and answer his and McIntosh's summons to surrender Fernandina.[25]

Just before embarking for the Patriot camp, Arredondo and Hibberson learned that Mathews was not at the Bell's River camp site of the rebels but in St. Marys.[26] Since they desired to question him, whom they recognized as the power behind the Patriots, before they saw McIntosh and Ashley, they went directly to Point Petre. At the Point a captain received them and led them to Mathews, who was in the Laval cottage near the post grounds. They offered Mathews a letter from Lopez, which was addressed to the commander of the

American forces, but the general refused it, stating he was only the commissioner of the United States with power to take possession of East Florida. At this point Laval entered the cottage, accepted the letter, and told the emissaries from Fernandina he would see them in his quarters on the post grounds, but would not say a word to them in the presence of Mathews.

Arredondo and Hibberson followed the major to his quarters. There Laval unburdened his troubles. The conduct of General Mathews, he said, had placed him in a most extraordinary and disagreeable situation, had compelled him to become a sentinel in his own camp, and forced his enlisted men to declare that they would not march into East Florida without definite orders from their commander. Laval assured the emissaries that he had refused, in spite of demands of his officers, and would continue to refuse to give such orders. In fact, he knew the acts of Mathews would never be approved by the great nation which he served. The major then withdrew to answer the inquiry of Lopez, and wrote: "I have the greatest satisfaction in informing you that the United States are neither principals or auxiliaries [in the planned invasion of Amelia Island], and that I am not authorized to make any attack upon East Florida; and I have taken the firm resolution of not marching the Troops of the United States, having no instructions to that effect."[27]

With this reassuring letter safely tucked away, Arredondo and Hibberson sought Mathews again. They found him with Isaacs and General Floyd, and in a mood to answer their questions.

"I have instructions from my government," he told them, "to receive East Florida or any part of it from the local authorities, or to take it by force to prevent its occupation by a foreign power."

"Do you, general, consider those rebels, who call themselves Patriots, the local authorities of East Florida?"

"I do," replied Mathews. "And furthermore, I have positive information of a British plan to land two regiments of Negro troops in East Florida."

"Who gave you that information?"

"A man in whom I have every confidence," stated Mathews. "He is a half-pay British officer and now a resident of Georgia."

Additional questions were answered with complete frankness. Mathews made clear his determination to take East Florida and emphasized his point by having Isaacs read the text of a treaty made with McIntosh as the commissioner of the local authorities of the Spanish province. Arredondo and Hibberson did not allow this fiction of revolution to pass unanswered.

"General Mathews," they said, "this is an American invasion of East Florida. Most of those in arms against us are Georgians, brought to our province by your promises of 500 acres of land. If you withdraw all guarantees of American support, we will drive these rebels pell-mell back into Georgia within a week. If we should fail to do that, Colonel Lopez will deliver Amelia Island to you."

Mathews made no reply and the emissaries left for the Patriot camp on Bell's River, where they found Ashley, McIntosh, and Cook at Low's Plantation. After handing Ashley the evidence of their commission from Colonel Lopez, they informed him that the colonel could not and did not wish to enter into any agreement or treaty with rebels. Neither would he surrender Fernandina without first testing them in battle.

McIntosh and Ashley were visibly shaken by the prospect of fighting. They knew Laval would give them no support and were uncertain of Campbell. Although they blustered and threatened, Hibberson and Arredondo remained calmly determined. If General Mathews, they said, wished to make a treaty in the name of the United States, Colonel Lopez would negotiate with him. Finally it was decided that commissioners from Lopez would meet with Mathews at ten the following morning.

It was past midnight when Hibberson and Arredondo returned to Fernandina. Lopez received them; many of the townspeople were awaiting their report, and responded to it with enthusiastic shouts. Major Laval's refusal to march on the town and the possibility of Campbell's remaining neutral gave the defenders of Fernandina more than an equal chance of defeating the rebels.

Meanwhile the revolutionists had not remained inactive. The main body of the Patriots moved down to Low's Plantation near the mouth of Bell's River. Their preparations for invasion and their rebel flag flying over their camp could be seen in Fernandina.

Shortly after seven on the morning of March 16 a messenger arrived with a letter from Campbell. Lopez frowned as he read: "I take the liberty of informing you that the naval forces of America near

THE CAPTURE OF FERNANDINA

Amelia, do not act in the name of the United States, but do in aiding and abetting, a large portion of your inhabitants, who have thought proper to declare themselves independent, and are now in the act of supplicating you, to unite with them in their cause."[28] Although Campbell never received the answer he desired from Mathews, by some unfathomable logic he decided his gunboats were no longer American property but free ships which could be used to advance the cause of revolution without involving the United States.

Whether the naval flotilla acted in the name of the American government or of the Patriots made no difference to the defenders of Fernandina. Campbell's decision changed the attitude of many who formerly advocated resistance. Nevertheless Lopez and his counselors authorized George Atkinson and Philip Yonge as commissioners to confer with Mathews.

As Atkinson and Yonge rowed across the Amelia River at ten o'clock that morning they saw the United States gunboats tacking into Fernandina harbor.[29] When the commissioners reached the bank of Bell's River at Low's Plantation, McIntosh and William Ashley blindfolded them and led them to a little house about fifty yards from shore. There they found Lodowick Ashley and George Cook but not Mathews. Since the general probably would not come, McIntosh suggested that Atkinson and Yonge negotiate with the Patriots. This proposal was promptly rejected. They agreed, however, to wait one hour for Mathews, and there followed a sixty-minute period filled with words of death, blood-letting, and other threats mixed with cajolery and promises.

On the last minute of the hour Mathews pushed the door open. Just behind him was his secretary, Ralph Isaacs. The Patriot leaders left the house, and the commissioners began by asking Mathews if he was authorized to take possession of East Florida by force.

"I am not," Mathews replied. "But I'm instructed to receive it from the local authorities, and I've accepted a part of it from the Patriots."

"Then, general, you consider the land we now stand on a part of the United States?"

"I do. The area from here to Rose's Bluff is American territory."

"Are the naval forces of the United States," Atkinson asked, "authorized to cooperate with the rebels who are now preparing to attack Amelia Island?"

Mathews hesitated for a moment. "No," he said, "the gunboats won't assist the Patriots."

"If we defeat the rebels will you then take Amelia by force?"

"I have orders from my government," replied Mathews, "to take possession of the island and of the rest of East Florida if it seems that Great Britain plans to occupy the province. I have proof that the British are sending black troops for that purpose."

"General Mathews, we know nothing about British occupation of East Florida. We do know that we must, and can surrender with honor if the American gunboats fire on us, but we shall never surrender to a Georgia rabble which we can repel."

"That's between yourselves and the Patriots," Mathews stated. "I have nothing to do with it. The United States vessels will not interfere unless the British ships in your harbor give you assistance. But if you accept aid from the British, Commodore Campbell will fire on you. Refugees from Fernandina told me that you've received cannon, muskets, and ammunition from the ships in your harbor."

"Great Britain is an ally of Spain, and we have a right to ask help from the British vessels. We have taken nothing from them by force."

"The English," stated Mathews, "have no right to interfere in this business. If you've received aid from them, and you admit it, the gunboats have orders to fire on you."

Atkinson and Yonge had their answer. Mathews knew of the British supplies which armed the townspeople, and, therefore, the American boats would bombard Fernandina if the Patriots were resisted.

The emissaries of Lopez tried another approach. "We are charged," they said, "to inform you that numbers of Georgians are with the rebels, and we demand that you order them home."

"I know nothing about them," Mathews said. "Even if I knew of American citizens in the Patriot army, I have no power over them. You should appeal to the governor of Georgia."

Atkinson and Yonge could get no satisfaction from Mathews and prepared to leave. Before they shoved off for the Amelia shore, they were handed a letter by Lodowick Ashley. In it he stated that only the humanity of the Patriots and their desire to avoid bloodshed had stayed their hand, but since friendly and reasonable overtures had struck no responding chord, all negotiations were at an end. "I charge you on pain of death," ran the letter, "to return to the Island and

THE CAPTURE OF FERNANDINA

inform the inhabitants, that I will this day make my landing upon it, and that I will not fire a single gun, or commit any disorder, if they do not fire upon me, but in the event that they do, we will show them no quarters and we will proceed to confiscate the properties of all those who should do so . . . but if they surrender I will obligate myself in the most solemn manner, to comply with my first proposals."[30]

As Atkinson and Yonge rowed back to Fernandina they saw the American gunboats anchored in the river and facing the fort. Three of them were within pistol shot of the garrison and their cables were sprung in readiness to shift the boats into desired fighting positions. In Fernandina the returning commissioners discovered the optimism and will to resist of the morning had changed to despair and talk of surrender. Many men had abandoned their assigned defensive posts. No inducements would persuade them to return in the face of the threatening guns of the American ships.[31]

Since Sunday the gunboats had been stationed at the mouth of Amelia River. On Tuesday morning, March 17, the ship commanders boarded Campbell's flagship and received written orders. They were to enter Amelia Harbor, approach the battery at Fernandina, getting as near as possible without grounding, and support the Patriots under McIntosh who were expected to attack during the day.[32] By nine o'clock five gunboats had entered the harbor.[33] Each boat carried a crew of fifty men and the ships' combined guns numbered thirteen: six nine pounders, six thirty-two pounders, and one long tom. Campbell anchored his flagship in Cumberland Sound within signal range of the gunboats; two other boats remained at the mouth of the Amelia River. The five gunboats approached the Fernandina battery in battle order with their crews at quarter, their guns loaded with canister shot, the tampions out, and matches lighted. Two hundred yards from land they stopped, threw out anchors fore and aft, and set the cables so the boats could be turned with ease. Everything was in readiness for a bombardment.[34]

As Campbell watched his gunboats in battle line before Fernandina his mind became more and more troubled. Only his respect and friendship for Mathews sustained him in his course.[35] The night before, Laval had sent him a message: "This is a damned rascally business, get your neck out of the halter as soon as possible."[36] The major's steadfast stand against Mathews worried Campbell. He decided to fire a signal gun and order his gunboats to withdraw from the harbor. Young, enthusiastic Winslow Foster, commander of gunboat 62, paid no heed. He yelled to another officer, John Grayson, "You may obey, but I shall remain." Grayson's and one other boat hoisted anchors and sailed back. Now only three gunboats remained. Campbell fired another signal gun and still another. He sailed his flagship up the river, passed Fernandina, and turned back toward the sound. Again the signal gun sounded. Sailors lowered a skiff and its crew rowed toward gunboat 62 with orders for Foster: under no circumstances was he to fire on the battery or aid the Patriots. The commodore fired another signal gun and sailed his ship north into Cumberland Sound.[37]

In Fernandina the people knew nothing of these last minute orders. They could see the Patriots loading flatboats on Bell's River in preparation for invasion. The signal guns of Campbell seemed to be synchronized with the movements of the Patriots.

On the shore a man yelled to the gunboat crews, "Keep off, or remain neutral until we decide the contest with the Patriots!" The voices of the people swelled into a shout of approval.

From over the water came the reply, "If you fire on them we'll fire on you."[38]

This answer threw the townspeople into confusion. While the cannon on the gunboats pointed toward the town, seven or more boat loads of Patriots were moving slowly toward the Amelia shore. A crowd formed around the commandant's house, where Lopez stood near the flagpole on which waved the banner of Spain. Almost as one man the people shouted, "Let Colonel Lopez decide!"

He pondered for a moment; then lifting his head, said, "We must surrender; resistance would be unavailing."

Lopez paused. It was almost three o'clock. He glanced toward the approaching Patriot boats. The people shouted, "Surrender – Resistance is impossible – Save our lives and property!"

"Who will take the flag of surrender?" Lopez asked. No one moved until George Clarke stepped forward. "I will," he said.

The people nodded and shouted their approval. The slaves and free Negroes dropped their guns and silently stole away. Not one of them wanted those Georgians to find them under arms.

Clarke got into a rowboat; a white flag flew on its bow. Out in the

THE CAPTURE OF FERNANDINA

river below Fernandina he met the oncoming Patriots, and offered Ashley the town.

About sixty Patriots landed at Fernandina Bluff, a mile below the town, and marched north in ragged file. Before the commandant's house they halted. It was four o'clock. Colonel Lopez stepped forward; tears ran down his cheeks. He offered his sword to Ashley, refusing in his humiliation to keep that symbol of his authority. Ashley buckled it around his waist. The Spanish flag was lowered, and on signal from Ashley, the Patriot flag was raised.

As the Spanish flag came down, the gunboats weighed anchor and sailed north to Cumberland Sound where they joined the other ships, and the flotilla moved leisurely through the water toward St. Marys. When the ships rested at anchor Commodore Campbell requisitioned his written orders of the morning from all the commanders. The purpose, he told them, was to record copies for his files. The orders were never seen again.[39] Thus Campbell eased his troubled mind. Later he wrote: "[the gunboats] took their station near the town of Fernandina, in a quiet and Friendly manner – the commanders of those Boats having orders not to fire a shot unless first fired on, and previous to the approach of the Patriots I gave a positive order not to fire a shot on any condition whatever – this measure had the desired effect of preventing blood shed which would inevitably have been the case...."[40]

On Amelia River, boat loads of Patriots continued moving from Low's Plantation to Fernandina. Eventually 180[41] tired, hungry men reached the town, men who had volunteered in anticipation of land and loot. Conditions were ripe for plunder, robbery, looting, but nothing happened. Not one chicken was stolen, not a single store robbed nor a house pillaged. It was an apparent miracle, a tribute to the leadership of Mathews and McIntosh and Ashley.[42]

At the commandant's house Lopez, McIntosh, and Ashley drew up articles of capitulation. Secretaries made copies, and Lopez signed them.

The terms were those which McIntosh and Ashley had promised. The commandant and his troops (all nine of them) were allowed the honors of war; upon delivering their arms and promising never again to fight the Patriots, they would be paroled within the limits of Fernandina. All real and personal property remained to the owners and no property was to be examined, touched, or destroyed. Within twenty-four hours Amelia Island would be ceded to the United States; but after the cession, the port of Fernandina would be exempted from American customs laws, and would remain open to British ships, to trading vessels of other nations, until May 1, 1813. Even in case of war between the United States and Great Britain this provision would be binding until the fixed date. All timber rights, grants, and other concessions of Spain would be continued and recognized as valid. Everyone who remained on Amelia Island was guaranteed his civil and property rights and those who chose to leave were free to go. The latter would have one year of grace within which their property could be sold without penalty or tax, and even should the United States fight Spain, agents would be allowed for those loyal to Spain.[43]

After Lopez had affixed his signature, George Clarke, his brother Charles, and George Atkinson placed their names on the document as representatives of the townspeople. McIntosh then signed as commissioner for the Patriots of East Florida.

On to St. Augustine

AFTER MATHEWS HAD FINISHED his conference with Atkinson and Yonge at Low's Plantation on March 17, he scurried north across the border. For a time he waited impatiently in St. Marys. From over the water came the sound of cannon fire. Fervently he hoped the naval vessels were not shelling Fernandina for that would involve the United States. Restlessness overcame him and from St. Marys he went down to Point Petre. With Smith in command of the post and Laval under arrest, the encampment was no longer forbidden ground.

There were few similarities in the characters or backgrounds of Smith and Laval. In the last years of the Revolutionary War, while Laval fought the British, Thomas Adam Smith was a child. In the 1780's his family migrated from Virginia to Wilkes County, Georgia, where his father, Francis, became the owner of extensive properties. Thomas Adam was brought up in Georgia, understood the Georgians' point of view and, as they, hated the Spaniard and the Indian.

Smith found his career in the Army. Entering it as an ensign he became a second lieutenant in 1803 at the age of twenty-two, and then in succession a first lieutenant, captain, major, and lieutenant colonel. From the first his men almost worshipped him; his superiors found him an obedient, respectful, courageous officer. He learned the army way: for him an order was to be obeyed, not questioned. He rose rapidly in the service.

Mathews knew Lieutenant Colonel Smith. In fact most prominent

Georgians knew the thirty-year-old colonel. Crawford and Troup were his intimate friends and Smith gave their names, William and George, to his sons. His brother-in-law was Peter Early, representative in Congress and later governor of Georgia. James White, founder of Knoxville, Tennessee, was his father-in-law and Hugh Lawson White, the brother of his wife Cynthia, was already prominent in the Volunteer state. On his paternal side Meriwether Smith, a famous Virginian, was his uncle; he could call George William Smith, who followed Monroe as governor of Virginia, cousin.

Thomas A. Smith had the lineage and attributes of an American. Furthermore, his striking appearance, his erect military figure, his handsome face, with heavy brows over dark piercing eyes, his strong chin and high forehead, and dark hair distinguished him. He could fly into a good Southern rage, "cuss" the army, and his superiors; but he knew when to cuss and when to be respectful.[1]

Mathews had no difficulty with Smith, for on the Florida question they agreed. Although the colonel followed Laval in not permitting American soldiers to volunteer in the service of the Patriots, there was no need for that now; and he readily agreed with the other plans of Mathews. Whenever the general should request troops for the peaceful occupation of East Florida or any part of it, they would be supplied. Smith would not question the authority of local officials, nor ask by what right they exercised that authority. He would obey the orders of President Madison's agent.

Anxiously Mathews waited through that long afternoon of March 17. Finally the returning gunboats brought the welcome news: Lopez had surrendered without firing a shot; the Patriots held Fernandina. Mathews smiled with satisfaction. His days of trial were almost over, his mission on the road to success.

Early in the following morning a request came from the "constituted authority of East Florida" asking Mathews, as the commissioner of the United States, to accept all the country lying between the St. Marys and St. Johns together with the coastal islands situated between the mouths of those rivers.[2] The general immediately called on Colonel Smith for a detachment of troops. Lieutenant Appling and a company of fifty men were ordered over the border with Mathews.[3]

On the afternoon of the eighteenth they sailed from Point Petre. As they disembarked at Fernandina, Mathews went ahead toward the commandant's house while Appling ordered his men into military formation. Mathews conferred with McIntosh and went through the formality of accepting the Spanish-Patriot articles of surrender. Then the American troops marched up in all their splendor and halted before the flagpole. On behalf of the Patriots McIntosh delivered the country to Mathews, who graciously accepted it in the name of the United States. He then delivered it to Appling, charging him with the duty of holding and defending it. A rifle salute was fired and the Patriots, massed behind the soldiers, cheered. A few of the watching townspeople joined in the shouting, but most of them remained sullenly silent.

Mathews was elated. The smart military appearance of Lieutenant Appling and his men, he reported, together with their good order and deportment, reflected honor on the United States. The entire proceedings commanded the respect of the "Dons."[4]

In the days which followed Mathews established the new order in Fernandina. He created a temporary customs district with a Mr. Lewis of St. Marys in charge as deputy collector. No goods, however, could be moved into the United States proper until President Madison approved the agreement made with the Patriots.[5] With the cooperation of Appling a police system was provided for the town and a few days later additional patrols came in when Captain John Williams came over from Cumberland Island with some marines.

The opportunity for loot in Fernandina tempted the adventurous rowdies among the Patriots. General Floyd estimated the value of property in the town at $200,000 and believed there was considerable specie hidden away; one British ship in port had a value of $150,000, and there were many other vessels in the harbor.[6] The troops, however, kept almost perfect order, no robberies were reported, and a peaceful calm hung over the town.

More essential for the grand scheme of conquest were plans for capturing St. Augustine. Even before they seized Amelia Island the Patriots were scouring both sides of the St. Johns for recruits. William Craig, Spanish appointed judge of the St. Johns district,[7] now threw his lot with the revolutionists. Zephaniah Kingsley, who had a plantation on the river and who, like George Clarke, had no scruples against cohabiting with Negro women, was dragged, he said, into camp.[8] Looking on from his comfortable though restricted quarters,

Colonel Justo Lopez could see no organization whatever in the Patriot ranks and concluded they would not succeed in their enterprise.[9]

Organized or not the Patriots were confident of success, and so was Mathews. While they prepared for a movement against St. Augustine, he requested troops and gunboats for their support. He informed Secretary Monroe of the absolute need for companies of infantry and artillery; he urged Governor Mitchell to send 250 Georgia militiamen (700 would be necessary if England aided Spain); he asked Campbell for gunboats on the St. Johns and off St. Augustine Harbor; and he told Smith of the Patriot plans, of new areas of East Florida which should soon be occupied by American troops.[10] Reluctantly Campbell complied in part with the general's request and Smith prepared to move the remainder of his command into East Florida.

Sunday, March 22, was the date set for the Patriot advance.[11] Actually the revolutionists, unorganized as they were, departed as quickly as boats could be found. Some left on Wednesday, more on Thursday, and the others followed shortly after. McIntosh and Ashley led the expeditions.

Between Fernandina and St. Augustine there was no real opposition. Three Spanish soldiers guarding San Nicholas at Cow Ford surrendered; the others (if there were others) fled into St. Augustine. On March 23 the Patriots arrived at Picolata, a post on the east bank of the St. Johns. Fourteen miles directly east lay St. Augustine and the Castillo de San Marcos. On the twenty-fifth, the advance guard halted near the San Sebastian River. Across the water, the Patriots could see the Castillo and the houses of St. Augustine.[12]

The revolutionists made a recruiting venture of their unopposed invasion. From St. Augustine Governor Estrada sent out an order: on the approach of the rebels every loyal man should destroy his property, burn his buildings, and run for St. Augustine. No one did. Though many fled into St. Augustine, the Patriots found houses intact, barns stored with provisions, and fat cattle on the range. As recruiting bands fanned out through the country, they persuaded or forced residents into their ranks. Kingsley refused their entreaties, requesting instead the status of a prisoner, but he learned that no prisoners would be taken; every man must either join the Patriots or submit to banishment and confiscation of his property.[13]

The exact number of Patriots who invested St. Augustine cannot be determined. One report gave 400 to 600, another 250, and still another 800; all of these were estimates.[14] The Patriots themselves never enumerated their force and the reports of Colonel Smith indicate 100 as a reasonable figure. A Spanish census of 1812 lists the names of 106 men as rebels and eighty-three who were either loyal or whose inclinations were unknown.[15] In addition to these residents of Spanish Florida there were the civilian and militia volunteers of Georgia.

Similar to their number, the organizational changes within the Patriot ranks are not easily followed. General Mathews, who should have known, reported that William Craig was elected president,[16] but every extant document indicates the general erred and that William Craig was never president of any organization. The only evidence of the Patriot government is in the signatures attached to proclamations and resolutions it promulgated. From these it is evident that some reorganization came after the capture of Fernandina. Daniel Delany, a wealthy East Florida planter, began serving with McIntosh as a commissioner. The military force of the Patriots was divided into two divisions with Lodowick Ashley as colonel commandant of the first and William Craig as colonel commandant of the second.[17] Sometime late in March a "Board of Officers for the Constituted Authority of East Florida" came into being, for Daniel Delany addressed a report to them.[18] Almost one month later William Craig signed, as chairman, a resolution of the Patriots.[19] Undoubtedly the governmental organization of the revolutionists remained a minor concern, for with the occupation of each additional foot of Spanish Florida an almost immediate delivery was made to the United States. Since the Patriots lost their power over the territory when the United States acquired title, there was no reason for a well organized Patriot government.

Whatever their organization, McIntosh remained the spokesman of the Patriots. On March 26, from the "Patriot Camp" near St. Augustine, he summoned Governor Estrada to surrender the town and the Castillo de San Marcos:

> The people of East Florida having long suffered under the Tyranny of an arbitrary government and being threatened that a body of merciless savages would be thrown into their country have unanimously with the exception of

St. Augustine declared themselves an independent people. They have organized themselves as a military body and have taken possession of all the country round St. Augustine . . . they have . . . offered to the commissioner of the United States to cede to the United States the province of East Florida under certain beneficial terms. Those terms are a full security of life, liberty and property; the establishment of all privileges, the payment of all debt due by the province and to the officers and soldiers; that the officers and soldiers of the Spanish army now in East Florida shall be received into the army of the United States in the same ranks as at present, or if they decline active service, they will be allowed a liberal pay during life; the Catholic as well as all other Christian religions will be protected and the fathers will be paid the same amount as now during their lives or residence in the country; all places of worship will be secured for the adoration of God in the same form as at present. We now demand the surrender of the town and citadel of St. Augustine in order that the people therein may participate in the beneficial consequences that must result from an annexation to the United States.[20]

If the governor expected aid from the Seminole Indians, continued McIntosh, he would be disappointed for their chief, King Payne, in a meeting with Patriot leaders at Picolata had assured them of his neutrality. Furthermore, many volunteers were assisting the people of East Florida, American troops were marching behind the Patriots, and American gunboats were sailing for St. Augustine. Since a prolonged siege would destroy life and property, yet accomplish no more than to delay the inevitable fall of the city, wisdom dictated surrender.

Loyal, courageous Estrada had not accepted the governorship of East Florida to liquidate the Spanish empire in southeastern North America. He would neither surrender nor confer with rebels. All told, he commanded about 300 men, some of them untried colored militia and others only volunteers from the town.[21] The reported neutrality of the Seminoles was a blow. He had sent them an appeal and hoped for their aid and that of the Negroes who lived in towns near the Indians. Reinforcements should arrive from Cuba, perhaps from the British colonies. Calls for help had been made, but he could not count on the day of their arrival. His situation appeared hopeless. But he bolstered his defenses, prepared to evacuate the town if necessary, and to retreat into the strong Castillo de San Marcos.

When Estrada defied them, the Patriots encamped near Moosa Old Fort. McIntosh and Delany retraced the way back to Cow Ford where, they hoped, Mathews awaited their formal cession of East Florida "to the walls of St. Augustine." However, a spring storm had prevented the movement of troops from Fernandina. McIntosh and Delany hurried on to Fernandina where they found Mathews, and on March 31, 1812, the papers of cession were signed.[22]

The text of the formal cession reiterated many of the agreements of record. It included provisions for the pay and pensions of Spanish soldiers, care of Catholic priests, guarantees of land and other property, and promises of civil liberties. Mathews emphasized the value of keeping Fernandina a free port until May 1, 1813; in fact, he thought the time should be extended until May, 1814, for this would appease the British and make them less likely to protest American annexation of East Florida. It would give Southern slaveholders a means of obtaining clothing for their Negroes, and bring in a considerable revenue for the United States.[23]

The cession terms more than adequately provided for the Patriots. All rights in land and timber were continued; trees on the public domain were free for the cutting until May 1, 1813; 500 acres of land would be granted each volunteer; the lax land grant policy of Spain would be continued unchanged; all individual loans would be repaid with interest; and the people would be protected from the Indians. Mathews bound the United States to establish a territory of Florida and eventually grant statehood when the territorial population should justify it.

The provision for the conquest of Mobile and Pensacola, Mathews stated, was not made with a view of committing the United States; but, he added gratuitously, it would be impolitic to leave them in possession of the Spanish. According to Mathews the sixth provision of the cession provided support for Secretary of State Monroe in his diplomatic explanation of American action.[24] In this provision the Patriots declared they were not rebelling against that which Spain fought for in Europe; but rather, if Spain succeeded and established herself as a nation of first rank, East Florida would be returned, if a majority of Floridians desired a restoration. The restoration would not be made, however, until Spain paid the United States for the spoliation claims, made good in full damages suffered by American citizens in consequence of the suspension of the right of deposit at New Orleans, and reimbursed the United States government for all expenses entailed in governing East Florida.[25] These broad conditions ensured that bankrupt Spain would never again hold the province.

After the commissioners had signed the cession agreement for the "Constituted Authorities" they set out for the Patriot camp. A storm born wind blew so fiercely from the south that four oarsmen could make no headway up the St. Johns River. At Maxey's Creek they hove to and walked. From Delany's Plantation they sent a messenger with the encouraging words, "Everything goes on to our wish."[26]

The rain and wind delayed action and the plans of Mathews. Both Campbell and Smith were awaiting clear skies before moving ships and troops. Gunboats numbers 62 and 63 were ordered to St. Augustine and their commander charged with anchoring as near the fort as prudence allowed; but he must not offend the town or garrison unless in retaliation for an insult to the American flag. Communication was to be established with Colonel Smith when he reached the outskirts of St. Augustine. If the Spanish objected, the commander should insist on the right, since East Florida had been ceded to the United States. Every assistance should be given General Mathews.[27] Three other gunboats would be stationed on the St. Johns, one near the bluff about fifteen miles from the river's mouth and two at Picolata.[28]

For Campbell's almost unquestioning obedience to Mathews, Smith was in part responsible. His wholehearted support of the Florida invasion bolstered the wavering commodore and eased his throbbing conscience. Smith complained of his shoddy troops—they had received no clothing for a year; of his equipment—rifles would not fire and there were no bayonets. Nevertheless he arranged with his contractor for provisions and prepared his command for duty, leaving a corporal's guard at Point Petre. On Friday, March 27, Mathews asked the colonel for occupational forces at points on the east bank of the St. Johns and for a sergeant's guard to accompany him on his journey south. Though knowing his small detachment could not hold the St. Johns line if the Spanish and Indians combined against him, Smith nevertheless pitched his tents in Fernandina; but for days the storm prevented further advance.[29]

Impatient Mathews took off from Fernandina on April 4 with the advance guard of Smith's command. Before he boarded the waiting boat he removed his three-cornered hat, and faced the watching soldiers and townspeople. The wind played through his red hair. He raised his battered hat. The crowd quieted.

"I go to St. Augustine," he said, "and from there our victorious

ON TO ST. AUGUSTINE

men move on Mobile and Pensacola. But we won't stop. On to Venezuela! We'll rout the autocratic Spaniards and plant the flag of freedom over all of South America."[30] Then with the stride of a Cæsar he moved toward the wharf and stepped gingerly into the small boat. It was his day of triumph and he enjoyed its every hour. He had a right to: his night of humiliation was on its way.

On April 7 Smith reached Picolata on the St. Johns. Mathews swelled with oratory as he delivered the place into the colonel's keeping. The following day Smith deposited stores at Six Mile Creek and prepared for his march on St. Augustine. On the eleventh, camp was made at Moosa Old Fort near the Patriots, two and a half miles from St. Augustine. The soldiers could see the housetops of the old city and even Spanish sentries on the parapets of the Castillo. Again the little pageant of occupation was enacted. At exactly four o'clock in the afternoon of April 12 the Patriots assembled, speeches were made, and Smith accepted Moosa Old Fort as American territory.[31]

Before reveille the following morning a Spanish gunboat was sighted on the river. On it came, firing one shot after another. One cannon ball hit a sandbank behind which a man slept, nearly burying him alive. Two more shots were fired and both passed over the American camp. When the United States flag was raised, the firing ceased and the boat turned back toward St. Augustine. On the fourteenth, Mathews sent Captain Massias forward with a flag of truce. At the Spanish lines he was ordered back on pain of death.[32] Estrada was still adamant.

General Mathews was a man bewitched. In this frame of mind he dictated a report on his mission. Heading his letters "Moosa Old Fort" he first addressed President Madison and apologized for not writing him before. The duties of his confidential mission and delicate trust had occupied his full time; but now that his mission was fast drawing to a successful conclusion, he could not refrain from giving his friend an account of the hardships, trials, and victories of the past year.

It is impossible to convey an adequate idea of the various embarrassments I had to encounter, the most trying and arduous proceeded from Major Laval's refusing to obey my requisitions after having pledged himself to do so, and also to support the persons engaged in the revolution, yet after they had passed the St. Marys which in relation to them may be called the Rubicon he without giving me the least previous notice in a clandestine manner sent word to them that he would neither support them or obey my requisitions – he is now under arrest – the charges I think will break him – the conduct of his however reprehensible respecting his deceiving me does not constitute any part of the charges exhibited as it would be the only means whereby the Government could be implicated in all this business, for I have not in any instance committed the honor of Government or my own reputation by any act – nor have I pursued any clandestine means to accomplish the objects of my mission with any subject of E. Florida. The applications were made to me to know on what terms the Government would receive them, to which I gave such replies as were justified by my instructions, and in every instance I conferr'd with men whose rank in society was respectable.[33]

Laval's perfidy, Mathews continued, forced him to promise much larger land grants than at first contemplated;[34] but there would yet remain a large and valuable country at the disposal of the United States, with sufficient live oak, cedar, and pine to build all the navy the nation would ever want, and there was also the large harbor of Tampa in which it could be anchored. The Indians would be a problem, and a treaty would be necessary for limiting their boundaries in East Florida.

The general did not forget his friends. As Laval was condemned so was Smith praised. McIntosh would make an excellent governor for the territory of Florida, unless Madison wanted General Floyd who was also most acceptable. James Seagrove of St. Marys or John P. Wagner of Kentucky, both old servants of Seventy-Six, deserved appointment as surveyor general; Ralph Isaacs should be attorney general; and Charles Harris of Savannah would make a good district judge.

Thus did Mathews create the territory of East Florida and reward his friends with its major offices. He reiterated his wishes by sending Secretary Monroe a list of recommended men: McIntosh for governor, Wagner for register of public lands, Seagrove for surveyor general, Isaacs and Harris for attorney and judge.

In his letter to Monroe, also of April 16, the general praised Isaacs for his work and informed the secretary of state that Isaacs could answer any question on East Florida. Isaacs, who would deliver the letters in person, had all the important declarations and agreements of the "constituted authorities" of the province. Mathews hoped the Senate would ratify the treaty of cession without delay. Before closing, the general mentioned with considerable pride his expense account; he had drawn only $2,000 during his entire mission.[35] It was a mere pittance in comparison with the wealth of East Florida.

Outside of the American camp and the back-slappers in the Patriot ranks, Mathews was almost the only man entranced by the revolution. Unsympathetically the editor of the *Charleston Courier* commented: "For ourselves, feeling as we do for the dignity and honor of our country, we must refrain at present from expressing our sentiments upon this transaction – we leave it to our Democratic brethren, who have inveigled with so much feeling and effect upon the attack on Copenhagen to furnish a justification for the part which the Americans have taken in this transaction."[36] This editorial might be dismissed as the party politics of a Federalist editor, but the *Georgia Argus* also sharply criticized provisions of the cession treaty and some of the promises of Mathews.[37]

Even Mathews' friend, the man who would make a good governor for territorial Florida, penned some harsh statements. "I regret exceedingly the *manner*," wrote General John Floyd, "in this hidden policy, all the sin of direct invasion rests on the Shoulders of the Government or its agent. And too against a weak, defenseless, unhappy Neighbor. . . ." Floyd would have approved a policy of taking East Florida by direct invasion, "but really the veil thrown over this Transaction, will not save appearances, and why resort to these means of causing a war with England, and by doing so make ourselves the aggressor. . . . Let the Government come out, draw aside the mask, it is too flimsy for deception, say they will have their provinces and it will be done, merit will meet its reward and the Government will only have to answer for the deed, which she will under Existing Circumstances have to do, with all the littleness attached to such a hidden transaction."[38]

Five days after writing this letter, Floyd was still critical of the invasion, but he also saw possibilities in it for good. If the Indians would only aid the Spanish, then, said Floyd, the Georgia militia forces would have an excuse for attacking and destroying the redskins and for wiping out the Negro towns, an evil which was encouraged by the Indians. But Floyd realized the danger facing Georgia. So many of his men had volunteered in the Patriot service, he was forced to call out the seventh and eighth battalions of his command for emergencies and an occasional scouring of those parts of East

Florida now in the United States' possession. He also knew of the danger confronting Mathews and Smith, for in his opinion the Patriots and the volunteers would run on hearing their first shot. His conclusion was simple: let the regular troops and militia openly take East Florida and obtain the honors and pecuniary benefits of the conquest.[39]

In those first exciting days the invasion of East Florida was a lark, an exciting adventure from family responsibility and old familiar places or from tiresome routine. The initial flush of victory brought additional recruits hurrying for the kill. Then, as quickly as it rose, optimism faded. The endless days and nights in a mosquito infested lowland, the inactivity, the terrible monotony of sameness, poor food, and inadequate shelter made men long for home. One by one they slipped quietly from the Patriot camp. Some men began corresponding with the Spanish in St. Augustine, reporting the strength and weaknesses of Patriot and soldier. Ships moved up the Matanzas River bringing supplies and perhaps reinforcements for the town, for Campbell's gunboats never blockaded the harbor. With reinforcements Estrada might sally forth and give the invader only sufficient land for a grave.

Early in April the Patriots realized the danger. Not knowing what else to do they issued a proclamation and Lodowick Ashley signed it. "Whereas, the inhabitants of East Florida did on March 13, 1812, declare themselves independent and assume the government in their hands and have a right to make laws for the defense and security of their life, liberty, and property; and, whereas, some evilly disposed persons are inciting disaffection, aiding and abetting resistance to the cause of freedom by correspondence with men in St. Augustine and are by vile and infamous deeds arming the barbaric Negro, they shall be guilty of high treason and on conviction, suffer death." But all lovers of freedom, even free persons of color and those previously refusing to unite with the Patriots, could yet join the cause. All who were not already Patriots must declare themselves at camp within ten days or be counted as enemies with the consequent confiscation of all real and personal property.[40]

The proclamation was as high sounding as it was useless. Almost every resident had already made his decision in favor of the Patriots or the Spaniards. Those who surreptitiously left the encampment could claim adherence to the cause and exemption from confiscation of property. It did give legal sanction for grabbing property of Loyalists and under its phrases many unscrupulous Patriots robbed for their own personal gain, making no distinction between revolutionist and loyalist.

Not only did the Patriots decrease in number but also their support by the American armed forces became weak and ineffectual. The gunboats at St. Augustine sailed back to St. Marys with unfavorable reports. A blockade of the town by sea was impracticable: ships could not withstand the winds and seas outside the bar; and an anchorage within the bar, beyond the range of the fort's guns, was impracticable because of the loose sand bottom and the high winds which would ground vessels on Fishers (Anastasia) Island. A blockade of St. Augustine hinged on occupying Fishers Island and control of Matanzas Inlet. Unless the Matanzas River, a twenty-mile arm of the sea separating Fishers Island from the mainland, was closed, St. Augustine could not be blockaded.[41] The possibility of British intervention could not be overlooked. Already the British warship *Calibri* had made threatening moves against gunboat 63 off St. Augustine and the American commander, expecting an attack, had ordered all hands to quarters, the guns loaded, and the matches lighted. For an hour the two ships maneuvered as though seeking position for battle.[42] This incident emphasized the danger from a British attack on blockading American gunboats.

Even if Colonel Smith had the authority, he could not take St. Augustine by assault. His effective force was 109 men; he needed artillery, and his men suffered from a lack of food and clothing. The nearby Patriot force did not exceed ninety-three while the Spaniards could muster 180 regulars, fifty colored militia, and 170 volunteers from the town. Well aware of all this, Colonel Smith expected an attack on his position.[43]

The Patriots made a bold front. On April 18 they allowed a Loyalist to leave camp with letters for Governor Estrada. The Patriots, he was informed, could never lay down their arms; for having declared their independence, the Spanish government would take their property and banish them from the land. They entreated Estrada to unite with them for a union that would increase property values in St. Augustine and enrich the governor tenfold.

Hidden in the folds of the first letter was a second of the same date in which the Patriots offered Estrada $5,000 and $1,000 for any five men he designated for an immediate surrender of the town. Payment was guaranteed, they told him, by a $100,000 secret appropriation of the United States and by wealthy Patriots who were assured repayment by the American government of all sums advanced in securing East Florida.[44] Estrada answered these appeals with silence: he would not sell his patriotism.

In April the Patriots had one reason for rejoicing. On the seventeenth the famous Georgia general, John McIntosh, strode into camp. Ashley, Craig, and Cook were men of limited military experience while John Houstoun McIntosh was no military leader at all. But his cousin John had fought the British, twisted the arm of Spain in East Florida, and was now a major general in the Georgia militia. He was experienced, commanding in appearance, well-known (surely his name would attract recruits), and he burned with hatred of Spaniards.

In the words of General McIntosh, he came for the purpose of investigating the Patriots' chance of shaking off the tyranny and oppression of the Spaniards and informing himself of the powers invested in General Mathews. After surveying the situation he planned on withdrawing. But the Patriots would not hear of it, and quickly elected him their commander-in-chief. When McIntosh hesitated, the rank and file declared they would abandon the revolution. Warmed by this display of confidence the egotistical old general accepted and immediately tendered his resignation as major general in the Georgia militia.[45]

General McIntosh sent Governor Mitchell an unfavorable report on the revolution. With Matanzas Inlet open, the Patriots could not blockade St. Augustine or the fort. Two British ships were sending provisions into the garrison and Great Britain was apparently planning on occupying the town. Under these conditions McIntosh could not understand why the American government did not rush reinforcements and take the fort while there was still time.

Exactly how long General John McIntosh remained with the Patriots is a conjecture. Late in April he gave Colonel Smith a disheartening report on the military potential of the revolutionists.[46] Undoubtedly his presence moved the Patriots to call for recruits, for on May 2, 1812, the constituted authorities of East Florida authorized

ON TO ST. AUGUSTINE

the raising of an additional force of 500 men. A committee headed by John Houstoun McIntosh with William Craig, Zephaniah Kingsley, and Buckner Harris was appointed to work with Commander-in-Chief John McIntosh on plans and ways of securing volunteers. The Patriots pledged all unassigned land in East Florida and all condemned property of Loyalists for payment of those who volunteered and for the expenses of the revolutionary government.[47] That the Patriots expected the recruits to come from Georgia was evident: they were to assemble at Ashley's Plantation on the St. Marys.

The influence of General McIntosh on the course of revolution was negligible. For a brief interval he acted as commander-in-chief of the Patriots, but it was a period of inactivity and waiting. Governor Mitchell refused the general's proffered resignation as major general of the first division of Georgia militia. It was well that he did, for the general and the militia were soon to be needed for defense against a more powerful antagonist.

The steadfast patriotism of Governor Estrada had defeated the Patriots. The hopes of those early months of organization and the promise of victory after Fernandina, faded before the walls of St. Augustine. The discouraged Patriots were no longer an invading army. The American gunboats became defensive weapons, for Colonel Smith's command could do no more than hold their advance and might be forced to retreat at any moment. By May, 1812, Smith, the Patriot leaders, and even Mathews knew the great adventure was over unless help came from Washington. Everyone awaited word from President Madison.

Revolution Denied

IN WASHINGTON JAMES MADISON squirmed in the presidential chair. Intellectual, scholar, political scientist of distinction, genius in a way, he was beyond his depth in the stream of American politics and the ocean of world affairs. His forte was in thought, in constructive reasoning, not in action.

Yet, by the spring of 1812, Madison was supreme in Washington. Behind him were three troublesome years in the White House — years of party strife, of bickering in his cabinet, of indecision in foreign affairs. In the country at large the Republican party continued its growth as American farmers became more politically conscious. Agrarians, not merchants or bankers or industrialists, populated America. Once these farmers had tasted victory at the polls and realized their potential power, there was no stopping them or the advance of their Republican party. Conversely the Federalists, outnumbered and undermanned, declined in power. In 1811, for the first time, the Federalists lost control of the executive and legislative branches of the Massachusetts state government. It was a sweet victory, though a narrow one, for the Republicans. For them it was a good omen of their growing invincibility; for the warlike section of the party it was a clear mandate for decisive action in foreign affairs.

These ardent nationalists within the Republican ranks were quick to seize their advantage. Although the "War Hawks" were a minority in the twelfth Congress, they made up for their lack of numbers by aggressive leadership and set determination. In December, 1811, they won the speakership of the House and throughout the long session from December to July, Speaker Henry Clay had the support of John Caldwell Calhoun, Langdon Cheves, William Lowndes, and David Rogerson Williams of South Carolina, Felix Grundy of Tennessee, Richard Mentor Johnson of Kentucky, and Peter Buell Porter of New York. Youthful, able, and drunk with the heady wine of nationalism, these men talked long and loud. In the cloakrooms and at dinner tables they won representatives and senators for their cause. No longer would they allow the United States to chart a yielding course between warring England and France in order to avoid war. In the opinion of the War Hawks, the United States of yesterday, which had been too proud to fight, was now a nation too proud not to.

They recited the wrongs heaped on America by England, France, and Spain. They upheld with fevered oratory every evidence of American resistance – the occupation of West Florida, the naval battle between the United States *President* and the English *Little Belt,* the defeat of the pro-British Indians at Tippecanoe. Country men who did not know the difference between a bill of lading and a letter of credit, who could not distinguish the bow from the stern of a ship, who thought of a sailor as a half-human animal of the terrifying sea, talked of neutral rights and impressments and freedom of the seas. But they did more than talk. They called for 10,000 additional regular troops, 50,000 volunteers, the outfitting of ships of war, and the arming of all merchant vessels.

In a way it made no difference whether war was declared against England or France. Both had been guilty of hostile acts against the United States. Yet, in reality, only a war with England made sense. France possessed no desirable lands in North America, while the spoils of a successful war with Great Britain would be Canada and the Floridas. By one clean cut of the sword the United States could sever all European influence in North America. Naturally it would be a short war: in the opinion of their planners all aggressive wars are short ones. A quick invasion would bring Canada into the fold; the Floridas presented no problem, since already they were virtually American.

Thus the South and West formed an unwritten alliance. The South would receive the Floridas and Canada would be added to the West. Felix Grundy envisioned the decline of Northern influence when Louisiana and the Floridas were peopled, but saw hope for the North in Eastern Canada: only by acquisition of the British provinces could the Northern people expand and retain their relative influence in the American union.

President Madison traveled the road of the expansionists. He did not lead their procession but he approved of their itinerary. When the Congress authorized an addition of 25,000 men to the existing army of 10,000, rather than the 10,000 which Madison had requested, he approved the measure. Encouraged by a chauvinistic Congress, the president grew firm and even reckless in his dealings with England. By the spring of 1812 war with Great Britain was set; only the time of the declaration remained to be determined.

The long smouldering revolution within the ranks of the Republicans had burst into flame. The mantle of Thomas Jefferson was torn into shreds. Authorization of a standing army in time of peace, when no foreign nation threatened attack and for the purposes of conquest, proclaimed the revolution.[1] A force of such size necessitated supporting militia, naval vessels, taxes, and loans. The Congress debated proposals to provide these, but the course of legislation was rough, the accomplishments few.

In 1812 Madison reached the apex of his administration. After twenty years of neutrality the United States would be pushed into a needless war, an aggressive and inconclusive war. At a time when Great Britain wanted peace and offered compromise, American leaders would succumb to the trickery of Napoleon; almost at the moment when Russia would turn on Napoleon and thereby doom his empire of the sword, the United States would declare war on Great Britain. And a few years later when Napoleon was exiled on Elba, the relatively small American state would be left facing a free and powerful England. By that time the British people, sick to death of almost a quarter century of war, would think peace more desirable than distant conquests and would allow the former colonies to go their way with no gains and, other than the costs and deaths of war, no penalties.

Early in 1812, chance and the clever machinations of a French adventurer, presented Madison and Monroe with what they thought would be a political bombshell. On a Boston packet ship outward bound from England in 1811, a British subject met the self-styled French Count Edward de Crillon. John Henry, the Englishman, confided his troubles to the sympathetic Frenchman. Back in 1808 and 1809, Henry said, he had served Governor General James Craig of Canada as a British agent in New England. Although the governor had welcomed his reports, Henry soon discovered Craig unwilling to reward his agent for such meritorious service. A personal appeal to officials in England and a proposal of $160,000 for his past services and future silence fell on deaf and ungrateful ears. Henry and Crillon entered into a partnership for mutual financial gain. They would sell the letters which described Henry's mission and work as a secret agent of Great Britain to the American government.

Crillon wrote to Louis Serurier, the French minister, outlining the situation of Henry and summarizing the contents of the letters. When the minister made no reply, Crillon hastened to Washington, won Serurier's friendship and gained an audience with Monroe. Almost without question Crillon was accepted and became a frequent guest of President Madison.

Crillon said he would sell the letters of Henry for $125,000, a high but not unreasonable price for documents of such importance. Monroe nibbled at the bait. The price was excessive, but it was the first offer of the Frenchman and he was willing to dicker. Finally on February 10 he accepted $50,000 on condition that the letters would not be made public until Henry could get out of the country. Both parties were satisfied: Crillon knew he had made an excellent sale, Monroe thought it a bargain.[2]

Impatiently Madison waited until March 9 before sending the letters to the Congress. These documents, the president stated in an explanatory letter, proved that a secret agent of Great Britain "was employed in certain States, more especially at the seat of Government in Massachusetts, in fomenting disaffection to the constituted authorities of the nation; and in intrigues with the disaffected for the purpose of bringing about resistance to the laws, and, eventually, in concert with a British force, of destroying the Union and forming an eastern part thereof into a political connection with Great Britain."[3] And this was done, Madison related, at a time when the British minister was professing his government's friendship for the United States.

The Henry letters by no means substantiated the statements of Madison. As outlined by Governor General Craig's instructions, Henry was employed to obtain accurate information on the wealth and population of New England, the ability and influence of its leading men, and their probable attitude on a war between the United States and Great Britain. He was to report on the relative strength of the two political parties and to give careful attention to the Federalists, for since they once controlled the country they might become a means of separating New England from the American Union. Though Henry was warned against operating as an agent of England, he could suggest, if sure of his audience, the possibility of transmitting communications from disaffected citizens to Governor Craig.[4]

Henry moved from Canada into Vermont, New Hampshire, and Massachusetts. Briefly he stopped in Burlington and Windsor, Vermont, and Amherst, New Hampshire, before he settled in Boston. His reports contained neither startling information nor lists of sympathetic Federalists. The people of Vermont opposed the idea of war with Great Britain and disliked the embargo laws. In the event of war the Massachusetts legislature would call for a convention and establish a government separate and distinct from the Federal Union. This observation, however, expressed only the opinion of Henry. Actually, he admitted, the common people of New England had for so long regarded the Constitution of the United States with complacency that they were disposed to treat it as a truant mistress whom they for a time had put away, but without greater provocation would not absolutely repudiate.[5]

Unquestionably the Henry letters made some Federalists tremble at the prospects of what they might reveal. Once their contents became public the Federalists breathed in relief and rose in counterattack. The American government had paid $50,000 for paraphrases of the original letters with a few mysterious asterisks introduced to excite curiosity and suggest damaging omissions. No Federalist was named; no Federalist knew of Henry's purpose or aided him in his mission; he never revealed his commission or instructions. Angered by the waste of public funds on these documentary duds, Federalists and Republicans demanded an investigation. A committee of the House of Representatives discovered that Henry, with the authorization of the government, was on his way to Europe; and Madison could not give the committee names of individuals who had "in any way or manner" countenanced the projects of Governor General James Craig, for Henry had named no one.

The irate Federalists did not uncover the French intrigue behind the Henry episode. Crillon appeared before the investigating committee but his masterful evasions and calm explanations buried questions with simplicity. Later, much to the amusement of the Federalists and the discomfort of Madison, Count Edward de Crillon was exposed as an impostor. The Crillon family in France had never heard of him; neither had the French government; and his checks for Henry "bounced," for they were drawn on the account of a man long cold in his grave.

The $50,000 given Crillon for Henry's letters was a poor national investment to be sure, but proved to be an excellent one for the Republicans. The publication of the letters and the innuendoes of party editors forced the Federalists on the defensive. Though in reality no more damaging than many of the printed articles, sermons, and orations of New England Federalists, the contents of Henry's letters raised questions about the national loyalty of Federalists. In an age of rising nationalism, suspicion of disloyalty was condemnation. No re iterated explanation, no later disclosure or denials received the publicity of the original disclosure and accusation.

The Republican party enthusiastically spread the Henry letters in the national press. Friendly editors composed barbed editorials on the Federalists and thundered at Great Britain. For a nation, a friendly nation at peace with the United States, to send a secret agent for intrigue with disaffected citizens – a foreign attempt to split the American Union and offer aid for that part of it which would go its way alone – stirred the passions of editors who commanded words of vituperation which they longed to use. During late March and early April the Republican press had a field day. Every defense, every explanation, every answer of Federalist editors brought on renewed outbursts from elated Republicans. The condemnation of Great Britain was complete: a government which would revolutionize the people of another country was beneath contempt.

The Henry letters served their purpose well. Politically they struck at the Federalists and nationally they were propaganda for a war with England. Since a declaration of war with Great Britain awaited the proper timing, the Henry documents covered actual issues with false ones and solidified the people against perfidious Britain.

As the Madison administration and Republican editors cut into the

British hide, the first reports on the Patriot revolution reached the desk of Secretary Monroe. On reading the hasty accounts from Mathews, he realized the awkward position of the government. In the excitement and thrill of the Henry letters had Monroe and Madison forgotten the detailed reports of Mathews, the explanations of Crawford, and the clear disclosures of Foster and Onís?

No matter the motivation for past action, they were now face to face with a difficult situation. Governor General Craig's acts paled in comparison with those of Madison: the reports of Henry were inconsequential compared with the deeds of Mathews. Here was no suggestion of encouraging disloyalty among the subjects of a friendly nation, here was no implied willingness to foment revolution, here was revolution and the use of American naval power against the peaceful colony of Spain. Mathews' acts could neither be disregarded nor explained away.

Reluctantly Madison and Monroe reached an inevitable conclusion. The national good took precedence over the welfare of an agent. Given authorizations could be withdrawn, instructions rescinded, deeds disavowed, agents repudiated. Nothing less than complete repudiation of Mathews would suffice. Even then the American government and the Madison administration would suffer in the circles of diplomacy and be derided by the Federalists.

Key senators and representatives were summoned for conferences. Representative George Troup shook his head but could see no alternative to repudiation. Shortly thereafter he received McIntosh's letter of March 12 and saw a ray of hope. Could the United States insist that the Patriot revolution was a legitimate one? McIntosh, Ashley, and the other leaders were subjects of Spain and revolution was a recognized remedy for unbearable conditions.[6] Could the United States disclaim all connection with the Patriots and bluff it through? But Monroe knew it was no good. Ships, eight armed vessels of the United States navy with their crews at quarter, their loaded guns pointed, their matches lighted for firing, could not be dissolved into the thin mist of imagination.

There was no other course. Unless Mathews was completely repudiated, the Floridas, at least for years, would be unattainable. By sacrificing the old general for the national good, the provinces might yet be secured. Of course Mathews was a hot-headed Irishman who had once played with the Federalists. A spirited defense of his action in Florida and the publication of his instructions and reports would give the Federalists potent political ammunition. But the risk must be taken. Perhaps Mathews would keep silent; he had a passion for the Floridas, he was a patriotic American, and in the secrecy of private letters and confidential messages much could be done to ease the humiliation of the wronged man. "Poor old Mathews," said Senator Crawford, "I am fearful will die of mortification and resentment when he is made sensible of the utmost extent of his disappointment."[7]

On April 4, 1812, Monroe dictated a letter to Mathews. "I am sorry to have to state that the measures which you appear to have adopted for obtaining possession of Amelia Island and other parts of East Florida, are not authorized by the law of the United States, or the instructions founded on it, under which you have acted. You were authorized," continued Monroe, "by law and instructions to take East Florida only on peaceful delivery by the governor or other existing local authority or to forestall occupation by a foreign power. In any case, a forceful wresting of the province from Spain was never contemplated, but only an occupation until a settlement could be reached by future amicable negotiation with Spain. The president," Monroe further informed Mathews, "has the utmost confidence in your integrity and zeal for the welfare of your country, and to that zeal he imputes the error into which you have fallen. But in consideration of the part which you have taken, which differs so essentially from that contemplated and authorized by the government, and contradicts so entirely the principles on which it has uniformly acted, you will be sensible of the necessity of discontinuing the service in which you have been employed. You will, therefore," Monroe concluded, "consider your powers as revoked on the receipt of this letter."[8]

Had the letter been dated in September of 1811, Monroe and Madison could not be criticized. Then, both the secretary and the president knew of Mathews' planned course of action. That was the time to stop him. Trusting, unsuspecting Mathews received the sanction of silence when he needed direction, the humiliation of repudiation when he accomplished his mission. And the needlessness of the president's caustic comment on Mathews in a letter to Jefferson was matched by its unjustness. "In E. Florida," Madison wrote, "Mathews has been playing a strange comedy in the face of common sense, as well as of his instructions. His extravagances place us in the most distressing dilemma."[9] This appraisal reflected more on the integrity of the president than on the wisdom of Mathews. Madison had been placed in a "distressing dilemma" of his own making.

So Mathews was sacrificed for the good of national expansion. From the war and navy departments orders went forward to Colonel Smith and Commodore Campbell. "Altho I am persuaded," Secretary Hamilton wrote Campbell," that you cooperated with Genl. Matthews [sic] from a conviction in your own mind that you were acting correctly: yet the proceedings of Genl. Matthews being unauthorized by the President of the United States are of course disapproved by him. I have it therefore in charge from the President to require of you to withdraw all the force under your command from the Spanish waters; and you will not in future cooperate with Gen'l Matthews."[10] In contrast with these definite orders of the secretary of the navy, the directives from the secretary of war were indefinite and inconclusive.[11]

Even before couriers sped on their way south with Monroe's letter of repudiation and the military orders for Smith and Campbell, editorials and reports appeared in Southern newspapers. The *Charleston Courier* editor agreed with former Secretary of State Robert Smith's castigation of Madison as the man responsible for a policy of taking East Florida by intrigue and bribery. "What will be these States at a more advanced age," asked the editor, "if at so early a period they have already fallen into corruption and decrepitude. The want of talents in a legislator may be lamented; ignorance may be pitied; but no apology can be made for *treachery and corruption*."[12] A few days later the *Courier* published the Henry letters and noted the similarity between the missions of Henry and Mathews.[13] Madison, reported the Charleston editor, took East Florida on the ground of expediency — the same idea motivated England in grabbing Copenhagen, Napoleon in overrunning Holland, Italy, and Switzerland. "The farce of receiving the Province from a handful of insurgents, assuming to themselves the glorious name of the Spanish patriots in the mother country, is disgraceful in the extreme. If Florida must be ours, let the arms of the U. States take it, and not receive it second hand."[14] At a time when the Patriots of Spain were fighting against the Corsican tyrant, the friends of America, stated the editor, must blush at this unprecedented conduct.[15]

Friendly editors explained the Fernandina fiasco in different ways. Many followed the *National Intelligencer* by giving as little space as possible and throwing all blame on Mathews for acting without the sanction or knowledge of the president.[16] The editor of *Niles Register* thought the officers and agents of the government acted on their own responsibility; but he admitted the possibility of administrative sanction to "root up and destroy this nest of *smugglers*" on Amelia Island. Although the government was not responsible for the invasion of East Florida, the editor urged the president to "disavow" the act and "promote" the persons who committed it.[17] No arguments or acts would convince the editor of the *Augusta Chronicle* that the Floridas should not be annexed by the United States as a recompense for American claims against Spain; he only regretted the delay in taking the provinces.[18] The *Savannah Republican* dismissed the problem with a demand for a fair and honorable cession of the Floridas.[19]

Knowledge of the repudiation of Mathews and the denial of the revolution brought divergent reactions from men in East Florida. Commodore Campbell, who first received intelligence of the disavowal, was elated. "By this days mail," he wrote, "I am honored with your instructions of the 8th Inst., which render me the happiest of mortals, and released me from a state of anxiety that no language of mine can express. I shall immediately with pride and pleasure carry into effect the orders of our much beloved President by withdrawing the Gun Boats from the Spanish waters."[20] Colonel Smith did not share the commodore's elation. He penned strong objections to a policy which would betray the Patriots who had been led on by American promises, and determined to give them every protection, even defending them in battle against the Spaniards, until he received positive orders for abandoning them.[21]

Major General John McIntosh could not comprehend the extraordinary act of the government and immediately decided on remaining as commander-in-chief of the Patriots in the hope of saving them from the wrath of Governor Estrada. "God only knows," stated the general, "what will be the consequence with the unfortunate characters involved in this transaction — I think the government can never abandon them to inevitable ruin, after being in some degree *invited* to *this revolution,* and formally ceding the Whole Province to the U. S. except the Garrison and town of St. Augustine."[22]

The Patriots sweated with anxiety and made a bold front. On May 4 John Houstoun McIntosh called for a regiment of volunteers to be composed of eight companies, each officered by a captain, two lieutenants, and an ensign, and made up of sixty-five enlisted men. In addition, commissions were provided for a colonel, lieutenant colonel, and two majors, with liberal land grants offered to all volunteers. These grants ranged in acres from 3,000 for a colonel to 1,000 for an ensign and 500 for a soldier. Those who brought in recruits would receive twenty-five acres for every acceptable man.[23] If the United States would not support them, the Patriots would go on unaided.

Next the Patriots turned to propaganda. Since they and their friends had been negligent in representing their cause and conduct with clarity, they would replace the lies of "Englishmen in heart and smugglers in practice" with the light of truth. They rebelled because they tired of the old order of corruption, were disappointed on not being made a part of the United States, and were fearful of being sold by Spain to England. Then they called on friends and neighbors, told them of the American desire for East Florida and of the United States law authorizing acceptance of the province. They exhibited the Foster-Monroe correspondence and informed them of the written and oral instructions of General Mathews. Under these conditions the Patriots threw off the yoke of Spain and liberated their friends on Amelia Island. Possessing no artillery, the Patriots asked that the American gunboats be used to neutralize and prevent the British from firing on the liberators and destroying the property and lives of friends in Fernandina. Thereafter the Patriots requested nothing from the United States. Without American aid they marched in glorious array to the walls of St. Augustine and won the unanimous approval, except for four or five miserable wretches, of the people along the way.

The revolutionists would never surrender. If fail they must, they would leave East Florida and abandon their property. The governor at St. Augustine might talk of pardon, but the Patriots knew of the dungeons and scaffolds prepared for those who had rebelled. "Policy or necessity might proclaim a pardon, but suspicion and revenge would never forget or forgive."

"To whom shall we then appeal," the Patriots asked, "but to the God above?" But as practical men they viewed the United States as nearer and a more helpful agent than God.

Wicked men, the Patriots stated, say the United States intends to abandon the revolutionists; but this could not be, for an act of Congress authorized President Madison to accept any part or parts of East Florida from the local authority. An American agent gave proof of his authority. Some say, however, the local authority mentioned in the law meant an authority existing over the whole of East Florida, but this interpretation could not be valid. Otherwise the Congress would not have explicitly included the clause "part or parts." Did the Congress contemplate accepting a part of East Florida from the old Spanish government? The weight of evidence was conclusive, the responsibility of the American government established; the United States would not desert the Patriots.[24]

Southern editors printed and reprinted this Patriot appeal. Though unsigned, it was evidently the composition of John Houstoun McIntosh. His friends in Georgia gave it publicity and commented favorably on the determination and courage of the revolutionists.

And what of Mathews? For days after all others knew of his repudiation he remained in happy ignorance. Whether the courier with Monroe's message missed the way or whether kind men wished to spare the general must remain unanswered. On May 1, General John McIntosh stated that "this thing [disavowal of Mathews] is Kept a profound Secret here."[25] Mathews was not at the Patriot camp near St. Augustine. Thoughts of an Indian uprising had troubled him and almost alone he had gone to the Indians for a conference. Thus the letters from Monroe did not reach him until May 9, 1812.[26]

When the two letters postmarked Washington, D. C., were handed to Mathews his body trembled with anticipatory excitement. At last, after months of patient and expectant waiting, he held an answer from the administration. That it could be bad news never entered his mind. As he read the letter blood rushed to his head and the earth spun about him. He read and reread the letter of dismissal. Then he turned to the second letter, the more personal note from Monroe also dated April 4, and weighed every word of its sentences.

This could not be. It was a fantastic dream, the figment of imagination, the hallucination of old age. On a man hit by so many disappointments fate would not, could not, deliver this final blow. His services in the Revolutionary War, his work in Congress, his contribution as governor of Georgia had almost been wiped from the memory of man by the Yazoo land frauds. The secretary of war had denounced him, senators had shied away from him, and President Adams had failed him. During those long and lean political years he listened for opportunity's knock. When it came in the evening of life, he had asked no questions, sought no favors, avoided no hardships; he had served his country with no thought of personal gain or political ascendency. In the territorial government which he planned for Florida he would seek no remunerative office. Honors and rewards he recommended for others. For himself the knowledge of service and the satisfaction of seeing the Floridas as American territory sufficed.

It could not be and yet it was. There alone in the solitude of a semi-tropical land Mathews finally realized the completeness of his repudiation, the magnitude of his disgrace. On a hot Florida day Monroe's letters killed George Mathews. Though for a time life remained in his body, his spirit was dead; fire no longer sparkled in his eyes, the spring in his stride was forever gone. In the weeks ahead there would be periods when his old patriotism reasserted itself and his anger flared high, but those moments would be little more than automatic reflexes from the past.

In his half-world of shadow between life and death Mathews thought of many things he could say and write in justification of his acts. Perhaps he smiled at Monroe's feeble attempt in the personal letter to appease an old servant of Seventy-Six and sneered contemptuously at the secretary's veiled threat. How could any man, plowman or president, think a reference to an old law of 1794, which provided penalties for American citizens who engaged in illegal political activities in neutral countries, could frighten and silence Mathews. Monroe should never have set the thought to paper. The patriotism of the general could be appealed to, but he could not be frightened.

Mathews did not know what he should do or how he should answer Monroe. Though his friends comforted him and urged him to expose the administration, he did nothing. For almost two months he waited before he trusted himself to dictate even an acknowledgment of Monroe's letters. Sympathy for the men who led the revolution, men who came in at his bidding and now would lose fortunes, stirred a feeble spark of life in him. He became a member of the Patriots and determined never to desert his fellow revolutionists.

And then suddenly during one of the endless days following May 9, Mathews realized that all was not lost. Colonel Smith's command remained in force at Moosa Old Fort and Commodore Campbell's gunboats rode the placid St. Johns. Was the revolution still on? For an answer to these questions Mathews awaited the arrival of Ralph Isaacs who was speeding south from Washington with dispatches and verbal instructions.

Revolution Revived

VACILLATION APTLY DESCRIBES the Florida policy of the Madison administration in March and April of 1812. Cognizant of Mathews' plan for conquest through revolution and of the inescapable consequences — American involvement — President Madison, nevertheless, indicated his approval by issuing supporting orders. The guns and supplies requested by General Mathews were loaded for transport; on March 28, 1812, Commodore Campbell was relieved of the over-all naval command of the southeastern coast and ordered to concentrate his attention on affairs in the vicinity of St. Marys, the scene of expected active operations, where it was essential to have a commander of skill and experience.[1] Mathews evidently had the complete confidence of Madison and Monroe.

Less than a week later neither the president nor the secretary of state questioned the necessity of repudiating the acts of Mathews. Disavowal of the old general was regrettable but unavoidable. For a time they believed the Floridas might be saved by sacrificing Mathews; but by April 6 they were convinced everything was lost, and ordered Campbell to withdraw his ships from Spanish colonial waters. On the same day, Monroe answered the protest of the British minister, Foster, by informing Onís of the repudiation of Mathews and assuring the Spanish minister that the troops would leave East Florida. Three days later the secretary of war ordered Colonel Smith "immediately to withdraw the troops under your command from Amelia Island and order them to reoccupy the former post at Point Petre."[2]

This order, however, was never dispatched, for between April 9 and 10 Madison again reversed his stand. Rather than give up East Florida without a struggle, he would continue the fight for its annexation. On April 10 new orders were forwarded to Colonel Smith. The instructions of January 26, 1811, which had authorized Smith to obey the requisitions of Mathews or McKee, were rescinded, and the colonel was directed to "obey any requisition or order of the governor of the State of Georgia...."[3] These directions were a contradiction of those contemplated the day before and provided for a change in overall command rather than evacuation of East Florida.

On the same day Monroe appointed Governor Mitchell as a special agent of the president. The instructions issued to Mitchell limited the disavowal of Mathews to personality and continued the armed occupation of East Florida. Mitchell was ordered to communicate with the governor of East Florida and in concert with him provide for an orderly evacuation of the Spanish province. Most of Monroe's letter appeared to be a straightforward denial of the revolution, but its last paragraph nullified every preceding sentence. Since the Patriots of East Florida had acted in expectation of support from the United States, Monroe thought the American government obligated to protect them from reprisal by Spanish authorities. Mitchell, therefore, must obtain "the most explicit and satisfactory assurance" of complete amnesty for the revolutionists. Monroe emphasized this point by praising the record and work of General Mathews.[4]

Thus officially the United States denied the revolution and at the moment of disavowal made a demand which would prevent evacuation of the occupied territory. If the Spanish governor should resent American interference with his exercise of sovereign powers, and it was a reasonable hope that he would, the Madison administration could present the world a picture of a contrite America, anxious to make amends, but checked by the revengeful desires of the Spanish government toward misled residents of Anglo-Saxon blood.

Monroe had more doubt about the possible action of Governor Mitchell than of the Spanish governor. If Mitchell accepted the first part of his instructions literally and ordered an immediate evacuation of East Florida, all was lost. The governor of Georgia had penned some sharp criticism of the government's policy in East Florida; for the safety of Georgia he might use his power to end the occupation.

The thought troubled Monroe but the risk was unavoidable. When Ralph Isaacs arrived in Washington late in April with the dispatches from Mathews, Monroe impatiently urged him to return south with written and oral instructions for Mitchell.

The enthusiasm of the secretary of state for the continued occupation of the Floridas surprised Isaacs. Before reaching Washington he had learned of the disavowal of Mathews and had concluded the Florida venture dead and buried. Monroe, however, quickly convinced Isaacs of his error, and offered him a job as liaison officer between the administration and Governor Mitchell. Though Isaacs requested release from government service, and pleaded for the pleasures of privacy and the opportunity to visit his daughter in New York, Monroe insisted.

In his conversations with Isaacs, Monroe clarified his ideas on the Floridas. "The East Florida Revolution has been extremely embarrassing," he said. "In all my years of service, the government has never before been placed in such a distressing dilemma."

Isaacs resented this reflection on Mathews but remained silent.

"But the province of East Florida must never go back to Spain," Monroe continued. "None of the revolutionists will be harmed. The Patriots must not suffer in person or in property for their acts. The American government will see to their protection."

Then the secretary gave Isaacs a copy of the instructions which were for Mitchell. Isaacs read the manuscript and remarked: "Mr. Secretary, your conditions will make a restoration of East Florida impossible. The Spaniards will never consent to these terms."

"Will Governor Mitchell understand that?" Monroe asked.

"He is not dull, sir," replied Isaacs.

"Tell him that the government is concerting measures to keep the province and save the Patriots. Tell the colonel" – Monroe always used the Revolutionary title of Mathews – "tell the colonel his disavowal was not personal but the necessary consequence of certain circumstances. The situation of the government absolutely prohibited any other action. Had it not been for peculiar circumstances, East Florida would have been accepted. Perhaps a few stipulations in the agreement between Colonel Mathews and the Patriots would have required attention, but on the whole there was considerable cleverness in the colonel's work."

"Mr. Isaacs, convince the colonel of the president's continued esteem. Mr. Madison has suffered much personal anguish in being the means of humiliating an old servant of Seventy-Six. In a private letter I expressed both the president's and my feelings for him. After delivering the instructions to Governor Mitchell, you must hasten to Colonel Mathews. Assure him that no reproach will ever be cast on him, that he will be reinstated with honor. Circumstances prevent an immediate acknowledgment of his clever work, but the president has not lost confidence in him, and the colonel will have convincing proof of it before long."

Intimate association with General Mathews had developed in Isaacs' heart a respect which approached hero worship. Disregarding the possibility of angering Monroe, Isaacs hinted at a question for which many men wanted an answer.

"The disavowal of General Mathews prevented me, as an employee of the government, from defending him," Isaacs stated. "But, Mr. Secretary, the general kept your department informed of his plans and advised you of every contemplated move. If he was in error, if he was misinterpreting his instructions, he could have been stopped. Surely, Mr. Secretary, some of his requisitions for arms reached your office. The letters I wrote for him, the ones forwarded by Senator Crawford, and the letter of the senator himself, were they lost in transit? Not long before the match was applied in East Florida a requisition for 250 muskets was made on your department, and the secretary of war ordered Major Thomas Bourke, the military agent at Savannah, to freight a vessel with them and dispatch the ship at once. The number and quality of arms ordered for delivery at Point Petre was in exact conformity with the requisition of General Mathews. Major Bourke conferred with me, for he had doubts, as the order for the muskets was in a post-script of a letter from the secretary of war, written in a different hand, and unsigned. But the major found the seal of the secretary's letter unbroken and, therefore, complied with the order."

During Isaacs' defense of Mathews, Monroe listened attentively but offered no explanation. When Isaacs ceased talking, there was a long silence, finally broken by Monroe. "Tell the colonel the president has not lost confidence in him. He will soon receive proof of the regard in which he is held."

Monroe quickly changed the subject. "Give Colonel Smith assurances that he was neither held responsible nor condemned for obeying Colonel Mathews' requisitions. Also give the Patriots the gist of our conversation and encourage them."[5]

Before Isaacs left Washington, Governor Mitchell was in St. Marys directing the forces in East Florida and laying plans for their withdrawal. Monroe's letter of April 4 authorizing the governor to act in the place of Mathews reached Milledgeville, the capital of Georgia, shortly after Mitchell had returned from inspecting the militia of southeastern Georgia.[6] The seriousness of the East Florida controversy worried the governor and convinced him 1000 volunteers were needed for protection of the state.

On March 28 Governor Mitchell received a sketchy report on the capture of Fernandina. The controversy between Mathews and Laval aroused the ire of the governor, who could not understand why the American government had not issued explicit orders to its military officers. In his opinion it indicated that Mathews had acted without authority; for the honor of the United States Mitchell hoped the government was not responsible for the revolution. As the executive of Georgia he was reluctant to mobilize the militia and entail large expenses on an already depleted state treasury. If, however, the consequences of American intervention was Spanish retaliation on Georgia, the militia must be called out for defense.[7]

When Mitchell had a more complete report of the incidents below the St. Marys from Senator Crawford, he was convinced he had no power to order Georgia militia into East Florida. It was now evident, Mitchell stated, that the Patriots had been misled by promises of aid from American regulars and Georgia militia. Although he personally regretted the situation in which such an able officer as Smith had been placed, he could not order militia beyond the state line. He did authorize General Floyd to hold the forces of his command in readiness for marching. If the general government should call for assistance, thereby relieving the Georgia executive of responsibility for making war without a declaration, he would order state troops into East Florida.[8]

The possibility of a Spanish-inspired Indian invasion of Georgia frightened the governor. On April 20 he wrote Secretary of War William Eustis of his fears and of Mathews' request for Georgia troops. Mitchell demanded prompt action on the Florida problem for the safety of his state and for the honor of the United States.[9]

A few days later the governor received his appointment as United States commissioner with powers formerly invested in Mathews. Without hesitation he cancelled all plans and on April 24 he set out for St. Marys. Three days later he was in Savannah, and, according to rumors, he would order an immediate evacuation of East Florida.[10] On May Day he reached St. Marys, lodging at Holzendorf's, where prices were high and quality in inverted ratio to costs.[11]

The governor was in a dilemma. He accepted his commission with the idea of terminating "the unpleasant business in which the United States have been made a party by the indiscreet zeal of their Commissioner."[12] But protests of Georgians and Patriots were hurled at him. If the British were throwing soldiers and supplies into St. Augustine, was it not his duty to take East Florida by force? In that event he would need the American gunboats, but Commodore Campbell held explicit orders for the withdrawal of his flotilla from Florida waters. If the Patriots remained in the Spanish province after American evacuation, how could he protect them?

David Brydie Mitchell was a man of decisive action. His past record proved it. Born in Scotland, he moved to Georgia as a youth of seventeen and inherited the property of an uncle who had died aboard a British prison ship during the Revolutionary War. Young Mitchell found Savannah delightful and remained in the city studying law in the office of William Stephens, a former colonial governor and a power in state politics. Under the tutelage of Stephens, Mitchell advanced rapidly in the Republican party. His spirited orations against the Yazoo land grants won popular approval and gained for him the post of attorney general of Georgia.

In the seaport city of Savannah many merchants and factors spoke their minds on Jefferson and his republicanism. Such criticism aroused Mitchell's anger for he staunchly defended his hero and his party. One heated argument with William Hunter, a leading merchant, went beyond words. On August 23, 1802, the men faced each other in the Jewish Cemetery. Hunter's first ball ripped along Mitchell's side; Mitchell's missed; Hunter's second shot cut through the clothing on his adversary's hip; but Mitchell's second aim was true, and Hunter fell with a bullet in his heart.

This exhibition of marksmanship and legal murder aided Mitchell's career. One year later he was commissioned a major general of Georgia militia; seven years later, at the age of forty-three, he won the governorship of his state. As governor of Georgia he led the liberal wing of his party, urging reforms and education and internal improvements. In his first year as chief executive he signed a bill which outlawed dueling.[13]

Mitchell was the logical successor to Mathews in the East Florida imbroglio. Able, courageous, and respected, he knew the frontier and possessed military as well as political prowess. As governor of Georgia, he could mobilize the state militia for defense and, if the administration's hopes materialized, for offense in East Florida.

Mitchell entered into his duties with no idea of directing an offensive action. In the beginning, he saw no contradiction in his orders from Washington; he blamed Mathews for the indefensible diplomatic strait of the United States. Later, after he had dealt with the Madison administration, which ignored him as it had neglected its first agent, he changed his opinion of Mathews.

During the first week of May, 1812, Mitchell's actions reassured the Patriots. He rescinded an order for the abolition of the customs house at Fernandina and told Smith to hold his position before St. Augustine.[14] Since Commodore Campbell had definite orders, he appealed to rather than commanded him to keep his gunboats on the St. Johns. Despite his previous expressions of elation on being ordered from East Florida, the commodore fell in line. An additional gunboat augmented the two already on the river. Campbell reported his reasons for disregarding his orders and received the approbation of the secretary of the navy.[15] These encouraging signs brought a temporary increase in the number of Patriots. Their morale revived and they talked hopefully of storming the Castillo de San Marcos at St. Augustine.[16]

Mitchell began negotiations with Governor Estrada. On May 4 he informed the Spanish governor of the disavowal of Mathews and the American government's desire for peace. He requested an answer, either written or verbal.[17] In his ambiguous letter Mitchell asked no question, and if any suggestion of terms under which the American troops would be withdrawn were made, Colonel Cuthbert, the bearer of the letter, made them. Estrada replied in cutting phrases: the newspapers had printed excellent reports of the repudiation of Mathews; because of that disavowal, he was amazed by the continued occupation of Spanish soil by American troops; until these troops were withdrawn he would not negotiate, and although he would regret any conflict, he recognized no authority south of the St. Marys but that of Spain; any conflict, whatever its immediate origin, would be the fault of the United States.[18]

Colonel Cuthbert conferred at length with the Spanish governor, and on returning to the American camp, informed Smith that the Spanish would not attack. Actually Estrada had made no such promise. The inconclusive letter of Mitchell had angered him; it purposely threw the burden of negotiation for evacuation of American troops on Spain, when the United States had been the aggressor. Estrada planned an offensive now that American support had officially been withdrawn from the Patriots. His considerable force in St. Augustine was eager to strike a blow for the honor of Spain, and Sebastian Kindelan, the recently appointed governor of East Florida, was en route from Cuba with reinforcements. At no time since March were conditions so favorable for Spanish success. One victory over the Patriots would discourage continued revolution and stimulate the Indians, who were divided on the advisability of remaining neutral or aiding the Spanish.

In St. Marys Mitchell knew nothing of the Spanish plans; he was too busy playing his own game. Since delaying tactics could work to the advantage of the United States, he had made no suggestion about evacuation of troops. He was playing for time, hoping for additional instructions from Monroe and an answer to his inquiry of May 2.[19]

When Colonel Cuthbert reported his interview with Estrada, he found Mitchell convinced that his duty was to hold rather than liquidate American territorial gains in East Florida. The anarchy and confusion within the province threatened the peace of Georgia; the insolence of the Negro population might have repercussions among Southern slaves, and British merchants in Fernandina waited in readiness to resume their illicit trade. Nevertheless, on May 16, Mitchell prepared a second letter, offering to withdraw the troops on receipt of certain assurances from the Spanish governor. "That such assurances will not be given I have some reason to believe," Mitchell stated with evident satisfaction.[20]

At the moment of his writing, the Spaniards were on the offensive. Colonel Smith with an effective force of 110 men was encamped near Moosa Old Fort. Once this fort had been the center of a Negro community and a part of the outer defenses of St. Augustine. Built on Moosa or Moses Creek it commanded the narrow neck of land between arms of the ocean, the North and Sebastian rivers. A mere shell remained of the fortification (which had been a coquina building with four bastions surrounded by a moat), for it had been destroyed during the inter-colonial wars and repaired only with timbers and boards.

A picket's guard occupied the old fort. Two hundred yards behind the ruins lay the main body of Smith's command, and farther back the Patriots. Without artillery or naval support Smith knew he could not retain his position in the face of a sortie from St. Augustine. However, he expected no attack.

On the morning of May 16 Smith watched a Spanish schooner and four launches move slowly up North River. At Moosa Creek the flotilla veered left, anchoring at the mouth of the creek. The schooner mounted two twenty-four pounders and other cannon of smaller calibre; the schooner and each launch were filled with soldiers. At ten o'clock the Spaniards opened fire with their large guns and Smith ordered reinforcements into the fort. After hours of intermittent, ineffectual firing, the Spanish vessels moved slowly up the creek toward Moosa Old Fort as if preparing for an assault.

Smith could not hold the fort. If the Spanish fire became too dangerous most of his men were to retire in such a way as to leave the impression of complete withdrawal. Fifteen men, however, well hidden behind stone and log ruins, were to remain as an ambushing party. When the Spaniards came within sixty yards, they would fire in unison, killing as many of the attackers as possible.

As the schooner neared Moosa Old Fort the twenty-four pounders found the range. The twenty-second shot of the bombardment pierced both walls of the fort and grape from the smaller cannon rattled against the timbers. As planned, the Americans beat a hasty and obvious retreat. The Spanish vessels now moved in with greater speed. Behind their protecting cover a sergeant and fourteen men waited, their muskets aimed, and their nervous fingers on triggers. In the tense excitement the sergeant misjudged distance. His men fired too soon. The ships were almost 400 yards away, not sixty, and the musket balls fell harmlessly into the water. The schooner and launches hove to and renewed the bombardment.

At this close range cannon fire endangered the American guard. As it retreated, the Spanish infantry landed and burned the wooden parts of the fort. For a time the cannon were turned on the American camp, but the distance was too great to be effective and the attacking party re-embarked for St. Augustine.[21]

From ten in the morning until four in the afternoon the Spanish force had shelled the fort and the American camp. It was a bloodless engagement: not a man was killed or wounded. The battle salved Spanish pride and infuriated Colonel Smith. He lived for revenge, for action, and called on his superiors for reinforcements and the opportunity for battle.

The incident released Mitchell from the dilemma of protecting the Patriots while evacuating East Florida. He accused Estrada of bad faith, of attacking when the United States offered amicable settlement, of choosing war rather than negotiation. Since he had decided on keeping troops in East Florida, he now had an excuse for delay. Until the Spanish governor accounted for his hostile action, Mitchell would not even consider terms for the protection of the Patriots.

The personal message which Ralph Isaacs brought from Monroe dissipated all doubt. After hearing Isaacs' account of the administration's wishes, Mitchell acted with confidence. The president wanted the revolution continued. The disavowal of Mathews had not been a general repudiation of the occupation of East Florida, but because of peculiar circumstances, a necessary diplomatic maneuver. To Mitchell his duty was now clear: he must continue occupation of the Spanish province and support of the Patriots with the least involvement of the United States. On June 7 he sent Isaacs into East Florida with instructions for Smith. Since the policy of the United States made it imperative to protect the property and persons of the Patriots, Mitchell ordered Colonel Smith to hold his ground, and if again attacked or fired on by the Spaniards, to dislodge and dispossess them of St. Augustine by siege or assault.[22]

Orders for attack were idle words without reinforcements. Mitchell sent his aide, Colonel Cuthbert, to Savannah for 100 militiamen, and accepted the Republican Blues and the Savannah Volunteer Guards.[23]

Colonel Daniel Newnan, of the Georgia militia, went into the piedmont area with orders for assembling volunteers at Dublin, Georgia.[24] Nearby were the militia of Major General Floyd and of Major General John McIntosh. From Commodore Campbell the governor secured a gunboat, 100 rounds of ammunition, and shot for six-pound cannon; two brass cannon from Point Petre were placed on board the ship. However, high winds prevented an immediate sailing.[25]

The militia trickled into St. Marys. In Savannah the Blues and Guards pitched their tents on the south common. Torrential rains dampened their equipment but not their spirits as they waited for passage. On June 12 they struck their tents and marched to the docks where gunboats awaited them. Detachments from the Chatham Artillery* and Rangers paraded with them and hundreds of cheering citizens braved the rain to wish them Godspeed. After a stop at Fernandina the volunteer troops re-embarked and on June 26 reached the American camp near Moosa Old Fort.[26]

In Milledgeville, volunteers assembled at the capitol for their orders. On July 1 they said their farewells and marched toward Dublin for a general muster of troops from central Georgia. "At 12 o'clock they assembled before the State House, surrounded by a large concourse of people, to exchange the parting salutations. . . . Tears, not the sickly effusions of cowardly apprehensions, but the pearly ethereal drops, which gild and adorn the generous cheek of Patriotism, were seen to steal from the eyes of many. Parents separating from their sons, wives from their husbands and connections, unfolded a scene affecting and sublime."[27] After wolfing refreshments, the militia marched "followed by three hearty cheers from the citizens which were reiterated by the volunteers with a zeal characteristic of Freemen." The Milledgeville Artillery accompanied them across Fishing Creek, where the sound of parting salutes told the people their heroes were on the way to high adventure and, perhaps, rewards in East Florida land.

By the last week of June more than 500 troops were reported en route for Colonel Smith's camp and an attack on St. Augustine. These Georgia troops – most of whom thought themselves heroic adven-

---

*The Chatham Artillery of Savannah has had its name attached to the famous Chatham Artillery punch. One quart of this delightful, potent drink will knock out nine admirals and even make an assistant professor slightly giddy.

turers – had enlisted for two months' duty. Before their terms expired, Governor Mitchell hoped other short term enlistees would take their places.

On June 11 the able, patriotic Sebastian Kindelan arrived in St. Augustine with almost 100 trained Negro colonials. Smith was planning defense rather than attack, for the new governor was a man of decision with a disposition to maintain the honor of Spain.[28]

The very day of his arrival Kindelan sent emissaries with letters for Smith and Mitchell. Captain Francisco Rivera went into the American camp with an invitation for an immediate conference and Jose de la Maza Arredondo carried a longer letter for Mitchell.[29] The continued presence of United States troops in East Florida could not be tolerated, Kindelan wrote, and unless the governor of Georgia ordered their removal, it would result in conflict and universal condemnation of the American aggression. In the name of Ferdinand VII and the Spanish nation, Mitchell was invited to evacuate Spanish territory within the next eleven days.[30] In effect Kindelan declared he would not negotiate as long as an American soldier remained in East Florida.

Colonel Smith answered by sending Captain Joseph Woodruff and Lieutenant George Haig into St. Augustine with information of Mitchell's over-all authority in the Southeast and a sharp reference to the unexpected attack of May which terminated previous negotiations.[31] Kindelan welcomed the men and then dismissed them with a curt note for Smith. Since the colonel lacked authority, the Spanish governor would waste no words on him; all he wanted of Smith was an immediate retreat beyond the St. Johns without giving further protection, active or passive, to those "banditti" who paraded under the name of Patriots.[32] As Smith read the note, his anger mounted. He penned a hasty reply: he would remain where he was, and warned the governor against allowing armed parties to leave St. Augustine, for they would be attacked by the American troops.[33] "I do not admit and never will admit to be dictated to for my troops," Kindelan replied, and added: "In the future abstain from sending any further communication here, for the bearer of it will be sent back without a hearing during the present differences."[34] Smith was furious. Although he could not attack he would hold his position as long as he had a man fit for duty.[35]

Meanwhile Kindelan's letter reached Mitchell at St. Marys. The governor replied with a lengthy review of past events and a condemnation of Spanish officials, whom he blamed for the existing situation. Because of the attack on Smith in May, when a frank explanation had been made of the American position, Mitchell knew Kindelan would not expect a proposal for evacuating the United States troops until a satisfactory explanation and apology for that unwarranted attack was at hand. If after eleven days the Spanish governor should attack, as he had threatened, he would find that the forbearance and peaceful spirit of the United States heretofore exhibited toward the Spanish stemmed from consideration of the weakness of Spain and a desire for peace and harmony with a neighbor.[36]

Kindelan fell into the error of answering Mitchell by giving an explanation of the attack. It was a mistake, he said. The rebels were occupying and fortifying a house on Moosa Creek, from which they could overlook the defenses of St. Augustine and obstruct the waterways near the town. The sight of the rebels infuriated the loyal subjects of Spain and made them defend the honor of their country. They planned no attack on the Americans. The Spanish sortie was directed solely against the rebels. Governor Kindelan would not insult the good name of the United States by believing American troops were among or aiding the banditti of East Florida. But, if some Americans, through ignorance or misdirection, were with the banditti, the blame fell only on them. Since this frank explanation evidenced his good faith, Kindelan called on Mitchell to reciprocate by adhering to his promise and giving an immediate order for the evacuation of East Florida. Such an order was an indispensable prelude to all further communication.[37]

In a long letter on July 6, Mitchell answered the trapped Spanish governor point by point and made additional charges. Mitchell admitted that the United States would have no cause for complaint had the attack on Smith come before the "friendly and sincere explanations" of Mathews' unauthorized action; but coming when it had, after the disavowal, and the expressed intention of making amends, the attack called into question the sincerity and the honor and the integrity of the American government. This incident therefore could not be passed off as a "trifling dispute." It was most serious: it required a full, faithful, and complete explanation.

REVOLUTION REVIVED

After reading the Spanish governor's letter, Mitchell felt certain that Kindelan, who was not in St. Augustine on May 16, had been misinformed as to the facts of the attack. The American troops, Mitchell told him, and not the Patriots, had occupied Moosa Old Fort. Furthermore the charge that Patriots blockaded the waterways near St. Augustine could not be substantiated. The revolutionists could not stop a rowboat, for they possessed neither boats nor cannon. Their only threat was their presence near St. Augustine. There was no reason for the attack, or at least no reason unless the Spanish wished to demonstrate their hostility toward the United States and question the sincerity of the American government in offering an explanation for its part in the invasion of East Florida.

Candor forced him to question also the use of black troops in East Florida. Kindelan knew the situation in the Southern section of the Union and the attitude of the people on arming Negroes. The bringing of Negro militia into the province as well as arming those already resident there was an act of hostility. The United States would not tolerate armed Negroes remaining on her southern borders.[38]

A hasty reading of Mitchell's letter convinced Governor Kindelan that further negotiation would be futile. He had fallen into a trap, and realizing it, he refused to play into his adversary's hands by additional letters and explanations, the purpose of which was delay and not settlement.

Almost six months passed before Mitchell received an answer. The Georgia governor's review of his trusteeship in East Florida in a legislative message brought a spirited response from Benigno Garzia, commandant of the military garrison at St. Augustine. Garzia stated that the Spanish attack was an act of defense, for the rebels, supported and encouraged by American troops, had captured Spanish fishermen and woodcutters within sight of St. Augustine. The Spanish governor naturally desired the evacuation of his province and welcomed Colonel Cuthbert, the aide-de-camp and official envoy of Mitchell. After a long conference, Cuthbert left St. Augustine and promised to return within six days with an answer from Governor Mitchell. When it became evident that this pledge would not be kept, the impatient Spanish soldiers defended their province by attacking the banditti. Obviously Mitchell procrastinated, intending to prolong the revolution; and had there been no Spanish attack, the governor would have presented some other subterfuge for keeping American troops in East Florida.[39]

Governor Kindelan acted wisely in ignoring Mitchell's letter. An answer would have brought additional charges with no resulting advantage for Spain. The Spanish governor left diplomacy to his country's minister, and concentrated on means of forcing the Patriots and the American troops from East Florida. Acting Governor Estrada had pinned his hopes of holding St. Augustine on Indians, particularly the Seminole Indians of the Alachua savanna west of the St. Johns.[40] If they would unite with Spain, their war cries would disperse the rebels and send them packing into Georgia. Without the food supplied by the revolutionists, and with his supply lines in danger of being cut, Colonel Smith could not hold his position before St. Augustine. At best he must fall back to the St. Johns under the protection of American gunboats; he might even be driven from East Florida.

Though slower and less satisfying than a Spanish assault on the Americans, the use of Indians was too advantageous to reject. It avoided the direct involvement of Spanish soldiers; and although the United States officials would accuse Kindelan of exciting and supplying the Indians, proof would be difficult. Spanish abetting of Indian forays would not be as obvious as American support of the Patriots. If Indian warfare kindled an aggressive reaction in Georgia, the resulting invasion of East Florida would hit the Seminoles, not the Spanish in St. Augustine.

While the Spanish governor plotted the defense of his province, Governor Mitchell considered the feasibility of attacking St. Augustine. Prospects were dismal. The natural and built-in strength of the Castillo de San Marcos was such that a small garrison could hold it against almost any assault. Washed by an arm of the sea on the north and guarded by a thirty-foot moat on the other sides, the fort presented a formidable obstacle with its fifteen-foot walls rising thirty feet high, and its six-foot parapets mounting sixty cannon. One thousand soldiers could live in its vaulted rooms and protected yard. Coquina, the shell-like rock of the walls, did not crack or break when hit by shot. Only by siege with absolute command of the ocean, could there be any hope of capturing the fort. Even then, in Mitchell's opinion, the cost of success would be more in blood and money than a similar reduction of the famed fortress city of Quebec.[41]

The Georgia governor was also disheartened by Monroe's silence. Bitterly he upbraided the secretary of state for not answering questions, for failing to inform him as to the sentiments and desires of Madison. In none of his letters had Monroe written a line about reinforcing Colonel Smith with Georgia militia, though the governor explicitly described the necessity of it. Mitchell's only order from Washington was sufficiently clear on one point: the troops must be kept in East Florida.[42]

The governor ordered his state militia into Florida on his own authority; but he did so as a temporary expedient, expecting regular troops of the United States to replace them. The Georgia militia saved Colonel Smith from attack and for the time being secured his advanced position,[43] but they could not reduce the fort.

By July, 1812, the Americans and Spaniards had reached a stalemate. Reinforced with Georgia militia the forces of Colonel Smith could not be driven back by the Spaniards, and the defenses of St. Augustine could not be reduced by the Americans. While Sebastian Kindelan sought Indian allies to throw the balance in his favor, David Mitchell expected a declaration of war against Great Britain, followed by congressional sanction for the occupation of Florida and the requisite military power for its conquest. Once committed to war, the United States would rush troops into East Florida before Great Britain could secure the province for her ally.

War and the Floridas

THE CENTRAL THEME OF THE first session of the Twelfth Congress of the United States was war. From the time of its convening in November, 1811, until its adjournment eight months later, bill after bill was introduced in preparation for war. The War Hawks rode hard in the saddle of national affairs. War with Great Britain was their goal, and only the timing of the declaration hung in question. Affairs in East and West Florida, possible British occupation of the Spanish provinces, Canada and the northwestern Indians, an increased army, naval bills, an armed merchant marine, additional taxes, and foreign affairs in general were the propaganda of war.

War demanded psychological preparation. Without a powerful stimulus a majority of the American people would remain indifferent to those who cried for vindication of national honor, for most men would endure much for peace. Unity of the people and support of the government required reason for fighting, something to fight for or something to defend. Repelling an attack would bring the desired unity, but without an attack, and when aggression and not defense was the purpose, the problem of psychological preparation became exceedingly difficult.

In 1812 the plan was for a war of aggression.[1] Citizens of the United States could not rise in defense of an invaded homeland. There was no invader; there was not the slightest possibility of invasion. Opportunity existed, however, for territorial aggrandizement. Canada lay almost undefended and the Floridas were hopelessly weak as England struggled with France for world supremacy and Spain fought for her existence. The chance to grab desirable English and Spanish colonies might never come again.

The United States had legitimate reasons for war with Great Britain: English interference with American trade, Great Britain's treatment of American seamen, her ubiquitous warships in and near American coastal waters, and her system of blockades warranted war. By 1812 the United States had valid reasons for a war in defense of her maritime rights, but the people could not be aroused by sailors' rights and freedom of the seas. Furthermore, the grievances of the United States against England did not originate in 1812. They came out of the past. They had been endured for years; endurance was preferable to conflict in the trader's mind and the farmer remained damnably uninterested. War, however justified by international morality, was inexpedient. This had been the cardinal policy of Jefferson.

For almost half a generation the United States had protested and endured the acts of Great Britain without fighting. Maritime offenses of Great Britain meant little to a country of farmers. Defense of seamen's rights had not stirred frontier enthusiasm for war. Furthermore, by 1812, Great Britain was ready for compromise, for she did not desire war with America. Therefore the United States had less reason for a declaration of war in 1812 than in 1809 or 1807 or in almost any year of the previous decade.

Desire for land was the main reason for war. Farmers and frontiersmen looked longingly at Canada and the Floridas. With that characteristic hankering of the Anglo-Saxon farmer for the land contiguous to his own, American agrarians could not resist the attractiveness of conquest and expansion. They were willing to fight for land, and were all the more anxious because the time seemed propitious. Since England and Spain could offer only feeble resistance, it would be a short, profitable war.

Aggression could not be put forward in justification of a declaration on Great Britain; so Madison fell back on the old maritime grievances. War could be justified as defensive on the basis of neutral rights.

On June 1, 1812, he sent his war message to Congress. Madison briefly reviewed diplomatic relations with Great Britain since 1803 and emphasized American efforts for peace. He charged Great Britain with repeated violations of the American flag on the great highways of nations, of impressing United States sailors, of stationing cruisers off the American coast and stopping incoming and departing merchantmen, of spilling American blood within the sanctuary of national waters, of plundering commerce under the flimsy excuse of a paper blockade, and of sweeping blockades under the name of Orders in Council. He emphasized the disastrous effects of these acts in cutting off the farmers' agricultural products from the markets of the world.

Only in one paragraph did Madison mention the West. He accused England of encouraging the Indians in a frontier warfare which shocked humanity and spared neither age nor sex. Not once did the president name Canada or the Floridas.[2]

Both houses of Congress debated the message in secret sessions, and the House of Representatives acted with dispatch. On June 3, John C. Calhoun presented a bill from the Committee on Foreign Affairs for a declaration of war with Great Britain. Immediately John Randolph of Roanoke rose in opposition, but his motion for rejection met with overwhelming defeat.[3] Every attempt of those opposing war and favoring an open debate was voted down. The minority decided that discussion in secret sessions of the House, whose members had long before made their decision, would be a waste of time. They would register their opposition by silence and a negative vote. Three days after hearing the presidential message seventy-nine representatives voted for and forty-nine opposed the declaration of war.[4]

Senators were more deliberate. They received the declaration on June 5 and referred it to committee. Three days later it was reported back with amendments, and after discussions in secret session, recommitted for further study. When the declaration again reached the Senate, Obadiah German opposed it. The Republican senator from New York admitted that Great Britain and France had given the United States cause for war, but he knew the proposed war against England was an offensive and not a defensive one. The United States was not prepared for an offensive war, German stated, and even if the nation possessed the requisite military power, conquest could not be justified by principles of right.[5] James A. Bayard, a Federalist from Delaware, agreed with his Republican colleague, and added: "No time has existed for years past when we had less cause to complain of the conduct of Great Britain."[6] Only these two senators spoke at length against the declaration though others attempted to kill it by delays. Except for their votes, proponents of war uttered hardly a word. Speeches were unnecessary, decisions had been made; on June 17 the Senate passed the declaration and on the following day President Madison signed it.[7]

Opposition to war centered in the mercantile states while the agrarian states favored it: Federalists desired peace and Republicans wanted to fight. Whenever congressmen crossed regional party lines the senators and representatives involved were more likely farmers within the Federalist party and merchants within the Republican party. In numbers, more lawyers cast votes in opposition to war than any other occupational group, and these lawyers were closely tied in with the mercantile interests of New England and the Middle Atlantic states.

War in 1812 was a Republican measure. According to the presidential message, the United States sought to protect the nation's traders and sailors; but the congressional vote for war came from Southern, Western and Northwestern congressmen, while the trading areas of the country favored peace. Those regions in which the wealthier, more satisfied people lived wanted no part of a war with Great Britain and the residents from the poorer, less satisfied sections saw in war a possible means of improving their economic status.[8]

With the declaration of war the Madison administration and its needlers, the War Hawks, achieved one of their twin ambitions. Invasion and annexation of Canada was now legalized by the action of the sovereign state, but authorization for seizure of the Floridas was yet to be accomplished. Although Great Britain and Spain were allies, a declaration of war against the former did not include the latter. The United States' claims against Spain could be used in justification for occupying the Floridas.

Consequently a declaration of war with Spain was not contemplated: the Floridas would be taken without it. On June 19 Representative George Troup of Georgia moved, and the House approved, a resolution requesting the Special Committee on the Spanish American Colonies to inquire into the expediency of authorizing the immediate occupation of East and West Florida.[9] Three days later, Samuel Mitchell of New York, chairman of the committee and one of the

Republican representatives who had voted against the war with Great Britain, presented a bill which empowered the president "to take possession of a tract of country lying south of the Mississippi Territory, and of the State of Georgia." Opponents of this bill fought its passage by demanding open debate, but by a vote of seventy-four to forty-four the House declared secret proceedings essential to the national welfare. On June 25 the House approved the bill by seventy to forty-eight.[10]

The first of two hurdles had been cleared with ease; only the Senate remained. President Madison and the War Hawks had powerful support from ex-President Thomas Jefferson, newspaper editors, and citizens' petitions. Jefferson, who had been hoping for action since March, wrote of the enthusiasm of his county's militia where 231 of the 241 on the rolls turned out for the first muster. "The only inquiry they make," Jefferson stated, "is whether they are to go to Canada or Florida. Not a man, as far as I have learned, entertains any of those doubts which puzzle the lawyers of Congress and astonish common sense, whether it is lawful for them [the militia] to pursue a retreating enemy across the boundary line of the union."[11]

The editor of the *Augusta Chronicle* looked with dismay on the possibility of allowing Spain to retain East Florida. In his opinion war with England justified seizure of the Floridas as a defensive measure, for they would be of more importance to England than all the other Spanish colonies in the New World. If Great Britain secured the Floridas, and the editor knew she would, then the weak and disaffected American territory bordering on the Mississippi could not be defended and the United States might as well bid "adieu" to it.[12] A restoration of East Florida to Spain would be "injurious to the United States and fatal to the lower part of Georgia."[13]

In a mass meeting on June 3, 1812, citizens of Savannah passed resolutions in favor of war with Great Britain and the immediate occupation of the Floridas. Ten days later a similar gathering in Milledgeville petitioned for war, and demanded, since the Floridas undoubtedly would be ceded to England, that the United States seize those provinces for the protection of the southern frontier. Without recorded opposition the people of the frontier states petitioned and demanded occupation of the Floridas.[14]

Secretary of State James Monroe agreed with these opinions and was confident the Senate would approve the House bill. In writing to an agent he stressed the American lien on East Florida, emphasized the danger of British occupation with the consequent Indian wars and smuggling along the southern border, and concluded with the statement that the United States must gain possession of the Floridas.[15]

On June 26 the House bill was introduced and read for the first time in the Senate. As passed by the House of Representatives, it authorized the president "to occupy and hold, the whole or any part of East Florida, including Amelia Island, and also those parts of West Florida which are not now in possession and under the jurisdiction of the United States." The chief executive was given discretional use of the military and naval forces and an appropriation of $100,000 for the occupation, but he was charged with preserving the social order in the provinces and guaranteeing the people religious freedom, and security of property and personal rights. The occupied provinces might be subject to future negotiations with Spain.[16]

After the second reading on June 27 the bill was referred to a committee of five for consideration and report. On the committee were Charles Tait of Georgia, William Branch Giles of Virginia, George Motier Bibb of Kentucky, James Asheton Bayard of Delaware, and Stephen Row Bradley of Vermont. Of these men only Bayard was a Federalist and only he had voted against war with Great Britain. Although Bradley had not voted on the war issue, he was a Republican from a frontier state and considered safe.

As expected, this committee reported the bill without amendment. On July 2, however, two amendments were added and the bill passed to a third and final reading. Unexpectedly, Senator Bradley moved postponement until the first Monday in November, but his attempt to kill the bill by delay met defeat by a vote of sixteen to fourteen.[17] This defeat brought smiles to the faces of those opposing the Madison administration, for it foretold their eventual victory. Republicans Bradley and Giles had voted for postponement, while Jeremiah Brown Howell and Michael Lieb, known opponents of the bill, had voted against postponement. In the final balloting they would undoubtedly shift their votes, and they did. The bill for the occupation of the Floridas was killed by sixteen to fourteen.[18]

This defeat stung the Madison administration. Republican bolting caused it: Senators Samuel Smith of Maryland, Michael Lieb of Pennsylvania, John Smith of New York, and Branch Giles of Virginia, all of whom had voted for war with Great Britain, joined four other Republicans, Nicholas Gilman of New Hampshire, John Lambert of New Jersey, Obadiah German of New York, and John Pope of Kentucky, all of whom had opposed the declaration of war. These eight, and Stephen R. Bradley of Vermont, broke party lines and in so doing killed the bill, for the six Federalist senators presented a solid front against the administration. Georgia, South Carolina, North Carolina, Tennessee, and Ohio stood unanimously with the administration; New Hampshire, Connecticut, Rhode Island, New York, Pennsylvania, Delaware, and Maryland voted solidly in opposition; and Vermont, Massachusetts, New Jersey, Kentucky, and Virginia delegations split their votes.[19]

Personal animosity and petty grievances defeated the administration. Samuel Smith of Maryland had often opposed Madison. After the dismissal of his brother, Robert Smith, and the appointment of James Monroe as secretary of state, Samuel Smith welcomed an opportunity to embarrass the president and his secretary. Branch Giles once hoped Madison would give him a cabinet post, and when that ambition went unrealized in 1811, he added the president to his list of personal enemies, a list which already included Monroe and Albert Gallatin, the secretary of the treasury. Lieb made the third member of the triumvirate which opposed the administration for personal reasons.[20] Pope of Kentucky had been read out of the Republican party by his constituents, whose opinions he did not represent, and had joined the Smith-Lieb-Giles faction.[21] The votes of any two of these men would have given Senate approval to the administration's cherished plan for acquiring the Floridas.

The course of political faction was strange. Hatred of Albert Gallatin was a cardinal tenet of the anti-administration forces, but Gallatin in his most enthusiastic moments could not stomach the plan to grab the Floridas.

Because of personalities, the Madison administration, already embarrassed by the over-zealous Mathews, had to backtrack again in East Florida. American troops were illegally occupying part of a Spanish province, and the Congress, in refusing to sanction the acquisition of the entire province, had in effect condemned holding a part of it. There was only one thing the administration could do. On

July 6 Monroe wrote Governor Mitchell: "Since the rejection of the bill in the Senate, the President thinks that it will be more advisable to withdraw the troops from East Florida. . . ."[22] Mitchell was instructed to secure the best possible terms from the Spanish officials for the Patriots.

Taken by themselves two paragraphs of Monroe's letter would have terminated the Florida project and abandoned the Patriots who had been incited to rebellion by Mathews' glittering promises. But neither Madison nor Monroe was quitting. Occupation of the Spanish provinces was not abandoned, Monroe stated in his letter to Mitchell, for the consequences of war with Great Britain might induce Congress, at a later date, to authorize invasion and annexation. Moreover, the law of 1811 which provided for the seizure of the Floridas to forestall foreign occupation remained on the statute books, and if the report of the British throwing reinforcements into St. Augustine was true, then Mitchell had authority for the conquest of East Florida. Monroe advised the governor in detail as to the proper explanation, if he should order the conquest of the Floridas: West Florida was the property of the United States by the Louisiana Purchase and East Florida was security over which America held a mortgage until settlement of the spoliation claims.[23]

The administration policy now became clear. Officially the troops were ordered from Florida, but there remained the expressed hope that unforeseen changes would soon force the Senate into reversing its stand. Implied in Monroe's letter of instructions was the desire for Mitchell to risk his own neck, just as Mathews had his, by continuing the occupation of East Florida.

Another means of acquiring the Floridas might be successful. Louis de Onís the unrecognized Spanish minister who resided in Philadelphia, had tired of his peculiar role in America. Although unrecognized, he communicated with the American State Department through the Spanish vice-consul of Alexander. Monroe had used this avenue of contact to suggest that Onís might use his influence in behalf of the Patriots of East Florida. On July 18 Onís declared Mitchell's demand of amnesty for the Patriots was in direct opposition to all laws of right and fair dealing. General Mathews, in disregard of the orders of his government, had seduced the loyal citizens of Spanish Florida, committed acts of hostility, and taken possession of East Florida in the name of the United States. Though Mathews had been disavowed by the president, the stolen property had not been returned.[24] A few weeks later Onís forwarded copies of the Mitchell-Smith-Kindelan letters of the past June – letters, Onís stated, which proved that the revolutionists continued their nefarious activities, aided and abetted by Colonel Smith's soldiers. Onís demanded the immediate, unconditional withdrawal of the American troops.[25]

In a moderate letter Monroe reiterated the often repeated claims of the United States and suggested that a peaceful cession of the Floridas would settle many problems. Onís took the dangling bait. Negotiation would enhance his personal position and might, if Monroe thought it a necessary preliminary to cession, speed the evacuation of East Florida. When he left Madrid, Onís informed Monroe, he had full powers of negotiation, and although those powers had been given by the old government of Spain, the existing Spanish authority, if the United States was friendly, would certainly again entrust him with authority over the Floridas. Onís would come whenever the president wished to receive him in Washington.[26]

Acquisition of the Floridas by treaty was a pleasant contemplation. It would bolster the declining prestige of the Madison administration and wipe from memory the Florida fiasco. Unfortunately the American government had hitherto withheld recognition from Onís: accepting the Floridas from him involved the government in an inconsistency.

Inconsistency, however, did not bother Senator Crawford. In August, 1812, he believed the United States, notwithstanding the repudiation of Mathews, should accept East Florida from the recently organized Patriot government.[27] By September Crawford thought that cession of the province from Onís should be accepted as it would confound the malcontents of the United States Senate and solve a touchy domestic and international problem.[28]

Encouraged by the influential senator's advice, Monroe walked down a road which had no terminus. Negotiation with Onís was futile. Madison saw this more clearly than Monroe. "Your interview with Onís will, I see, be fruitless," Madison told his secretary. "It is clear that he has no powers now, if he ever had, and improbable that he ever had them, to cede Territory. The general terms of his commission prove nothing. . . . His object is to bring himself into importance and to gain time."[29] But this positive opinion of the president did not stop Monroe. Late in November Monroe advised a congressional committee against another attempt to secure a law authorizing the occupation of East Florida, giving as his reason the possibility of cession by Onís.[30] Before the new year, however, the secretary of state conceded defeat and urged action by Congress.

Meanwhile Governor Mitchell had more than fulfilled Monroe's fondest expectations. Though he began his mission planning the evacuation of East Florida, the governor became one of the strongest advocates of occupation. By July, 1812, his ardor for annexation warped his accustomed ethical standards. However much he may have objected to Mathews' instigation of the rebellion, that revolt and the partial occupation of the Floridas had, in his opinion, made occupation of all imperative. Mitchell worked assiduously in securing Georgia militia for service in East Florida. Hundreds of Georgians volunteered for sixty days and moved south in high, adventurous spirit. They aided the meager forces of Colonel Smith, but they were not reliable soldiers. When their sixty days expired, almost to a man they headed back home. Impatient Smith fretted while waiting for a declaration of war on Great Britain. Mitchell, also confident of a forthcoming authorization for the subjugation of the Floridas, anticipated the arrival of regulars and siege guns.

To him the Senate's denial of the Florida project was legislative treason. The governor stated in answering Monroe's letter of July 6: "You may therefore judge of my surprise and mortification at the information . . . that the Senate had rejected a bill . . . authorizing the immediate occupancy of the entire provinces." In his surprise Mitchell passed over those instructions which ordered evacuation of the army detachment and informed Monroe of the Georgia militia en route to Smith; these volunteers would enable the colonel to maintain his position and to be ready for assault when so ordered. "I have carefully avoided making any proposition for withdrawing the troops, under the fullest conviction that such a step was not intended . . .,"[31] the governor stated, and thereby demonstrated his insight into the thoughts of Madison and Monroe.

Mitchell willingly accepted a responsibility for which he had no authority and for which he might lose face, if the Madison administration ever saw the necessity of disgracing him as it had Mathews.

The governor knowingly took that chance, feeling it a duty of citizenship owed to the United States and to Georgia. Spaniards had armed every able-bodied Negro of St. Augustine and had brought two companies of black militia from the West Indies — nothing could anger Georgians more. Negroes should never be allowed the opportunity of handling guns or of discovering they could fight. In Mitchell's opinion the white men on the southern frontier would rise in rebellion unless Colonel Smith remained in East Florida to contain the black scourge.[32]

Governor Mitchell believed his services were needed more at the state capital than at St. Marys. After informing Monroe of his intention to keep the armed force in East Florida, he departed for Milledgeville but before he reached the Georgia capital he was burning with fever and for weeks on end he could accomplish nothing.

Others took up the task of the sick governor. In mass meeting the citizens of Greene County petitioned President Madison. England and Spain were closely allied, they stated, and the United States could hurt Great Britain most by conquering her possessions in the North and her potential colonies in the South. The Patriots of East Florida had rebelled and declared themselves independent with the understanding that the United States would support them, and if they were abandoned, they would throw themselves into the arms of England, knowing they would be treated as rebels by Spain. If the United States evacuated East Florida, Great Britain would step in and acquire bases for commercial raids and smuggling, incite the "merciless and unrelenting savages" against Georgia, and induce rebellion among the black population. The citizens of Greene County proscribed the ill-advised action of the Senate, but in their opinion the law of 1811 gave the president ample power for occupying East Florida. If the United States did not occupy it, Great Britain would, "And shall we tamely and quietly sit by, and suffer our open and avowed enemy to possess herself of those provinces and thus increase her means of annoying us? No, let us not wait till the blow which seals our destiny is given. What will now be the work of a few days, and the loss of little blood, may if delayed, cost us the lives of thousands, and the labor of years."[33]

The Patriots reacted by putting their affairs in order and petitioning Monroe for aid. A convention of delegates framed a constitution and elected John Houstoun McIntosh "Director of the Territory of East Florida." On July 30 he appealed to the secretary of state and the president by reviewing the history of the revolution, describing the suffering of quondam Americans under Spanish rule, dwelling on the promises of Mathews, emphasizing the effect of the Foster-Monroe correspondence, and declaring that the white population of East Florida outside of St. Augustine, other than a few smugglers and slave traders of Fernandina, favored the revolutionists. Although Mathews had been repudiated, McIntosh continued, the Patriots knew they would not be delivered into the vengeful hands of the arbitrary, jealous, and vindictive Spaniards whose promises of amnesty meant nothing. The revolutionists had already learned that United States troops and gunboats were their only security. Americans would discover this also, for

Our slaves are excited to rebel, and we have an army of negroes raked up in this country, and brought from Cuba, to contend with. Let us ask, if we are abandoned, what will be the situation of the Southern States, with this body of black men in the neighborhood. St. Augustine, the whole Province, will be the refuge of fugitive slaves; and from thence emissaries can, and no doubt will be detached, to bring about a revolt of the black population of the United States. A nation that can stir up the savages round your western frontiers to murder will hesitate but little to introduce the horrors of St. Domingo into your Southern country.[34]

As portentous as the situation was for citizens of the United States, the plight of the Patriots was worse. They could not move their slaves across the St. Marys without violating American law. "Some of us have been accustomed to the sweets of affluence, and most of us to the enjoyments of plenty," McIntosh avowed. "We, in common with other citizens would willingly have sacrificed all we have, had it been in defense of the United States; but to be beggard [sic] and branded as traitors is wretchedness indeed to men who thought they were acting as some of their forefathers had in 1776."

McIntosh entreated the president and his cabinet to take council; to consider the Patriot's unhappy, unexpected, and unmerited situation; and to hold the army in East Florida until a cession was accepted or Great Britain threw troops into St. Augustine and compelled the United States to decisive action. Responsibility for the revolution rested on the United States, and, McIntosh concluded: "Upon the principles of justice and humanity, we call for the protection of the United States; with it we become free and happy; without it, we must become wanderers upon the face of earth, or tenants of loathsome dungeons, the sport of cruel and inexorable tyrants."

Monroe ignored this impassioned appeal; but, undaunted, McIntosh wrote again on October 3 enclosing a copy of his previous letter, and addressing the secretary as a private citizen who had confidence in American justice. Though the people of East Florida were dispersed and their houses in ruins, they had not lost faith in the United States. "Our situation every day becomes more critical," McIntosh stated, "and though we hope, we have no certain information to cheer our spirits."[35]

Neither Madison nor Monroe could answer the letters of one who claimed an executive position in an unrecognized, rebellious government. Without reason, however, Monroe failed to acknowledge Mitchell's letters or to give the governor, a commissioned agent of the United States, additional instructions. Left to his own resources Mitchell ordered Colonel Smith to hold his ground and meet attack with attack. Volunteers from Georgia and gunboats of Commodore Campbell guarded Smith's supply lines, but the colonel's situation became more precarious with each passing day. Illness reduced his effective force while reinforcements strengthened the Spanish garrison in St. Augustine. Indians and Negroes of the interior played on their war drums. Smith's meager force could be surrounded and destroyed.

Mitchell knew it. Yet he had done everything within his power, and more. On September 19 the governor sent Monroe a long letter, explaining the problem in detail and requesting the president to retain the troops in East Florida.[36] Before time permitted an answer, Mitchell wrote again: affairs in East Florida had assumed a serious and alarming aspect; Governor Kindelan had won the Indians, Smith's supply line had been attacked, and the colonel had withdrawn from St. Augustine. Reinforcements must be sent immediately.[37]

A day before Mitchell dispatched this urgent appeal, Monroe had at last written. The president, Monroe stated, regretted the evident lack of cooperation by the governor of St. Augustine, who persisted in his refusal to give a satisfactory amnesty to the Patriots and who was inciting the Seminoles to war. "The conduct of the governor of

East Florida has excited much surprise," Monroe continued, "more especially when the liberal and friendly conduct of this government towards Spain is taken into consideration." He explained the entire East Florida affair by contrasting the honest ethics of the American government with the underhand methods of Spain. "As soon as it was known that General Mathews had transcended his powers, the President revoked them and committed them to you, with authority to restore the territory to the governor of the province, on the condition, that satisfactory assurance should be given you, that the people who had acted . . . on the faith of the United States, should not be punished or molested."

"On a full view of your conduct," Monroe continued to Mitchell, "I am happy to communicate to you the entire approbation, and thanks of the President. In accepting the trust, you gave a proof of patriotism, and the discharge of its duties has been distinguished by ability and judgment which the nature of the case required." Failure to forward full instructions to him did not reflect negligence, Monroe assured Mitchell, but rather mirrored the president's confidence in the governor.[38]

Mitchell had gambled and won. He had correctly interpreted the wishes of Madison and Monroe, and, unlike Mathews, suffered no disgrace for his insight. The administration approved his orders for retaining American troops in East Florida.

Monroe soon relieved Governor Mitchell of his duties in the Floridas and transferred his powers to Major General Thomas Pinckney. The reason, however, was not dissatisfaction with Mitchell, but the need for his services as governor of Georgia in aiding the war effort. Also the importance of East Florida and the new plot brewing for its annexation required the over-all command of a ranking army officer.

More than six months after the repudiation of Mathews and more than three after the Senate rejected the House bill for seizing the Floridas, American troops remained in the Spanish province. From the Georgia border past the St. Johns, East Florida was governed by the United States. The Madison administration had recovered from the defeat inflicted by recalcitrant senators in July; expansion southward had again been placed on the agenda.

Life in the Occupied Land

OCCUPATION, THE AMERICANS discovered, was more difficult than the conquest of East Florida. Smugglers and slave traders evaded laws; British warships supported English merchants; Patriots demanded special privileges; and Spanish Loyalists resented American authority, reporting their grievances to diplomatic representatives. Repeated changes in command and the Madison administration's negligence in giving orders for governing the occupied area added to the confusion. Soldiers and militia passing to and from Colonel Smith's camp near St. Augustine, contractor's agents scouring the country for cattle or demanding immediate transports for supplies imported from the United States, and Indians roaming the outskirts of civilization magnified the problems of occupation. The hot, wet climate and semi-tropical diseases made shambles of projected plans.

Fernandina, the unofficial capital of occupied Florida, was a madhouse. That first peaceful conquest of the town by restrained Patriots belied the era of confusion which followed. Old General Mathews foresaw the problems. To meet them he appointed Lewis, the former deputy of St. Marys, as collector of the port, declared Spanish law void, and replaced Spanish officials with his personal appointees.[1] Yet Mathews was uncertain of his powers and of his responsibilities. For a time he kept trade checked in the once busy port, waiting for additional orders from Washington. But before leaving on what he hoped would be a triumphant conquest of St. Augustine, he restored trading rights and provided for the collection of customs, the income

LIFE IN THE OCCUPIED LAND

from which was to be reserved for repayment of those who financed the revolution.

Supporting the civil establishment of Mathews was a Marine detachment of sixty men under Captain John Williams, which came down from the Cumberland Island base with orders to hold Fernandina. Theirs was the double task of protecting the supply line of Colonel Smith and keeping order in the occupied town; for despite the appointees of Mathews, Captain Williams ruled Fernandina, holding and exercising complete authority over the people, who enjoyed only those rights which he allowed them.[2]

Most Loyalists accepted the new order but some worked to undermine American authority. Mathews complained about the latter and Smith instructed Williams to arrest and imprison individuals on demand by the collector of the port or any civil magistrate.[3] Rumors of the undercover activities of Loyalists were on the lips of every Patriot: they were arming Negroes, communicating with captains of foreign ships, and maturing a plan for the massacre of Americans by inciting a general insurrection of slaves. Though Colonel Smith discounted these rumors, he nevertheless warned Williams that vigilance was essential.[4]

It was the Patriots, however, and not the Loyalists, who gave Williams the greater trouble. In their opinion he should recognize their right and authority in Fernandina. Instead he placed Patriot and Loyalist on the same footing: both must obey the rules and regulations. The Patriots countered by accusing Williams of favoring citizens with anti-American and pro-British inclinations, of being a drunkard, of conduct unbecoming "an officer and a gentleman," and of suggesting the impending disavowal of Mathews. These accusations nettled Williams, but Smith reassured him by rejecting them.[5]

Captain Williams was an able commander. Before the repudiation of General Mathews, the captain's difficulties were limited to malicious gossip, but news of the general's disavowal elated the Loyalists. At a mass meeting on May 13, they elected Joseph M. Arredondo their chairman and stated that three-fourths of the revolutionists had been forced into rebel ranks by a few designing, scheming men. Arredondo, Philip R. Yonge, and James Cashen were appointed as a standing committee with power to summon the people for defense in periods of danger.[6]

Though the Loyalists thanked Williams for his gentlemanly conduct during his command, they now considered his authority terminated. Emboldened by the renouncing of Mathews and organized as they were for resistance they no longer accepted the insults and highhanded actions of the Patriots.

British and Spanish sea captains sensed the change. The Spanish *Fernando,* which had been seized after the fall of Fernandina, hoisted sail on May 15, and, ignoring the orders of Commodore Campbell, sailed from the harbor. Lieutenant John Hulburd, commander of an American gunboat, hailed the *Fernando,* but the British brig *Sappho* signaled him to keep away. Hulburd fired two shots at the *Fernando,* the second hitting her quarter sail, and when the ship hove to he boarded her and ordered her captain to wait until a prize master could be placed aboard. The *Sappho* came up quickly, and Hulburd was ordered away under threat of the destruction of his gunboat. Since the *Sappho's* battery numbered eighteen large guns, the American gunboat put back into Fernandina harbor, while the *Fernando,* escorted by the *Sappho,* sailed away into the Atlantic.[7]

This British defiance of American authority dismayed the Patriots as much as it cheered the Loyalists. Not only had General Mathews been renounced by his own government but also a British naval officer had protected a Spanish merchantman. These acts and rumors of an immediate evacuation of East Florida gave Loyalists hope for revenge on the Patriots, but the revolutionists had not accepted defeat. A detachment of Patriots moved toward Fernandina with orders for the arrest and imprisonment of the Loyalists leaders.[8]

Governor Mitchell arrived at St. Marys before these Patriots had accomplished their mission. His first orders turned confusion into anarchy. As yet unbriefed by Monroe's intermediary, Isaacs, the Georgia governor ordered Captain Williams to conduct himself as the commander of an American military post and leave Fernandina alone.[9] Mitchell suspended the civil officials of General Mathews and chaos held sway as Loyalists and Patriots battled for supremacy. A few undisciplined Negroes plundered property and assaulted whites, and law was so generally disregarded that Mitchell reported East Florida in a complete state of civil war, anarchy, and confusion.[10]

The governor rectified his error. Loyalists, and other men of property who foresaw complete ruin, petitioned Mitchell for a restoration of the former Spanish laws and their enforcement by the American military commander, and their petition was granted.[11] Civil officials were reinstated, order restored, and customs collected. Captain Williams, who was ordered by Colonel Smith to obey Mitchell and be guided by his instructions for the governing of Fernandina, worked in harmony with the Georgia governor.

The blundering inefficiency of the administration in Washington shattered this peace. After Mathews had been rejected, the secretary of the navy ordered the recall of Captain Williams' marine detachment. This order moved slowly from superior to subordinate, and although the situation had changed since April and Smith's force remained encamped before St. Augustine, the naval order finally reached Williams, who prepared for the immediate withdrawal of his Marines to their Cumberland Island base.

Mitchell countermanded the order and Williams remained in Fernandina — but the damage had been done. When Colonel Smith learned that Williams had been ordered from Fernandina, thus leaving the colonel's command without a guarded communication and supply line, he shook with anger. He momentarily blamed the marine captain and informed Williams no more instructions would be given him or any further authority exercised over him. Smith's anger swayed his judgment: Williams was reminded of the unfavorable reports received about him as commander of Fernandina; he was replaced by Captain Fielder Ridgeway.[12] Smith later regretted this exercise of temper. He and Williams became friends, but the order had been given, the damage done. An incompetent took the place of an able man at Fernandina.

A loyal army man could not be proud of Captain Fielder Ridgeway of the riflemen. His glib tongue served him well as a recruiter and his promotion from a lieutenant to captain was the reward for his success in enlisting men. As a commanding officer, however, he handicapped a company. Army life on the frontier bored him, drink attracted him, and the company of obeisant soldiers pleased him more than association with fellow officers. He had been court-martialed and tried at Point Petre, but was freed on a technicality. Smith cannot be excused for appointing a man like this, but it must be said in his defense that he realized his error and quickly replaced Ridgeway.

Ridgeway received his orders late in June and hastened from Point

Petre, where he had been confined, to Fernandina.[13] Here he made the most of his opportunity. Fernandina was civilized: it had liquor and women, and he was in command. He wanted the Fourth of July celebrated in a patriotic manner by the East Floridians, but anticipated trouble. On July 3 Ridgeway ordered a search of all houses in Fernandina and the confiscation of everything which could be used as a weapon.[14]

Ridgeway's tenure was brief. On July 6 Captain Abraham Massias was appointed commander at Fernandina and five days later he occupied his post.[15] Ridgeway left the same day for active duty with Colonel Smith, but within four months he again faced a court-martial, charged with being drunk on three occasions and with reporting himself sick when in reality he was drunk while serving as officer of the day. He escaped condemnation only to run into difficulties on the northern front in 1814, which resulted in his being cashiered from the army.

Captain Massias was courageous, aggressive, and respected by all except those with anti-Semitic prejudice. Smith would have kept him in the field had it not been for one thing – Massias was a sick man. This illness, from which he slowly recovered during a tenure of ten months at Fernandina, did not prevent his ruling with an iron but just hand. Mitchell encouraged him, instructing him to maintain strict discipline, prevent violence, allow arms only to Americans, protect the property rights of the residents, watch all Negroes and imprison those who could not prove their free status or who were not vouched for by their owners.[16]

In complying with these instructions Massias made many rules and regulations. His men assembled under arms every morning and night and could not buy liquor without permission. Soldiers and non-commissioned officers patrolled the town in groups of three, reporting to sentries every half hour during the day and every fifteen minutes at night. Every soldier not in rank and under arms at the third tap of the drum in the morning and who did not continue under arms until a man could be seen at 300 yards faced a severe penalty. Each evening at nine, when the drum sounded, all liquor and grog shops were to be closed and not reopened until sunrise. Slaves and free persons of color found on the streets between nine and sunrise would be imprisoned unless they had written passes signed by owners, guardians,

LIFE IN THE OCCUPIED LAND

and employers. No tavern keeper could sell liquor to an enlisted soldier at any time and sailors from naval or merchant vessels were required to leave the town before nine in the evening. Every ship entering the port should anchor before the battery for inspection. Even fishing boats were prohibited from sailing before sunrise and had to return for inspection before sunset.

Massias later taxed store and shopkeepers of every description twelve dollars per year, payable quarterly in advance along with a twenty-five cent fee for the notary, Samuel Betts. This tax was the same as the former Spanish levy, and all income from it, as in Spanish days, would be used by Philip Yonge in caring for the poor. Because of the number of disputes over lot boundaries, land claims had to be submitted to George J. F. Clarke, the former surveyor general of East Florida, for adjudication. Town beautification was encouraged: trees should be set out at least eight feet from front lot lines; stumps and obstructions must be removed from the street. Every resident was personally responsible for keeping the street by his property clean; garbage should be collected daily and dumped into the Amelia River. Elemental sanitation was necessary for health, Massias proclaimed, and warned that these sanitary regulations would be enforced by the officer of the day. Furthermore the owners of mules, horses, and hogs should keep their animals outside the town limits.[17]

Enforcement of regulations brought bitter protests from smugglers, Loyalists, and Patriots. Many residents of Fernandina petitioned the United States for relief from the onerous rule of Massias and indicted him for appropriating customs duties for his personal use.[18] An accounting was demanded from Massias of all taxes collected; and after an investigation, Colonel Smith was convinced the accusations were made by enemies of the United States – men desiring a less vigilant commander who would not interfere with their smuggling activities.[19] If Massias deserved censure, Smith believed it would be for his leniency in dealing with the Loyalists.

The Patriots heartily agreed. Since the reinstitution of Spanish laws in Fernandina, Massias had given more and more responsibility to former Spanish office holders. His dependence on Philip Yonge and George Clarke, leaders of the Loyalists, maddened the Patriots. Month after month Massias paid less and less heed to the men who had engineered the revolution. He refused to grant them the recognition they demanded and finally threatened to turn his military forces against them.

For the latter action Colonel Smith was responsible. His daily contact with the Patriots developed a dislike which he frequently expressed in his letters. In September he wrote Massias: "The Patriots having acted so ungratefully toward my Detachment it will be well in no instance to acknowledge them as a Public body, but afford all the aid in your power to deserving individuals."[20]

The revolutionists, however, had in fact done yeoman service for Colonel Smith. They scoured the country for food, carried his dispatches, and by force of numbers frightened the Spaniards and Indians. When the United States declared war on Great Britain many Patriots enlisted, while others acted as informers and through their information many British merchantmen were captured.[21] Smith thought so well of the Patriots in June that he was hopeful of capturing St. Augustine with their assistance and presenting the Spanish town to the nation as a birthday gift on July 4. He later recommended acceptance of the active, hardy revolutionists as enlistees in his detachment.[22] The *None Such,* a privateer authorized by John Houstoun McIntosh, partially blockaded St. Augustine and captured vessels en route to the Bahamas with appeals from Governor Kindelan to the English for men and supplies.[23] With Patriot sanction privateers from the Carolinas hovered off the Florida main intercepting materiel destined for St. Augustine.

As the influence of General Mathews waned in their councils, the Patriots lost their effectiveness. The more turbulent, impatient revolutionists raised their voices; with Mathews no longer in control, unity disappeared. Revenge and selfish desires replaced the old motives and Colonel Smith could no longer depend on organized bands of Patriots for cattle. Individuals stole and sold goods for personal gain. Uncouth adventurers, dissatisfied with their loot, shouted like children in the light of fires needlessly set.

Not all of the Patriots acted so wantonly. Those who fronted the rebellion for Mathews longed for annexation, but they were disappointed and discouraged by Madison's shifting policies, and by the American agents in East Florida who ignored their claims for recognition. Thoughtful leaders searched for a way out of their predicament. A more definite governmental organization might be the solution, McIntosh thought; so he called for a constituent convention to frame a constitution.

At the beginning of their revolution the Patriots adopted a temporary government without a constitution, a legislature, or an executive. A formal government was unnecessary, for the revolutionists would cede East Florida and the United States would create a territorial government for the occupied parts of Florida. No need existed for officers other than a commander of troops, who would receive conquered territory from the Spanish, and a commissioner, who would deliver the province to the United States. For a time this makeshift organization answered the Patriots' needs, but after the repudiation of Mathews, a regular governmental organization, which could be recognized by the United States, became essential. A working government would demonstrate the earnestness of the Patriots and speed the annexation of their province.[24]

On July 10, 1812, the revolutionists elected fifteen delegates and empowered them to frame a constitution and organize a government.[25] When the delegates assembled, they elected John Houstoun McIntosh as president of the constitutional convention and William Hamilton as secretary. Among the thirteen other delegates were Lodowick Ashley, William Craig, and Buckner Harris, men who had been associated with the Patriots almost from the beginning of the revolution.[26] Working in harmony, the delegates unanimously approved of a document entitled the "Constitution of East Florida."[27]

In approximately 4,000 words the constitution outlined a frame of government. It began with a preamble or recital of grievances of the Patriots; mentioned their fear of being sold to Great Britain, their desire for union with the United States, and their successes against the corrupt Spanish regime. In three articles and twenty-nine sections the constitution provided for a government with separation of powers: a director or executive, a unicameral legislature or council of fifteen, and an elaborate system of courts. All free white males, twenty-one years of age and residents of East Florida, could vote; but only those who possessed property valued at $1000 or more could serve on the council, and those who held a minimum of five hundred acres of land and at least $1500 in other property would be eligible for the position of director. The powers and duties of officials and the rights of citizens were similar to those of the people of the United States.

The constitution makers again and again entitled their country the "Territory of East Florida." Patriots wished neither independence nor statehood in the United States with all the consequent cost and taxation of a sovereign state or commonwealth. They desired immediate annexation by the United States, and the "Territory" in the name of their country connoted their ultimate goal within the American Union. So there could be no misunderstanding of their purpose, as the fifteen convention members stated: "It is expressly and unequivocally and unanimously declared by them that it [the provisional government of East Florida] is intended to exist and be in operation only until the United States shall acknowledge this Territory as a part of the United States." Attached to this positive avowal was an expression of confidence in American justice, a justice which would result in the ratification of the treaty of cession previously made by General Mathews.

As provided by the "Constitution," elections were held on Saturday, July 25, and the "Legislative Council" assembled at Zephaniah Kingsley's plantation on the following Monday. John Houstoun McIntosh received his reward for past contributions in service and money by being named "Director of the Territory of East Florida."[28] The council favored an appeal to the American government and agreed on the necessity of a more unified, aggressive policy in East Florida.

Director McIntosh penned his letter of July 30 in the hope that Madison and Monroe would recognize the new government. His expectation was in vain. The Madison administration could give no more recognition to this farce of a government parading under the name of the Territory of East Florida than it had given the previous makeshift fathered by Mathews.

The Patriots had no success with the local agents of the United States: Governor Mitchell ignored them, Colonel Smith grew increasingly bitter toward them, and Massias threatened them with the American army and navy. He had cause for his threat. As Director of East Florida McIntosh demanded all duties collected at Fernandina since the establishment of a customs house there. Massias refused. McIntosh pleaded, mentioning the promise of these funds as made by Mathews, and the financial straits of the revolutionists. Pleas became demands and demands threats, but Massias remained adamant.

With the customs duties denied them, the Patriots decided on taxation and confiscation of property as a source of revenue. Since the revolutionists had already given personal service or money and the Spanish had destroyed Patriot resources, it seemed equitable to make the Loyalists pay the costs of government. Unfortunately, however, the wealthier Loyalists resided in Fernandina where Massias brooked no interference with his authority. Late in September, 1812, McIntosh conferred with the captain. At the conclusion of the conference Massias requested naval assistance from Commodore Campbell, and the commodore ordered Commander Winslow Foster of gunboat 62 to aid and assist Massias by every means within his power.[29] On learning of this order McIntosh wrote Campbell a letter filled with bitter emotion. Would the commodore send a gunboat against the Patriots, who planned nothing more than the confiscation of some horses belonging to Loyalists? There had been need for a gunboat on the St. Johns when the Indians and Negro mercenaries of Spain had been pillaging and murdering, but Campbell had not sent a ship to protect the Patriots. "Good God!" McIntosh exclaimed. "If your Government have [sic] any disposable force will you send it to protect a few paltry horses of men, who are declared enemies to your country, while the scenes which I have related are allowed to be transacted without even your pity on the innocent wives and children of men, who, for the love of your Government have risked everything they owned to become subjects of it? Shall I add, of men, who were persuaded by your authorized commissioner to take up arms against their oppressors and who have been promised, publickly promised, protection?"[30]

The Patriots had ceded East Florida to the walls of St. Augustine, and, in the opinion of McIntosh, if a part of this area was to be protected by the United States, then all of it should be. Since the cession had been refused he could not understand why American officers exhibited such concern for Loyalists – men who opposed the United States and therefore had no fear of their allies, the Spanish, Indians, and Negroes, while the Patriots had been despoiled of their property by these same wretches without aid from the United States. American officers had been given Amelia Island, McIntosh declared, and accepted it, promising the Patriots all taxes secured by customs. That promise had been broken. Massias should give equal protection to all residents of East Florida or else confine himself within his garrison bounds.

McIntosh next appealed to Monroe. The Anglo-Spaniards on Amelia Island were exulting at the misfortunes of the Patriots, boasting that the United States gave protection to Loyalists, who would soon confiscate and possess the estates of the revolutionists. Can the Patriots be censured for wishing to levy some contribution on them? asked McIntosh. The Loyalists in Fernandina were in regular correspondence with Governor Kindelan, McIntosh stated, and the Patriots believed the threat of burning their houses would make them appeal to the Spanish governor and force him to give up his barbarous warfare on the wives and families of the Patriots. This threatened retaliation, and it was only a threat, had been suggested in a conversation with Massias; and although McIntosh admitted he may have said more in the heat of passion, he knew he had not made false accusations and foolish threats.[31]

Monroe ignored his letter, but Campbell sent a brief explanatory note in reply to his. The commodore stated there had been no gunboat available when McIntosh had requested one for protection of the Patriots. No one felt more concern for the revolutionists than he, declared Campbell, but he could not comply with requests or orders made by an authority unrecognized by the United States.[32]

Fortunately for the already discouraged McIntosh, he did not see the postscript attached to the copy of Campbell's letter sent to Washington. The Patriots were the authors of their own misfortunes, Campbell stated for the benefit of the secretary of the navy, for instead of remaining in camp near St. Augustine, they abandoned their camp in a shameful manner, leaving Colonel Smith to fight their battles. In Campbell's opinion McIntosh was responsible for most of the difficulties; for the Director of East Florida claimed all credit for the revolution, belittled the work of General Mathews, and acted in a manner just short of madness.[33]

McIntosh and the Patriots continued their make-believe government, but their hour was spent. Brigadier General Thomas Flournoy almost recognized them in December, when he ordered the release of four Spanish soldiers who had been captured by the revolutionists, and requested that a copy of the order be delivered to "John H. McIntosh, Director of the Territory of East Florida." Quick to seize even this slender straw, McnItosh graciously acquiesced.[34] If he anticipated more recognition as the result of this cooperation, he was disap-

LIFE IN THE OCCUPIED LAND

pointed; he was fighting for a lost cause and for discredited Patriots. Finally, realizing the farce of the revolutionary government and thinking only of himself, late in 1813 he sought repayment in Washington of the money advanced for the revolution.

Colonel Smith could have used a well organized force of Patriots, for as the summer of 1812 advanced, his position before St. Augustine became increasingly precarious. With a maximum force of 120 men and a long supply line, and faced with the ever present danger of an Indian uprising, Smith could not relax for an instant. Repeatedly he informed his superiors of his critical situation. Mentally he was torn by doubt, his pride in himself and the army wounded; he had conquered a country without firing a shot in battle and had been forced into boring and inglorious inactivity.

Hope alone sustained him. The certainty that war with Great Britain would bring orders for action made June bearable. Enthusiastically he wrote of the militia coming to his aid: 175 men arrived at Cow Ford on June 24, Colonel Daniel Newnan was marching with two troops of dragoons and 250 infantrymen, and six barges with forty to fifty men each were en route from North Carolina.[35] With these reinforcements and authorization for an attack, the army's prestige would be restored by the capture of St. Augustine. But war with England did not affect Florida. Reinforcements were only a fraction of the reported numbers and militiamen were poor excuses for soldiers.

The Savannah Blues and Volunteer Guards, who left their native city with cheers ringing in their ears, found neither vacation nor glory in East Florida. The voyage down the coast became a nightmare. They were crowded like hogs in the leaky transports, and the incompetent crew of one vessel was directed by a careless, drunken commander. At the St. Johns the volunteers disembarked and marched for fourteen hours under a burning sun, with only a biscuit for food and swamp water for drink. The weary, disillusioned militia reached Smith's headquarters at nine o'clock on the evening of June twenty-sixth.[36]

The Georgians erected their tents beside the camp of the regulars. Behind them the Patriots rested in disarray; before them the Spanish drums sounded, and cannon salutes shattered the quiet of night. On July 5 Smith learned of the declaration of war with England, and on the following day he and his staff of officers moved in for a closer examination of the Castillo. Plans were drawn for the coming assault, but authorization for attack never came, and one hot, dreary day succeeded another.

Heat, rain, privation, and boredom made the Savannah volunteers long for home. They demanded transports for their return voyage since they had volunteered for only two months and claimed they should be in Savannah for discharge on or before sixty days from the date of original enlistment. On July 24 the Volunteer Guards and some of the Blues slipped quietly into Savannah; the remaining Blues straggled in nine days later.[37]

As the Savannah militia thus ended their expedition ingloriously, the volunteers from central Georgia under Colonel Newnan marched into East Florida. These men differed from the pallid city-dwellers of Savannah. They smelled of the great outdoors. They were independent, full-blooded Americans who got their information from stump speeches, pulpit preaching, and an occasional newspaper. With their muskets they could hit a squirrel at fifty paces, aim at and kill an Indian varmint by smell alone. Some lacked shoes, but their feet were tough; others were without guns, but they would wrestle muskets from the enemy. They feared no one but God, and Him only on Sundays.

In building the American tradition they should have been unconquerable. After a few weeks in East Florida, however, these frontiersmen were conquered just as their city cousins had been subdued by Florida. Some stole away from camp, for two months of service was too long for them. Colonel Smith told Newnan to drum the men caught planning desertion out of camp with ropes around their necks.[38] Disgusted, Smith wrote a friend: "In truth I am truly tired of this Damned Province and would not remain (if it rested with me) one month longer in my present situation for a fee simple to the whole of it."[39]

The literate officers and men found surcease in letters. Captain Ridgeway, who joined Smith after his brief rule in Fernandina, was the most prolific correspondent in camp. He complained to his brother in Maryland of having had no news from him in almost two years, and wanted to know of home, "How the people stand the War . . . how is the sale of Produce, who is dead and who is married and who is not . . . ?" Ridgeway described his suffering which was caused by warm weather, bad water, and insufficient provisions. He entreated his brother, "Let me know if Miss Elizabeth Weems is married or Miss Mary Parron, and [about] all the Young ladies."[40]

Ridgeway distrusted the regular contractor and wrote friends in St. Marys for supplies. Since he had not tasted butter for many days, he requested Sergeant John Tally "to procure me 4, 5 or 10 pounds Also chicklings Duck if they can be had. I will be glad if you can sent me a small roast Pigg."[41] Ridgeway sent no money for he had no loose coins and could not get a bill changed.

William Kinnear, a homesick lad from Virginia, was more concerned with his dismal Florida surroundings than with food. East Florida was "a fit recaptacle for savages and wild beasts, the scenery of the country exhibiting nothing except disart – pine barren and vast regions of untrackless swamps where nothing can be heard by the lonely traveller save the screeching of the owl or howling wolf." Yet this was the place, Kinnear told his mother, where the American soldiers stood in daily fear of their lives. "The atmosphere is likewise coeval with imperfections of the country, pregnant with sickness and death."[42]

Unfortunately some other soldiers found time for adventurous exploration. Five of them, while rowing on North River, discovered some Minorcan girls on the river bank about two miles from the American camp. Descendants of the poverty stricken inhabitants of Minorca, whom Doctor Andrew Turnbull brought as indentured servants to New Smyrna in 1768, these comely girls presented an appealing picture to five lonesome soldiers. The girls with their jet black hair and sparkling eyes, their high breasts, their lithe and supple figures were a powerful lure. They signaled the soldiers, indicating a desire to escape from the Spanish area. The men, anticipating much, rowed with swift, powerful strokes toward shore, beached their boat and ran forward. They never reached the charming Loreleis. Successive volleys of musket fire from the underbrush felled the soldiers. Four of their bodies were discovered later, three with scalps missing, and one corpse was never found.[43]

Danger always lurked beyond the encampment, and in camp too. Drenching, intermittent rains and a hot, blistering sun took a severe toll. Bad food, inadequate shelter, and the ever-present mosquitoes laid man after man low. Colonel Smith's letters monotonously listed the number of ill men. Often a third of his entire command failed to stand reveille in the morning because of sickness. Captain Ridgeway believed he would never get well in Florida's climate, but he sometimes confused illness with the hangover from excesses of the previous night.

To improve conditions Smith ordered the building of log huts with thatched roofs. These gave protection from rain and sun, but moisture clung to clothing and bedding. The dampness crept in everywhere, even, it seemed, into one's bones. Sun and a bath in the river afforded temporary relief. Then the heat and perspiration made one damp and smelly all over again.

Soldiers lolled in the shade of trees and huts. Here a group listened while a literate companion read a newspaper, and the men laughed uproariously at the naive editorials of Georgia editors. "The military profession is made a lucrative one . . .," one publisher declared, for a five-year volunteer would receive $300 in pay, a cash bounty of sixteen dollars, and separation pay of fifteen dollars and 160 acres of land. A frugal soldier could save $300 from his total pay of $331 and have 160 acres of land all for five years of patriotic service."[44] The soldiers hooted at the idea of spending only thirty-one dollars in five years. "Did that editor know how much a gallon of whiskey cost?"

Other men listened intently to the reader. The theater in Augusta was offering the celebrated comedy *Heirs at Law* and the favorite pantomimic interlude in one act called *Harlequin Hurry Scurry or The Devil among the Tradespeople*, to be followed by the farce *Jew and Doctor*. That would be a grand event, for civilized people would be there – girls with their long curls. Lonesome soldiers longed for the sight of them.

Accounts of events back home eased the pain in the hearts of most enlisted men, but on some the news had a different effect: they deserted and headed for home. A few of these were caught and punished. John Walker of Captain Ridgeway's company left with the plate, bed, and table linen of one household, and the clothing and $500 in gold of another; one Marine joined the Spaniards in St. Augustine; Private Holder was shot. Private Day was brought to his place of execution, made to kneel at the foot of his already prepared grave, and then his pardon was read.[45]

Colonel Smith hoped these examples would deter others from deserting. He did not censure the mass of his men, for like them, he was sick of East Florida, of the heat and rain, of the inactivity. His was a responsibility which could not be thrown off. He felt personally dishonored and believed the reputation of the United States Army tarnished by the enforced stand of his detachment.

The increasing hostility of the Indians indicated action might come soon. If the Indians raised their tomahawks, Smith would be in jeopardy of capture by concerted attack from front and rear by Spaniard and Indian. He realized the danger, but preferred action with its accompanying danger and possible glory to existing humiliation.

The General Retires

IN HIS HOUR OF TRIUMPH, AFTER Fernandina fell and after the investment of St. Augustine, far-seeing George Mathews had feared the Indians and their Negro allies. He had turned back from the walls of the old city, foregoing its possible fall and a consequent victory celebration, to hold a talk with the Indian chiefs. While on this duty he had received Monroe's letters of disavowal and appeasement.

For a time the shocked old man wandered in a daze, at times believing himself still the accredited agent of the government, and then again the full realization of his disgrace would burst from his subconscious into his conscious mind. Feeble as it was at first, sanity returned and with it twin determinations: he would continue in the Patriot service and he would vindicate his honor.

The first was more pressing. Governor Kindelan was an aggressive, patriotic Spaniard, who would defend his country's province to the limit of his power. With St. Augustine partially blockaded by sea and almost surrounded on the land, the governor's only possible allies were the Seminole Indians. Mathews conceived his duty to be in counteracting the Spanish influence with the Indians by warning the savages that the consequences of intervention would be extermination. In June he met King Payne and a delegation from the Seminole tribes at Picolatti. The resulting talks were inconclusive, but Mathews left the conference convinced of Indian neutrality. From Picolatti he returned to the Patriot camp before St. Augustine.[1]

Ralph Isaacs found him there.[2] As Isaacs later reported, Mathews was in a "most unhappy frame of mind."[3] It was an understatement. Since May 9 the repudiated agent had thought again and again of the ways and means of vindicating himself. By mid-June he had reached one conclusion: neither the power nor exalted station of Madison would screen the president from exposure or deny the general a just "ravange." He would publish his instructions from former Secretary Robert Smith and his own letters to Monroe which gave detailed reports on his plans and activities; he would release a full account of his conversation with Madison on January 1, 1811, and the "backstairs" instructions which he received from the president; he would send out copies of the secret appropriation act for $100,000 which was earmarked for the corruption of Governor Folch.[4]

But time and tact calmed Mathews. Isaacs appealed to his patriotism, emphasized the harm such an exposure would do the United States, and declared it would certainly prevent a quick annexation of the Floridas. Mathews' patriotism conquered his personal resentment.[5]

Isaacs pushed his advantage. He reported the encouraging words of Monroe; declared the president believed Mathews had been actuated in Florida by as laudable a spirit as when he had fallen at the head of his regiment in the Revolutionary War; and told of the administration's determination to occupy the Floridas. Complimentary reference to his war service always touched a responsive chord in the general's heart and the acquisition of the Floridas was his greatest ambition. Isaacs' appeals were reinforced by the receipt of a letter from Senator Crawford, who wrote Mathews about the passage by the House of the bill for occupying the Floridas and of prospects of favorable action by the Senate. In Crawford's opinion, the annexation of the Floridas was in the offing and Mathews would be tendered the governorship of a territory created from the province.[6] Appointment as governor of Florida would both vindicate and honor the general.

The explanations of Isaacs, the encouragement of Crawford, and above all the renewed hope of acquisition of the Floridas, the fondest desire of the general, turned Mathews from his course: he would neither publish his instructions nor write defenses of his conduct; he would do nothing which would embarrass the president or the government. With these assurances Isaacs left for St. Marys with dispatches for Governor Mitchell and a report on the critical situation of the American detachment before St. Augustine.[7]

Mathews remained in the Patriot camp, where he listened as scouts told of unrest among the Seminoles. The more aggressive braves were advocating war. Though some of the Indians could not resist the inducements offered by Governor Kindelan, Mathews knew that others, including King Payne, opposed their chauvinistic brothers; so with McIntosh he again conferred with the chiefs.

This conference was the general's last effort in Florida for the Patriots. He yearned for a long talk with Senator Crawford, and since the Congress had adjourned, the senator would be at his home in Georgia. Mathews headed for St. Marys, and from there proceeded with Isaacs to Lexington, Georgia, to confer with Crawford. On August 4, 5, and 6 Mathews and the senator talked.[8] Crawford described the last weeks of the recent congressional session, damning those recalcitrant Republican senators whose desertion of party had defeated the bill for occupying the Floridas. Mathews gave an accounting of his acts and brought Crawford the latest news of the revolutionists. He outlined the government set up by the Patriots and convinced the willing senator that their political independence should be recognized by the United States. They agreed that Crawford would write Monroe, and the general would hasten to Washington and lobby for recognition of the Patriots.

Latent anger lingered in Mathews because of his repudiation. Crawford explained the Henry incident and declared it accounted for the disavowal. By playing politics with the Henry letters, Madison and Monroe had placed themselves so they could not approve the work of Mathews, however much they might have admired it. For the first time the general learned the secrets of the Henry affair. Now he understood why he had been repudiated and it angered him even more. Monroe's ineptitude in exploding a political dud when he knew of Mathews' undercover activities in East Florida, was inexcusable incompetence. Were not the Floridas of greater importance than the discrediting of a few Federalists whose party had already spent its finest hour?

But Mathews would say nothing. Crawford assured Monroe of that. "Upon the subject of the disavowal the genl. will not speak, when with you or the President unless you mention it, and in that event you must prepare yourself for some harshness of expression."[9] The senator thought Mathews more concerned for the Patriots than moved by his own vanity: "If they could be secured from loss and injury, and especially if the country should be taken and retained by the U. S., I believe he would be reconciled to the mortifying situation in which he has been placed by the disavowal of his conduct."

Accompanied by Isaacs, the general moved toward Augusta and the main stage route for Washington. Mathews was almost seventy-three, and he could no longer laugh at distance or the hardships of travel. It was a long, painful trip. But he tortured himself by veering to the left for a conference with Benjamin Hawkins at the Creek Agency. The Indian agent promised he would send a delegation of Creeks to the Seminole Indians; and satisfied that this plan of using the Creeks to contain the Seminoles offered hope for peace, Mathews moved on. The unmerciful August heat was broken by torrential rains, but flooded streams had to be forded.[10]

Late in August the general reached Augusta. Once there he crawled into bed. By morning his fever had mounted – he could not rise. The hot, humid air of the river town pressed on him from every side. As he tossed with fever day after day, he must have relived his past in delirium. Tradition-makers later wrote of his outbursts of temper and his threats against Madison: he would give the president a personal beating; he was on his way to Washington, where he'd "be dam'd if he did not blow them all up."[11]

However, the general was dying. His fever continued unabated, and his once strong muscles could barely move his emaciated body. On Sunday, August 30, he would be seventy-three years of age. Sunday came and Mathews still lived, but as though that birthday were a goal of major importance, he achieved it and could go no further. Hot-tempered General George Mathews was dead.[12]

The funeral procession formed on Monday afternoon. At its head the Independent Blues walked by their horses and the Rangers with guns reversed followed. Behind them came Charles Mathews, John Forsyth, Ralph Isaacs, and Freeman Walker. City officials, citizens of Augusta, and a company of artillery completed the procession. Minute guns were fired as the mourners paced the distance to St. Paul's Church; in the churchyard, as the body of Mathews rested in the grave, three shots were fired by artillerymen and three volleys by the infantry.[13]

The militia of Augusta agreed on the propriety of wearing crepe bands and Governor Mitchell issued a call from Milledgeville for all military officers in the state to wear black crepe armbands for thirty days as a mark of respect to the memory of Mathews.[14] In commenting on the general, Mitchell stated: "By this demise, another hero of the Revolution is gone. Whatever political errors he may have fallen into, in the course of a long public life, let them rest in oblivion. He has carried with him to the grave, many scars from wounds he received fighting battles of the Revolution — let us, therefore, pay that respect which is due to the memory of a soldier, who often braved death to establish the independence of our country."[15]

Augusta editors paid the general a more loving tribute. They reviewed his achievements and failures, and expressed their admiration of his "kind, benevolent, sincere, just, tenacious" personality: a man who lived as a "stranger to adulation, equally above the smiles and frowns of power"; and one who, "though his heart was stung by some recent transactions, yet never was his patriotism more conspicuous, than when he made every feeling of personal resentment subject to it."[16] A historian later described him as the "victim of a covetous but vacillating administration which he had served faithfully according to his lights and as the sequel proved, far too well for his own future."[17]

The Black and Reds

MATHEWS DIED BEFORE THE FULL horror of Indian warfare burst around the Patriots. Planters along the St. Johns and St. Marys, frontiersmen beyond the limits of civilization, and lumbermen deep in the forests lived in constant fear of attack. Mathews had shared their fears. An Indian uprising would send timid revolutionists flying to evacuate their families and movable possessions, the more courageous to protect their homes and children. In either case the Patriots would be dispersed and useless as a fighting force.

Even before the investment of St. Augustine in April, 1812, rumors of a forthcoming Indian war shook the residents of East Florida, and some used their fears as excuses for not uniting with the Patriots. If they left their homes, the Indians, with Negro slaves and free persons of color, would run wild. Plundering and burning of property, scalping of old men and women, abduction of babies in arms would be everyday occurrences. East Florida would revert to wilderness, and property accumulated by years of hard work would disappear overnight.

Mathews and the Patriot leaders anticipated the danger and sought to forestall it by calling the Seminole Indian chiefs into conference at Picolatti. These Indians lost little love on the Spaniards. Traditions of the tribes recalled days of the past British era of Florida when Cowkeeper, the head chieftain, made annual visits to St. Augustine. There he paraded before the white men, showing off his retinue of wives with their copper colored bodies shining with bear grease, and received honors and presents from the English governor. Around his neck hung the "Great Seal" which the Great White Father across the ocean, George III, had sent as a symbol of friendship and authority. When Spain regained the Floridas in the 1780's, Cowkeeper swore eternal hatred for the Spaniards. On his deathbed he voiced his regret at being called away before he had killed 100 Spaniards, and made his sons promise to account for the fourteen still needed for the achievement of his desire.[1]

In 1812 one of Cowkeeper's sons ruled the poorly organized, decentralized Seminole nation. By this time the son, Chief Payne or King Payne, was an old man who had seen his people prosper; he wanted peace, not war, and especially opposed a war which would aid Spaniards. His younger brother Bowlegs, or half-brother, was full of vigor and exuberant manhood. Bowlegs offered Mathews and the Patriots more than neutrality: he would join the white Americans in war.[2] Though he made the offer with the pride of an Indian chief he was treated like a common cur. The white men wanted no Indian allies; the Indian chief should mind his own business and leave the American and Spaniard alone. Bowlegs bristled with anger. Although he would follow King Payne on neutrality, the rebuff rankled in his heart.

Satisfied with their work, the complacent Patriots announced that peace and friendship had been established with the Seminoles on a permanent basis and upon the grounds of mutual interest.[3] Mathews was not so optimistic. Neither did the Spanish governors accept the conference results as final: Estrada sent Negro emissaries into the Indian councils, and Kindelan, after his arrival, spread imaginative but plausible conjectures of what the Georgians would do with Indian lands after the Spaniards had been thrust from East Florida.

This propaganda from St. Augustine fell on fertile soil, and the more aggressive Seminoles rallied under the leadership of Bowlegs in a demand for war. The opportunities for plunder and scalps, the chance to hit back at land-hungry Georgians who had been pushing closer and closer on their hunting grounds, fired the Indian imagination. War involved only a minimum of risk, for Kindelan promised aid and the United States had repudiated Mathews. The Patriots and unauthorized Georgia volunteers could be destroyed with ease. In addition there was the financial reward offered by Kindelan for scalps.

Mathews heard of this growing dissatisfaction. Without hesitation he met the challenge by calling a second conference, inviting twenty-seven chiefs for a talk at Forbes' store in Picolatti. There he reiterated his position: the fight in East Florida was a white man's quarrel; Indian interference would not be tolerated; war would bring swift, dire punishment. He distributed presents and assured the Indians that their lands would not be invaded.[4] Mathews concluded by urging Payne "to set you down at home and mind your business, and I will be your friend."

A few chiefs muttered their disapproval, saying the American's talk was "to amuse and deceive them." But Payne shook his head: he thought Mathews spoke with truth. The young warriors protested again: "We will go home and put our children away," they said, "and prepare for war."

Another officer, probably McIntosh, asked for peace. "You suspect us, you are wrong; sit down and take care of your women and children. The head of the American government has put us down here with arms in our hands to defend ourselves. We have nothing against you, and believe us your friends; we are so, and wish well to you." The Great White Father in Washington sent men into East Florida against the Spaniards, McIntosh stated, and not against the Indians. "You have large stocks of cattle, when we want beef we will send to you, do you send them down, and we shall have something to pay you for them."[5]

The Indian chiefs heard the "talks" quietly and remained in disagreement among themselves. Payne, however, brought them in line. There was no enthusiasm for the white man, no cordiality even from those chiefs supporting Payne, but the Indians did promise continued neutrality. Indian promises, like the white man's, were made under the exigencies of the moment and could be broken with facility. Disquieting rumors penetrated the Indian councils and Spanish agents told the Indians that in their July convention the revolutionists had made plans for partitioning the Indian lands.

These reports bolstered the war party, for Indians feared the Americans. Northern white men ruined hunting with their farms and their idea of individual ownership of land. They lived in towns where many thousand people busied themselves within a small space of ground; but the Seminole was a wild and scattered race, he swam the streams and leaped over the logs of the wide forest in pursuit of game, and was like the whooping crane that made its nest at night far from the spot where it dashed the dew from the grass and flower in the morning. More than fifty summers had seen the Seminole warrior reposing undisturbed under the shade of his oak and pine in Florida, and the suns of many winters had risen on his ardent pursuit of the buck and the bear, with none to question his bounds or dispute his range.

Young warriors would not give up their forests without a struggle. They deprecated traditional animosities against Spaniards and rebelled against the do-nothing policy of King Payne. Spain was weak. Her colonists could hardly hold St. Augustine; but Americans were strong, vigorous, and greedy. Unchecked they would take the Indian land.

Agents of Kindelan continued to play upon Indian apprehensions. The conquest of St. Augustine would prelude the conquest of the Floridas. Hordes of Americans would descend with sharpened ax and pointed plow, trees would fall, deer and other game would disappear; and the Indian would die or be pushed from the home of his fathers. Thus it had been in the Carolinas and Georgia. Thus it would be in Florida, unless the Indians struck in time. Today Spain could back them, and behind Spain was Great Britain. But tomorrow, after Spain was conquered, the Indian would stand alone, hopelessly alone.

Kindelan blamed Americans for disrupting the Indian trade and preventing delivery of the annual presents for the chiefs. He told the warriors that they could recoup their losses by fighting, for he would give them one thousand dollars for the scalp of John McIntosh and ten dollars for every other scalp.[6]

The desperate Spanish governor found able allies among the Negroes of East Florida. In July a Negro who had left the Seminoles for a job with a white man returned with the secrets of the Americans. An officer had ordered him to tell the Indians that as soon as St. Augustine capitulated, the Patriots would turn and sweep the red people from Florida. Another officer had asked the Negro, "When are you going home? I shall see you again for I will soon be eating beef at the Seminole village."[7]

A Negro from St. Augustine warned King Payne that Americans spoke with twisted tongues. "These fine talks are to amuse and deceive you, they are going to take your country beyond the St. Johns, the old people will be put to sweep the yards of the white people, the young men to work for them, and the young females to spin and weave for them. This I have heard," the Negro swore, "and this I tell you."[8]

Negroes of East Florida held an important stake in the outcome of the Spanish-American quarrel. Back in the 1730's when England and Spain had fought for Georgia, a colony of runaway slaves found haven in St. Augustine. They settled north of the town at Gracia Real de Santa Teresa de Mosé, where a fort was erected for their protection, the ruins of which the Americans referred to as Moosa Old Fort.[9] Spanish officials armed the ex-slaves and treated them as free men. When Great Britain won the Floridas in 1763 slaves could no longer gain their freedom by running into the settled areas of Florida.

The Seminoles, however, offered that which the British denied. Important chiefs, who had observed the power and affluence of white owners of slaves, bought some Negroes, paying for them in cattle, hogs, and horses. But possession of slaves did not bring the contemplated prosperity. In fact they became a problem. An Indian could not be bothered with the supervision of the choppers of wood and hoers of corn; so he set them apart in Negro villages, gave them tools, and demanded token payments as evidence of his overlordship.

Left in freedom the Negroes prospered. They built and planted, acquired cattle and horses, and filled huts with corn. In return for moderate rent they were protected by their Indian masters and had almost complete freedom of person. For ambitious Negroes it was a heavenly state compared with their old status. Word of their way of life spread throughout the lower Southland and escaped slaves trickled into the Florida peninsula. Once there the fugitives became members of a Negro village near some Seminole tribe.

These Negroes dressed for work in Indian fashion with a minimum of handmade clothing or prepared skins, but on festive days there appeared moccasins and leggins, a colorful long smock, a brilliant shawl or bandanna turban. and glittering metal ornaments. With his superior training in agriculture, the Negro surpassed his lenient master in producing corn and potatoes, rice and beans, and other edible products. In his palmetto log house with palmetto thatched roof he made a home and reared a family. He was free in all but name. Firearms were his, hunting and fishing his rights. When danger threatened he fought with the Seminoles as any freeman would fight for his home.

Continued freedom depended on Spanish retention of East Florida. American control would bring former owners seeking their slaves, unscrupulous men claiming what they never possessed, or raiders capturing Negroes for a lucrative market. These village Negroes of the Seminoles saw the Spanish as a bulwark against re-enslavement, and other free Negroes in and near St. Augustine appreciated Spain's protection. Governor Kindelan treated Negroes as men. The Negro loved this as much as the Georgia farmer hated it, and consequently free colored men volunteered for the defense of St. Augustine while able Negro advisers urged the Seminoles to take the warpath.

Georgians and Carolinians mentioned Negro soldiers in guarded whispers. They deprecated the soldierly qualities of the colored race and declared the Negro incapable of fighting; but Charleston and Savannah editors carefully deleted every reference to the colored militia in St. Augustine, leaving an asterisk in the blank and informing the reader that the deletion had been "for reasons of local security." Though he said the Negro could not fight, the white man shook with fear at the thought of armed Negroes rising in rebellion. The Negroes of East Florida were a standing menace and Southern men would pay a high price for the destruction of the Negro towns. Some men welcomed an Indian war with all its resulting destruction; for, as Governor Mitchell expressed it, an Indian uprising would "afford desirable pretext for the Georgians to penetrate their country, and Break up a Negro Town; an important Evil growing under their patronage."[10]

Patriots, whose properties and families in East Florida would bear the brunt of an Indian attack, demanded peace. For the third time Mathews and McIntosh went to the Indians, meeting King Payne in his Alachua village. This time they threatened rather than appealed: if the Indians took the warpath, they would be driven from Florida. "General Mathews told Payne, in the square at Latachwo," according to a Spanish report, "that he intended to drive him from his land." To the absent Bowlegs, McIntosh sent a message "that he intended to make him as a waiting man. . . ."[11]

These threats called the Seminoles' hand. A continuation of lukewarm neutrality would not satisfy the Americans: there must be positive assurance of peace or they would attack the Indians. King Payne preferred peace but Bowlegs beat the drums of war. When he was again in the Indian town he told a council that the Patriots had destroyed Indian trade and prevented Governor Kindelan from sending presents; he repeated the stories told by Negroes of the American intentions, and he declared the white men would attack as soon as St. Augustine fell. Since neutrality would not save the Indian from destruction, he urged his listeners to strike first while the Americans still had Spanish foes.[12] King Payne again called on the young braves for peace; but when they rejected his pleas, he raised his voice saying, "Go and fight, and if you are able to drive the white people go and do it, if you won't take my talk."[13]

Indians from several of the upper Creek towns joined the Alachua and Alligator tribes who could put almost 200 Indian and forty Negro "gunmen" on the warpath. The smaller number of Indian allies from the upper towns included some who had been banished for crimes, and other curious warriors who desired adventurous excitement.[14]

Their decision made, the Indians moved swiftly. From their towns in the hammocks beyond the St. Johns they sped through forest and swamp to fall on nearby houses and plantations. On Saturday, July 26, they killed a white man and five Negroes, and captured thirty-two slaves.[15] The following day they moved within four miles of Smith's camp, leaving two scalpless bodies. In less than a week they killed eight or nine men and liberated eighty to ninety slaves.[16]

These attacks accomplished all that Governor Kindelan had anticipated. Patriots threw their muskets over their shoulders and fled in haste from their camp, leaving Colonel Smith with his American soldiers, almost half of whom were ill, to face the Indians and Spaniards. Some of the Patriots reorganized at Hollingsworth's (later Camp New Hope) on the St. Johns, but most of them hurried home, where they packed wagons or loaded boats with movable property. Smith damned the Patriots for leaving him and Patriots damned the revolution as they scurried in flight.

Only Kindelan smiled. On August 9 he reported the investment of St. Augustine broken, and with the Patriots gone, his Negro militia established contact with the Indians who drove cattle into St. Augustine where the people had been on short rations. In winning the Indians Kindelan saved the town, but he needed guns, ammunition, and presents for his red allies. He appealed to the captain general of Cuba and the British in the Bahamas for assistance.[17]

The Indians wreaked havoc along both sides of the St. Johns as their mounted raiders went as far north as the St. Marys. They skirted the American supply depots at Picolatti and Davis Creek but attacked and burned plantations on both banks of the river north of those points. Occasional war parties cut between Smith's camp and Picolatti, endangering his supply line.

Colonel Smith was at Point Petre where Georgia volunteers were in sufficient number to check the Indians, but the colonel did not have a single musket, cartridge, flint, or haversack for them.[18] Sending them into East Florida would be a futile gesture, for the munitions and supplies there were less than needed for the regulars and militia already in the province.

In the face of Indian danger Smith sped back to his detachment before St. Augustine. At New Hope (now Jacksonville) he saw the miserable remnant of the Patriot army and concluded: "From their rapid decrease, having dwindled away to nothing, it is doubtful whether the 'Patriot Army' will ever revive again."[19] At Davis Creek he ordered Lieutenant Elias Stallings to construct a blockhouse and allow refugees the privilege of building cabins nearby. Smith left his boat at Picolatti for the dangerous overland journey east to his detachment near Moosa Old Fort where he found one-half of his men too ill for duty. Although he dispatched small reconnoitering parties in search of the Indians, the elusive redskins evaded the soldiers.

While Smith was sailing the St. Johns, Indians committed atrocity after atrocity. Early in August they attacked "Laurel Grove" where Zephaniah Kingsley with seven men fought them from his plantation house. Before giving their departing war whoop the Indians killed three Negroes and captured twenty-six more.[20] Two Patriots, James Hollingsworth and Daniel Pritchard, left Picolatti with dispatches for officers at the American camp. Only a few miles from Moosa Old Fort, they dismounted to water their horses. An Indian raiding party surprised them and American soldiers later found their bodies, scalped and tomahawked, with a painted warknife left lying nearby.[21] On August 12 Lieutenant Stallings sent a rifleman from the blockhouse with dispatches for Colonel Smith. A patrol found the soldier's body about three miles from the river. "From the appearance of the body, which was left lying in the road, he had been flogged, his nose, one ear, and privates cut off. He had three shot wounds in his body and his scalp taken."[22] Signs around the dead soldier indicated a party of ten Negroes and Indians had ambushed the rifleman. This atrocity aroused the soldiers to such a degree that Smith admitted he could not control his men should an enemy be captured.

The soldier had not died in vain. The ambuscade of Indians and Negroes who killed him had lain in wait for the supply wagons which moved between Fort Stallings, the blockhouse on Davis Creek, and the American encampment near St. Augustine. A fortunate circumstance saved the supply train. On the morning of August 12, wagon drivers worked for hours to get the oxen moving and this prevented the wagons from leaving at the appointed hour. The near success of the Indians forced Smith to send a military guard with the supply wagons.[23]

In their angry excitement Indians attacked friend and foe indiscriminately. All white men, and even Negro slaves, when they aided their owners, were endangered. When Dublin, the slave of Francis Philip Fatio, warned his master on August 13 of an approaching band of Indians, Fatio shrugged his shoulders. He had always been a friend of the red men, and they had often visited his plantation at New Switzerland on the St. Johns; he was an ardent Loyalist, a fact well-known by the Indians. He would pacify them with words. Since Dublin had seen the dancing Indians and knew they could not be reasoned with, he grabbed Fatio, despite his protests. With Dublin and Scipio, another slave, the nine members of the Fatio household hastened through their garden to a small creek and a ready boat. Eleven people, including the children, crowded into the little skiff and the slaves pulled hard at the oars. Before the Indians discovered the escapees, they had reached the broad St. Johns. Shots from Indian guns fell close as the Fatios rowed away.[24]

The escaping party met a detachment of 130 men from the volunteers of Colonel Newnan who were headed for Fort Stallings. Captain Tomlinson Fort, their commander, landed them at the blockhouse fort on August 15, much to the relief of the small guard stationed there. These timely reinforcements prevented an attack on the supply depot, but the Indians remained hidden in the nearby forests.

Fifteen Patriots discovered the lurking danger. They had come from Camp New Hope with Captain Fort, and once settled they foraged for food. On one such sortie they sighted a melon patch at a distance and hastened on, heedless of danger. Just as they reached the objective, the Indians charged. One man was killed and scalped almost in front of the Patriot leader, and one Indian fell dead from a well aimed musket ball. The Patriots ran, then re-formed quickly to fire on the charging Indians. These tactics of running, reloading, and firing were repeated many times. On the final charge the Patriots used their last ammunition. Fortunately the Indians did not know this, and retreated into the forests.

The Patriots still wanted those melons. In a second expedition Indians met them as before and one lieutenant received a mortal wound. The firing could be heard at Fort Stallings and Captain Fort marched to the rescue. His detachment met the running Patriots, with the Indians in pursuit, yelling their blood curdling whoops. On sighting the volunteers, the red men broke for the safety of forest and swamp.[25]

The arrival of Captain Fort at the blockhouse, and soon after of Colonel Newnan with the remainder of the volunteers, checked the Indians. They could not meet the Georgia militia, almost 250 of them, with any hope of success. Newnan's arrival not only cowed the Indians but also excited the anticipations of Colonel Smith. Since the first Indian outburst the colonel had planned on striking them in their towns and destroying their homes, property, and their "evil system of Negro villages." Lack of men and munitions had prevented the execution of well-laid plans.

Smith chafed while waiting for reinforcement. The aggressive Indians and Negroes had killed ten of his men, including the Patriots associated with the regular army and had captured more than a hundred slaves. They had laid waste the settled areas along the St. Johns. The audacious Bowlegs had raided the plantations between the St. Johns and the St. Marys. Only on Amelia, Talbot, and Fort George islands could former residents of the interior breathe in safety and even on the islands many lived in dread, for Bowlegs had moved across the St. Marys, killing a young man at Traders Hill in Georgia.

Bowlegs had made only this one quick thrust into Georgia. On August 18 he attacked a refugee planter encamped on the Florida side of the St. Marys, attempting to free or capture the planter's Negro slaves.²⁶ Some of the Negroes ran; others were forced into the river. Slaves in the neighborhood of Florida heard of the Indian successes. They already knew of the Florida haven among the Seminoles and lately there were rumors of additional inducements for escape. Governor Kindelan would bestow Spanish citizenship and arms on every Negro who joined the Spanish.²⁷ Hundreds of ex-slaves were already in the Indian towns of Florida, and Colonel Smith believed immediate action necessary to check the Indians, for otherwise slaves would flock into the back country of Florida and so strengthen the redskins as to make their reduction extremely difficult.²⁸

Smith had had his share of troubles. His health was threatened by the heat and insects of Florida. Inaction troubled him and he blamed the Spanish, "the most cowardly as well as most cruel of human family," for not beginning a fight. The more than 200 black troops in St. Augustine needled him, especially since Kindelan would not send them out for battle, and, because of orders, Smith could not attack. The colonel, however, was not discouraged, for with Newnan's volunteers, 250 or 300 men would be ready in a week to burn and destroy the Indian settlements.²⁹

By the morning of August 21 Smith smelled victory in the air. He ordered Captain Fort to take command at Picolatti, destroy the boat used by Indians and Negroes in crossing the St. Johns at Buena Vista, and then march against the Indians to destroy their towns, cattle, corn, potatoes, and other provisions.³⁰ Georgia volunteers would deter the Indians from attacking his line of communication and avenge the brutality of the past month. But Smith faced another disappointment. Captain Fort could not proceed against the Indians until Colonel Newnan arrived with the remainder of the volunteers. When the Colonel did reach Fort Stallings, he found the supplies for his force missing. Smith could not provision him or send him iron mills for grinding corn, and without food Newnan's militia detachment could not advance. Smith ordered him to camp somewhere along the St. Johns, the site to be determined by the availability of grist mills, corn, and slaves.³¹

The Georgia volunteers pitched their tents on the east bank of the St. Johns just below Picolatti. Almost immediately Newnan reported an alarming discontent among his men. The soldiers under Captain Fort demanded transports for a return home. Since the trip from St.

Marys to Picolatti had consumed almost half of their sixty-day terms, an immediate departure must be made or else the soldiers would not reach home before the expiration of their enlistment. Sadly Smith wrote: "If you cannot effect the objects that brought you in the Province in consequence of desertion . . . what a disgraceful story it will be to go abroad."[32]

Smith urged Newnan to strike one blow. Two parties of seventy-five men each could destroy two or three of the nearest Indian towns. Captain William Cone with forty Patriots, men who knew the Indian country, would accompany Newnan. By striking the Indian towns and then marching swiftly to waiting transports on the St. Johns, the volunteers could be returned to Georgia before expiration of their enlistments.[33] Immediately after Smith dispatched his letter to Newnan, a rider came with information that Captain Cone had been ordered from Kingsley's plantation to Camp New Hope.[34] Without experienced guides Newnan's volunteers could never find the Indian villages and the contemplated expedition must be delayed until Cone could reach New Hope, receive new orders, and arrive at Picolatti.

There were other delays: Colonel Newnan had too few horses for an expedition into the wilderness; thirty-seven volunteers lay ill and the colonel himself burned with fever. But he was determined. "If I thought the scoundrels I command would not desert, and would extend their terms of service –," Newnan wrote, and then stopped, for he knew all of them would go home. Nevertheless, he thought there would be time for a short foray into Indian country. He would march as soon as food could be collected, although he admitted "that any officer who trusts his honor and reputation to the three months militia alone, will be in danger of losing both."[35]

Newnan camped at Fatio's plantation a few miles south of Picolatti, waiting for horses and recuperating from fever. Most of his command were too debilitated for an active campaign without assistance from cavalry.[36] Colonel Smith chafed because of the delay. An expedition into the Seminole country would pull the Indians back into the wilderness and relieve him from possible entrapment. He complained bitterly that "Volunteers for one or two months only add to the difficulty of procuring supplies without rendering any essential service, as by the time arrangements can be made for any important enterprise their term of service will have expired."[37]

But Smith admitted his debt to the volunteers. Their presence prevented the Indians from cutting his communication line to the St. Johns. Even so, he found it advisable to send a strong military escort with every wagon train. This reduced his force before St. Augustine and he realized the impossibility of holding his position, for an attack would be sudden – it might come at any hour.[38]

On September 9 a Spanish deserter slipped into the American camp. The soldiers thought him a spy, but he told a straightforward story of an attack on Picolatti in which twenty-six Indians participated. After burning the buildings there, the Indians disappeared into the swamp east of the St. Johns. It was inconceivable, Smith thought, that twenty-six Indians would be so bold when the camp fires of the 250 volunteers could be seen from Picolatti. Nevertheless he asked Newnan to investigate and also to set the day when he would march against the Seminoles.[39]

However amazing the story seemed to Smith, it was true. Indians had suddenly appeared in Picolatti, their war whoops throwing the picket guard into temporary confusion. Before the men rallied, the storehouse and "skinn house" were in flames. In the ensuing attack one Indian fell and the others ran into the woods where they lurked, a potential danger to the supply trains which moved between the American camp and the St. Johns.[40]

Also on September 9, Armstrong, a Patriot employed in supplying cattle for Smith, met an Indian scouting party. The cattle driver's body, mutilated and scalped, was found less than three miles from Colonel Smith's headquarters. Indians and Negroes were growing bolder in spite of the volunteers.

Nevertheless optimism reigned in the American camp. Captain Fort arrived there on September 11 with information that Newnan at last had horses and would march for King Payne's town the following day. A wagon train was scheduled for departure on September 12 to load supplies which had arrived at Fort Stallings. On that afternoon drivers stood by their two wagons ready for the difficult twenty-mile trip to Davis Creek and Fort Stallings on the St. Johns. Marine Captain John Williams with one non-commissioned officer and twenty privates held the bridles of their mounts. Captain Fort, who was returning with dispatches for Colonel Newnan, made the twenty-second man of the guard. For some miles on the route west the small party traversed rough dry terrain and then the swamp closed in around them. Twelve miles of alternating stretches of mucky land and sand lay ahead. The rough road twisted and turned to keep on higher ground. As the wagons entered Twelve Mile Swamp the sun faded away in the west, and in the ensuing deep twilight the experienced teamsters skirted the swampy places, guided mainly by their knowledge of the trail. Lights were forbidden since their glow might bring an Indian attack.

Unknown to Captain Williams a detachment of seventy Negroes and six Indians had already spotted the train. Cautiously they followed the creaking wagons and snapping whips of the teamsters. When light from a rising moon outlined the American marines, the Negroes closed in for attack. At the command of their leader, a free Negro named Prince, they charged the American rear, and the deep guttural shouts of the Negroes almost drowned the shrill war whoops of the Indians.

The attackers directed their first fire at the horses and officers and numbers of wounded and dying horses blocked the path ahead. The advancing Negroes were only twenty paces behind. Captain Williams ordered a charge, but as the men began to move, he fell severely wounded; and though he urged his marines forward, other shots struck him as Captain Fort carried him from the line of fire. Fort made a pallet for Williams and assumed command of the guards. Then he ordered another charge; but the regulars, lacking confidence in a volunteer officer, held their ground.

The Americans fell back, carrying Captain Williams and leading the few uninjured horses. During the retreat Captain Fort fell and Williams quivered as additional musket balls thudded into his body. Wounded Captain Fort made the cover of the nearby swamp, and there the soldiers re-formed for defense where their position afforded excellent protection. Behind them lay an impenetrable swamp, trees gave cover from the Negro fire, and moonlight outlined the attackers.

One man failed to reach the swamp. This non-commissioned officer was shot and scalped in sight of his horrified men. On the trail, the Negroes ransacked the wagons, raising angry cries on finding them almost empty. Led by Prince they charged directly toward the swamp, but as they came within twenty paces, Captain Williams miraculously revived and ordered a charge. His men responded nobly; their shouts, shots, and bayonets threw the Negroes back in confusion, yelling like devils.

The entire action lasted only twenty-five minutes. During the remainder of the night the Negroes and Indians milled around the captured wagons, while the Americans nursed their wounded in the swamp. A few soldiers mounted the horses and slipped away for Fort Stallings and help, while the others remained as guards for the wounded. Near morning the Negroes and Indians placed their injured men in the wagons and headed for St. Augustine.

A detachment from Fort Stallings found the battered Americans that morning. In addition to the scalpless non-commissioned officer, five privates and Captain Williams were wounded. Captain Williams suffered from eight wounds: a broken right arm, a ball in his thigh near the groin, his stomach punctured, three holes in the right hand, one in his shoulder, and one in his left leg. Gently he was taken to Fort Stallings and from there by water to Camp New Hope. The courageous marine officer and former commander of occupied Fernandina wrote a friend: "You may expect that I am in a dreadful situation, though I hope I shall recover in a few months."[41] He was beyond hope, however, but lingered in excruciating pain until September 29, when he found peace in death.

The marines' defeat cut Colonel Smith's supply line. With Negroes boldly operating from St. Augustine, supplies could not reach the American detachment at Moosa Old Fort unless guarded by a large force. Since Colonel Smith did not have such a force at his disposal, a retreat to the St. Johns, where Commodore Campbell's gunboats controlled the river, was his only recourse.

On learning of Captain Williams' fate Smith dispatched an express rider to Newnan. "I wish you without delay to join me with eighty or ninety of your men and all the horses you have or can obtain," Smith ordered: "Without your aid I shall not be able to secure our baggage and save the sick, fifteen or twenty of which are unable to march."[42] Colonel Newnan moved quickly. At ten o'clock on September 14 Smith burned his thatch-roofed huts and began his retreat. Spaniards in St. Augustine danced joyfully on sighting the rising smoke. That night the colonel reached Fort Stallings safely with all his men and most of his equipment, though some essential camp baggage was destroyed because Newnan had not sent a sufficient number of horses.[43] Had Kindelan with his superior forces attacked the retreating Americans, a catastrophic rout, if not capture of the entire force, would have resulted.

The Spanish governor was content, for he had more than won his point. Three months before, Kindelan's demand on Smith for an immediate withdrawal to the St. Johns had been answered by the colonel with threats of death on Spaniards venturing out of St. Augustine. Without firing a shot, without using a soldier who could be identified as Spanish, Kindelan forced Smith to lift the siege of St. Augustine and seek safety on the St. Johns.

Indians and Negroes accomplished the feat for the Spanish governor. While he remained in St. Augustine, they had destroyed the Patriots as a fighting and food-gathering organization. Then with supplies furnished by Spain they had struck Smith's life line, and, undaunted by the presence of 250 Georgia volunteers, had won by their boldness. The American detachment of regulars nursed its sick and wounded in its camp on the St. Johns, protected by gunboats riding the river, while the disillusioned Georgia volunteers made preparations for a return home.

Newnan Meets Defeat

AFTER HIS RETREAT FROM ST. AUgustine, and smarting from wounded pride, Smith dreamed paper plans for an offensive. In letters he praised the bravery of volunteers and soldiers in East Florida. All the marines of Captain Williams' defeated guard acted well except Hampton, whom Smith described as being "I fear of the dunghill family."[1] With all the praise he bestowed on individuals and companies, the fact remained that an American detachment had been outmaneuvered and defeated.

Smith cried for revenge, for an opportunity to regain lost prestige. He desired 300 additional men to augment his detachment of 120 and the 150 volunteers. With a total force of 570 and some reserves as allowance for the "sick, lame and lazy," he could again invest St. Augustine. He would station twenty men at Picolatti, forty at a supply depot on Six Mile Creek, forty at Twelve Mile Swamp, and 150 at his former encampment before St. Augustine. Nearer the town he would send 220 men with heavy cannon to build redoubts opposite Solano's Ferry. With his forces thus stationed his supply lines would be secure and communications between the Indians and Spanish could be prevented by mounted scouting parties. If British ships threw supplies into St. Augustine, Smith could act under the congressional authorization to preoccupy East Florida; St. Augustine would be starved and bombarded into submission.[2]

Only an act of Congress and a large reinforcement, however, could secure the capitulation of defensible St. Augustine. In reality Smith's position near Fort Stallings on the St. Johns was tenable only because of American naval control of the river. One British brig off the St. Johns bar would send Smith in precipitant, disastrous retreat overland for the Georgia border. Almost half of his regular soldiers lay ill and useless. Tens of the volunteers with him were sick, and most of Colonel Newnan's 250 militia were packing their haversacks for a return home. Rather than taking the offensive the colonel would be pressed to hold his place in East Florida. Newnan, on the other hand, urged his Georgians to extend their services for one campaign against the nearby Indian towns, and with booty and honor, march home as heroes. But most of them had lost faith in him as a commander. Reports of desertions in the volunteer ranks reached Governor Mitchell in September and he concluded that the Georgia troops would not advance into the Indian country.[3] Newnan, Colonel Smith stated, "had become so unpopular with the Detachment that they could not be prevailed on to volunteer under him a few days longer to go against the Indians."[4] Indeed, the Georgians would not remain as guards while Smith built his camp huts on the St. Johns and reorganized his forces. The term of the volunteers expired in a week, and regardless of need or honor they would sail for home.

Newnan, however, would not admit failure. After guarding Smith's regulars in their retreat from Moosa Old Fort, Newnan hurried back to Picolatti and set September 19 for the beginning of his offensive march.[5] Adamant refusal of his men to extend their term of enlistment forced a change in plans. Every persuasive effort of the colonel touched responsive chords in only seventy-five of his 250 men.[6] Although Smith thought an expedition foolhardy unless most of the volunteers would re-enlist for ten or fifteen days, Newnan would not listen. "He certainly does not exercise his thinking faculties much," was Smith's caustic comment.[7]

The morale of the Georgia volunteers which was so high when they departed from Milledgeville and Dublin had progressively declined with each week of service. Their voyage down the Georgia coast to St. Marys had been easy compared with the hardships previously endured by the Savannah Blues and Volunteer Guards. On July 29 Newnan's men, encamped at Point Petre, were briefed on the duties ahead. As almost a month had passed since their original sixty-day enlistment, a movement into East Florida depended on their willingness to extend their terms or re-enlist.

Newnan bombarded the volunteers with propaganda. He dwelled on the barbarous cruelty of Indians, the danger facing Georgians as long as Indians and Negroes remained in East Florida, and the heroic welcome awaiting those who participated in the coming victory. He appealed to the volunteers' economic interests. Besides service and honor the Georgians would divide and appropriate the fertile Indian lands. It was reported that Governor Mitchell had promised victorious militiamen the land, and this was "a powerful inducement for re-volunteering."[8]

Georgians had heard many reports of the territory in possession of the Seminoles. According to rumor the Indians held two large areas: Big Hammock, situated along a river which flowed into Tampa Bay, and Lotchaway Hammock, a fifty-three mile long and sixteen-mile wide strip in Central Florida. "The salubrity of the Air of East Florida, the facility with which the tropical plants might be introduced and naturalized to its climate, the great variety and quantity of fish in its Rivers and on its Sea Coast, and its many other advantages are so notorious, that as soon as the Country becomes a part of the U. States, the contention will be, who shall first locate the lands in it."[9]

Newnan clinched his appeal with one final argument. He had the requisite instruments with him for surveying land, and the sight of these surveying instruments "stimulated his men not a little."[10] Without exception the men re-enlisted for sixty days from July 29. One impressed volunteer wrote an appealing letter to his friends back home: "many idle men should join us. . . . If re-inforcements can reach us by Sept. 20 or Oct. 1st it will be in time. Such another opportunity will perhaps never present itself for young men to advance their fortune in so short a time."[11]

Transports moved a detachment of eager men under command of Captain Tomlinson Fort into East Florida and up the St. Johns River, while Newnan with the remaining volunteers marched overland to the same river.[12] Mid-August passed, however, before the Georgians bivouacked a few miles south of Picolatti. There the volunteers went into camp on the east bank of the St. Johns within striking distance of the Alachua Indian towns. A three-day march would bring the Georgians into the heart of King Payne's country.

Newnan met Colonel Smith at Moosa on August 21 and so impressed the colonel that he wrote Thomas Bourke, the commissary agent at Savannah: "His men are stout, active fellows and will fight well, but they have no shoes, canteens or camp equippage of any kind. I have ordered them to Picolatti to prepare for their march against the Indians, but I am fearful their term of service will have expired before they can procure the necessary equipments."[13]

When Newnan rejoined his command his troubles began. August, of all months, was a poor season to introduce men to the charms of Florida. Heavy rains which pelted them en route gave way to a blistering sun which steamed the wet earth. Many of the men were dismayed at the appearance of the land, for although the topsoil was apparently deep and filled with humus along the river banks, thousands of matted roots lay under the surface, and back-breaking work with ax and grub hoe would be a prerequisite to farming. Yet reports of cleared land and plain in the Indian hammocks, ready for the plow, encouraged some of the volunteers.

Of more immediate concern was food. In a country reputedly overrun with game and with willing Patriots to round up and slaughter the myriads of cattle, little attention had been given the problem of feeding 250 men. The Patriots had been dispersed by Indian attacks and deer had disappeared into endless forests of pine, oak, and scrub palmetto. Visions of fertile Indian land did not fill a present emptiness of stomach.

Newnan could not obtain sufficient corn or mills to grind what he had. Food, camp supplies, and ammunition for a week-long expedition into the Indian country could not be found. Without horses and pack animals the volunteers would be unable to move with the necessary speed. Director McIntosh of the Patriots answered Newnan's plea for horses by attempting to confiscate those of the Loyalists in Fernandina and immediately ran into a feud with Captain Massias. Until horses arrived Newnan was immobilized at Picolatti.

Detailed accounts of Indian barbarity and boldness disconcerted men who had been fearless in the safety of their Georgia homes. Tempers became short. Newnan severely reprimanded one of his captains as a "conceited, opinionative [man] and wanting in the feelings . . . and even the courage necessary for an officer. . . ."[14] From that time Captain John Humphries, the disciplined officer, agitated against Newnan, and the volunteers split into antagonistic camps.

Soldiers became disgusted with the few Patriots who hung around camp. As one volunteer expressed it, "if the whole world were drained to the last dregs, there could never be found such another collection as the constituted authorities of this province, I mean the *Patriots* — although we protect their lives and property, they would willingly receive every soldier's knapsack in the detachment for a quart of milk."[15] Patriot leaders had run to Georgia and had given such examples of timidity that the people were driving their cattle over the St. Marys. "I wish to God an end could be put to our troubles in some way," exclaimed an unidentified Patriot; "I am almost ready to set fire to my house and go off by the light to some other country."[16]

Georgia volunteers were ready for some country, any country other than Florida. Between thirty and forty lay ill with "inflammatory complaints" and others sweated with fever.[17] Feeble and hardy alike turned away from Newnan's pleas for re-enlistment. Almost 175 of them refused to follow their colonel, demanding instead transports for home.

Yet by September 24 Newnan had increased his volunteer force more than fifty per cent over his original seventy-five men. Nine additional Georgians, who had either experienced a change of heart or had been left by the departing transports, signed on for three weeks. Against his better judgment Colonel Smith sent Newnan twenty-three militiamen, and Captain William Cone with nine of his Patriots volunteered as guides. In all, Colonel Newnan's force numbered 117 and his slave Isaac, a young boy.[18] This detachment was adequately supplied with powder and shot, but had only twelve horses and food for only four days. Optimistic Newnan expected to find an ample supply of food in the corn cribs and cattle of King Payne. With his small force Newnan planned to hit the Alachua towns after a lightning march, destroy as much property as possible, and retreat before the Indians mobilized against him. His expedition "was courageous but ill-conceived — the force too small, the distance too great, and the provisions insufficient."[19]

On Thursday afternoon September 24 Newnan crossed the St. Johns and headed southwest toward the Indian country. Men marched in Indian file with Captain Humphries' company of riflemen in the lead; Captain Fort's company, which in the absence of the wounded captain served under Lieutenant Abram B. Fannin, occupied the center position. Newnan and his slave boy Isaac marched with Fannin's men. Behind them Lieutenant John H. Broadnax, who commanded Captain Thomas Coleman's company, and Captain Cone's Patriots, protected the rear of the advancing detachment. Not far from the west bank of the St. Johns, Newnan bivouacked for the night. The three remnants of once full companies encamped in a rough triangle, in the center of which the baggage and camp accouterments were deposited, while the soldiers of each company occupied the angles of the triangle. Men slept with their feet pointed outward from the camp center and bedded down fully clothed with their muskets within reach. If guards sounded an alarm during the night, the officers were instructed to bring their companies up on the right and left of the company facing the enemy and fight in Indian style until ready for a concerted frontal and enveloping attack on the foe.

That night's sleep, however, was disturbed by nothing more than the sounds of curious, frightened animals of the forest. In the morning Newnan briefed his officers. An advance scouting party would precede the main force, a rear guard would follow behind, and whenever thick palmetto and scrub necessitated, scouts would fan out on the right and left flanks of the marching column. Should the advance scouts sight Indians, Humphries' riflemen would file off to the right, Fannin's company would move forward to occupy the center, and Broadnax's men would file off to the left. When the detachment formed a crescent and the order was given, the soldiers would charge the Indians. In that charge the left and right would endeavor to circle the enemy's flanks and close in upon him from all sides.

These arrangements for bivouacking at night and marching during the day were faithfully executed. Because of the open pine forests, flanking guards or scouts were seldom needed. At times thick growths of palmetto or canebrakes closed in on the marching men and at other points along the route of march high, firm land became a narrow strip between two lakes or swampy areas. Scouts approached such natural places of ambuscade with vigilance, but as each point was passed without sign of Indians the soldiers relaxed. On Friday and Saturday the detachment marched deeper and deeper into the Seminole country.

As the volunteers broke camp on Sunday morning officers issued warnings. Guides who knew the country well estimated the first Indian town only eight miles distant. Conferences and mapping of an attack delayed the morning march, and it was almost ten before the advance guard moved ahead. Fifteen minutes later they sighted a big swamp which extended for miles on their left and at the same instant they saw the Indians. As prearranged, Captain Humphries' company filed off to the right and in so doing circled too far. Between them and the approaching Indians lay a sink hole which effectively protected Humphries' men and also eliminated them as a factor in the ensuing battle. (Newnan later wondered if the wide circling was chance misadventure or planned calculation.) The two other companies moved forward as scheduled.

Before them seventy-five or more Indians waited in shocked surprise. Some of the braves were mounted. King Payne, erect and warlike on a prancing white horse, barked orders. As the Americans saw Payne in action they questioned the reputed age of the octogenarian chief. Evidently the Indians had no forewarning of an American expedition, for their bodies were unpainted, their packs were on their backs, and their guns were not loaded. The destination and purpose of the Indian party remains a conjecture — perhaps they were headed for St. Augustine and a conference with Governor Kindelan or even planning a raid on the St. Johns plantations.

As Newnan's men formed a battle line, the Indians prepared for action by falling back, "unslinging their packs, priming their rifles, and each man taking his place." Trees gave individuals protection. Indian warriors found cover and the advancing Americans ran from pine to pine. When the two forces were 130 yards apart the Indians commenced firing. Newnan ordered a charge, which was accomplished so swiftly, the soldiers firing all the while, that the yet unprepared Indians retired "with the greatest precipitation." But they soon held. In less than 200 yards they found protection behind trees and checked the American advance.

For hours the battle raged. Newnan's volunteers made repeated charges, reorganizing between each assault for another advance. Some Indians circled the American flank, seeking to recapture their packs, and ran into Captain Humphries' men, who prevented the braves from securing their lost supplies or getting at the American wounded and war materiel. By early afternoon the Indians held a half-mile line along the swamp. Since the Indians rested with their backs to this impenetrable morass the battle ended in sporadic musket fire.

The engagement lasted two and one-half hours. Nine Americans were wounded, two of them mortally, and one man lay dead. The enemy's losses were considerable. Newnan saw seven of them fall, two near the swamp; but "the rest our men had the curiosity to scalp." Payne was among the wounded. He fell like a stricken eagle and his men pulled their injured chief behind the cypress trees of the swamp.

Newnan's detachment remained among the pines just beyond musket range. In the shadows of big cypress trees the Indians took out their war paint and adorned their bodies in color of death. From time to time chieftains gathered as in conference. As the afternoon shadows lengthened small parties of Indians and Negroes reinforced their painted brothers – Newnan estimated the total enemy force at 200 or more.

For five hours the battlefield was unnaturally quiet. Occasionally a rifle sounded and an Indian responded by discharging a gun. As the sun sent its last rays through the trees, abruptly from the swamp came an indescribable frenzy of sound, as though all the animals of Florida had assembled in convention. The cry of the panther and wildcat mingled with that of wolf and bear. Here was the roar of the alligator and there the squawk of the hawk. To the accompaniment of this crescendo of animal calls an Indian chief, probably Bowlegs, advanced on his haunches, weaving to right and left as a serpent approaching an unsuspecting field mouse. Animal cries changed to war whoops; Indians and Negroes charged. In the twilight, and except when in motion, it was difficult to distinguish them from stumps. At 200 yards they halted and commenced firing.

These antics brought no response from the Americans, and the Indians moved closer, making all the while the most "frantic gestures." Then from behind trees and logs the soldiers opened fire and the Indians withdrew into their swampy fortress.

Newnan debated the advisability of ordering a charge. Advantage rested with the Indians. Their force outnumbered his almost two to one, they held a half-mile defensive line which could be approached only by direct charge, and their towns with supplies were nearby; while Newnan, who had planned on eating Indian corn and beef, had no source of food. From time to time the Indians made other advances, direct and flanking movements, the latter being directed at the camp accouterments and the wounded. Fighting continued until almost eight o'clock when in the darkness random shots were answered by fire directed at the preceding flash until finally all was still.

After fighting, waiting, and fasting the entire day soldiers welcomed the night. Two more men were killed and one wounded in the twilight engagements. The uninjured flopped behind their covering trees worn out by nervous exhaustion. But there was no rest. Throughout the night they worked or stood guard. By daybreak they had thrown up a breastwork of logs and earth with portholes for defensive muskets. Now it would be difficult for the Indians to take the Americans by assault, and equally, if not more difficult for the volunteers to retreat from their fortification.

Newnan realized his plight. During the night he sent an appeal to Colonel Smith by Captain John Whitaker who rode away on the best of the twelve horses. In the confusion and darkness six other men, one of them the doctor, mounted horses and spurred them toward the safety of civilization. Newnan was left with only five horses, not enough to carry the seriously wounded. Food supplies were almost gone and with Indians roaming the forests, securing game was impossible. Men would not suffer from thirst, for water lay a few feet underground; but they could be starved into submission.

On Monday morning, September 28, the day following the battles, soldiers waited in excited dread of an attack. None came. On Wednesday, however, Indian snipers fired into the fort and continued to harass the embattled Americans day after day.

Haggard, discontented, hungry men talked of deserting in the night rather than facing another and another day, to die eventually of hunger or be captured by the Indians. Scheming Captain Humphries encouraged disaffection by whispering of the hordes of Indians in Florida; more and more soldiers were ill with fever and others would soon be too weak for marching; rain and wind presaged a hurricane and colder weather, and relief would never come from Colonel Smith. Holding a breastwork in the wilderness in expectation of that possibility was a stubborn, futile act.

Newnan heard the rumblings of discontent. On Friday he dispatched another letter to Smith. "I am now intrenched within six miles of the [Seminole] nation and must sacrifice the sick and wounded or perish for want of provisions, unless you can send me a reinforcement immediately." Newnan concluded his appeal with a short, meaningful sentence: "We commence eating horses tonight."[20] Horsemeat quieted the men temporarily. Then Indian sharpshooters killed the remaining horses. As soon as the bones of animals were picked clean, starvation would be the only alternative to capture.

Captain Humphries now found an attentive audience. Newnan held out for delay: by leaving the breastwork the detachment would give up all hope of aid; by not keeping faith with the promise made to Captain Whitaker, the expected relief party might be surrounded and cut to pieces by Indians. Newnan talked in vain. Reluctantly he admitted defeat. He had a choice of leading his men in retreat or remaining alone.

He ordered litters constructed for the seriously wounded men. Humphries objected. Better to let the wounded die, he said, than endanger all by attempting to save them. On this point Newnan refused to budge – the wounded would be evacuated.

At nine o'clock on Sunday night, October 4, the retreat began. Soldiers took turns carrying the five litters with wounded men. Three other men hobbled along each painful step supported by companions. Within a few hours men who had complained of staying in the fortification began to grumble about the hardships of moving through Florida forests in darkness. After eight miles the soldiers halted and Newnan ordered the construction of log breastworks.

Sergeant Major John C. Reese and one private sped quietly on through the night with another dispatch for Smith. Newnan promised Reese that the volunteers would remain on the spot until aid arrived from Picolatti.

Had Newnan and his men known one secret, they would have hanged Captain Humphries on the most available oak limb. Captain Whitaker, who had been sent back for help on September 27, delivered Newnan's letter to Smith. The colonel could spare few men, for more than 100 Indians and Negroes in the vicinity of his camp were planning an attack.[21] Yet Smith answered the call of men in distress. By using every available horse, he mounted twenty-five men and sped them to Newnan's rescue. On October 1 a wind of near hurricane force prevented the men from fording the St. Johns,[22] but they crossed the river a few days later and spurred their horses forward. Two hours after Newnan's detachment left the breastwork on Sunday night, the horsemen galloped into the abandoned camp. They came by a different route from that used by the departing volunteers; and although Newnan had had the forethought to send two men along the path which the relief party used, they either missed the mounted men or took to the woods for safety without a thought of accomplishing their purpose. When the twenty-five horsemen discovered the evacuated breastworks, they hastened back along the route of their arrival.[23]

Smith had also ordered Midshipman T. W. Wyman, commander of gunboat 164, to anchor his vessel at Picolatti and remain there five or six days.[24] This order was altered later; Wyman would remain at Picolatti until the fate of Newnan was known. At reveille and tattoo the heavy guns of the boat should be discharged as a signal to Newnan.[25]

Meanwhile the volunteers at their second breastworks revived in spirit with the dawn of October 5. Captain Humphries renewed his mutinous agitation. He approached a number of privates and even Captain Cone, who suffered from a slight wound. Retreat during the previous night had been untimely, he whispered, for the Florida terrain was too difficult to traverse in darkness. In daylight miles could be covered with speed, and the rushing wind and beating rain of the hurricane would prevent an Indian attack.

Newnan pleaded with his men: marching through timberland during a raging hurricane was in itself dangerous, for they had already attempted one march and found it unendurable; by remaining where they were Sergeant Reese would find them. Then horses would be provided for the wounded and food for the hungry.

The soldiers could not be convinced. Wet, hungry, hopeless, they demanded movement. Newnan again faced the alternative of leading them or remaining alone.

About three that afternoon the march began. As before, soldiers manned the litters in turn. Newnan himself was so weak from fever that he could not shoulder his own gun, and he marched with the rear guard, while his little slave boy ran ahead with the scouts. After five miles of snail-like progress the detachment entered an area where the hurricane force had snapped off many pine trees. Hundreds of them lay on either side of the trail, affording excellent protection for Indians. And sure enough heads appeared and disappeared among the fallen pine branches.

Without waiting for the main force of volunteers the Indians began a premature fire. So sudden was the attack that the soldiers were caught defenseless and four of the advance guard fell at once. The Spanish guide was killed instantly, and two others, one of them the boy Isaac, were mortally wounded. The fourth man escaped but at a horrible penalty. A musket ball hit him a glancing blow and while he lay unconscious an Indian neatly lifted his scalp with swift, skillful strokes of a hunting knife.

Newnan saved the wounded man, for when the colonel heard the first shot he ordered a charge. The volunteers put the Indians to rout, many of them dropping their guns, and the small attacking party ran off without rallying for a second attack. Fighting was over in less than fifteen minutes. Newnan ordered a temporary breastwork thrown up as a precaution against a possible renewal of battle.

When the Indians failed to reappear, the volunteers pushed through fallen timber in search of killed or wounded redskins. They found three dead, and while they were scalping these Indians, the wounded volunteer revived and called for help. His companions found him, scalped but alive. This scalpless wonder made it back to Picolatti and safety, where he became the cynosure of all eyes.[26]

At ten o'clock on October 6 the volunteers broke camp. After a march of five miles they camped between two ponds and constructed defense works of logs and dirt to protect their front and rear. By this time the men were too worn out for protests or rebellion. They willingly waited for relief, while living on "gophers, alligators, and palmetto stocks."

Meanwhile Sergeant Reese had reached Picolatti. Only fifteen horses could be secured for a relief expedition and on October 7 Smith ordered fifteen men away toward Newnan.[27] A few days later fourteen of the horsemen found him and food and medical supplies resuscitated the hungry and wounded. With horses for the sick and injured the volunteers proceeded to the St. Johns where gunboat 164 convoyed them to Kingsley's plantation.

They disembarked about noon on October 11,[28] eighteen days after they had set off from Picolatti. For most of that time they had endured terrific hardship in the Indian country, fought three battles, and suffered from almost a week of sniping fire. By Newnan's own account he had eight men killed, nine wounded, and eight missing. He estimated the Indians killed and wounded at fifty, but actually specified only fourteen instances when Indians fell from the Georgians' fire. The expedition was a miserable failure.

Human nature, however, has a remarkable facility for twisting fact into fiction. Within a few days the volunteers had won a glorious victory and Kingsley's Laurel Grove Plantation "was hansomely decorated with scalps" by the celebrating Georgians.[29] They claimed as many as forty Indians killed and a total of seventy killed and wounded.[30] King Payne had been killed, according to laudatory newspaper accounts, Bowlegs wounded, and three other principal chiefs slain.[31]

The actual number of Indians killed and wounded was unknown. For more than a century the fiction of King Payne's death has been perpetuated in historical lore. In reality the aged chieftain recovered from his wound and died a few months later of old age,[32] although his wound undoubtedly weakened his body and hastened his death. In this sense it may be said that he received a mortal wound in battle with the volunteers.

An unanswered question remains. Why did the Indians allow the volunteers to escape? If the warriors which Newnan surprised on September 27 were on their way to join the Spaniards in an attack on the American regulars, as Smith believed,[33] why did they not annihilate the Georgians? The probability is that Payne lacked ammunition and was on his way to St. Augustine for the guns and powder promised by Governor Kindelan. In the first attack on September 27, unprepared Indians dropped their packs and lost almost all of their reserve ammunition. For almost five hours after termination of the initial battle Indian guns were silent. The braves were probably out of powder and waiting for men from their towns to come with a meager supply. After the second attack, the Indians did not fire on the Georgians for two days.

Additional reasons partially explain the Indian failure. Georgians behind log and earthen fortifications aimed their muskets accurately. Notwithstanding reports of their ability, Indians were poor fighters; even Newnan admitted the Negroes gave him the most trouble. "Negroes, who are their best soldiers" was Newnan's succinct description of colored troops, which by Georgia theory could not fight. The wounding of Payne and Bowlegs (if he was wounded) would account for some disorganization among the black and red warriors. The hurricane might be a more logical reason for their allowing Newnan's escape. When the gods were angry, superstitious Indians took no chances with fate.

Newnan fled from the wrath of the Indians and ran into that of Smith. During those endless days and nights in the forest with warriors eager for their scalps on all sides and the rain pouring down upon them, men wondered why Colonel Smith did not rush a relief party. When finally it came there were only fourteen horsemen, an insufficient number to carry all the sick and wounded who considered themselves too feeble for marching. When Smith had called for aid on September 12 so that he could retreat from St. Augustine in safety, Newnan had given everything from his command. The contrasting actions of the two commanders may have loosened Newnan's tongue.

At least this was reported to Smith, and the colonel flew into a violent rage. He penned Newnan a blistering letter. The reported observations, Smith stated, injured his reputation as an officer and, added to the disrespectful way Newnan had acted in other instances, demanded an explanation. "Be assured, sir," Smith concluded, "whatever may have been my forbearance for the sake of harmony, my prerogatives as an officer and feelings as a man shall be respected."[34]

Newnan read the letter with amazement. He conquered his feelings and replied calmly but firmly. He wrote of his high regard for Smith, of the colonel's interest in the safety and reputation of the Georgia militia, and of their mutual desire for harmony. "I know what is due to the prerogatives and feelings of a superior officer," Newnan stated, "and if I have violated either it was unwillingly done and proceeded from the irritation of the moment; at the same time I must believe that you are as willing to respect the feelings of an officer under your command as to exact a regard for your own."[35] Newnan forwarded his letter by Captain Cone, who was to explain everything to Colonel Smith.

The Georgia commander did more than explain. In his desire to avenge his defeat, he persuaded forty of his volunteers to re-enlist for a second campaign. These together with forty-two mounted Patriots and the 100 militia which Major General Floyd was bringing into East Florida would assure a second expedition against the Indians and the destruction of their towns. Colonel Smith was a soldier – severe, impatient, quick to take offense, and also quick to forget it. Newnan's letters and his ambition to lead a second expedition against the Indians completely won the army colonel. "For your bravery and that of your men all due credit is given and honorable mention has been made of them in all my communications to Head Quarters," Smith told Newnan. He also informed Governor Mitchell, "The Colo. has certainly acquitted himself well as a fighting character. . . ."[36] In harmony the regular and militia colonels made plans for a second Seminole expedition.

The mercurial Indians, however, now sued for peace. After they had thrown Newnan back in confusion, their wounded King Payne nursed his injury while he planned a general Indian uprising. Heretofore only a few tribes with their Negro allies had participated in the fighting. A union of all Florida Indians would bring together more than 1,000 warriors. With supplies from St. Augustine, they could destroy the whites in East Florida.

When Payne recovered he called a general conference.[37] Chieftains of all the Seminoles attended and the Wolf Warrior, headman of the Mickausee Indians, spoke for his tribes. Wolf Warrior rejected the idea of union, and even the Seminole chiefs at best, were lukewarm. The Indians could see little profit in war. All white settlements in East Florida except those on the islands had already been looted and destroyed.

The feeble chief accepted defeat. If he could not secure unity in war, then the only recourse was a mission to Benjamin Hawkins with a request for peace. On this plan the assembled chiefs agreed. Emissaries hastened to the Indian agent Hawkins; the Seminoles would deliver all property, including slaves taken from Georgians, if Colonel Hawkins would secure peace. While the Indian delegation conferred with the agent, news arrived of the sudden death of King Payne.

Although his passing did not seriously deter peace negotiations, it did break the heart of his brother, Bowlegs. At his instigation Payne had led the Alachua and Alligator tribes against the white men. However often Bowlegs assured himself that his brother had not died of battle wounds, the disturbing thought remained that, had it not been for war, Payne might still be alive.

That Bowlegs gave the Indian funeral oration for his brother is within the realm of possibility. "Do not grieve," he told the assembled

Indians. "Misfortune will happen to the wisest and best men. Death will come and always comes out of season. It is the command of the Great Spirit, and all nations and people must obey. What is passed and cannot be prevented should not be grieved for.

"What a misfortune for me," Bowlegs whispered, "that I could not have died this day, instead of you. What a trifling loss our people would have sustained in my death; how great in yours.

"I shall wrap you in a robe and hoist you to a slender scaffold where the whistling winds shall take your spirit to the happy hunting grounds."

Bowlegs turned again to his people and spoke with the strong, powerful voice of command. "Go and rest, my people. This is not Payne. It is a body of clay which I shall care for, not from love of it but from memory of the spirit which once dwelled in it. Go and rest, my people."[38]

Thus ended one phase of the Indian conflict. Payne was dead and his Indian people had tired of war. The Georgians and other Southerners, however, had only begun to fight. They were determined to avenge the defeat of Newnan and possess the Indian land. In these twin goals they were supported by Colonel Smith and, after some hesitation, by the Madison administration.

Plan of Conquest

Newnan's enthusiasm for a second expedition against the Seminoles pleased Colonel Thomas A. Smith. A man who was undaunted after more than two weeks of hardship and insubordination in the Indian country, and who could persuade almost half of his men to re-enlist after their humiliating defeat, had those "never say die" qualities of a soldier and an officer. Never again would Smith question the motives and abilities of Newnan; instead he assigned him an important place in a second expeditionary force.

On October 20 Smith advised Mitchell of his plans for destroying the Indians and capturing St. Augustine. McIntosh and the Patriots were moving with renewed vigor; already forty of their mounted men camped near New Hope. Major General John Floyd with approximately 120 men was expected within a few days. Floyd's militia, the Patriots, Newnan's forty volunteers, and a small detachment of regulars would make a force of more than 200 men. With most of this detachment mounted, Smith considered the destruction of all the Indian towns in East Florida a certainty.[1] On concluding a successful campaign against the Seminoles, the American forces would surround and capture St. Augustine.

Floyd reached Camp New Hope during the last week of October. A count of his men together with Patriots and Newnan's volunteers disclosed a maximum of 170 soldiers fit and willing for duty. Since estimates of the Alachua and Alligator Indians with their Negro allies ran as high as 240, Floyd refused to lead an expedition. If he struck the Indians, he wanted to give them a devastating blow. By making a horrible example of those who had taken the warpath, all the Indians of East Florida would be cowed into neutrality. An inadequate force with a consequent disastrous result might bring the various Indian tribes into a militant alliance, for the red man's martial spirit thrived on prospective victory. Therefore wisdom dictated defense unless an offensive could be overwhelming.

Smith, however, would not abandon his project. On receipt of orders "not to act offensively against St. Augustine,"[2] he threw his full weight behind an Indian offensive. Since he had American gunboats protecting his communications and most of his men had recovered from their summer complaints, he felt secure from a possible Spanish thrust. He therefore "volunteered" forty of his regulars for service and placed his best subalterns at the disposal of General Floyd. Assured of 220 men and adequate supplies, the Georgia militia general now agreed to march on Monday, November 2, against the Seminoles.[3]

As had happened so often in past months the plans of Smith never materialized. On October 25 the colonel was called to Point Petre for a conference. Before his departure from Camp New Hope he expressed his confidence in the ultimate outcome of an expedition led by "so able an officer" as Floyd.[4] But the contemplated offensive never advanced beyond its embryonic stage. Floyd undoubtedly was faced with violent opposition from his militia, the core of the proposed expeditionary force. Invariably a few weeks in Florida brought scores of men down with inflammatory complaints and fever. Others found life in East Florida sufficiently rough without opposition from Indians, and volunteers were not in the category of regulars – their commander paid more heed to their complaints and desires. Then too the actual number of Patriots and Newnan's volunteers evidently fell short of the estimates made by optimistic commanders.

Meanwhile at Point Petre Smith ran into valid reasons for the continuation of a defensive policy. Rumors of a cession of the Floridas by Onís and of an Indian peace offer, though recognized as possibly false, checked the urge for battle. Even Smith with his desire for revenge and military glory was not so callous as to expose regulars and volunteers for sheer love of fighting. He also received an important letter from Major General Thomas Pinckney advising the colonel of a change in over-all command – Pinckney, not Mitchell, was now in charge of East Florida affairs.[5] Until the recently appointed commander issued orders, Smith thought it best to hold his force together at Camp New Hope. This decision was supported by a letter from Adjutant General Flournoy advising Smith that new orders had been issued by the War Department.[6]

The colonel remained at Point Petre for almost a month. During that time he busied himself in organizing and supplying the reinforcements which Governor Mitchell moved toward the Florida border. Smith's correspondence was replete with requests for guns, ammunition, cannon, and accouterments. Not once did he indicate a passing thought of retreat from East Florida and a restoration of the province to Governor Kindelan. Rather his efforts suggested the reoccupation of his old camp at Moosa Old Fort as a preliminary step in the subjugation of St. Augustine. Conquest of the Castillo de San Marcos and the overthrow of Spanish rule were more enticing prospects than the defeat of a few hundred Seminoles. With the Spanish expelled from East Florida, the Indians would be a minor problem.

In the midst of his dream of conquest a letter from General Pinckney brought Smith a prospect of release from East Florida. The rifle regiment and dragoons of Smith's command were ordered to the northern front, Pinckney stated, and the colonel would proceed to Knoxville, Tennessee, to await further orders. A few days later Pinckney informed Smith that these orders had been suspended for the moment insofar as they related to the colonel, but the riflemen and dragoons must march north immediately.[7]

Smith was now left in East Florida with a hollow command. As his regulars moved away he commanded few men other than the militia which Mitchell was sending from Georgia. Colonel Smith realized there was no plan or policy now in Washington. Unexpected reverses on the Canadian war front forced a concentration of troops in New York state. The War Department, however, planned an extensive movement toward New Orleans in anticipation of a British thrust at that point or a British expedition into Spanish Florida. Monroe still played with the idea of securing the Floridas by negotiation with Onís. Administrative officers worked at cross purposes and President Madison hesitated.

Unlike the halting administration in Washington, Governor

Mitchell in Milledgeville knew exactly what he wanted. Colonel Newnan's defeat had frightened the governor. He blamed Kindelan for the Indian uprising and feared that Seminole war parties, supplied from St. Augustine, would plunder his Georgia frontier. Furthermore, the defeat of Georgia troops by Indians and Negroes, especially the Negroes, endangered the Southern slave system and brought horrible nightmares of Negro insurrection.

From July 30, when he left St. Marys,[8] until late in September Governor Mitchell's illness had prevented aggressive action in support of Smith. When the Georgia governor realized the impending failure of Newnan and learned of Colonel Smith's retreat, he moved with surprising speed. He ordered ten companies of Georgia militia to Point Petre and told General Floyd to reinforce Smith without delay.[9] From all over the state Mitchell ordered troops south, paying no heed to the Canadian front, for in his opinion the South was of more importance.

Without hesitation or consideration of his powers Mitchell ordered Smith to use the Georgia troops. "If your prospects are flattering at any time of being able to take St. Augustine and they will volunteer, as I have no doubt they will, I advise you to carry the whole for that purpose. . . . You may rest assured that I shall not recall you," Mitchell promised Smith, "and if the general Government issue any peremptory orders to that effect, they must find some one else to execute it, for I never will, believing as I do that it would be disgraceful to do so under existing circumstances. No! Satisfaction must be had for the blood already spilt, and that satisfaction must be taken at the point of the bayonet."[10]

If the United States would not subdue the Spaniards and Indians in Florida, Georgia would act alone. Mitchell issued a general order authorizing General Floyd to collect and deposit at Traders Hill provisions for 500 men and horses. Floyd was instructed to publicize the purposes of the forthcoming expedition as one against St. Augustine, but actually he would destroy the Seminole towns first and then turn on Kindelan.[11]

This order for mobilizing a mounted expeditionary force reached Floyd at Camp New Hope where he was gathering volunteers for a foray against the Indians. Floyd returned to Georgia and during the first weeks of November he bought supplies – corn at one dollar per bushel, flour and jerked beef at five cents per pound. At Traders Hill he sought storage houses for these provisions and space for men and horses. Floyd eagerly assumed command and warned Mitchell that immediate action was necessary; for unless the savages were checked, robbery and plunder would increase. The general hoped the Georgia legislature would make adequate appropriations for the expeditionary force.[12]

Mitchell anticipated Floyd's thought. On November 2 the governor reviewed the course of events in East Florida in his message to the legislature. Negro militia in St. Augustine could not be tolerated by Georgians, Mitchell stated, and the Spaniards' use of Negroes in warfare was "so savage and barbarous that it is impossible for an American to hear it without feeling the utmost indignation and resentment against the power who commands or even permits it." Mitchell had expected occupation of the Floridas as a consequence of war with Great Britain; and notwithstanding the failure of the United States Senate to approve conquest, it was his "sincere and candid opinion, that the peace and safety of this state will be hazarded if the occupancy of East Florida by our Government is relinquished, or much longer delayed." President Madison was stopped by the Senate, Mitchell averred, but Georgia must not wait for congressional approval. Therefore he had ordered a detachment of 500 mounted men mobilized at Traders Hill. This executive act required the immediate attention of the legislature.[13]

Mitchell voiced the sentiments and demands of Georgians. On the night of October 5 citizens of St. Marys had boarded a boat, which was loading ostensibly for Havana but in reality for St. Augustine, and ruined the cargo. The following morning they entered into a fixed and determined resolution to hold up to public scorn anyone directly or indirectly aiding the Spaniards, who were employing savages of "different shades" in war against the Georgia militia.[14] On Sunday night, October 18, Savannah blades burned the sloop *Alpha* which had been trading with St. Augustine. The *Alpha's* crew, in resisting the attackers, mortally wounded Isaac Delyon and injured Andrew Griffin, two respectable young men of Savannah.[15] The *Augusta Chronicle* described the citizens as "justly exasperated" with those who traded with Spaniards and stirred the ire of Augusta citizens by reporting three Savannah men killed by the *Alpha's* crew.

Although the *Chronicle* editor deplored mob action, he admitted that taking the law into one's own hand was necessary in certain instances.[16] Angry Georgians demanded action in East Florida.

Legislators in Milledgeville sensed the feelings of their constituents. On November 9 the senate received a bill, the provisions of which authorized Mitchell to occupy East Florida and vested in him full authority to organize sufficient militia for the investment and reduction of St. Augustine. The bill further provided for acceptance of volunteers and payment of all expenses of an expeditionary force.[17] Realistic senators admitted one difficulty: the United States Constitution prohibited a state from keeping an army or making war unless the state was invaded. But Georgians declared the Negro militia near their border was so unusual a provocation that some senators favored 1000 men rather than Mitchell's 500 volunteers for service in East Florida. The proposed act was referred to a joint committee on that part of Mitchell's message which related to East Florida.

On November 20 this committee presented its report. The committee members unanimously favored immediate and decisive measures by either the federal or state government for the occupation of East Florida. Since the Senate of the United States had for some inexplicable reason rejected the House bill for occupying the Floridas, the state of Georgia must act. Public safety combined with urgent necessity overshadowed all other considerations and justified by every legitimate and universally recognized principle of the law of nations the seizure of East Florida. The committee report cited two instances when a state could keep troops in time of peace: when a state was actually invaded and when a state was in such imminent danger as to admit of no delay. In the opinion of the committee, the use of Indians and Negroes in warfare made danger imminent and gave the Georgians the right to occupy and hold East Florida until the time when the national government assumed its responsibility for the security of Georgia.[18]

To make war on Spanish Florida without sanction of the federal government was a drastic act. Sane legislators realized that and voted down independent Georgia action, but the legislature did adopt a strong resolution calling for federal seizure of East Florida and threatening state action unless Georgians were protected.[19] A second resolution authorized Governor Mitchell to use a voluntary cavalry patrol on the border for defense against marauding Indians, and for offense against St. Augustine in cooperation with the forces of the United States.[20]

While Georgia legislators and citizens accepted Governor Mitchell's report on East Florida at face value, officials in St. Augustine protested with vigor. Benigno Garzia, commandant of the Spanish garrison, charged Mitchell with misrepresentation, with mixing truth and falsehood to justify an infamous aggression on a friendly power. Garzia stated that Georgians had forced Spaniards into war by starving women and children in St. Augustine, by using "banditti, and by proscribing free people of color who were a part of the Spanish militia." After such conduct Governor Mitchell had no right to blame Spain for the soldiers used, no more right than a midnight ruffian to insist that his intended victim throw away his blunderbuss. If Georgians had been frightened by defeat, Garzia told them, all their fears could be dissipated by retreating from East Florida. In that event Spain would not send an army across the border. In reality, Garzia avowed, there was a hidden motive in Governor Mitchell's legislative message, a motive known throughout the civilized world: "It had been a long time since Georgia had a slice of Indian or Spanish land and the fever was again at its height."[21]

Mitchell shrugged away Garzia's accusation and worked the harder in securing volunteers. Because of the opposition of state legislators he gave up his plan for invading East Florida, but Georgia would be ready when the United States finally acted.

Although Mitchell had been relieved of his duties as presidential agent, he held to the hope that Colonel Smith would have the opportunity of conquering the Floridas. Georgia would contribute everything in its power, the governor told Smith, and warned the colonel to keep secret any intention of going against the Indians; for if forewarned, they would "carry off all their women and children, destroy all the provisions they cannot secrete, and take shelter in Spanish Garrisons, or prowl about the woods like wolves, and occasionally shoot down some of their enemies, when they will themselves be invisible." Mitchell stated that he was relinquishing command over Florida affairs because of ill health and the press of duties as governor of Georgia.[22]

When Mitchell gave ill health and his executive duties as reasons for relinquishing his commission he told a partial truth. These considerations had influenced Madison and Monroe, but in reality they had dismissed him and replaced him with Major General Thomas Pinckney. From Charleston, where he commanded the southeastern military district, Pinckney had found considerable difficulty in providing for Colonel Smith without stepping on the toes of Mitchell. Again and again the general mentioned that "delicate subject," namely noninterference with the powers of the Georgia governor.[23] These niceties of etiquette placed additional burdens on Pinckney. Monroe knew this, and since the Florida question was primarily military, efficiency dictated the vesting of Mitchell's diplomatic and Pinckney's military power in one man.

On November 3, Monroe informed Pinckney of his selection as successor to Mitchell. In a brief letter the secretary of state characteristically said little of the duties of the commissioner or of the administration's plans regarding the Floridas. Monroe promised to forward copies of the instructions to and correspondence with the former commissioners; and these, the secretary stated, would guide Pinckney in executing his highly important trust.[24]

Major General Thomas Pinckney was another old soldier of Seventy-Six. In the seventy-two years since his birth at Charleston, South Carolina, on October 23, 1750, he had moved from his aristocratic wealthy, though provincial, environment into national and world affairs. After serving in the Revolutionary Army, he became governor of South Carolina in 1787, and four years later President Washington sent him as minister to the Court of St. James, where he represented his government until called for extraordinary duty in Spain. At Madrid in 1795 he successfully negotiated the treaty of San Lorenzo el Real (Pinckney treaty), which fixed the northern boundary of West Florida at the thirty-first parallel and gave American citizens the right of deposit at New Orleans. Pinckney returned home a famous man, but his fame could not stem the rising tide of Jeffersonian republicanism. In 1796 he was defeated as the Federalist candidate for the vice-presidency. After two terms in Congress, he foreswore politics and settled down in Charleston as a lawyer and gentleman farmer. He came out of retirement in 1812 when President Madison commissioned him as a major general in the regular army.

Pinckney was tall and spare in figure. His clean-cut features, erect carriage, and air of poised self-control marked him as a man of distinction. His courteous manner and personal dignity were combined with bold aggressiveness and persistent, even obstinate determination. Pinckney was an individualist with a keen mind, who expressed his opinions freely without regard for personal advantage. Although in stature below the great men of the Revolutionary era, he could complete an assigned task with surprising facility. In accepting any appointment he insisted on a clear statement of his duties.

When Monroe lightly skipped over the powers and duties of the commissioner for Florida, the general responded by enumerating his conception of the assignment. Pinckney stated that he was not accepting a separate diplomatic appointment but an additional military duty, and in accordance with President Madison's wishes, would keep American troops in East Florida until Governor Kindelan gave satisfactory assurances as to the persons and property of the Patriots. Pinckney requested of Monroe orders concerning Colonel Smith: was the colonel to remain at Camp New Hope or was he to reoccupy his former camp site at Moosa Old Fort? Until definite instructions were in hand, Pinckney would keep Smith at New Hope; for if the reports of refusals by militia to cross the Florida border were accurate, Smith could not reoccupy Moosa as there were less than 1700 regular troops in the Southern military district and many of these were untrained recruits.[25]

Pinckney could not resist the impulse to comment on the Florida project. In a private letter he informed the secretary: "My opinion is that we are not justified in withholding any part of the Province of East Florida upon the ground that the Spanish Government refuses to pardon the offenses committed against it by their subjects." Although the Patriots had been encouraged by an American agent, Pinckney believed the United States could do no more than use amicable means of securing favorable treatment for the revolutionists. "I do not understand," he continued, "that because we cease to injure the Spaniards an obligation attaches to them to comply with our demand that they should forgive subjects criminal to them. . . ."[26] Pinckney did not know whether the United States had just grounds for claiming or occupying the Floridas, but he did know, no matter the legality of the action, that if the administration was set on capturing the provinces, sufficient force should be provided to accomplish the end in view without additional hesitation. In effect, Pinckney told Monroe, the United States should either occupy all of East Florida or evacuate it.

Madison and Monroe would not consider evacuation. Yet without congressional authorization the president could not act; by keeping the troops in East Florida he was stretching his power to the limit. Monroe still retained hope of a cession through Onís, yet each day of delay increased his suspicion as to the power and willingness of Onís to cede the provinces. Monroe was also burdened by additional duties, as military reverses and quarrels within the administration brought cabinet changes. On December 3, 1812, William Eustis resigned as secretary of war; and Monroe, though retaining his state department portfolio, became acting secretary of war. In his dual capacity he had little time for tedious negotiation with an unrecognized minister whose authority was in question. If the Floridas were to become American property, direct invasion and occupation should not be delayed.

In December, 1812, president and secretary hatched the egg of conquest. The aggressive attitude of Governor Mitchell in his November legislative message, and the response of the Georgia legislators and people encouraged Madison. Newspaper editors gave editorial support to Georgia's demands. "We believe the opinion is becoming very prevalent," stated the *National Intelligencer,* "that the safety of the Southern frontier, as well as every motive of general policy, requires that East Florida should be added to our territorial possessions."[27]

Subjugation of the Floridas would compensate for the dismal failure of American arms on the Canadian front. The record of the army on the northern border approached national disgrace. Thomas Jefferson thought General William Hull should be shot for cowardice and treachery, and Major General Stephen van Rensselaer of the New York militia dismissed for incapacity.[28] Southern editors wrote vitriolic comments about Northern militiamen who refused to cross the national boundary and fight the enemy on his homeland. Boundaries, these editors avowed, would not be used as excuses for cowardice in the South. In a short winter campaign, when troops could not be used effectively in a frigid North, Southerners would conquer the Floridas and cover the stain on national honor with the glory of success.

PLAN OF CONQUEST

This rising tide of sentiment for action in Florida washed up gold in Washington. Monroe forgot his scheme of obtaining the Floridas by cession. Late in November the secretary had advised a House committee against congressional enactment of a law authorizing conquest of the Floridas and unequivocably stated that Great Britain would not occupy the provinces.[29] On December 8 the secretary informed Pinckney of the same old conditions, either of which would permit seizure of East Florida: amicable arrangement with local authorities, or use of force to forestall English intervention. In elaborating on the duties of Pinckney, Monroe evinced a different opinion on probable British intentions from that previously expressed to the House committee. The secretary emphasized the inherent danger in English control of the Floridas, warned Pinckney to be vigilant, and ordered Colonel Smith's forces retained at Camp New Hope while an army was collected at Point Petre. How long the existing state of affairs on the southern frontier would be permitted, Monroe could not state, but he intimated forthcoming changes and decisive action.[30]

Two days after Monroe's letter of December 8, Senator Joseph Anderson moved in secret session that a committee be appointed to investigate the expediency of authorizing the president to occupy and hold East Florida.[31] As Senator Anderson was an administration stalwart, his advocacy of this Florida measure had the backing of Madison and Monroe. The Florida project had been defeated in July by but two votes, and the president and secretary believed the Senate would now approve conquest. In Philadelphia Onís received reports that the president had promises of a majority in favor of annexing the Floridas. The American government, Onís warned British Admiral John Warren, had made plans for the conquest of East and West Florida.[32]

Without waiting for the Senate, the administration began moving troops toward the southern border. Popular Andrew Jackson was to march from Tennessee to New Orleans and then move east into Mobile, Pensacola, and St. Augustine. Soldiers from Pinckney's military district were to mobilize at Coleraine and Point Petre, where they could be rushed into East Florida; and should Pinckney's forces meet too much resistance, Jackson's volunteers would be within striking distance of St. Augustine. Commodore Campbell's naval flotilla would blockade the Spanish town.[33] These powerful military and naval forces could destroy the Indians and push the Spaniards out of Florida.

For Congress Monroe outlined American military needs for 1813. He requested a minimum of 2,000 regular troops for Savannah and East Florida, 2,500 men for New Orleans, Mobile, and other Gulf settlements. In the secretary's opinion special provision should be made for Savannah and East Florida whether the latter remained in the possession of Spain or was occupied by the United States. It would require no greater force to hold East Florida should possession be taken, Monroe stated, than to guard the United States against British intrigue and invasion from a vulnerable southern frontier.[34]

By late December newspaper editors noted with approbation the general movement of troops. "The prospects of a winter campaign to the southward is daily getting stronger," wrote the editor of the *Augusta Chronicle*.[35] General Flournoy was already in Florida, Pinckney and his staff were en route, and both regular and militia soldiers were massing in southern Georgia. Colonel Smith would soon have 1000 men; with them he could advance to his former encampment at Moosa Old Fort.

General Pinckney asked Governor Mitchell for copies of his instructions and a report on his negotiations with Governor Kindelan. After studying them, Pinckney concluded it inadvisable to have further communication with the Spanish governor. If an offer should be made for withdrawing the American troops upon receipt of guarantees of amnesty for the Patriots and then Congress should authorize occupation of the Floridas, the negotiations would bear the character of bad faith. With shocking honesty Pinckney told Monroe he would resume negotiations with Kindelan, if authorized to tell Kindelan that President Madison was keeping American troops in East Florida with the expectation of congressional sanction for the conquest of the province.[36]

Pinckney believed Madison and Monroe had made unalterable plans for conquering the Floridas. To protect his flank and his line of communications he planned an expedition against the Indians as preparation for a siege of St. Augustine.[37] Soldiers corralled horses, built carriages for thirty-eight cannon, and collected provisions for a campaign. Pinckney knew he had insufficient cannon, clothing, and shoes. Even in mild Florida he could not order half-naked and barefooted men into battle. Because of deficiencies the general thought it would be the middle of March before St. Augustine could be assaulted. He hoped Madison would not announce the intention of the government before that time or before the army was ready for an advance.[38]

Although General Pinckney personally opposed the reduction of St. Augustine, he would obey the command of superiors. His orders from Washington were unequivocal. On November 27, 1812, he was instructed to concentrate at Point Petre all disposable forces south of Virginia and he was told that these troops would probably be used in East Florida.[39] Less than a week later he was ordered by command of the president: "Col. Smith is to retain his position on the River St. Johns: – that he is to be reinforced: – that the Seminoles who have committed murders and depredations on our Citizens are to be subdued: – and that a force is also to be embodied, as advanced by my letter of the 27th of November, for offensive operations, preparation to the entire possession of the Province of East Florida."[40]

Pinckney answered this letter by pointing out that the Castillo de San Marcos was a "regular fortification with a good ditch." Its reduction could be accomplished only by famine or direct assault. In either case heavy ordnance and considerable ammunition would be indispensable. Sufficient troops and supplies should be in East Florida so that St. Augustine could be captured before the hot summer season.[41]

On January 13, 1813, Monroe assured Pinckney: "It is intended to place under your command an adequate force for the reduction of St. Augustine, should it be decided by Congress, before whom the subject will be in a few days. From the number and character of troops in the Garrison (at St. Augustine), it is hoped that its reduction will not be attended with much difficulty or delay."[42]

Patriots and Georgians looked forward with eager anticipation to the conquest of East Florida. McIntosh and Buckner Harris had never given up hope of eventual American aid. In December they set up a court on the banks of Bell's River opposite Fernandina and outside the jurisdiction of Captain Massias. There Judge Buckner Harris passed sentences of confiscation upon the property of those who had left the province. With the United States again on the march, Patriot leaders felt secure as they visualized ultimate success. Their forces in the field, who were scouting for Colonel Smith, reported Chief Bowlegs ready to renew a war in which neither age nor sex would be spared.[43] This false propaganda aroused Georgians, and as the Patriots expected, increased the possibility of invasion.

By January, 1813, Patriots, Georgians, and administrative leaders believed the conquest of Florida near. With troops marching into Point Petre from the far reaches of the southern military district and Jackson's volunteers en route from Tennessee, the awaited occupation of the Floridas could not be long delayed. Such leaders as Jackson and Pinckney made victory certain.

As Spaniards in St. Augustine saw the approaching might from the north they knew their day of rule was almost over. The possibility of additional reinforcements from Cuba was slim, and Great Britain had never promised aid for the Florida provinces. Hopelessly St. Augustinians awaited their fate.

17

The Tennessee Volunteers

IN FLORIDA THE UNEXPECTED took precedence over anticipated events. So it had been in 1812 and so it was to be in 1813. With Pinckney's forces moving toward East Florida and Jackson's toward West Florida, apparently it was a question of which army would first invade the Spanish provinces. The answer was neither. Rather, from Tennessee a mounted force of volunteers, uncalled for and unexpected, reached the southern border of Georgia and moved into East Florida before either Pinckney or Jackson mobilized their men on the frontier.

Tennessee militia prided themselves on their courage and prowess in battle. Their proximity to the powerful Creek Confederation and their natural hatred of Indians made them respond with alacrity when danger threatened. Most renowned were the men of middle and west Tennessee who had answered the call of their leader Jackson and marched off to battle redskins. Eastern Tennesseans had little in common with their wealthier, plantation-owning compatriots. In the rugged hills of the east there were few plantations and consequently few slave owners. In economics and in politics the Easterners lived apart from Westerners, yet despite the meager slave population in their section, the Easterners had an interest in slavery. In their opinion Negroes could only be held in check by the peculiar institution: slavery was a necessary method of control. The Easterner also met the Westerner on common ground in a mutual fear of the Indian.

Therefore when men of East Tennessee read of the Indian and Negro uprising in Florida, they did not wait for state or national call to arms. An expedition into the Spanish lands offered adventure, and more than that, an opportunity to kill Indians and nip in the bud a possible uprising of the Creeks. A general taking-of-the-warpath by the Creeks would endanger East Tennessee. Already some Indians were robbing and killing within striking distance of Knoxville.

In October and November, 1812, Colonel John Williams, adjutant general of Tennessee militia, selected aides and signed up some volunteers. On November 10 he published a general call to arms, stating:

> The latest newspaper accounts show a want of troops in East Florida to check the hostile Indians. 'Tis shameful that Georgia alone should bear this burden. All those who have enrolled themselves with me, are directed to parade, at Knoxville, on Tuesday the first day of December next, prepared with a supply of provisions to take them to the point of destination.
>
> The patriotic freemen of Tennessee, who have not enrolled themselves, are requested on that day, to come forward well mounted, and prepare to march to Saint Johns, where the troops of the United States are stationed, and where the Indians are said to be assembled, in such numbers as to threaten the destruction of our troops. . . . War now rages in our land – A deranged Monarch, venal Prince, and a corrupt Ministry, have driven us to assert our rights, at the point of the bayonet. They have enlisted under their banners the savages, those hell hounds fitted only for deeds of ferocity, who seek victory by the indiscriminate slaughter of all ages and sexes.
>
> Our females and property are in a place of security – our brethren in a sister state need our aid, will it be withheld! . . . Let us march to their relief – Let us give decided evidence that while others talk we are prepared to act –Let us go to the scene of action, and there present ourselves ready to share with our brethren, the dangers and glories of the field – Let us not wait the slow formality of being dragged from home by compulsory orders – Freemen ought to risk something – Let us go on our own expenses in the first instance – If we can thus be useful to our country, we will be more than compensated.[1]

Every man was to be mounted on a strong horse and should bring a rifle or musket, a brace of pistols, a tomahawk, and a butcher knife. Since uniformity of dress would enhance the military appearance of the volunteers, pantaloons, a black hunting shirt, a black hat, and boots or shoes with leggings were required. The expense of furnishing his horse and equipment rested with the individual.

In response to Williams' appeal 165 men assembled in Knoxville on December 1, 1812.[2] Among them were representatives of the best families of East Tennessee. One newspaper correspondent described the volunteers "as hardy, robust and brave a body of men, perhaps, as ever trod the tented field."³ The youngest man was eighteen and the oldest eighty. Most of the volunteers were men of independent fortune, liberal education, or lucrative professions "who like the best Romans in the purest days of the republic, have cheerfully and promptly abandoned all to aid in preserving and supporting the honor and independence of our country."⁴ They tethered their horses and pitched their tents on the campus of the University of Tennessee.⁵

While his subordinates completed preparations for the march, Williams penned a letter to President Madison. "Late intelligence shows a want of troops in East Florida, to check the hostile savages," he informed the president. "A considerable part of the Georgia militia, it is said, have refused to afford relief to the troops of the United States, stationed at St. Johns, from a fatal exposition of the constitution relative to the militia." Since Tennesseans believed the American government would occupy the Floridas, the volunteers, Williams stated, would march on December 4 for the St. Johns, where it would give them pleasure to execute the orders of the president. "In executing your orders, not a man in this corps will entertain constitutional scruples on the subject of boundaries."⁶

Governor Willie Blount, who had been informed of the proposed expedition, supported it in a letter addressed to the secretary of war. "The volunteers of East Tennessee," he proudly proclaimed, "have armed and equipped themselves at their own expense, are composed of men as respectable and as well attached to the government as any to be found in Tennessee or any other state of the Union, and had they been willing to wait, would have been 1000 men." Blount urged the secretary to use the Tennesseans well and not chill their enthusiasm by cold neglect.⁷

With praise and plaudits ringing in their ears the volunteers mounted their horses on December 4 and headed toward Asheville, North Carolina. There a Mrs. Erwin had beeves butchered and barbecued for the hungry men. She and another patriotic woman of North Carolina collected and presented the volunteers with 100 dollars for their expenses.⁸ For only three nights of the first seven out of Knoxville the men paid for their provisions; on four days people along the route or in Asheville showered them with food.

After two days in the North Carolina town the volunteers marched again on December 12 as snow drifted from the ashen sky. The snow fell rapidly as the temperature dropped to nine above zero. That night a fierce, chill wind blew off hill and mountain, but the soldiers were well-tented and blanketed. In daylight their horses covered mile after mile with quick, sure steps. On December 19 the volunteers, now totaling 240 as additional men joined them en route, camped at Washington, Georgia. Townspeople supplied them with staples and tasty tidbits.[9] The local editor saluted them by asking, "Georgians! Does not such evidence of patriotic zeal inspire you with the spirit of your visiting brethren?"[10]

On Sunday, December 20, the Tennesseans broke camp. Before the new year they approached the Florida border where they halted while Williams tendered their services to General Flournoy. From St. Marys Flournoy sent a guide to lead the volunteers to Camp Pinckney, near Coleraine, and Magrith's Ferry on the St. Marys. Flournoy promised to meet Colonel Williams on January 7 in Coleraine and make arrangements for an expedition against the Seminoles.[11]

Williams had not forgotten to advise Governor Mitchell of his purpose. While the volunteers camped in Asheville, the colonel sent privates Pleasant A. Miller and Enoch Parsons with a letter which informed the governor that help was on the way.[12] The offer of aid placed Mitchell in an embarrassing predicament. He could not welcome the Tennesseans wholeheartedly, for their expedition implied the failure of Georgians as Indian fighters and an official could not admit such a damaging fact. On the other hand, Mitchell could not ask the Tennesseans to return home and let his people subdue the Indians – that would be inhospitable – moreover, the Newnan expedition and the futile efforts of the past months contradicted any claim of military prowess which Georgians might advance.

Governor Mitchell handled his problem with tact. He thanked Williams for his patriotism and welcomed him to Georgia. In fighting the savages, both red and black, of Florida, Mitchell stated the Tennessee volunteers would be uniting with Georgians who would share the danger and glory of battle. Only the central government's policy had prevented Georgia militia from destroying the Seminoles. The governor hoped the United States would authorize an expedition against the Indians, and if Washington did not, Georgia would act alone.[13]

The editor of the *Milledgeville Journal* was more blunt. Although he appreciated the patriotic motives which inspired the Tennessee riflemen, he decried their lamentable lack of knowledge of the strength and resources of Georgia. Conquest of East Florida and the annihilation of the Seminoles would be a small matter for Georgia citizens. They could defeat any force in East Florida, but the general government would not authorize offensive action. Let the federal government give the word, proclaimed the editor, and Georgia legions would advance.[14]

Governor Mitchell, who had been so vociferously determined on destroying the Seminoles in November, 1812, experienced a sudden change of heart. Since the Indians had sued for peace, war was unnecessary and the Tennessee volunteers should return home without disturbing the negotiations being conducted by Benjamin Hawkins. Knowledge of the Indian attitude was well-known in the South. *Niles Register* carried an article on the subject and the *Charleston Courier* reprinted a long editorial from the *Georgia Journal*. "The Indians have offered to lay down their arms and submit to any terms, even the most humiliating, which the United States might think proper to prescribe. Of this fact there can be no doubt," avowed the *Journal's* editor. "A more ardent desire for peace, we may venture to affirm, was never manifested by any people whatever. They propose to restore not only the property of the whites, but to deliver up all offenders against our laws. Could we ask – could they do more? Why then make war upon them? Why drive them from their homes and firesides, perhaps to utter ruin, a poor, defenseless, miserable race of beings, who are supplicating, as it were, mercy upon their knees?"[15]

Indian agent Benjamin Hawkins asked General Pinckney to stop the expedition against the Seminoles. In reply Pinckney expressed his pleasure in learning of the Indians' peaceful inclinations, but stated that his instructions were to chastise the red men. Since Hawkins had communicated the Seminoles' desire for peace to President Madison, and as sufficient time had elapsed for the president, if he had desired, to rescind the order for an advance, Pinckney could do nothing other than allow the Tennessee volunteers to proceed unless word came from Washington. If, however, Hawkins could secure an immediate submission on all terms demanded by the United States and also Indian hostages equal in number to American citizens killed, Pinckney would suspend hostilities until the pleasure of Madison was known.[16]

FLORIDA FIASCO

On January 12, 1813, General Pinckney informed the secretary of war that the volunteers would be provisioned and used against the Seminoles unless orders to the contrary were received from President Madison.[17] Indeed there had been time, ample time, for Madison to stop aggression. Yet Pinckney held the volunteers at Coleraine for almost a month. Then he could delay no longer. When Madison and Monroe ignored the question by remaining silent, Pinckney assumed his duty lay in ordering an advance into the Indian country.

During that month of delay the rabid Tennesseans were bitterly resentful. Some went into St. Marys and presented their case to General Flournoy; others castigated Benjamin Hawkins for his interference. One volunteer wrote Governor Blount that the volunteers had been stopped by the "Chief of the Creek nation, to wit Ben Hawkins." This volunteer promised Blount a detailed explanation of the arts employed by Hawkins to prevent chastisement of his red subjects, and expressed the hope "that some one of the Tennessee Volunteers will plant the American eagle on the walls of St. Augustine before we return."[18] A semi-literate volunteer wrote his wife: "I forgot to tell you as how we ar gwine to fight the Ingins and Spaniels – I believe they live sum whare about aunt Marys or sain Johns but lord whod go thare."[19]

The volunteers were going there. That was the wish of Madison and Monroe, for their silence had a purpose. By striking the Seminoles, the danger of an attack on Pinckney's forces or Jackson's, when they should enter East Florida, would be eliminated. It is evident, therefore, that the Madison administration purposely refrained from answering Benjamin Hawkins or issuing Pinckney orders. Long after the volunteers should have proceeded on their mission, the secretary of war informed Pinckney: "When the mounted volunteers under Col. Williams shall have performed the duty which you have assigned them against the Indians, you will consult your own judgment, and either continue them in service with the Regular Troops assembling at St. Marys, or dismiss them, as the good of the service may require."[20] The unquenchable thirst of the Madison administration for the Floridas had blinded it to right: Indians suing for peace would be given the sword because their destruction was part of a plan of conquest.

The Tennessee volunteers crossed the St. Marys on February 3 and rode toward the St. Johns. From Camp New Hope Colonel Smith marched south with 220 men.[21] The two forces were to rendezvous near Payne's town in Alachua from which a joint campaign of extermination would begin. General orders from Flournoy commanded Smith to punish those Indians who had taken the warpath, burn all their property which could not be transported, drive as many of their cattle back as possible, execute without mercy Negroes captured under arms, and take all other Negroes as prisoners.[22] On completion of the mission Smith would return with his force to Camp New Hope and Williams with his to Coleraine.

With less than a day's notice Smith marched down the east bank of the St. Johns. At Kingsley's plantation he camped and secured some horses and additional supplies. There he used Kingsley's flatboat in crossing the river. He proceeded down the west bank until Picolatti was sighted across the river, then veered toward the southwest, and followed the trail of Newnan. Smith pushed his men hard, for unavoidable delays had thrown him behind schedule. The junction with Williams' volunteers had been planned for twelve noon on Saturday at Newnan's battleground.[23]

On Sunday, February 7, Smith's detachment met the Tennesseans about thirteen miles from Payne's town.[24] In conference the commanders decided to split their forces and send one detachment against Bowlegs' town and the other against Payne's. By quick simultaneous thrusts both Indian villages would be destroyed. They abandoned this strategy, however, for not a single guide knew the way to Bowlegs' town.

The joint forces moved toward Payne's town and camped about three miles from the Indian settlement on Sunday night. At four o'clock Monday morning the expedition moved forward; scouts advanced cautiously toward the town and flanking details spread to surround the village. At dawn the nervous soldiers charged into the settlement and found an abandoned town. Evidence of recent habitation could be seen everywhere – provisions in storehouses and pots over still-warm ashes. The Indians had been warned by friendly Creeks, and taking their Negro slaves, had left their old habitat.

Smith bivouacked his men on the village site. Colonel Williams' volunteers rode down an Indian trail which they hoped might lead into Bowlegs' town. Within a few miles they spotted two Indians, one of whom they killed, and the other, though wounded, escaped into a thick hammock. The volunteers spurred their horses down the trail and ran into a small camp of Indians. Without investigating or calling for surrender, the Tennesseans fired with rapidity. At the first volley two squaws fell. One old man was killed and seven prisoners captured.

The captives gave Williams disappointing news. Payne's people and those of Bowlegs, king of the Seminoles since his brother's death, had left the area three weeks ago. The Indians in the neighborhood belonged to different tribes from the Alachua and Alligator clans, and a settlement of these peaceful Indians was located less than two miles away.

As the cold rain had chilled his men and darkness was approaching, Williams ordered his detachment back to Payne's town. His forces camped there on the eighth and ninth of February; on the tenth they rode away in search of the Indian town, convinced that it was the village belonging to Bowlegs. Five miles from camp they ran into musket fire which came from Indians concealed in a large hammock and swamp. One horse fell dead but not a man was wounded. Williams formed a battle line some distance from the hammock and placed his riflemen on his flank. Then he ordered a charge followed by a hasty, disorganized retreat, hoping by this maneuver to pull the Indians into the open so the riflemen could cut in behind them. Then, caught between the cross fire of the two Tennessee forces, the Indians would be cut to pieces.

Wily Indians did not fall for this trick. When they remained behind the trees and thick scrub of the hammock, Williams stationed his riflemen behind trees on the right and left of the enemy. A detachment of musketmen rode away, dismounted, and worked their way behind the Indians as the riflemen kept up an almost continuous fire. This strategy also failed, for the musketmen returned after finding the hammock and swamp impenetrable.

The battle settled into an exchange of fire. Incessant musket fire blanketed the overcast sky with layers of smoke, and rifleballs whistled through the air or thudded into trees. Occasionally the stocky, thickset Indians wearing little other than their war paint ventured from cover. Their appearances and war whoops sent chills down soldiers' spines, but some soldiers, as if to prove their courage, charged the enemy. Militia Major Henry Stephens galloped toward a venturesome redskin, overtook him, and at the moment of bayoneting the running Indian, was shot in the hip. Lieutenant John Smith was killed by a stray bullet. From time to time Indian war whoops were cut short as rifleballs found yielding flesh. Slowly, the accurate fire of the Tennesseans drove the Indians from the margin of the hammock into the thick underbrush.

After four hours of fighting, darkness began closing in on the contestants. A rider informed Williams that Smith's force was marching on the double to the scene of battle. As continued firing in the semidarkness would be a waste of ammunition, Williams pulled his volunteers back, met Smith's advancing column, and the combined forces camped together that night.

They remained in camp on the tenth and eleventh. During the night of the eleventh four prisoners, two Indian squaws with suckling babes, stole from the camp. As they approached the outer picket lines the whimpering, frightened babies broke into lusty crying. One squaw quieted her child, but the other, Williams reported, "in order to facilitate her escape inhumanly strangled to death her infant child." Soldiers buried the little body next day, and rode away in search of bigger Indians to kill.

As they approached the previous battlefield Indian warriors checked their advance. While Colonel Smith's forces held the Indians, the volunteers proceeded to what they thought was Bowlegs' town, where they camped from the twelfth until the seventeenth. Every day detachments scoured the surrounding countryside for horses, cattle, swine, and concealed mounds of corn. After all portable provisions had been secured, the huts and palmetto buildings were fired. Rolling pillars of smoke issuing from the devouring flames hung over the land and the Indian town was left in ashes.

On February 17 Colonel Smith ordered a general withdrawal. Together the Tennessee volunteers and the colonel's force moved back to Payne's town, burned it, and backtracked along the path of original advance. Near the St. Johns the forces split. By February 24 Smith was back at Camp New Hope and the volunteers were encamped at Coleraine, Georgia.

In a campaign of three weeks the volunteers had destroyed Indian property by wholesale. They burned 386 houses, consumed or destroyed from 1500 to 2000 bushels of corn, collected 300 horses and 400 cattle, and brought back or ruined 2000 deer skins.[25] Most of the horses and cattle wandered into the woods and swamps during the long march back to Georgia. Twenty Indians were killed and a number, including squaws, wounded.[26] Nine Indians and Negroes were captured, four of whom escaped and five were brought back. A twelve-year-old Indian boy, whose father had been killed, became a charge of the men at Camp New Hope; a wounded woman, an aged Negro man, and one Indian squaw with her child were displayed in Coleraine as booty of war.

The combined American forces suffered few casualties. One volunteer was killed and seven wounded, but Smith's men escaped without injury. The volunteers celebrated their victory. They described how the Indians had taken the bodies of Newnan's unfortunate soldiers, cut off their heads, and nailed them on trees in the Indian villages. An elderly volunteer named Wildear displayed his son's scalp, which he found in an Indian hut.[27]

The victorious volunteers could return home where families and friends would sing their praise. "You have rendered an essential service to the public," Flournoy wrote Colonel Williams, "and merit for yourself and the officers and men under your command, the praise so justly due to brave and patriotic men."[28]

Colonel Smith returned to Camp New Hope with mixed emotion. For the first time in almost a year he had participated in a campaign. That gave him some satisfaction. But as a military man, despite the resulting praise of the expeditionary force, he found little honor in winning against feeble opposition, killing and wounding old men and squaws, and capturing a few women and children. Now that he had had his taste of action, he demanded a transfer to a more active field. "I have been near Twelve months in this Province, a period in which if no Perils were encountered, excessive perplexity and vexation were sustained," he wrote Flournoy. "The purposes of Government, as for the eight months past, are yet indefinite in relation to East Florida."[29] Smith had only contempt for the Spaniards, saying that those "Scoundrels with whom we have to contend will never attempt to remove us, even if they should perish with famine in their fortress." The colonel had determined to use all his "influence to take leave of this damn'd barren Country immediately and forever."[30]

Thoughts of a furlough in Tennessee and then duty on the northern front, where he might acquire some practical knowledge of military affairs and also render a service to his country, excited Smith's imagination. Before leaving Florida he requested General Flournoy to do something for the medical service at Camp New Hope, where Dr. Dusenberry had "by his ignorance killed one or more men and wasted the greater part of the Hospital Stores. Every officer at the Post are [sic] so well convinced of his ignorance that they will not willingly trust him to attend their men."[31] Shortly after writing this letter, Smith received his furlough. He delivered his command to Major Lawrence Manning, and after some days at Coleraine, left Florida and southern Georgia, as he wished, forever.[32]

The furloughed colonel escaped the controversy over the Indian expedition. On March 2 Governor Mitchell sent General Pinckney a letter of protest. Georgia had the means, will, and courage to chastise the Indians, Mitchell stated. Colonel Newnan's expedition had proved the ability of Georgians to defeat the Seminoles, and "This conflict convinced the Indians of their inability to contend with Georgia and produced propositions for peace upon terms entitled to consideration. . . ." Mitchell was surprised and astonished when the Tennessee volunteers and Smith's troops marched against the Indians, most of whom were peaceful and who had refused to unite with or give any assistance to the hostile Seminole tribes. This unjust expedition had been sent without informing or consulting Georgia officials. As a result Mitchell feared the friendly Creek Indians, witnessing the white man's perfidy, might rise and endanger the people of Georgia.[33]

Mitchell had penned a strong letter and Pinckney had a difficult task in answering it. He assured the governor that Colonel Smith was ordered against hostile and not peaceful Indians. Furthermore, he wrote, every effort was made to get definite orders from Washington. On his own responsibility he delayed the expedition in the hope of receiving a countermanding order from the secretary of war. When he received no additional instructions from Washington, Pinckney explained, he had no choice but to follow his original orders, namely, to subdue and chastise the hostile Indians.[34]

As unfair as it had been, the job done by the Tennessee volunteers was a thorough one. Their destructive expedition left the Indians of central Florida facing starvation, forced them toward the west coast, and eliminated them as an enemy in the planned conquest of the Floridas. Pinckney's gathering forces and Jackson's volunteers could proceed without fear of Indian attack on their exposed flanks. The first step in the conquest of the Floridas was an accomplished fact.

Jackson's Volunteers

WHILE MEN OF EAST TENNESSEE displayed their military prowess in Florida, those of Middle and West Tennessee rallied around their leader, Andrew Jackson. For him they would go into Canada, Florida, or anywhere. In their opinion the national government had delayed too long in calling Jackson and his Tennesseans.

Idleness was not the choice of Jackson. Long before the declaration of war against Great Britain he had called his men to arms; immediately after the declaration he proffered President Madison the services of 2,500 volunteers. Madison accepted the offer, but the summer and fall slipped by while the Tennesseans, their names inscribed on muster rolls, remained inactive.

In the 1812 master plan of war Andrew Jackson was given little consideration by Madison and his advisers. General Henry Dearborn was to storm the fortress at Quebec and General James Wilkinson was to guard New Orleans. While others received important commands, Jackson vegetated in Tennessee. In Albany, New York, Aaron Burr told young Martin Van Buren, "I'll tell you why they don't employ Jackson; it's because he is a friend of mine."[1]

Jackson was indeed a friend of the suspected and discredited Burr. He had defended the reputation of the former vice-president and condemned those who had prosecuted him. Jackson had also expressed a preference for Monroe over Madison as the successor to President Jefferson. These acts, however, were not the cause of Jackson's unemployment in 1812. Madison wanted men of proved ability, men who had attained military stature in the Revolutionary War. Secretary of War Eustis, an old soldier of Seventy-Six himself, concurred in this policy. Furthermore, Eustis could not see the temperamental Jackson, who had called the secretary "an old granny," as the man for an important command.

The humiliating, disastrous failure of American arms in Canada forced Madison to reconsider the military situation. With the North secure, Great Britain might invade the Gulf ports and the lower Mississippi. To guard against this possibility Eustis requested 1,500 volunteers from Governor Willie Blount of Tennessee.[2] Jackson, however, would not command, for by order of the president these volunteers would reinforce General Wilkinson at New Orleans.[3] That at least was the official destination of the Tennesseans. Once in New Orleans they would be moved east toward Mobile, Pensacola, and St. Augustine.

When Governor Blount received the order from Washington, he called in his friend Jackson. As he read the order Jackson realized that Eustis was not calling the volunteers who had already tendered their services; he was either excluding Jackson or placing him under General Wilkinson. "There appears something in this thing that carries with it a sting to my feelings that I will for the present suppress," Jackson told Blount. Jackson assured the governor that he would sacrifice his own feelings and lead the volunteers wherever Blount commanded. "All I ask," Jackson stated, "is that we may be ordered to a stage where we may partake of active service, and share the dangers and laurels of the field."[4]

Reassured by Jackson's cooperative spirit, Blount gave the general a letter which authorized the organization, provisioning, and transportation of 1,500 volunteers. On November 14, 1812, Jackson published the governor's letter and informed prospective volunteers that they would defend the Mississippi valley. They should rendezvous in Nashville on December 10 with the men dressed in dark blue or brown uniforms and the officers in the prescribed uniform of the United States Army. Each volunteer was expected to bring a gun, ammunition, blankets, and general camp equipage. Reimbursement from the federal treasury was promised for all supplies and equipment furnished.[5]

As posters and newspapers spread the news throughout Middle

Tennessee, the people gathered in county-wide meetings where local orators urged volunteers to sign for duty. Milling crowds congregated around county courthouses for the ceremonial muster of troops. Those who could not volunteer wished their brothers Godspeed and contributed money for equipment. In Franklin and Williamson counties $500 was collected for this purpose.[6]

Eighteen miles below Nashville the people of Williamson County assembled in the town of Franklin on December 3 for the muster. A larger than expected crowd, drawn by the fame of Gideon Blackburn, the "Chrysostom of the pioneer pulpit," thronged the courthouse square. Blackburn was famous for his fiery delivery and his wealth of illustrative anecdote: when his voice thundered, sinners cried and the devil cowered in Hell. Blackburn was more than a Presbyterian minister and teacher: he was an Indian fighter of repute, the defender of the American frontier way of life. When he migrated into Tennessee he came "equipped for double warfare as with Bible and hymnbook, knapsack and rifle, he set out with a company of soldiers to defend a fort at the place where Maryville now stands."[7] There he organized a church and then, his work accomplished, he moved westward into Middle Tennessee where he became the friend of Jackson and the minister of the general's wife, Rachel.

On December 3 Blackburn, inspired by his audience, warmed to his task; his ardor stirred his listeners and their enthusiasm stimulated him. He waved the American flag and castigated the enemies of the United States. He directed most of his discourse at the civilians before him, thus setting the stage for his final sentences of encouragement and advice for the volunteers. Turning toward the soldiers he threw the full force of his powerful voice at them.

"You might touch at Pensacola, and alight, like the Eagle of prey, at St. Augustine – recalling the blood of the brave Captain Williams, and the difficulties of Newnan and Smith. You might scale their ramparts and spread the wings of the Eagle of liberty on the summit of their fortifications, chastising the slaves of monarchy, and eternally enslaving the black renegades."

The thunder of his voice rumbled away. Quietly, solemnly, in a hissing whisper, he warned the volunteers: "Need I advise you not to return ingloriously . . . ? You fight in the view of the female patriots . . . who have *petticoats* in reserve for cowardly officers."

The Reverend Gideon Blackburn paused. As pre-arranged the volunteers stepped forward to mass around the flag. Blackburn stretched a long arm forward, his bony finger almost touching the wind-blown emblem, as his voice rolled out over his audience. "Behold the flame of liberty waving in the air. Behold the flame of liberty painted on the cheek of your brothers. See! the heroes are collecting around the standard of liberty—the sound of the drum invites you to your station."[8]

Williamson County men heeded the drum beat. So did hundreds of men from other Tennessee counties. After inspiring orations and warm, tearful farewells, they marched toward Nashville and the general rendezvous.

As days dragged on toward the general muster of December 10, Tennesseans waited in uneasy anticipation. Would the men of Tennessee respond? The president was calling for 1,500 men to volunteer for service in a distant country. New Orleans by way of the Cumberland, Ohio, and Mississippi rivers was almost 1,300 miles away; Mobile and Pensacola, the probable points of destination,[9] were 200 miles farther; and St. Augustine lay 400 miles toward the east. Volunteers would have to conquer a wilderness inhabited mostly by savages and capture a country outside the limits of the United States. Would 1,500 Tennesseans appear in Nashville? That question weighted many minds on the night of December 9.

It was bitterly cold the following morning. During the night a piercing north wind sent the temperature near zero, and as the day advanced snowflakes fell faster and faster until Nashville was blanketed by a driving heavy snowstorm. Men shook their heads and asked, "Would volunteers appear in such weather?" But before eight o'clock some companies marched into town and by noon the public square was crowded with volunteers. At four o'clock the joyful news was out. The patriotism of Tennesseans could not be questioned, for 1,800 volunteers thronged Nashville.[10] People went mad—men of all classes congratulated one another and sang the praise of Tennessee's loyal sons.

The volunteers pitched their tents on the hills overlooking Nashville. Some men cleared away snow with their broganned feet, while others chopped wood, kindled fires, or brought water for cooking. Near dusk Governor Willie Blount, accompanied by exuberant citizens warmed by toasts drunk to volunteers, paraded through the streets. From the frozen, snow covered thoroughfares the crowd thrilled to the twinkling campfires on the nearby hills.

On those tented hills Andrew Jackson and his lieutenants worked without ceasing in caring for soldiers. Quartermaster William B. Lewis had provided a thousand cords of wood for the expected men. Ordinarily this fuel would have lasted until embarkation for New Orleans, but every stick of wood was burned that first night to keep the men from freezing. "From dark until nearly daylight the General and the quartermaster were out among the troops, employed in providing for this unexpected and perilous exigency; seeing that drunken men were brought within reach of a fire, and that no drowsy sentinel slept the sleep of death."[11]

About six in the morning, after a night of tramping in the snow, General Jackson entered a local tavern. Civilians and soldiers hovered around the open fire of a grog shop. One Nashville man, who had spent the night in a comfortable bed, was berating the authorities for having called so many troops without first providing adequate shelter for them.

"It's a shame," he told his companions, "that soldiers should be out on such a night, while the officers are quartered in the best houses of the town."

Jackson rushed forward and confronted the speaker. "You damned, infernal scoundrel!" roared the general. "You're sowing disaffection among the troops. Why, the quartermaster and I have been up all night, making the men comfortable. Let me hear no more such talk, or I'm damned if I don't ram that red hot andiron down your throat."[12]

Even the general's anger and threats did not still the rumblings of discontent. For three days the cold wind and low temperature continued unabated. Tents afforded little protection from the piercing wind, and there was an average of one blanket for three men. Twenty-seven to thirty soldiers slept side by side in tents, using the available blankets and their neighbor's body for warmth.

Information that five additional companies were en route toward Nashville warmed the spirit of the volunteers.[13] Eventually 2,070 men answered the call to arms, and Tennesseans pointed with pride to this exhibition of patriotism.

Warmer weather quieted the voices of discontent. On New Year's

Day Captain William Carroll's company of Nashville volunteers paraded in full dress for three charming guests. The Misses Lewis, Dudley, and James presented the captain a standard upon which was inscribed "God Armeth the Patriot." The girls whispered that their prayers would ever be for the success of their heroes, the Nashville volunteers.

Accepting the standard and holding it high for all to see, Captain Carroll said, "This reflects honor on the female patriot."

Then he turned toward his massed company: "Who would not fight for his country's cause under colours painted with taste; and [bowing toward the girls] by *your hands!* He who would not, deserves not your smiles, nor his country's plaudits! Under this banner, what foe dare we not encounter? What valorous deeds can we not achieve? It shall float in triumph, or be surrendered only with our lives.

"Fellow soldiers! Our country's wrongs and violated rights, prompt us to step forward in her defense – the smiles of the fair attend you. This is the signal for heroic exploit – designed by the loves and presented by the graces. The Gods are with us. Under the snow-white wave of this banner we 'conquer or die.' "[14]

Not every event in Nashville was so pleasant. Oliver Bush was drummed out of the service. An elderly man sneaked through the encampment urging men to desert. Jackson reprimanded him and let him go because of the loyalty of a son in the volunteers.[15] Men lost patience because of delay, demanded the opportunity of fighting – or at least of being on the way to battle – and an end of close order drills. Others complained about their pay, asking why some soldiers received their pay before others. "Why," asked Jackson, "if the love of Country have drawn you from the bosom of your families, such anxiety about who shall be first paid? Do you not know that all cannot be first? Can you not exercise a little patience? Take care how you indulge this reckless disposition, least [sic] the world should say that you are *ostensible* patriots, but *real mercenaries.*"[16]

Mercenary motives were alien to Jackson, who had borrowed hundreds of dollars on personal notes and used the money for the volunteers. He worked long days in speeding the accumulation of supplies and charting the expedition's course. Finally all was in readiness. Before leaving Nashville Jackson wrote the secretary of war: "I have the pleasure to inform you that I am now at the head of 2,070 volunteers, the choicest of our citizens, who go at the call of their country to execute the will of government, who have no constitutional scruples; and if the government orders, will rejoice at the opportunity of placing the American eagle on the ramparts of MOBILE, PENSACOLA, AND FORT ST. AUGUSTINE, effectually banishing from the southern coasts all British influence."[17]

On January 10, 1813, the volunteers embarked. The Nashville company, which Jackson selected as his guard, arrived at the general's headquarters that morning. Governor Blount was there; the judges of the superior courts and other leaders of the state were onlookers. From headquarters Jackson, the principal staff officers, and the guard marched to the Cumberland River where troops were boarding anchored boats. Minute guns were fired as the cables were loosened, and the spectators responded with shouts of encouragement and farewell. "The huzzas made the shores of the Cumberland resound, and the high Cliffs re-echo'd the melancholy of the parting scene!"[18]

That Sunday at sundown the boats anchored a few miles below Nashville. On January 12 the boats reached Harpeth River, forty miles below Nashville, where infantrymen who had left Nashville on January 7 awaited the flotilla. A count disclosed insufficient boats for transporting all the men and supplies. This deficiency was caused by a contractor, who, because of religious belief, had not sent his transports down Harpeth River on Sunday. The mouth of the river was frozen over; solid ice now prevented boats from being brought down river. Consequently many soldiers marched overland toward Clarksville.

Day after day the transports moved down the Cumberland toward the Ohio. Clarksville and Palmyra were left behind. On Sunday, January 17, one of the quartermaster's boats sank but the horses aboard and most of the corn were saved. Later in the morning Chaplain Blackman went from boat to boat preaching short sermons.

Two days later the flotilla reached the Ohio, where cakes of floating ice made navigation of that waterway impossible. For four days the volunteers camped on the banks of the Cumberland and then on the fifth day the river was clear; men boarded their vessels and pushed into the swift river current, and within four more days they sighted the ice-covered Mississippi. It was bitterly cold, but the river was rising and breaking its covering of mud-colored ice. During the night of January 29 the Mississippi rose four feet and the next morning the river was clear.

From the Ohio the transports moved into the broad, muddy Mississippi where driftwood and concealed snags endangered boats. As Captain John Wallace's ship passed Island 35, a snag stove in one side of his boat. In a few minutes the vessel was entirely covered with water, and its crew stood knee-deep in the cold current, expecting at every moment that one of the dark, rolling river waves would engulf them. Captain Harry Newlin was close by but he ordered his men to row away from the danger. Luckily for the endangered crew, Captain Brice Martin was cut from different cloth. His men propelled their boat with Herculean strokes, rescued the frightened men, and salvaged the wrecked vessel.

On the morning of February 16 the cliffs of Natchez came into view and the boats were anchored two miles above the town. Small fieldpieces were discharged in salute as General Jackson was rowed toward the shore. In Natchez he dined with Thomas M. Winn and received dispatches from General Wilkinson.[19]

Wilkinson requested Jackson to camp at Natchez, for neither quarters nor provisions were ready for 2,000 men in New Orleans. British forces were not in the vicinity of New Orleans or the Gulf, Wilkinson stated, and he required no reinforcements. Evidently the New Orleans commander was miffed. He had received no orders respecting the Tennesseans; he knew nothing of their probable destination, and certainly would not yield his command to Jackson until so ordered by a superior authority.

Jackson replied with a brief letter. He agreed to remain at Natchez and to await additional orders from Washington. He disclaimed any desire to outrank Wilkinson, stating: "I have marched with the true spirit of a soldier to serve my country at any and every point where service can be rendered."[20]

The volunteers disembarked on February 17, marched through Natchez, and made camp just beyond the town. After the freezing weather en route the warm Mississippi sun came as a welcome relief. But rain descended in torrents on February 20 and roads became quagmires of mud. The long voyage, unbalanced diet, and bad water populated hospital tents.

Jackson waited impatiently for orders. He informed Wilkinson that the volunteers would be kept in readiness for movement to any point at which an enemy might appear. The general, however, was thinking of conquering Florida, for he told Wilkinson, "My eyes are turned to the south East."[21] Colonel John Coffee reported Natchez an ideal campsite with a central location, from which the army could move quickly to the east and take the Floridas.[22]

After two weeks of idleness Jackson's patience was worn threadbare. He could not keep men imbued with the martial spirit at their peak by daily drills without an idea of when they would march. "Would it not be important to the Government to turn this section of the army to the frontiers of Canada?" he asked Secretary of War Armstrong. "I presume the Detachment under my command was ordered to this country in anticipation, that the Government would be authorized by a Law of congress to occupy the Floridas. But private advises say that such a law will not be passed and the object of the Expidition [sic] will be lost."[23] Jackson mentioned the embarrassment to himself and General Wilkinson because of indefinite instructions from Washington. As had Mathews and Mitchell before him, the Tennessee general discovered that the Madison administration chested its cards in the play for Florida.

Two more weeks dragged on before dispatches came from Washington. On Monday, March 15, an express from Secretary Armstrong reached Jackson. The general ripped open the letter, and read: "The causes of embodying and marching to New Orleans the corps under your command having ceased to exist, you will, on the receipt of this letter, consider it as dismissed from public service, and take measures to have delivered over to Major General Wilkinson all the articles of public property which may have been put into its possession. You will accept for yourself and the corps the thanks of the President of the United States."[24]

Jackson was dazed. He could not believe what he read. Termination of the Florida project was not unexpected, for he had received advance information on that possibility. But the troops were needed elsewhere – on the Canadian front, on the eastern seaboard. Surely 2,000 men could be used by a country which had suffered defeat after defeat. Even if the Tennesseans could not serve, they should not be dismissed in Mississippi, hundreds of miles from their homes.

Were the volunteers dismissed as of that day? Were they to march back home on their own, without supplies, arms, or ammunition? Jackson did not know. Again he read Armstrong's letter: "On the receipt of this letter, consider it [the volunteer force] as dismissed from public service." There it was in black and white – to him the most idiotic order yet from those bureaucrats and armchair generals in Washington.

Jackson would not accept the order. Returning home without a chance to fight was bad enough and he could not dismiss his loyal soldiers so far from home. If necessary, he would march them back as an army and pay all expenses. With Armstrong's letter before him Jackson penned a blistering reply. "If it was intended by this order that we should be dismissed eight hundred miles from home, deprived of arms, tents and supplies for the sick, of our arms and supplies for the well, it appears that these brave men, who certainly deserve a better fate and return from their government, was intended by this order to be sacrificed. Those that could escape from the insalubrious climate, are to be deprived of the necessary support and meet death by famine. . . . Was this the language of the act calling on the citisans [sic] to rally round the government of their choice, which brought this band of heroes the best citisans and wealth of our country into the field, and whose attention to order discipline and harmony forbode ample services to their country, who tendered their services to march and support the Eagles of their country to the heights of Abraham on the North, or the burning and unwholesome climate of the South. These men had no constitutional boundaries but that of their insulted Government, its rights privaliges [sic] and its laws."

Andrew Jackson praised his militia. "I have no hesitation in giving the lie to the modern doctrine that it is inefficient to defend the liberties of our country, and that standing armies are necessary in time of peace." He concluded his letter by stating: "I mean to commence my march to Nashville in a few days at which place I expect the troops to be paid and the necessary supplies furnished by the agents of Government while payment is making, after which I will dismiss them to their homes and families."[25]

There was a Nemesis which dogged the heels of those who served Madison and Monroe in their Florida schemes. Mathews, Mitchell, and Smith found disgrace, dissatisfaction, and boredom in Florida without accomplishing the desired goal. Jackson was not allowed the opportunity of even reaching the Spanish provinces before he received a curt dismissal.

In Washington anticipated acts had not become laws. Madison and Monroe had moved too quickly. The unexpected always conquered the expected in Florida affairs.

Recalcitrant Senators

IN DECEMBER, 1812, MADISON AND Monroe believed congressional sanction for occupation of the Floridas a foregone conclusion. The Senate defeated the measure by only two votes in July. Since that date the United States had been denied success in Canada, and two senators from the recently admitted state of Louisiana had been seated. Louisiana's senators naturally favored the annexation of the Floridas, and the people of the country demanded a victory somewhere. The promise of an easy conquest together with Southern agitation would undoubtedly bring a few maverick Republican senators back into regularity. Those close to the administration assured the executive of swift senatorial approval of the project which had for so long been dear to the hearts of Republican leaders. Without hesitation or a full consideration of possible consequences, the president and his secretary set in motion the troops and supplies requisite for conquest.

Their friend, Senator Joseph Anderson of Tennessee, moved on December 10, 1812, in secret session, that a committee be appointed "to consider whether it be expedient to authorize the President of the United States to occupy and hold the whole or any part of East Florida, including Amelia Island, and also those parts of West Florida which are not now in the possession and under the jurisdiction of the United States, with leave to report by bill or otherwise."[1] Anderson's proposal was debated in the Senate on Tuesday, December 15, but further consideration was postponed until Monday. On the following day, however, Senator Michael Lieb of Pennsylvania moved that the president be requested to lay before the Senate information on British plans for occupying the Floridas, the desires of the people of East Florida to be under the protection of the United States, and the American and Spanish forces in or near the Spanish province.[2] Three days later Senator Chauncey Goodrich demanded complete information on recent negotiations for the settlement of differences and claims between the United States and Spain along with proposals made by any person or persons exercising, or claiming to exercise, power from Spain to cede East Florida.[3]

On December 22 Senator Samuel Smith of Maryland advocated postponement of the Florida proposal, but his motion met a quick defeat. Senator Anderson's resolution was accepted by a vote of eighteen to twelve. Lieb's request for information, as amended by Goodrich, also won approval of the Senate. Senators Anderson, Goodrich, Smith, Charles Tait of Georgia, and Joseph Varnum of Massachusetts were appointed as a committee to investigate the advisability of authorizing the seizure of the Floridas.[4] The committee was a "safe" one, for Chairman Anderson, Tait, and Varnum were administration stalwarts.

Debate on the Florida project was suspended until receipt of the requested information. On January 14, 1813, President Madison transmitted the report of Monroe on Florida.[5] Monroe answered one by one the questions raised by Senators Lieb and Goodrich. There was no precise information on movement of British troops toward East Florida, he admitted, for if Great Britain planned to occupy the province, "the intention and the act will become known at the same time." As Great Britain was at war with the United States and therefore needed troops in Halifax, the West Indies, and other parts of the Western Hemisphere, "it will be easy for her to disguise the destination of any particular embarkation, until it reaches our coast." British soldiers could land at St. Augustine, Monroe stated, or at any other port of Florida without opposition from American forces.

As to the feelings and disposition of the people in East Florida, Monroe knew their attachment to the United States was beyond question. The revolutionary movement in that Spanish province and the cession made to General Mathews evinced their longing for American occupation and protection. He also summed up all the negotiations for the cession of the Floridas and reiterated the claim of a mortgage which the United States held on East Florida. Since the Spanish government would not settle its just debts, the United States must take the province, for eventually Great Britain or France would control Spain. With East Florida in possession of either of those powerful countries, the United States could not acquire it or secure compensation for the spoliation claims.

On January 19 Senator Anderson's committee reported a bill which authorized the president "to take possession of a tract of country lying south of the Mississippi Territory and of Georgia." Section one empowered the executive to occupy and hold that part of West Florida which lay west of the Perdido River. The second section was the heart of the bill. It provided for the seizure of "all that part of West Florida east of the Perdido, and the whole or any part of East Florida, including Amelia Island." Sections three and four authorized the use of military forces and made appropriations to cover the expense of conquest and occupation. The final section of the bill dealt with the establishment of a temporary government after conquest, and instructed the president to preserve the existing social order and grant residents of Florida complete personal, religious, and property rights. This section also designated that the area east of the Perdido might be subject to future negotiation with Spain.[6]

The proposed act passed a first and second reading without opposition. On January 26 Samuel Smith moved that section two be stricken from the proposed measure.[7] Since this section was the important one, it was agreed to debate the motion and then vote on it. The outcome of the Florida project hung on the acceptance or rejection of Smith's proposal. If administration forces succeeded in defeating it, the whole of East Florida would be seized and annexed.

The opposition rallied its forces. Debate continued for days with the opponents of occupation speaking most often. As the argument continued the Madison supporters appeared to be in the majority. Samuel Smith reluctantly admitted defeat. In his opinion the administration senators had the necessary votes for passing the bill and they would not change their ideas, no matter what might be the logic and truth presented by their opposition. Senator Tait of Georgia took the floor. He presented a memorial from the legislature of his state and denounced those who opposed the general welfare of the United States and the particular good of Georgia.

RECALCITRANT SENATORS

Federalist Senator William Hunter of Rhode Island responded for the anti-administration senators. He reminded the assembled senators of the July, 1812, vote and the rejection of an almost identical proposal for occupying the Floridas. Had any new proof of necessity, additional statements of reason, or further explanations of cause for occupation been advanced? Hunter asked. He declared they had not. The same old refuted arguments had been reiterated — arguments which had been rejected less than seven months before by the Senate. Consistency should be the guiding principle of the legislator, Hunter stated, unless reason, valid reason, made change necessary.

Although some senators had denied that the proposed conquest of East Florida would be war, Hunter declared it would be and he supported his contention by citing Vattel's definition of war. Based on the writing of this recognized authority on international law, Hunter told his audience: "I say this is not only war, but an offensive war; not only an offensive but an unjust war; not only unjust, but I am, for the honor of my country, [forced to say].... It is a wicked war; it is robbery." These were strong words, Hunter admitted, but added that the people of Georgia and South Carolina needed strong words to awaken them. If he were a resident of Georgia, Hunter would get on his knees and pray for defeat of the occupation bill, for war would bring an invasion of the South by the black militia of Spain. The Negro, "that unhappy species of population, which prevails in our southern country, aroused to reflection by the sight of black soldiers and black officers, may suspect themselves to be fellow-men, and fondly dream they likewise could be soldiers and officers.... Take care," Hunter warned, "that while you are pursuing foreign conquest, your own homes are not devastated."

Some men preferred to take the Floridas rather than obtain them through diplomatic channels, Hunter stated. Should the United States grab East Florida because renegades, banditti, or Jacobin revolutionists opposed the regular Spanish authority? "Does a really deep, honest, spontaneous revolutionary movement exist there? Is it not, on the contrary an artificial, concerted, contrived, petty, patched-up, miserable treason, paid for by our money, fomented by our people? Who caused this movement? Was it not solely occasioned by American interference — by American instigation? When the names were read, from Matthews [sic] communication and the other papers, could the gravest among us forbear to smile at the paucity of Spanish names?"

Hunter wanted it understood that he was not condemning General Mathews. He had boundless sympathy for the memory of that abused individual. "I cannot but believe that he thought he acted with perfect good faith to the Government, strictly in virtue of his private, if not public instructions, and that he counted, not only on the support, but the applause of Government. Cruelly disappointed in the result, he conceived that he had just cause of complaint. He considered himself the victim of a temporizing, vacillating, insidious policy." Hunter turned and addressed Senator Crawford, "I ask the honorable gentlemen from Georgia, did not Matthews [sic] die with such sentiments trembling to the very last on his lips? The averment of his own honor and innocence – of the tergiversation and pusillanimity of his employers? Was he not hurrying on to Washington, literally for his vindication, when, fortunately for those he had in his power to expose, death arrested his course?"

Sarcastically he asked his listeners if American honor had been besmirched by the attack on Smith's forces at Moosa Old Fort. "Moosa," he cried, "where is it? Within two miles of the fortress of St. Augustine. And, if you had the camp of an enemy at Georgetown, threatening the Capitol – the existence of your government; a foreign force, combined with domestic traitors, to overwhelm you, to throw you neck and heels into the Potomac ... would you not attack?" The firing on Moosa was the most miserable of all the reasons advanced for seizing East Florida, Hunter shouted. "Good God! Where are we? In what age do we live? In what country, when it is made a crime to extirpate the invaders of our native soil? In what age, in what country, when it is made a virtue for a nation, itself in war for neutral rights, to invade an inoffending, helpless, friendly, neutral country?"

The senator told his colleagues that he had exhausted himself but not his subject. In conclusion he requested each senator to ask himself again and again what right the United States had to East Florida. "Is it any other than the right created by desire – the right suggested by ambition – the right of taking advantage of the troubles of our neighbors – of plundering weakness, of imposing on misfortune, of oppressing the oppressed?"[8]

At the conclusion of Hunter's speech, the legislators demanded a vote. The question was: shall section two, which authorized the seizure of East Florida, be eliminated from the bill for occupying the Floridas? As the senators answered the roll call, opponents and proponents hastily computed the possible outcome. The final tally was nineteen to sixteen for deleting section two of the bill. The pro-administration forces had picked up two votes more than their total of fourteen in the July, 1812, contest, but their opponents had gained three.[9]

Six Federalist senators and thirteen Republicans had combined to reject once again Madison and Monroe's plan for annexing the Floridas. Senators from Louisiana, Georgia, South Carolina, North Carolina, and Tennessee unanimously favored occupation; senators from Rhode Island, Connecticut, New York, New Jersey (only one senator voted), Pennsylvania, Delaware, and Maryland were unanimously opposed; and senators from New Hampshire, Vermont, Massachusetts, Virginia, Ohio, and Kentucky were divided. The anti-administration faction of Giles, Lieb, and Samuel Smith, aided by Federalists and commercial interests succeeded in tearing the heart from the Florida bill.

On February 5 the emasculated bill, which now authorized nothing more than occupation of those as yet unseized areas between the Perdido and Pearl rivers in West Florida, passed by a vote of twenty-two to eleven.[10] The House of Representatives accepted the Senate bill and President Madison signed it on February 12.[11] The act added nothing to the president's power. Long ago the Congress had authorized occupation of West Florida from the Perdido west, claiming that area as a part of the Louisiana Purchase. The status of the Floridas east of the Perdido remained the same on the statute books of the United States: the president could occupy and hold it to forestall foreign occupation or accept it from the local authorities.

For a second time within less than seven months the plans of president and secretary of state had been rejected by recalcitrant senators. After July, 1812, and in spite of the Senate, excuses had been found for keeping troops in East Florida. Would the Florida subject be abandoned, or would another scheme be hatched for annexation?

Retreat of the Invader

THE PERSISTENT OPPOSITION OF senators forced Madison and Monroe to give up their plans for conquering the Floridas. In the face of congressional disapproval the administration could not maintain troops in East Florida.

For almost a year since that day in March, 1812, when Colonel Smith's regulars moved from Point Petre to Fernandina, American troops had been stationed on Spanish colonial soil without congressional authorization or international sanction. Always there had been hope—hope that local officials would surrender the province, that Great Britain would invade it, or Congress would permit conquest of it. None of these possibilities had been realized. East Florida remained as desirable as ever; but it must be obtained, if it still could be secured, by some means other than conquest. American troops had to be withdrawn.

Madison delayed the inevitable order for evacuation, but he cancelled preparations for conquest. Four days after section two of the Florida occupation bill had been deleted, the secretary of war ordered Jackson to dismiss his volunteers. Monroe did not issue this order. On February 5, 1813, he surrendered his office to John Armstrong, and confined his activities to directing the Department of State. Armstrong, a military man and former minister to France, dictated the curt letter of dismissal which had angered Andrew Jackson.

Recall of Jackson did not imply the evacuation of East Florida. Three days after Armstrong dispatched the Jackson letter, the secretary gave General Pinckney discretionary power to dismiss or retain the East Tennessee volunteers in service when they returned from the expedition against the Seminoles.[1] Thus a week after Senate rejection of the Florida occupation bill, the administration was not contemplating evacuation of the Spanish province. On February 15 Armstrong wrote Pinckney: "The late private proceedings of Congress have resulted in a decision not to invade East Florida at present."[2] Pinckney was ordered to quarter his troops in such a manner as to promote their health and discipline. Removal from East Florida was not ordered. On the contrary the implication was clear – American regulars were to hold their position until such time as invasion was authorized.

Armstrong's letter puzzled Pinckney. He had assumed that the Senate's action foreshadowed evacuation of East Florida, and was surprised when he received no definite orders for withdrawal. The general requested further instructions. Was he to continue occupation of the St. Johns and Amelia areas, or was he to evacuate the American troops? If retreat was planned, should he communicate with Governor Kindelan in hope of securing amnesty for the Patriots?[3]

Some time between February 15 and March 7 President Madison reached a decision. The trend of the administration's thinking was indicated on March 6 by a letter of Armstrong's. In it the secretary answered Pinckney's inquiry of January on the problem of allowing the Tennessee volunteers to proceed against Indians who had sued for peace. Belatedly the secretary stated, "It is the spirit of the National policy to give peace to any enemy asking it in sincerity and good faith. The Seminoles do not form an exception."[4] This was the spirit in Washington in March, but it had not been the attitude in December and January when Hawkins, Mitchell, and Pinckney had pleaded the cause of the Indians. This statement of high principle came too late to save the lives and property of the Indians.

A new policy on Florida was announced on March 7. Onís had given Monroe assurance of amnesty for the Patriots along with a copy of the general pardon approved by the Cortes in Spain. This amnesty act was sent General Pinckney, who was authorized to communicate with Governor Kindelan. If the governor verified and promulgated the amnesty, Pinckney was ordered to withdraw American troops from the St. Johns and Amelia Island.[5]

Evacuation, however, was not a renunciation of the Florida project. Madison and Monroe would yet obtain the province through diplomacy, and opportunity came in a Russian proposal of mediation of the differences between Great Britain and the United States.

In the changing European scene Russia had broken with Napoleon and allied herself with Great Britain and Spain. As the ally of Great Britain, Russia had a vital interest in terminating the American war which lessened British power in the joint effort to defeat Napoleon. In September, 1812, Count Nicholas Rumanzoff called in John Quincy Adams, the United States minister at St. Petersburg, and questioned him about American reception of a Russian mediation offer. Adams assured the count that it would be well received. The American minister expressed doubt as to the British attitude, but was assured that Great Britain had been consulted and the prospect for peace appeared favorable. On September 30, 1812, Adams informed Washington of the proposal.[6]

It was March of the following year before Monroe received the offer. Russian minister André Daschkoff presented Rumanzoff's proposal and Monroe eagerly accepted it. Since the war against Great Britain had not progressed as planned, the confused Madison administration welcomed the possibility of a face-saving peace. There was even a chance of gaining a diplomatic victory, for Great Britain faced a formidable foe in France. If urged by the Russians, the British might concede much for peace with the United States.

Peace and the Floridas became twin goals of Madison and Monroe in 1813. The president appointed John Quincy Adams, Albert Gallatin, and James Bayard as ministers plenipotentiary to meet British representatives in St. Petersburg, and with Russian aid, negotiate a treaty. Since Adams was in the Russian capital, Gallatin and Bayard were briefed by Monroe, who saw the negotiation with Great Britain as a means of securing the Floridas. He ordered the American ministers to insist upon a recognition of United States ownership of West Florida beyond the Perdido River as a part of the Louisiana Purchase and the American right to East Florida as an indemnity for the spoliation claims. Gallatin and Bayard should keep in mind that Mobile would be occupied by United States troops; "And as the Law authoriz[ing] the President to take possession of East Florida, in case an attempt should be made by any foreign power to occupy it, is still in force, it will be proper for you to have the object of law in your recollection in your negotiations."[7]

Monroe knew of Secretary of the Treasury Gallatin's distaste for the Florida annexation project. It was no surprise, therefore, when he received a protest from the secretary. Why was it important to take immediate possession of Mobile, asked Gallatin, when the United States could occupy that town at any time? Seizure of Mobile was of minor importance, but grabbing it from Spain, the ally of Russia and Great Britain, might impede negotiations. "You know that to take by force any place in possession of another nation, whatever our claim to that place may be, is war," Gallatin explained; "and you must be aware that both Russia and Great Britain will feel disposed, if not to support the pretensions of Spain against us, at least to take part against the aggressor."[8]

Gallatin also requested official information on the evacuation of East Florida. In his opinion the order for withdrawal of American troops could be used advantageously. It might smooth the ground in preliminary negotiations and could be exhibited as an expression of Congress on the Florida question. It would in effect do much toward counteracting the unfavorable opinion of the United States in Europe which had developed as a result of the invasion of East Florida.

Monroe answered Gallatin with a curt, pointed letter. Orders had been issued for the occupation of Mobile, he stated, and if they had not already been carried out, they would be before the American ministers reached St. Petersburg. "That is a question settled," the secretary informed Gallatin. An order had been given for evacuating East Florida, and Monroe promised he would make an effort to send the ministers a copy of it before they sailed.[9]

Gallatin made one more effort. He acclaimed the evacuation order but urged Monroe to leave East Florida alone until the appearance of British troops there gave proof that Spain had ceded it to Great Britain. He scoffed at rumors of British acquisition of the Spanish province. If Great Britain ever occupied East Florida, he believed it would be at the request of Spain and because of American aggressiveness. The withdrawal of American troops would kill any British pretext for occupying St. Augustine.

The occupation of Mobile still worried Gallatin. It might bring war; and he warned Monroe that should it involve the United States in a war with Spain, it would disgust every man north of Washington. Annexation of the Floridas was a Southern scheme. Northern men disliked it and it should be buried. In the existing critical situation of the United States he saw need for prudence to preserve and invigorate the American Union.[10]

Gallatin's admonition fell on deaf ears. Orders for seizing Mobile were not rescinded; instructions for demanding the remaining parts of West Florida and East Florida were not altered. The American ministers sailed with definite instructions to prevent Great Britain's acquisition of the Floridas and to claim the whole of those provinces for the United States as recompense for the spoliation claims against Spain.

As Gallatin and Bayard prepared for their mission, activity increased along the Georgia border. General Pinckney received the order to evacuate East Florida on March 18, 1813. He planned to leave his headquarters in Charleston and move to St. Marys where he could supervise the retreat from Florida.[11]

Before leaving Charleston Pinckney sent his aide to Governor Kindelan with information of the American desire for a settlement of differences. If the governor would honor and promulgate the amnesty act of the Spanish Cortes, the United States forces would be withdrawn from East Florida. The general believed a personal meeting would facilitate American evacuation and Spanish reoccupation of the province.[12]

Kindelan gave the general's aide a warm welcome. The governor sent Pinckney a certified copy of the amnesty which had already been promulgated, and assured the general that all revolutionists who appeared in St. Augustine would be given a complete and unconditional pardon. As much as Kindelan would enjoy meeting the American general, he thought it improper as long as United States troops remained in East Florida.[13]

Governor Kindelan complied with the letter of the amnesty as promised by Onís. By the proclamation, "Don Sebastián Kindelan y Oregon, Knight of the Order of St. James, Brigadier General of the National Armies, Civil and Military Governor of the City of St. Augustine," made known that the captain general of Cuba by order of the regency of Spain had granted an amnesty to the insurgents who had cooperated in the invasion of East Florida. A general pardon with oblivion of the past was granted all who would in the future demean themselves as good and faithful subjects of the constituted

Spanish authorities. Each insurgent had a four-months period of grace within which time he should either leave the province or appear in St. Augustine for his pardon.[14]

General Pinckney read the proclamation at Savannah where he had paused while en route to St. Marys. Without hesitation he accepted Kindelan's statements as evidence of good faith. On April 7 he informed the governor that American troops would be withdrawn with all possible speed. A preparatory order for evacuation had already been issued, Pinckney stated, and he would soon be in St. Marys where he could communicate more easily with the governor.[15]

Before he reached St. Marys the general had issued orders dismissing the East Tennessee volunteers and disbanding the Georgia Militia.[16] As the Tennesseans desired to return home by different routes, $2,000 was given Colonel Williams for the expenses of his several detachments.[17] Pinckney planned to withdraw the regular troops from Florida to the post at Point Petre near St. Marys.

The general arrived at the Georgia town during the second week of April. He received an inquiry immediately from Kindelan. On what day would the American troops leave St. Johns and Amelia? the governor asked. He wished Spanish soldiers to march in as the Americans departed and thus prevent robbery and bloodshed by "persons of no character or vagabonds from the State of Georgia," who might compromise the peace between Spain and the United States.[18] Pinckney promised to evacuate the St. Johns on April 29 and Amelia Island on May 6.[19]

Spaniards celebrated this announcement of intention. General Pinckney was pleased to be the agent who could atone in part for past wrongs, but Georgians and Patriots shouted their anger. The latter bombarded Pinckney and other officials with protests.

Quick-witted Buckner Harris solicited Governor Mitchell's interposition in behalf of the East Floridians. As those below the St. Marys had been reduced to extreme want they would be forced to "go off in a state of beggary." This would materially affect the state of Georgia, Harris stated, for Floridians would seek refuge there.[20]

Harris, who had the title of "President of the Legislative Council of the Territory of East Florida," conferred with Patriot council members. In the absence of "Director" McIntosh they called a special council meeting. Harris and his advisers unanimously determined to defend East Florida "to the last extremity." Though short of money, they planned on selling their personal property and pledging the unappropriated lands of East Florida as security to those who would lend the Patriots money. Would Georgia give money, provisions, and munitions, Harris asked Mitchell. The example set by France during the American Revolution could be imitated by Georgia, and by so doing the state would avoid the charge of direct interference in Florida.[21]

The Patriot legislative council convened on March 30 and addressed an appeal to Pinckney. The history of the East Florida revolution was recounted and emphasis placed on the agency and promises of General Mathews. Even after the general's disavowal, Patriots discovered the American troops still protected them. Smith's regulars, Newnan's volunteers, and the East Tennessee volunteers were convincing evidence of continued American occupation. Encouraged by these favorable signs, the revolutionists had prepared their land and planted their crops. Then the blow fell. Their only promise of protection was in a Spanish proclamation of amnesty. In the opinion of Patriots, that pardon originated in St. Augustine, not Spain. It was a hollow and deceitful subterfuge which would not be honored in practice by Kindelan, for the Patriots expected neither truth nor mercy from officials who used blacks and mulattoes as soldiers. As soon as the American troops evacuated East Florida the revolutionists would receive no mercy — "the result can easily be anticipated and is dreadful to think of."

Since Pinckney knew the record of the "vile Spanish government" in the Netherlands and elsewhere the Patriots requested the general to stay his orders for evacuation. Or if he had determined on withdrawal, then each military position in East Florida should be given the revolutionists, who had originally captured them from Spain and ceded them to the United States. In all fairness the customs duties collected at Fernandina should be handed the Patriots, for they had seized that town and delivered it on promise of receiving all duties collected there.[22]

In addition to its appeal to Pinckney, the Patriot council vested John Houstoun McIntosh with dictatorial powers.[23] He received specific authority to receive the customs funds, disperse them as he saw fit, and make agreements or treaties.

McIntosh and the council also issued a counter proclamation in answer to Kindelan's amnesty offer. They viewed with "disdain and abhorrence the proffer of pardon by the corrupt government of St. Augustine," and pledged their property and reputations for their "glorious cause." "*Patriots of East Florida*," ran the proclamation, "weak must be the mind that can have the least dependence upon a promise so hollow and deceitful" as the pardon of Kindelan. "Can anyone believe, that such a corrupt, jealous and arbitrary government will adhere to promises however sacredly made? Will they not screw every title to your property . . . [from you]? Aided by a venal judge, supported by a cruel government, your enemies will harass you so long as a cent remains with you. . . . *Can you!* Will you in poverty become the sport of slaves and the abhorred army in St. Augustine." From now on, the Patriots proclaimed, there could be but two parties in East Florida — friend and enemy.[24]

Pinckney was disgusted by the offensive language of the proclamation.[25] He ignored the appeal of those who claimed authority. The general did answer a letter in which Zephaniah Kingsley and thirty-four other private citizens of East Florida stated evacuation would leave them at the mercy of black and red savages.[26] Citizens of East Florida had no right to expect continued protection by American troops, Pinckney replied, for the United States had never recognized the acts of Mathews. The American government would not allow a foreign power to interfere with the internal problems of the United States and conversely would not interpose its authority between a foreign power and its subjects. The United States had continued the occupation of East Florida after disavowing Mathews by using the spoliation claims against Spain as a shield with which to protect the Patriots. At the cost of many lives and by the expenditure of much money the American government had secured an amnesty for the revolutionists. The United States could do no more; the troops would be withdrawn; and although he would regret it if Kindelan did not fulfill his promises, Pinckney advised the Patriots their appeal should be made to the Spanish government, "the government of your nativity or of your choice," for protection.[27]

John Houstoun McIntosh conferred with Pinckney on April 12, the day he arrived at St. Marys.[28] "General, we have heard rumors of evacuation," McIntosh said. "When your aide passed through St. Marys en route to St. Augustine, he refused to tell us his purpose. He did promise that President Madison would give us ample time, if the troops were withdrawn, to sell our property, or remove it from East Florida. We thought your aide's mission favored us. Now we hear the troops will be withdrawn – that the amnesty proclamation of Kindelan has been accepted as real."

"It has," replied Pinckney. "Mr. Secretary Monroe secured it from Spain through the agency of Mr. Onís. The Patriots are assured a general and complete pardon."

McIntosh made a gesture of hopelessness. "You know the nature and character of the Spanish government," he exclaimed. "Do you, general, believe any Spanish government will fulfill its promises? This pardon is fallacious and treacherous."

"My duty is not to pass judgment on Spanish veracity," Pinckney stated. "Because it felt a partial responsibility for Mathews' acts, the United States has protected you. Governor Kindelan has met American demands and East Florida will be evacuated."

"But we'll be left destitute," exclaimed McIntosh. "Spaniards have made repeated threats against us. They will violate every promise, for ignorance, venality, and bigotry are ingrained in their character, and they will surely find pretexts to despoil us of our property, of our lives."

"If that should occur, I shall be sorry," Pinckney stated.

"It will happen," said McIntosh. "Could you hold the troops in East Florida until you can represent us to President Madison? We do not believe a government for which we have risked everything will deliver us to our former tyrants merely on the declaration of an impotent Cortes in Spain – a declaration suggested by the Spanish minister in Washington."

"Wait a few weeks, general," McIntosh pleaded. "Don't deliver us to an enraged and vindictive enemy without giving us one more opportunity of calling on your government for safety and protection."

Pinckney shook his head. "My orders are definite," he said. "The troops will be withdrawn."

"We knew continued occupation of East Florida requires some legislative sanction," McIntosh stated. "But on your recommendation, President Madison would demand some pledge, some assurance that the general pardon will be observed in practice."

"I do not have discretionary powers," Pinckney said. "My orders leave me no latitude. I have already made arrangements with Governor Kindelan for evacuation."

McIntosh knew he had failed. As a soldier Pinckney would obey orders, but would he, as a farmer? McIntosh appealed to him as a fellow planter.

"We have plowed and planted our lands. We have four months in which to accept pardon or leave East Florida, which will not give us sufficient time for harvest. Those of us who are determined to be American citizens need some protection. If the grace period under the amnesty could be extended, it would help us."

Pinckney considered this appeal, for property and property rights were dear to his Federalist heart. Even revolutionists should not suffer so extreme a penalty as the loss of planted crops.

McIntosh had struck a sympathetic chord. The general would not delay evacuation, nor appeal to President Madison, but he would request an extension of time from Kindelan.

This appeal was not what McIntosh had in mind, but he could obtain nothing more. On the day following his conference he summarized his arguments in a letter. Pinckney replied with a firm, friendly manner which gave the Patriots little cause for hope. The general promised to forward McIntosh's appeal and letter to President Madison.[29]

Discouraged but indefatigable McIntosh addressed a letter to Monroe. "We have been most cruelly disappointed," he stated. "After all our expectations and hopes, after all the assurances we have received from Genl. Mathews and Governor Mitchell and others, that we would never be abandoned by the U. States Government, we are surrendered on the declaration of a crazy imbecile Cortes (which the president refused officially to acknowledge) at the most critical unfortunate period that has existed since we have attempted to throw off oppression. . . ."

In 1812 the Patriots had produced few crops on their farms, McIntosh declared, and in 1813 they would be unable to gather those which had been planted on the assurance of continued American occupation of East Florida. To talk of moving into Georgia was idle fancy. "Genl. Mathews found me with a numerous family, possessed of affluence to give them the best education and to carry them in the most fashionable circles in America, but I owe it to the memory of

Genl. Mathews to declare, that I was warmed by his honest zeal, I revered his virtue and shall ever respect his memory. Genl. Pinckney will leave me poor and without the means of living anywhere, but in retirement."[30]

McIntosh was not financially destitute, and Pinckney did befriend the Patriots. The general forwarded the Patriot appeals to Washington and he planned to delay the evacuation to give them a few more days of grace.[31] On April 18, he informed Kindelan of the hardships faced by those who were unwilling to remain under Spanish authority. Unless they were allowed sufficient time to harvest their crops and sell their property they would burn their houses. Such destruction would benefit no one. If Governor Kindelan would extend the grace period from four to seven months, Pinckney believed peace would be quickly restored, as former revolutionists would have economic reason for behaving themselves.[32]

The pardon was general and unlimited, Kindelan replied, but those who would not accept it could not remain in East Florida longer than four months. He could not extend this period beyond the limit set by the Cortes. He would, however, allow the insurgents the additional privilege of naming agents who could supervise their farms and sell their crops during the 1813 season. These agents must be native or naturalized Spaniards acceptable to the governor, and in exporting property and produce the regular export duties would be levied. Furthermore, Kindelan concluded, insurgents who accepted this offer must never again set foot in East Florida.[33]

This concession did not satisfy the Patriots. Only American annexation of East Florida and validation of their land claims would have satisfied them. In a final attempt to gain American support the Patriots spread rumors about the mistreatment of former revolutionists and the possibility of English occupation of East Florida.[34]

General Pinckney brushed aside this Patriot propaganda. The evacuation was carefully planned to make it appear as a restoration of neutral territory which had been held until Spanish officials complied with demands made by President Madison. Therefore destruction or removing of property was banned. American army officers were to act as disinterested neutrals as they withdrew from the St. Johns on April 29 and from Fernandina a week later.[35]

These orders were not fully executed. Major Manning embarked from Camp New Hope three days before the appointed time, and as the Spanish soldiers knew nothing of this altered plan, the Patriots occupied the camp. Before withdrawing they burned camp huts and nearby plantation houses, destroyed agricultural equipment, and killed farm animals. Kindelan complained of the American breach of faith. An embarrassed Pinckney rebuked Major Manning who defended himself by declaring the date on his letter of instructions appeared as April 26 rather than April 29. This explanation did not satisfy Pinckney who favored a formal inquiry of the Major's action.[36]

Captain Massias evacuated Fernandina on May 6 as planned.[37] Commodore Campbell's gunboats convoyed the retreating troops from New Hope and Fernandina to St. Marys, where the naval vessels anchored. American naval and military forces were all withdrawn from East Florida after one year and fifty days of occupation.

Fernandina acclaimed the restoration of Spanish rule. Cannon boomed welcoming salutes as Captain Francisco Rivera and forty men reoccupied the town. Happy men read the posted proclamation of Governor Kindelan: East Floridians were promised the rights and privileges of the "Holy Charter" of 1812, the recently promulgated liberal Constitution of Spain. On May 8 the citizens massed around a hastily constructed pavilion and swore their fealty to Spain and the new Constitution.

Philip Yonge accepted provisional appointment as *Capitan de Perdido* of Amelia Island. Kindelan knew Yonge only by reputation. He had demonstrated his loyalty by resisting the rebels and sending food to St. Augustine during the siege. Although born to parents who had moved from Scotland into Florida during the British period, Philip Yonge was a native of East Florida and had the confidence of English-speaking residents of Fernandina. He was one of the Anglo-Spaniards who had mastered the Spanish language.

Governor Kindelan had more trouble securing native Spaniards for the St. Johns area than for Fernandina, for outside of St. Augustine there were less than twenty-five Spaniards in East Florida. Many of these had joined the rebels or had relatives among the revolutionists. On the St. Johns Kindelan found only two men who had not supported the insurgents. These were Farquahar Bethune, a Scot, and Francisco Fatio, a Swiss, and as loyal naturalized subjects they were appointed captains of the lower and upper St. Johns districts.

265

Problems other than appointments faced Kindelan. East Florida was a ravaged, despoiled land. Charred remains marked former houses and barns, cattle and work animals were scarce, plows and other farm tools could not be found; even seed for planting was difficult to procure. A country which had been fairly prosperous in March, 1812, was almost barren and desolate in May, 1813.[38]

The anarchy created by revolution, invasion, and Indian wars was not terminated by the American retreat. Former Patriots contested Spanish authority below the St. Marys; adventurers from Georgia and other Southern states raided the Spanish province for slaves and movable property; and smugglers and slave traders renewed their illegal activities. Spanish officials complained of the raids and American officials of the smuggling.

A few weeks in St. Marys convinced General Pinckney that the East Florida problem had not been solved by evacuation. It would be advantageous to purchase the province at a price much higher than its estimated value, he told Monroe, for the United States would save money acquiring it. With its possession the American army on the border could be reduced by seventy-five per cent. Smuggling and the loss of customs duties could not be checked without ownership or control of East Florida. Furthermore, acquisition would prevent criminals from justice and fugitive slaves from escaping, provide security against the Indians, and give peace of mind to Southerners.[39]

As the military and civil governments of East Florida were a heavy financial burden on Spain, Pinckney believed tactful diplomacy would bring desirable results. The military establishment, as poor as it was, cost Spain $30,000 a month. Pinckney expressed a willingness to suggest negotiations to Kindelan who, although he could not cede East Florida, was in position to describe conditions within the province in their true light for those who had the power of cession.[40]

After advising Secretary Monroe of this important affair of state, Pinckney asked for instructions on a pressing detail. The prisoners of war captured by the East Tennessee volunteers were a nuisance. Governor Kindelan had offered his services in getting them back to the Seminoles; but as Pinckney did not wish to furnish the governor with a means of liberating the prisoners and thereby winning Indian acclaim, the offer had been declined. Pinckney admitted they could be restored to their homes by an American expeditionary force but it would be a costly gesture. Continued supervision of the captives, however, was also expensive. The federal marshal at St. Marys could imprison them but he refused responsibility for them.[41]

Time solved the problem. By July, 1813, only two of the five prisoners remained alive, for the old Negro man, the squaw, and her child had died. The little Indian boy had left the post with an American officer. The surviving Indian woman had been shot through the leg before capture. She had fully recovered from the wound, but sat silent and alone day after day, as if waiting for release by death. It was as distressing to see her bowed in despair as it had been to witness the passing of the other unfortunate captives.[42] The general's conscience was soothed by releasing the woman. With freedom, her appetite and spirit returned and she probably found her way, determined but alone, to her people in Florida.

Less heartrending but more vital were the defenses of southern Georgia. Pinckney established thirteen small garrisons along the border. One hundred soldiers guarded the ferry near Coleraine and a few men occupied each of the other twelve posts. About 800 reserves were kept in training at Point Petre,[43] which would be available should Great Britain occupy East Florida and invade Georgia.

General Pinckney advised purchase of the Point Petre camp site which was for sale at a reasonable price.[44] As the United States was paying an annual rental of $1,000 for the land, Pinckney's advice was taken. However, the military establishment at Point Petre became of less and less importance for most of the troops were withdrawn and moved into defensive positions on the Atlantic coast. Commodore Campbell sailed the gunboats from St. Marys harbor for more northerly ports. By 1814 the military establishments at Point Petre and St. Marys had been reduced to their weak condition of 1812 before Colonel Smith had followed General Mathews into Fernandina.

Rampaging Rebels

EVACUATION OF EAST FLORIDA confused and divided the Patriots. As McIntosh had predicted, most of them made their peace with Governor Kindelan. In St. Augustine those who would not leave their land and property gave their oaths of allegiance and received their pardons. Some former revolutionists found sanctuary with relatives in Georgia, and others, who had assets north of the border, returned to former homes and lands within the United States. But a few unpropertied individuals who could not find haven in Georgia because their past unsavory financial or criminal records made that state forbidden territory, remained in East Florida and refused the proffered amnesty.

John H. McIntosh was among those who moved into St. Marys, where he dogged the heels of General Pinckney, always complaining, ever protesting. He hated the general. Mathews had been a friend of the Patriots; and, McIntosh recalled, Mitchell had been won by the revolutionists. Only Pinckney had refused all pleas and, therefore, in the opinion of McIntosh, he was responsible for the Patriot defeat and McIntosh's losses.

These financial reverses preyed on McIntosh's mind. By his own account he had advanced the Patriots thousands of dollars and had had approximately $100,000 in property destroyed. As he contemplated his losses, he lost interest in the revolution and sought restitution and reimbursement from the American government.[1]

While McIntosh sulked, others continued the revolution. Buckner Harris assumed direction of the remaining irreconcilable Patriots.

With fifteen men he moved from plantation to plantation and from farm to farm threatening to burn the property of those who accepted pardons. Intimidation deterred the fainthearted and fear made others break their sworn oaths and rejoin the Patriots.[2]

Harris had plans. With support from Governor Mitchell he would make a treaty with the Seminoles and on the land secured by treaty the Patriots would develop a prosperous frontier settlement, free of Spanish control and always ready for annexation by the United States.

In May Harris conferred with Mitchell at Milledgeville and approached the Georgia governor with flattery. Had it not been for the brave band of victorious Georgians under Newnan, Harris told Mitchell, the fate of the Patriots would have been utter ruin. The revolutionists again needed aid. Not men this time but money. With it a settlement could be made in Alachua, the Seminoles would be pushed deeper into Florida or exterminated, and the frontier of Georgia would be safe from Indian raids. Then fugitive slaves could find no haven in East Florida, for the Patriot settlement would be between them and the Indians. If Mitchell would underwrite a loan for the revolutionists, Harris promised to solve the East Florida problem.[3]

The governor was interested but the fiscal affairs of Georgia were in a precarious condition. Mitchell, however, endorsed the idea of a peace treaty and suggested a meeting with Benjamin Hawkins. After receiving letters from Mitchell addressed to the Indian agent, Harris rode south and found that Hawkins had concluded a conference with twenty Indian chiefs the day before. They had come from Tampa Bay, Hawkins said, and had asked whether the white men planned on renewing hostilities. They avowed their desire for peace and stated that the Florida Negroes lived on a hammock near Tampa Bay, apart from the Indian towns.[4]

Hawkins believed Harris could overtake the chiefs. With a note of introduction from the agent, Harris, Patriot Major Francis R. Sanchez, and Daniel Delany hastened into East Florida. They overtook a few chiefs who grunted approval to everything Harris suggested. They would return every captured Negro slave, make satisfactory settlements for property destroyed, cede the Patriots' land in Alachua, and avoid contact with Spaniards. The Indians solemnly promised to meet Harris on July 13 at Underwoods Mile, twenty miles from Traders Hill, Georgia, for the formal signing of a treaty.[5]

Harris sent Delany to Governor Mitchell with the good news. As Indians respected military might, Harris suggested that a detachment of Georgia militia be at the forthcoming conference. He renewed his request for a loan. Money was even more essential now for the Indians expected presents. The conference would be expensive but a lasting peace was worth almost any price.

As Delany rode toward Milledgeville Harris galloped east to St. Marys. He urged General Pinckney to send a United States delegate to negotiate with the Indians, but the general refused. He had neither appointive nor treaty making powers.[6]

While securing funds in St. Marys Harris encouraged Judge William Ashley in his propaganda offensive against the Spaniards. Ashley recorded the case histories of former Patriots who had accepted pardons. James Hall had found Governor Kindelan sincere but the people of St. Augustine vindictive. Hall had not been allowed to secure his fugitive slaves and other property in illegal possession of St. Augustinians. Fear of personal injury and even death had made him seek safety in Georgia. Abner Broodway claimed he had been kept in a loathsome dungeon during most of 1812, and although acquitted of the false charge against him, had been reincarcerated on the demand of citizens of St. Augustine. James Black reported that the Spanish Negro militia were running wild. A party of them under command of the former slave, Dago John, were scouring the country searching for horses, cattle, and provisions. These colored barbarians, Black stated, welcomed two escaping slaves at Cow Ford on June 5, and gave them twelve dollars and a pass into St. Augustine.

Judge Ashley forwarded the statements and affidavits of these Patriots to Governor Mitchell. Black troops of Spain were out of control, the judge stated, and unless they were checked their actions would have a baneful influence on slaves in Georgia. Ashley urged Mitchell to support Harris. Since the United States would do nothing, Georgia should aid the Patriots and thereby establish peace along the border.[7]

Impatiently Harris awaited the promised Indian conference and treaty. As July 13 neared he headed west for Underwoods Mile and for days he camped at the site of the proposed conference ground. Not a single Indian appeared. The shrewd Indians never intended to keep their date with the Patriot leader, but promising him everything to be rid of him, had led him on a snipe hunt and left him holding the bag.

Harris returned east breathing fire. He assembled his followers on the mainland west of Amelia Island and threatened to plunder East Florida.[8]

For all his plans and exertions he had accomplished nothing. The Indians had deceived him and Governor Mitchell finally rejected his pleas for financial aid. Judge Ashley's propaganda had not fooled the governor, for Mitchell knew the truth was not in Ashley or his court. "I hear that the utmost cordiality and friendly intercourse subsists between those in command on both sides the St. Marys," Mitchell stated, "and I must believe that it is founded on the fullest confidence and honorable views of both governments."[9] General Pinckney confirmed the governor's statement. In his opinion Kindelan was manifesting every disposition to fulfill the amnesty granted the revolutionists.[10]

The Patriots' task was obvious. They must destroy this mutual confidence between American and Spaniard and create incidents which would incite passion and brew border disturbances. The Patriots began their work with an eager vengeance on their old enemies, the Loyalists of Amelia Island.

A Patriot force of sixty men occupied and fortified Lodowick Ashley's plantation house on the St. Marys.[11] General Harris, as his followers called him, sent pillaging detachments east and south to seize movable property as well as slaves. Anything which could be converted into cash became fair booty.

Pinckney informed Monroe of these depredations. The Patriots, he also stated, had spread false rumors of a Spanish force en route from St. Augustine to invade Georgia.[12] He alerted his frontier guards and ordered the capture of insurgents who used Georgia as a base in their forays against East Florida.

As American troops could not attack the Patriot camp below the St. Marys and Governor Kindelan did not have the men for an offensive, Fernandina Loyalists organized a militia guard. Citizens of Amelia Island, Negroes, and even sailors from ships anchored in harbor volunteered, and in less than a fortnight the Loyalists forgot their defensive plans. They would invade the Patriot stronghold and run the rebels into Georgia.

On Sunday, August 8, sixty men crossed from Fernandina to the west bank of the Amelia River. There the force split. Thirty men in four boats rowed up Bells River toward Watermans Bluff[13] while other volunteers marched west. Between these river and land forces the rebels would be surrounded and captured.

As the boats approached Watermans Bluff a few armed men appeared on the river bank. Their numbers rapidly increased, and soon muskets pointed down on the advancing Loyalists. Before they reached the bluff they were hailed and ordered to surrender. The Loyalists answered with a volley of shot and the Patriots poured a deadly fire into the open boats. For almost fifteen minutes the Loyalists responded with an ineffectual fire. Then with two-thirds of their force killed or wounded, the men lay prone in their boats. Oars fell overboard and the wind and current slowly pushed the boats out of range.

The victorious Patriots turned to meet the advancing land force of Loyalists. There was no fight. Outnumbered by two to one the Loyalists ran for their boats and rowed across the Amelia River to Fernandina. Six Loyalists were killed and fourteen wounded in the river battle, three of whom later died.

In Fernandina the people expected an invasion of their town. Some moved their families on board vessels in the harbor and others sailed or rowed away to St. Marys.

The Patriots won their victory without the loss of a single man killed or wounded. General Harris, however, did not want Fernandina, for his heart was set on advance into the former Seminole country. There the Patriots would found a colony of workers whose prosperity and wealth would attract hundreds of other settlers. Spaniards and Indians would be overcome by this influx of white settlers and East Florida would be conquered by the plow.

General Harris sent Governor Mitchell an account of the Patriot victory and their plans. The Indians, Harris stated, were returning to their former lands and ways. Recently they had attacked Kingsley's plantation and taken his "black wife and his two children." In the absence of "Director" McIntosh, Harris planned an expedition against the Indians preparatory to a settlement in Alachua.[14]

John Houstoun McIntosh took no part in the summer activities of the Patriots. He was too busy with personal problems, as more and more his thoughts turned toward Washington. As Congress would reconvene in August, McIntosh timed his arrival with that of returning legislators.

Secretary Monroe received the "Director of the Territory of East Florida" but President Madison was indisposed and at Montpelier. Monroe's cordiality and frankness made up for the absent president. Almost immediately the conversation turned to Pinckney, as McIntosh recounted the evacuation of East Florida and the suffering of the Patriots.

"Mr. Secretary," he said, "General Pinckney arrived in St. Marys as prejudiced against the Patriots and their cause as he was against President Madison's administration."

"The general is a Federalist who places his country before his party," Monroe replied.

"Did he have the national good at heart when he evacuated East Florida?" McIntosh asked. "We knew nothing of his plans. A fortnight before his arrival in St. Marys, the general sent one of his aides to St. Augustine. The purpose of that mission was kept a profound secret and we were left in ignorance until General Pinckney informed us of the agreement with Governor Kindelan and the amnesty – an amnesty, Mr. Secretary, which has not been fulfilled."

"The general pardon for all the revolutionists was secured by negotiation with Mr. Onís," Monroe stated. "The president believes it will be observed."

"Patriot after Patriot has testified under oath of mistreatment, although each complied in full with Governor Kindelan's terms," McIntosh said. "Even the valid observation of the amnesty would have been unjust, for some of us preferred poverty as citizens of the United States to wealth as puppets under Spanish tyranny. We could not gather our crops and remove our property in four months. We begged General Pinckney not to withdraw the troops until we could move our property, but he refused. Most of the Patriots had no choice. To save their property they had to accept pardons."

"That was unfortunate," Monroe said. "The president regrets it all the more because so many were led into revolution by the mistaken zeal of Colonel Mathews."

"Without his promises we would not have taken arms against our oppressors," McIntosh said. "But we were fond of him. He made us believe the United States would help us. He gave us hope."

"The colonel was a patriot," Monroe stated.

"And so are we, Mr. Secretary. For that reason we believed General Pinckney should protect us, but he said he had definite orders."

"The general had discretionary powers," Monroe said.

"He told us he had orders which could not be disobeyed," McIntosh cried.

"His instructions gave him considerable leeway," Monroe said. "The president and I regret the haste with which the general acted. But what has been done cannot be undone. Without congressional sanction the president cannot order reoccupation of the Floridas."

"East Florida can be conquered without American intervention," McIntosh stated. "Most of the Patriots who accepted pardons were not given any real security. They are ready to take up arms again. Money is all they need."

"The United States cannot be involved," Monroe said.

"It would not be," McIntosh promised. "General Mathews guaranteed us the customs collected at Fernandina. The collector appointed by the general accepted bonds in lieu of money, but Captain Massias demanded cash payments. I understand he collected almost $4,000. If this sum, which is really ours and less than the amount I advanced the Patriots, were turned over to us, we could finance a settlement in the abandoned Seminole country."

"But, Mr. McIntosh, that would involve the government," Monroe said. "The United States would be inconsistent in denying the revolution and at the same time giving the Patriots monies collected during the revolution. Tell your friends," Monroe concluded, "that the president and I have done, and will continue to do, everything which can be done with propriety to get possession of and to annex East Florida."[15]

Monroe gave President Madison a detailed account of the meeting with McIntosh. "The case of McIntosh may be a hard one," the president replied, "but there is great difficulty in relieving it. If the occupancy of the country be acknowledged as a wrong to Spain as is done by the act restoring it, the collection of money during the occupancy must be a part of the wrong; and to restore the money not to Spain, but those in arms ag'st her, would be considered by her as an aggravation of the wrong."

Madison thought the central question was how far the United

States was bound to indemnify those who suffered because of Mathews' promises. The president, however, could not resist the opportunity for a sly maneuver. "In the meantime if the money could be got from the hands of the collector into those of McIntosh so as to form an item in the general acc't open between the U. S. and Spain, it might not be amiss. But can that be done?" Madison asked. "Reflect on the subject if you please and let me know the result."[16]

McIntosh never saw Madison's letter. The "Director" of East Florida returned to St. Marys where he supported General Harris in the scheme to found a colony in Alachua, though he never became a leader in the plan. He had lost heart for adventure in Florida. From September, 1813, his interests in life were in making a home near St. Marys and collecting his claim against the United States.

Meanwhile Harris spent much of the fall of 1813 in the Alachua area, exploring it, and fighting a few skirmishes with the Indians and Negroes. Between times he collected money and stored provisions for the coming settlement. As he worked toward his goal, another and completely irresponsible leadership directed men who assumed the name of Patriots, but who in reality were bandits and thieves.

Samuel Alexander, a Georgia adventurer, led these slave stealers and pillagers. With almost sixty men he cut through East Florida in September, October, and November. They stole three Negroes from Farquahar Bethune; hijacked three other slaves who had been taken by George Morrison, a former overseer of McIntosh's plantation, and sold them in Georgia.[17] For five days James Cashen was held a prisoner in his own house while Alexander's band looted the plantation. Cashen listed the names of his stolen slaves in advertisements and accused John Smith of Abbeville, South Carolina, John Harris of North Carolina, James Kinderick of St. Marys, and three other men identified only as Diamond of Neuse River, North Carolina, Pierce and Bartlet of Kentucky, as the individuals who were offering the Negroes for sale.[18] Adventurers and robbers from distant points had found good stealing in East Florida.

Their atrocities hurt the Patriot cause. The editor of the *Augusta Chronicle,* who advocated the annexation of East Florida, could not stomach such criminal action. "The report lately handed us from that quarter [East Florida], under the signature of Samuel Alexander, Col. Com., we consider as a burlesque on military operations, and of course did not publish it," the editor stated. "We believe . . . that their views are neither friendly to law or liberty, and that no object favorable to them or honorable to us, can possibly result from so polluted and corrupt men as are assembled in Florida. . . ."[19]

The Harris faction of the Patriots countered this adverse publicity with anti-Spanish propaganda. They reported an expeditionary force of Spaniards, Negroes, and Indians en route for an invasion of St. Marys. Bowlegs had drawn arms and supplies for 200 men in St. Augustine and had promised to raid southern Georgia. Colonel William Scott of the Georgia militia investigated these rumors and declared them false.[20]

There were men who had tired of the anarchy below the St. Marys. Joseph Hibberson appealed to Charles Harris, the United States district attorney at Savannah. The reports of colored troops had been exaggerated, he stated. There were only forty-two on Amelia Island, twenty-five of which had been stationed there after the robbery of James Cashen, and seventeen men who were shipwrecked while en route to St. Augustine. The facts were clear, Hibberson said. The so-called Patriots were armed with United States muskets; they were encouraged by Judge William Ashley of Camden County; they took or put off the name Patriot at convenience, and among them were less than six men who had ever been subjects of East Florida. Hibberson requested the district attorney to bring legal action against these robbers and slave stealers.[21]

Philip Fatio informed Peter Early, Mitchell's successor as governor of Georgia, that the rebels had plundered and laid waste the entire country between the St. Marys and the St. Johns. They had even crossed the St. Johns, burning Fatio's plantation buildings, and stealing his slaves. He estimated his losses at more than $10,000 and the destruction of two crops. The rebels spread false rumors of Spanish invasion of Georgia to cover their own villainy. Fatio asked whether the governor could recall one act of aggression by Floridians against their neighbor.[22]

Judge Francis Hopkins of McIntosh County, Georgia, forwarded the governor a number of affidavits which gave evidence of the sincerity and honesty of Spanish officials. Georgians who sought escaped slaves on Amelia Island had found the Spaniards cooperative and helpful. They "act with the utmost good faith in endeavoring to apprehend, secure and restore to the citizens of Georgia any and all negroes which have fled to [East Florida] for protection and [the Spanish government gives] ten dollars for all such Negroes taken up."[23]

Unfavorable publicity and the plundering of self-styled Patriots did not stop Buckner Harris. His determination to found a colony in the Seminole country of Alachua never wavered. If this could be accomplished with Indian and Spanish sanction, he would be pleased; but with or without approval he would lead the Patriots to their promised land. As a realist he did first attempt negotiations with Governor Kindelan.

In August Patriot Captain William Cone suggested a conference to his friend Fatio. The misunderstandings between the Patriots and the Spanish could be settled, Cone stated, for the breach was not too wide for an understanding and the re-establishment of peace. The Patriots requested removal of Negro troops from East Florida, a land grant in Alachua as recompense for losses, and amnesty for all past offenses. The revolutionists were fighting for liberty and security, Cone avowed, and they did not wish to harm loyal Spaniards of East Florida. Since the Patriots were increasing daily in number they could soon expel the Spaniards from Florida, but they preferred peace to war.[24]

Harris and James Dell continued the peace offensive begun by Cone. They proposed an immediate armistice to Governor Kindelan and the appointment of a commission to settle all outstanding differences. The representatives of Kindelan should be empowered to cede the Patriots such unallotted parts of East Florida as were reasonable.[25] McIntosh endorsed this proposed armistice. He and Daniel Delany told the Loyalist Samuel Betts that Fernandina would be destroyed unless negotiation resulted in a satisfactory settlement.[26]

For more than two weeks the Patriots waited for a reply which Kindelan had no intention of making. Then Harris sent the governor a long letter explaining the thought and attitudes of the revolutionists. Those people who professed to be Spanish subjects in East Florida were mostly sycophants who continuously whined about Kindelan's appointments and concealed from the governor the true condition of the country. These men urged the use of Negro troops against the Patriots.

Harris credited Kindelan with honesty and a sincere attempt to fulfill the amnesty act. The pro-British faction and Negro troops, however, by vile acts and the burning of houses had defeated the governor's good intentions. Reluctantly, according to Harris, the Patriots had been compelled to meet force with force. In defensive fighting they had grown strong and were ready for offensive operations. As long as the existing conditions continued no Spaniard would be safe outside the walls of St. Augustine and those harboring Negro troops would be given no mercy. Sooner or later the enemies of the Patriots would meet with the vengeance of an aroused people. Harris again suggested a conference between the Patriots and Governor Kindelan.[27]

The Spaniard ignored the appeals, threats, and misrepresentations of the revolutionists. He warned his government of the plans being laid by the enemy, but he could not defend the far reaches of East Florida with the troops under his command. On Amelia Island, in the area east of the St. Johns, and of course in St. Augustine, Spanish soldiers guarded the loyal subjects of Spain. The remaining sectors of East Florida were open for settlement by those who could face the Indians.

The Patriots knew of Spain's weaknesses. Notwithstanding their propaganda to the contrary they knew the Indians had moved southwest from the Alachua country and there was little immediate danger in squatting on former Seminole lands, where opportunities for profit were tremendous and the possibilities of interesting the United States were good.

Reports of Spaniards arming the Indians made Monroe toy with another move for annexation of the Floridas. "The late conduct of the Spanish Authorities in E. Florida, in furnishing the Indians with ammunition and arms for the express purpose of making war on the U. States, forms a new cause" for action, Monroe stated.[28] Whenever Congress permitted, the secretary thought the bayonet would be used in East Florida and negotiation be used elsewhere. Thomas Jefferson agreed with Monroe. As Spanish conduct would probably force the United States to seize the Floridas, Jefferson hoped Congress would take the provinces, for "their inhabitants universally wish it, and they are in truth the only legitimate proprietors of the soil and government."[29]

As Harris assembled his men in southern Georgia during December, 1813, and January, 1814, he had reason for optimism. Although each volunteer came for private gain and the promised 500 acres of land,[30] they were eager for enriching adventure. Success would attract others and likely bring American intervention in their behalf.

On January 10, 1814, Harris led seventy hopefuls across the St. Marys. Additional recruits joined the Patriots as they marched through the back country of East Florida and they numbered ninety when they stopped at Payne's old town in Alachua on January 16. Two days later the sound of hammers and axes split the Florida air as construction was begun on a twenty-five-foot square, two-story blockhouse. While some men busied themselves with building others surveyed the land for individual allotments. Before the blockhouse or survey had been completed more than 160 men were in camp and others were expected.[31]

They named their fort in honor of former Governor Mitchell. It stood approximately 100 miles south by southwest of Coleraine, Georgia, at latitude twenty-nine degrees and fourteen minutes.[32] Within seven miles of Fort Mitchell lay a large lake, with its surrounding soil of deep, fertile loam. Large numbers of fat cattle roamed the woods and prairie. Wild vegetables grew in abundance and orange blooms of untended Indian groves perfumed the air.

The blockhouse at Fort Mitchell was built on a prairie which was seven or eight miles wide and twenty long. Farmers thought the land well suited for sugar cane. Corn, potatoes, melons, every crop, would grow like wildfire, the Patriots said. Cattle and hogs would run wild, multiply, and feed on nature's foods. Nearby lakes and streams afforded excellent navigation.[33]

After the Patriots had established themselves on the former Indian land, they assembled on January 25, 1814, as a legislative body. McIntosh, Clark, the Ashleys, Craig, and other former leaders of the revolution had severed active connection with the Patriots. In the place of McIntosh, Buckner Harris was confirmed as "Director." Francis R. Sanchez became "President of the Legislative Council" and James Dell was the "Colonel Commandant" of the military force. The assembled Patriots declared their community a continuation of the 1812 revolutionary force and entitled their country "The District of Elotchaway of the Republic of East Florida."

Harris addressed the "Legislative Council" and recommended legislation. He congratulated them on being the first legislative body in a territory once the lurking place of the "most inveterate and troublesome savages." Although the revolution of March, 1812, had produced distressing calamities, Harris proclaimed the day of triumph near. The Patriots had been injured and abused, persecuted and slandered by Spaniards and their allies, smugglers, pro-British agents, Indians, and Negroes; but, the speaker stated, the perfidy of the enemy was known in Washington. United States troops would soon be active in East Florida. Therefore Harris advised sending a minister to President Madison, and vesting in the emissary power to cede Alachua and ally the Patriots with the United States in the war against Great Britain.[34]

As the executive, Harris outlined legislation for the encouragement, support, and protection of the people. A code of laws should be enacted, officers appointed, courts established, and judges selected. A contractor should be appointed and arrangements made for trade with Georgia. The "Legislative Council" responded with a resolution approving an address to President Madison. In the address the legislators reviewed the course of revolution since 1812, dwelled on their desire for American citizenship, and requested the United States to accept "The District of Elotchaway" as a territory of the American Union. They gave an optimistic account of their settlement and their prospects of growth. The Patriots would hold the country against Spaniards and savages of all color, or die like men. "We dread no enemy," they proclaimed. Only the United States could rout them, but they knew their brothers would not war against them.[35]

The "Council" and "Director" gave Wilson Connor the necessary credentials as minister to the United States and sent him toward Washington. This "minister plenipotentiary and envoy extraordinary" was an unlettered, part-time Baptist minister, who covered what he lacked in education and polish with voice and vigor. Connor was a giant of a man, brawny, forceful, and daring. His enthusiasm for the cause stimulated his natural aggressiveness, and if anyone could present the Patriot causes to Madison and Monroe, he could.

Harris informed General Pinckney of Connor's mission and sent the general copies of the Legislative Council's resolutions and address. If General Pinckney had the power, Harris urged him to occupy Alachua and enroll the revolutionists in the service of the United States.[36]

Pinckney ignored the Patriots, but Governor Kindelan did not. Before January 27, 1814, he had complete reports on the Alachua settlement. As this violation of Spanish sovereignty might lead to conflict, Kindelan requested Governor Peter Early to strike at the roots of such illegal and unwarranted proceedings.[37] The Georgia governor advised Kindelan that the insurgents in East Florida were outside the jurisdiction of Georgia. He condemned the illegal activities of the revolutionists but disclaimed all responsibility for Harris, who was a fugitive from a debtors' court in Georgia, and many of his associates were of similar or worse character. Early told Kindelan to capture these lawless men or drive them across the border where they could be prosecuted in Georgia courts.[38]

Benjamin Hawkins also feared the consequences of a white settlement near the Seminoles and on land which the Indians regarded as their communal property. After inspecting the Patriot camp he inquired of Early as to Georgia's official position. "You can with truth assure the Seminoles," the governor replied, "that the government of Georgia gives no countenance to the patriots of East Florida in their unwarrantable procedures."[39]

The Patriots worked in Alachua unperturbed by this criticism and unchecked by Spanish military force. As they had an ample supply of provisions for a year, seed and equipment for farming, they surveyed their extensive lands and prepared for planting. Harris looked over his domain and swelled with pride: "Our enemies have all fled," he stated; "our numbers are increasing."[40]

While his fellow revolutionists tilled the soil in Florida Wilson Connor rode through Georgia and South Carolina. In his pouches was his commission as minister, dated February 15, 1814, and an outline of his duties in ceding "The District of Elotchaway." He hoped to reach Washington by the first of March, but crawled into bed at Louisburg, North Carolina, where for almost two weeks a fever racked his powerful body. After the fever abated he was too weak for travel. On March 15 he advised Secretary Monroe of his mission and forwarded his commission and official documents.[41] For three weeks he waited. Then he penned another letter begging for a reply.[42]

On April 19 Monroe acknowledged receipt of Connor's letters. "The United States being at peace with Spain," Monroe replied, "no countenance can be given by their government to the proceedings of the revolutionary party in East Florida, if it is composed of Spanish subjects – and still less can it be given to them if it consists of American citizens, who, so far as their conduct may fall within the scope of existing laws long enacted and well known and understood, will be liable to censure."[43]

Thus Monroe finally denied the revolution fomented by General Mathews, supported by American military force, and encouraged by President Madison's administration. The denial was late by more than two years. Such a simple, direct, and unequivocal statement as that sent Connor in 1814 would have nipped in the bud the activities of Mathews in 1811. Destruction and death would not have blighted East Florida. General Mathews would not have ended his days as a disgraced, broken, vindictive old man, and the honor of the United States would not have been smeared with the charge of aggression.

Had Monroe or Madison changed their attitude on East Florida? In 1811 and 1812 they had shared the optimism of the young nationalists when Canada and the Floridas were so attractive and apparently so easy to grab. By 1814, however, the question was one of retaining existing territory rather than enlarging the American domain, for British warships and armies threatened the life of the United States and dissatisfaction was widespread in New England. The year 1814 was not a year for aggression. It was a time for defense.

As Monroe's denial killed hope for American intervention on behalf of the Patriots, avenging Indians and Negroes destroyed "The District of Elotchaway of the Republic of East Florida." In his eagerness for more land Buckner Harris explored the borders of Alachua. Often he went alone, or with only a few men, seeking rich loam and suitable sites for settlement. On May 5 a scouting party of Indians and Negroes waylaid and killed him.[44]

The Patriots as an organized band died with Harris, for he was the "whole support of the cause."[45] The settlers broke and fled for Georgia, and within two weeks Fort Mitchell was deserted. Its former occupants were in Georgia or hiding in the back country west of Amelia Island and south of the St. Marys. The Patriot remnant in East Florida remained as an unorganized band of robbers which, from time to time, slipped across the Georgia-Florida border at its unguarded points to raid both American and Spanish farmers.

Unwanted in Georgia, except by the police, and condemned by Spain, the former Patriots became wanderers. Some found seclusion in sparsely populated Georgia frontiers, others lost their former identity in the American West. A few remained along the St. Marys waiting for that day when the United States would take East Florida. Those who were not under indictment in Georgia collected evidence of their losses and made claims against the United States for damages resulting from a revolution created and encouraged by an American agent. Never again did they assemble as a body claiming themselves to be the constituted government of East Florida. Some of them later united for one battle, and reassuming the name Patriot, fought the British invader along the St. Marys.

Tommies and Tars

THE DEATH OF BUCKNER HARRIS and the flight of the would-be empire builders from Alachua were almost simultaneous events. Leaderless and quaking with fright the land-hungry settlers fled in precipitant haste. Their fear was of more than the Seminoles. Even with their Negro allies the Florida Indians might have been held in check. It was the possibility of a general uprising of all Indians in the southeastern region which sent the Patriots scampering toward Georgia.

Even more frightening were rumors of British activities. Occupation of the Floridas had been justified by the administration in Washington as a defense against expected British aggression. By the summer of 1814 England was apparently ready to accept the role which had been assigned to her by American nationalists.

As the power of Napoleon was reduced in Europe, Great Britain turned on her audacious and presumptuous former colonies in North America. In 1813 Admiral George Cockburn appeared off Chesapeake Bay with a powerful naval force. His looting and destruction foreshadowed coming events which by the summer of 1814 would make the Chesapeake a British lake. The capture of Paris on March 30, 1814, and the confinement of Napoleon on Elba released British military and naval forces for the war in North America. With power to spare, Great Britain planned to strike the United States in the north, along the Atlantic, and on the Gulf.

In May a squadron of English ships with invasion barges lashed to their sides appeared off the St. Marys River. British sympathizers welcomed landing parties on Amelia Island where proclamations were posted on trees and buildings.¹ His Majesty's army and navy were on their way. Georgians prepared their defenses in feverish haste and made conjectures as to the point or points of attack. Above all they feared British agents would arouse and supply the Indians.

Georgians had cause for dread. In time English forces would invade the relatively unimportant St. Marys area, but at the moment Indian allies were the paramount aim of British leaders. On July 1, 1814, Vice-Admiral Alexander Cochrane sent Colonel Edward Nicholls with a detachment of officers to the Indians of West Florida. The admiral forwarded two field pieces, 2,000 guns, and 1,000 swords, and promised arms for every warrior who would fight the Americans. He urged the Indians to encourage the flight of Negroes from Georgia and the Carolinas and ordered Nicholls to clothe, supply, and arm the Negroes. *"The King Our Father* having with his allies subdued the French and sent their Emperor Napoleon a prisoner to a little Island," Cochrane stated, "has determined to chastise Mr. Madison, and his worthless associates. . . ."²

The Indians rallied to the British standard. They gave Nicholls the title of commander-in-chief and urged Cochrane to keep a British post on the Gulf. "The Spaniards are Weak frail friends," the Indians reported; "in our distress they turned us to the Woods like dogs, but since your Sons came here we walk like men in their Streets." Indian chiefs assured Cochrane that they would enlist Negro warriors, unite the redmen, and crush the "wicked and rebellious Americans."³

Admiral Cochrane expected many Negro allies from East Florida and Georgia. He emphasized the fighting qualities of former slaves. They were excellent horsemen, he declared; and mounted on their masters' horses, clothed and armed by Great Britain, and instructed in tactics, he believed they would be the equal of the Cossacks of the Russian army and more terrifying to Americans than any other troops. "I have it much at heart to give [the Americans] a complete drubbing before Peace is made . . .," Cochrane stated.⁴ Although the British high command ordered him not to encourage slave insurrection, the admiral planned to welcome escaped Negroes and offer them the choice of enlisting as soldiers or settling in some English colony.⁵

Cochrane's appeals and promises alarmed and quieted the Georgia expansionists. The most ardent, land-grabbing Southerner would not risk his life in East Florida while British agents encouraged the Indians and supplied them with guns and ammunition. Governor Peter Early penned frantic appeals to Secretary of War Armstrong for the defense of Georgia. The state had only 3,500 militia with which to meet the British, Indians, and Negroes.[6]

During the summer and fall of 1814 Georgians expected the worst — invasion, Indian warfare, slave insurrection. They watched as a British flotilla entered Chesapeake Bay, captured Washington, and burned the principal governmental buildings. They became frantic as a naval squadron sailed south from Chesapeake, and sighed with relief as it moved around Florida and into the Gulf. But Georgians knew their situation remained critical. Colonel Nicholls and Captain George Woodbine, another British agent, were bringing the Indians into union. Many chiefs of the Floridas and Georgia brought out the war paint and shouted for revenge on the Americans.

Admiral Cochrane aided his agents with proclamations and appeals. "Come forth, then ye brave Chiefs and Warriors, as one family," he said, "and join the British Standard. . . . If you want covering to protect yourselves, your wives, and your children, against the winter's cold, — come to us and we will clothe you. If you want arms and ammunition to defend yourself against oppressors, — come to us and we will provide you." And what did Great Britain wish in return for this bounty? Cochrane asked. Nothing more than help in regaining the Indian lands for the red men — "the lands of your forefathers, — from the common enemy, the wicked People of the United States...."[7]

British agents found the Indians and Negroes more cooperative than the Spaniards. Governor Kindelan suspected the motives of Great Britain. The Floridas, he knew, could fall as a prize of war to either England or the United States, and as the governor of East Florida, he saw neutrality as the only course for Spain in North America. He informed George Woodbine of Spanish neutrality and protested against the presence and activities of British agents in the Floridas.[8]

Great Britain could forego Spanish support. With or without Kindelan's consent the Indians welcomed representatives from King George, the Great Father from across the wide, deep water. They recalled the years of British control of the Floridas; the presents and food, the medals and honors which they had received from English governors were pleasant recollections. British military advisers foreshadowed the return of those past idyllic years in addition to checking the advancing Americans, if not regaining occupied lands from the avaricious Southerners.

Confidently the British expedition moved into the Gulf, feinted toward Mobile, and sailed for the Mississippi. Two American vessels, the *Caroline* and the *Louisiana,* under the command of Commodore Daniel Patterson contested the way. Above them on the east bank of the river General Andrew Jackson's militia volunteers were forming into a defensive army. On December 27, 1814, hot shot from British cannon penetrated and burned the *Caroline.* Two weeks later massed English regulars marched in perfect formation against Jackson's defense works, where they fell in bloody, humiliating defeat.

As one British expeditionary force moved on New Orleans another sailed into Georgia waters. On December 13, 1814, ships from Admiral George Cockburn's fleet anchored off Cumberland Sound.[9] The Georgia coast was surveyed during the following weeks as additional ships augmented the flotilla. By January 11, 1815, two ships of the line, each with seventy-four guns, seven frigates, numbers of smaller armed vessels, and nineteen barges hovered off the coast.[10] This naval force and the 1,500 colonial and Negro troops on board the warships could overpower any possible Georgia resistance. Governor Early thought the day of payment had arrived. In return for past aggressiveness Georgians would suffer the horrors of British and Negro warfare on their coasts and British-led Indian raids on their frontiers.[11]

On January 11 the British occupied Cumberland Island and established camp near the abandoned marine installations. Two days later barges filled with troops crossed the sound toward the St. Marys River and before noon the first barge was pushed aground near Point Petre. On the Point and in St. Marys Captain Massias' thin force of ninety-six men stood their ground momentarily against overwhelming numbers. A detachment of thirty-six men suffered fourteen casualties before they abandoned Point Petre, and Massias fell back from St. Marys to form a defense line near Barrington with Colonel William Scott's eighty-man militia force at Jefferson on the Satilla River. A scouting party of former Patriots patrolled the St. Marys River and spied on the enemy.[12]

British colonials and Negroes pillaged the little seaport town. "We had some fine fun at St. Mary's," an Englishman informed a friend, "and had plenty of plunder. How are you off for tables and chests of drawers, etc.?"[13] Another British soldier happily proclaimed that he and his compatriots grabbed property worth fifty thousand pounds in ransacking St. Marys.[14] Thomas Cochrane complained of a fate which prevented his arrival in time to share in the looting, but consoled himself with the thought that scarcely thirty thousand pounds would be realized from the property seized.[15]

Few of the townspeople were molested. Archibald Clark and Doctor Ross were imprisoned on the frigate *Primrose* where British officers questioned them day and night about the specie of the customs house. The Negro troops, which the Georgians feared more than any others, conducted themselves in an exemplary manner while on duty in the town.

On scouting details the Negroes fought bravely but often forgot humanity in the excitement of battle. "Blacky had no idea of giving quarters," an Englishman reported, "and it was with difficulty the officers prevented their putting the prisoners to death. The Yankee riflemen fired at our men in ambush. Blacky, on the impulse of the moment, left the ranks and pursued them into the woods, fighting like heroes. A poor Yankee, *disarmed,* begged for mercy, Blacky replied, 'he no come in bush for mercy,' and immediately shot him dead."[16]

Fear of the Negroes and rumors of 600 Indians under Captain Woodbine advancing from Florida toward Georgia sent the frontiersmen scurrying for coastal towns above St. Marys. Settlements on the St. Marys, Satilla, and Altamaha rivers were abandoned as frightened families fled in panic. On January 22 Governor Early declared martial law in Savannah in an attempt to control a people made senseless by fear – an overpowering fear created by rumors of 6,000 British troops marching on the city and of Indian-Negro war parties bent on raiding the frontier settlements.[17]

These rumors were groundless. At Ghent in Belgium a treaty of peace had been signed in 1814 on the day before Christmas. Forewarned of the impending treaty, the British had not planned a full invasion of Georgia. On January 24, 1815, they burned the barracks at Point Petre, seized and towed away all the vessels in the St. Marys, and returned to their camp on Cumberland Island,[18] where they awaited the expected report on the ratification of the peace treaty. A bored officer expressed the sentiments of his countrymen by stating: "I think we have had quite enough of war for some years to come...."[19] For more than twenty years the people of Great Britain had been fighting France, and peace was more important than the conquest of Georgia or of the entire United States.

Cumberland Island was an uninteresting stretch of sand covered by vegetation and infested with insects of every description. British tars and tommies escaped its monotony by sailing to Fernandina where grog shops and women offered forgetfulness and momentary thrills. Yet those who made the hard trip in search of such pleasures found unfriendly officials. Already warned by Governor Kindelan, responsible citizens of Fernandina requested their visitors to leave and dissuade their friends from entering the town. Spanish citizens would not give the United States excuse for later complaints. Arms, food, pleasure, or anything else which could in any way assist the British were denied them under the rigid neutrality ordered by Kindelan.

The governor protested vigorously every attempted breach of neutrality. Furthermore, he complained of the protection which the British gave escaped slaves of Fernandina. Admiral Cockburn reminded the governor that Cumberland Island was under English law, a law which prohibited slavery. Though only a few slaves had sought refuge within the British lines, the admiral granted their former owners free access to Cumberland Island and permission to persuade but not force the slaves to return home.[20] Allies, though they were in Europe, Spain and Great Britain, were poles apart in the New World.

Cockburn disliked these petty controversies. His contest with the imprisoned Archibald Clark was also a nuisance. Clark knew (or should have known) where the gold and silver of the St. Marys customs house was cached. If Admiral Cockburn could secure that specie before peace was declared his invasion of Georgia would augment his personal fortune by a gratifying amount. Day after day Clark was questioned and every means short of physical injury was used to loosen his reluctant tongue. Cockburn damned the silent American and ordered an expeditionary force to burn Clark's mill and other property on the St. Marys River.

On February 24 a task force of 250 men boarded six barges. Sails and oarsmen propelled the unwieldly carriers across Cumberland

Sound, up the St. Marys past the ruins at Point Petre and the almost deserted town of St. Marys, and on toward Camp Pinckney near Coleraine. There the British planned to land and march overland to Spanish Creek on which Clark's sawmill stood. As the first barge neared the landing shots rang out from the Florida bank of the river, where, hidden behind towering pines, about thirty Patriot riflemen began to fire into the open British boats.

Quickly the barges veered toward the Georgia shore. The trees from that bank seemed to spout flame as twenty or more Georgia militiamen of Colonel Scott poured a withering fire into the boats. Oarsmen pulled the barges into mid-stream, but this position was almost as perilous as hugging the shore, for bullets from Patriot and Georgia muskets reached the defenseless Englishmen. Resistance was virtually useless, for trees and scrub covered the musketmen on both river banks. With no thought of completing their objective, British officers ordered a hasty about-face. In turning the unwieldly barges they neared the Florida shore where Patriot marksmen fired deadly volley after volley into the confused British.

As the barges were headed downstream the current and flashing oars soon sent the craft out of range. The British had literally been cut to pieces. While the barges moved slowly with the current the Englishmen tended their wounded and counted their dead, and guided their craft by the most direct route, now nearing one shore and then the other, thereby following a reasonably straight course down the winding river. Since the enemy had been left behind the officers thought all danger past. But they were mistaken, for Patriots and Georgians had not given up their prey. By cutting directly across the necks of land formed by the crooked river they out-distanced the barges and awaited their coming.

The barges sailed down the seemingly interminable St. Marys. Again and again the riflemen were left behind only to appear once more at a lower river bend. Never did men more warmly welcome the sight of Cumberland Sound and security from those deadly musket balls than did those Englishmen on that January afternoon. Two-thirds of the unfortunate men had been killed or wounded, according to the report of John Houstoun McIntosh; and Colonel Scott informed Governor Early that the English had suffered between 100 and 160 casualties. And later, in the tradition of American exaggeration, the number mounted until the dead reached 180 and the wounded a like figure. Thus in the folklore of Georgia those Patriot and militia riflemen had surpassed perfection by killing and wounding 320 of the task force of 250 men.[21]

Despite these later exaggerations the engagement was a severe blow to English prestige. Admiral Cockburn, whose selfish greed had caused the defeat, swore he would send a force of sufficient strength into Georgia to burn every building between the St. Marys and the Altamaha rivers. Before he could carry out his threat he received orders to cease hostilities, for Great Britain and the United States were at peace. The British force on Cumberland Island was withdrawn, and except for a few ships which cruised off the Georgia coast as protection for English merchantmen, the admiral's fleet sailed for British ports.

One final serious but ludicrous incident of the war was in the offing. During the occupation of St. Marys Admiral Cockburn had seized an American barge and a dismantled gunboat. When Commodore Campbell received notice of the peace treaty he ordered sailing-master John Hulburd from Savannah to St. Marys with a request for a return of the boats.

Hulburd sailed from Tybee bar at one o'clock on the afternoon of March 16. His was a peaceful mission in a little gunboat manned by a skeleton crew. At three-thirty the lookout sighted a sail to the southeast; apparently it was a Russian or Swedish merchantman plying between Fernandina and Savannah. As a smoky haze hung low on the horizon little attention was given the vessel until forty minutes later when it loomed up on the right of gunboat 168 and a cannon ball zoomed over the fore gaff of the American boat. Hulburd hoisted his colors, and veered left as the unidentified vessel raised British colors.

It was the rocket ship *Erebus,* commanded by Captain Bartholomew, which followed and fired a second shot passing just behind the main rigging of the gunboat. As the *Erebus* pulled up on the starboard tack, its Captain Bartholomew picked up his trumpet.

"You damned rascal," he shouted, "if you don't lower your boat and come aboard immediately, I'll fire into you. I'll sink you, God damn you!"

John Hulburd was silent. His men pulled at the square sail.

"Why don't you heave to?" Bartholomew asked. "God damn you, I'll sink you. I'll fire a broadside into you."

"This is a United States vessel from Savannah bound for St. Marys with dispatches for Admiral Cockburn," Hulburd said.

As he shouted the last words a musket was fired from the *Erebus*. The ball whistled near Hulburd's shoulder and almost hit the helmsman. The spent bullet struck the water thirty feet away.

"This is gunboat 168," Hulburd yelled. "If you desire information you may come aboard."

"I don't care a damn for your dispatches nor Admiral Cockburn either," the captain yelled. "God damn them and the United States too. I'll fire a broadside into you and sink you if you don't lower a boat and come aboard, you rascal."

Hulburd turned his vessel and ran close under the lee of the *Erebus*. "This is United States gunboat 168," he repeated, "with dispatches for the admiral off St. Marys. If you have doubts, send over a boat. I'll heave to as soon as I clear sufficiently to lie to."

"If you heave to on the starboard, I'll send my boat over." As Bartholomew completed the sentence he raised his hands high and shouted: "No! No! No! No!" as though ordering his men not to fire. Then turning toward Hulburd: "God damn you. Come aboard or I'll sink you. I'll fire thunder into you."

"If you do, I'll return your compliments with lightning," Hulburd replied.

Hulburd pulled up on the starboard. A lieutenant and crew in a small boat came alongside.

"If you don't come aboard the captain will take every one of you into Charleston," the lieutenant said.

"Tell your commander that I'll not lower a boat," Hulburd said. "Not an officer or man will leave this vessel except by force."

"If you don't obey," the lieutenant stated, "you'll be sunk. I advise you to go –."

"I want no advice," Hulburd yelled. "I have orders from my government. I obey them only. Tell your commander that his highhandedness shall not pass with impunity."

The rowboat turned back toward the *Erebus*. As it neared the British ship, Bartholomew asked, "Won't the damn rascal come?" The lieutenant shook his head.

"Then come alongside and let me sink him. I'll sink him," Captain Bartholomew repeated; "I'll fire a broadside into him."

A cannon boomed. The shot pierced the mainsail of gunboat 168, barely missed the mast, and cut away one of the stays. Hulburd looked at his crew. They stood at battle station apparently eager to fire. He looked at the *Erebus* with her twenty-two guns showing and twenty closed ports which possibly hid additional cannon. Resistance was useless and the gunboat could not outsail the enemy.

Hulburd fired one shot over the bow of the *Erebus,* sank the signals, and lowered his colors.

A small boat put away from the British ship. A lieutenant boarded the American gunboat and Hulburd formally surrendered his vessel.

"I'm only a lieutenant," the Englishman said.

"Then send the proper officer over," Hulburd replied. "The officers and men are your prisoners."

The lieutenant ordered Hulburd to the *Erebus* where he was met by the angry captain.

"This is my sword," Hulburd said. "That is the United States gun vessel number 168. I surrender it as your prize; myself, my officers, and crew are your prisoners."

Bartholomew ignored the words. "How dare you refuse to come aboard His Majesty's ship?" he asked.

"I do not know or acknowledge your right to order me on board, or interrupt my sailing along the American coast," Hulburd replied. "I shall report this flagrant abuse of power to my government. Had I the crew ordinarily aboard my vessel, you would not have forced me on board until a few thirty-two pound shot marked your ship. If I commanded a vessel of twenty guns, I would take satisfaction right now."

Bartholomew was silent for a time. Then he said, "I only wanted to warn you off the coast. I have orders from Admiral Cockburn. Do you wish to see them?"

"As I am governed by orders from the United States, I can have nothing to do with those of a British admiral," Hulburd said.

"I thought you might be from the Cape of Good Hope," the captain said. His eyes were twinkling and there was a faint smile on his lips.

"You could not believe that," Hulburd exclaimed. "You see my ship has no quarter-deck, has not been at sea long, and her boats are not stowed for a long voyage. You know, had I been on a long cruise, I would not run past Savannah and expose my vessel to British warships."

"Upon my honor," Bartholomew said, "I believe the whole thing was an accident. If you had not been running away from me, the last shot would not have been fired."

"You cannot believe that," Hulburd shouted. "You saw both my jibs to windward and the helm a-lee."

"Upon my honor," Bartholomew repeated to himself, "I don't know whether the gun went off by accident or was fired. I gave no order to fire."

Bartholomew walked the quarter-deck for a few minutes. Then he asked, "Will you see my orders to warn all vessels off the coast?"

"No," Hulburd replied. "I have nothing to do with them and no desire to see them."

"If you think this will cause any dispute between our governments," the captain said, "I will accompany you to Admiral Cockburn and have it settled."

"I do not feel authorized to receive any satisfaction you can offer for such a wilful insult to the United States," Hulburd replied.

Captain Bartholomew had tired of his fun. Suppressing his mirth he ordered Hulburd away and gave him free passage into St. Marys. Gunboat 168 sailed into Cumberland Sound, but Admiral Cockburn had left the Georgia coast and Hulburd delivered his dispatches to Captain Hamilton aboard the British ship *Ceylon*. Then the irate sailing-master penned a detailed account of the hour-and-a-quarter engagement for his superiors.[22]

The last scene of the War of 1812 had been acted off the Georgia coast near the scene of its preliminaries along the Georgia-Florida border.

The Revival of Anarchy—and Peace

YOUNG ARDENT LIEUTENANT Hulburd begged for a ship and permission to scour the seas for the *Erebus*. He would teach haughty Bartholomew a lesson; but the lieutenant pleaded in vain, for the needless war begun in 1812 had been concluded on December 24, 1814, at Ghent, Belgium. Jackson's overwhelming victory at New Orleans, the skirmishes along the St. Marys, and the incident off the Georgia coast were as unnecessary and as inconclusive in final effect as was the war itself.

The peace had been long in the making. Tall, handsome James Bayard and short, bald-headed Albert Gallatin sailed for Europe in May, 1813, with Madison and Monroe hoping for peace through Russian mediation. In St. Petersburg the American envoys found that Lord Castlereagh of Great Britain had rejected the Russian proposal. The controversies between the United States and England, Castlereagh said, were problems of internal government and, therefore, not proper subjects for mediation. In other words the American-British conflict was a family affair which should be settled by direct negotiations between Great Britain and her former colonies. A renewal of the Russian offer brought a counter proposal from Castlereagh: emissaries would be appointed to treat with representatives of the United States in London or in some neutral city.

Gallatin, Bayard, and the third peace commissioner, John Quincy Adams, had no authority to negotiate directly with Great Britain. Until additional instructions came from Washington the Americans could do nothing. Adams was occupied with his diplomatic duties at

St. Petersburg, but the other commissioners twiddled their thumbs during the summer and fall. Meanwhile the United States Senate turned down the appointment of Gallatin as peace commissioner because he had retained his position as secretary of the treasury. Expecting Gallatin to return to Washington, President Madison appointed Adams, Bayard, Henry Clay, and Jonathan Russell to represent the United States in direct negotiations for peace. But Gallatin preferred his diplomatic mission and resigned his cabinet post. Thereupon Madison appointed and the Senate confirmed him as the fifth member of the peace mission.

It was January, 1814, before Gallatin and Bayard escaped from chilly St. Petersburg. By permission they stopped in London where Gallatin argued with the slow-moving Castlereagh, who would not be pushed. He would appoint commissioners and discuss peace, but at his convenience. The impending defeat of Napoleon and the coming European settlement occupied Castlereagh's thoughts. Finally Gallatin and Bayard sailed for Ghent, the Belgian city selected for negotiations.

There the five-man American commission waited for British representatives and argued among themselves. The younger, inexperienced Clay questioned every contention of Adams, the nominal and unpopular head of the commission. Gallatin poured "oil on the troubled waters" and by tact and ability became, in fact, the spokesman for the Americans. On August 8 Lord Gambier, Henry Goulburn, and William Adams, puppets of Castlereagh and men of little political stature, arrived in Ghent. From August until Christmas Eve the British and Americans contended for a favorable peace.

In the United States rumors of impending decisions found an eager audience. Southern newspaper editors did not waste words on the probable treaty with Great Britain, for they knew the United States could secure neither Canada nor the Floridas from England. The question was: would Spain cede England the southern provinces in the general peace settlement? Even before the American commissioners had sailed in May, 1813, Southerners feared Great Britain would acquire the Floridas.[1] From that date until the final peace agreements editors speculated on the implications of British occupation of the Spanish provinces. The prospects were discouraging. The Floridas under Spain would eventually become American property but they could not be wrested from powerful Britain. Had American aggressiveness forced Spain into ceding the Floridas to Great Britain?

Southern editors thought so. A Charleston journalist reported Ferdinand VII of Spain had ceded the Floridas, but the governor-general of Cuba had refused delivery to Great Britain until the Spanish Cortes ratified the cession.[2] An unidentified correspondent at St. Marys described the arrival of Colonel Nicholls and Captain Woodbine at Fernandina on June 7, 1815, where eager pro-British townspeople asked if they were prepared to take formal possession of East Florida. "Not yet," they replied; "we have not received the money and supplies requisite for occupation." Fernandinans were convinced that British troops would soon be in East Florida.[3]

On December 1, 1815, the editor of the *Augusta Chronicle* concluded that all was lost. "We have always believed," he stated, "that if Spain ever indemnified England for her exertions in this cause, the Floridas would naturally form a part; first, because, being detached from all the other Spanish colonies, and maintained at a considerable expense on the treasury of Spain, they have ceased to become valuable to her. Since the U. States became possessed of Louisiana, the Floridas no longer serve as a barrier to the frontier of her richer colonies, and the probability is, and we are sorry to believe the report, that the Floridas have been ceded to Great Britain."

The Augusta editor disagreed with those who blamed Mathews, Mitchell, or other aggressive American agents for the catastrophe. Rather he decried past indecision which had prevented occupation of the provinces. "We had once a good claim on the Floridas, and justifiable cause to take and hold possession, at least until our differences and claims were amicably adjusted with Spain; had we done so, we would have saved the colonists of Florida from the ravages and plunder of a band of free-booters, who nowhere left the vestiges of civilization behind them, and at this day would have stood on a better footing with Spain than we now are."[4]

Secretary Monroe gave credence to the repeated rumors of cession. "East Florida in itself is comparatively nothing," he wrote John Quincy Adams, "but as a post in the hands of Great Britain it is of the highest importance." As the Florida peninsula commanded the Gulf of Mexico and its tributary waters including the Mississippi, the outlet for much of the most fertile and productive soil of the United

States, it could be used by Great Britain to control essential American trade. Furthermore, the secretary feared British agents stationed in Florida would incite the Creeks and other Indians, aid escaping slaves, and stifle westward expansion. "It is believed," Monroe concluded, "Great Britain has accepted the cession of East Florida and of it only, that she has done it with the intention to establish a strong post there and to avail herself of it for all the purposes above suggested."[5]

Had Great Britain accepted the Floridas? The editor of the *London Chronicle* thought so. The question of an indemnity for British aid to Spain was a problem, he admitted. Although England preferred and demanded free trade with the Spanish-American colonies, the wily Spaniard had rejected it and thrust the Floridas on Great Britain. The editor regretted this. He saw no advantage in the ownership of sandy East Florida and unhealthful West Florida. England had been happily rid of them in 1783, the editor declared, and now they were even more worthless than they had been. They were an expense which cost Spain more than $150,000 annually. Their inhabitants would eventually demand annexation by the United States. Great Britain had lost by acquiring the Floridas, the editor stated, for Spain had given that which was not worth keeping, and indeed that which could not be retained for long against an expanding United States. It would be better for Great Britain to forget the Floridas, the editor concluded, and protect Canada.[6]

That was a logical conclusion. Those English and American citizens who feared Great Britain would accept the Spanish provinces were reassured by the general European peace settlements. Spain retained her colonies although the part of West Florida lying beyond the Perdido River was under the jurisdiction of the United States.

The peace left this problem of boundaries unsettled. Since 1808 the United States had refused official recognition to Spanish minister Luis de Onís. With the restoration of diplomatic relations in 1815, Onís suggested the re-establishment of the 1808 boundaries between West Florida and the United States.[7] As compliance with this request would mean the evacuation of those sections of West Florida which had been occupied in 1810 and 1813, Monroe rejected the proposal in a strongly-worded letter. The United States had suffered many wrongs from Spain, Monroe declared; some of them originated before 1808 and others after that date. The spoliation claims and

THE REVIVAL OF ANARCHY — AND PEACE

Spain's rejection of the convention of 1802 were old grievances which demanded attention. More recently British troops and agents had been allowed in the Floridas where they incited the Indians and injured the United States. Because of valid claims, grievances, and a well-founded right to the territory west of the Perdido, Monroe stated that his country would retain the disputed area until all controversies between Spain and the United States were settled by a friendly, honest negotiation.[8]

Onís emphatically denied Spanish responsibility for British activity in the Floridas. Officials of those provinces had had strict orders to maintain neutrality. They had done this to the best of their ability; British agents and soldiers had entered the provinces against the will of Spain. His country had done nothing since 1808 to harm the United States, Onís declared. Could the American government make the same statement about its relations with Spain? he asked. Furthermore, the United States and not Spain had severed diplomatic relations in 1808. Onís proclaimed his country had been and was eager to settle differences by fair negotiation.[9]

Denials, protests, accusations gained nothing for Spain. That long, narrow stretch of land west of the Perdido River was the only territorial addition from the war era. Neither Madison nor Monroe would relinquish it. By the Treaty of Ghent the United States won nothing from Great Britain in territory or in commercial rights. Territorial demands, neutral rights, impressments, freedom of the seas, sailors' rights, and paper blockades were conspicuously absent in the wording of the Treaty of Ghent. The United States had only one thing to boast of — the land west of the Perdido, and that would be held.

England emerged triumphant from the Napoleonic wars but Spain saved little of her once vast new world empire. One by one her rebelling colonies established their independence. Although she retained the Floridas east of the Perdido, it was a hollow victory. Weakened and impoverished by decades of conflict Spain could spare neither the men nor the money to govern the provinces. In and near St. Augustine the authority of the Spanish governor was generally respected; in Fernandina, law was observed at times; but in the back country anarchy reigned. Robbers from Georgia, smugglers, slave traders, and Indian raiders operated almost at will. What government there was stemmed from men who organized themselves for the purpose of defense and who received little support from St. Augustine.

Governor Kindelan knew that Georgians were responsible for the lawlessness in East Florida. In December, 1814, he asked Governor Early to disperse or punish individuals who planned a raid into Florida from Coleraine.[10] The Georgia governor ordered Colonel Scott to investigate and suppress the raiders and assured Kindelan that Georgia and the United States would not aid and encourage troublemakers.[11] Rather, both governments desired peace on the border and would punish those who created disturbances. Since Spain lacked the military power to check the Indians and the British agents, the governor thought Kindelan should not object if Georgia militia entered Spanish territory and destroyed the hostile Indians.[12]

English agent Edward Nicholls spoke out for the Indians. He accused Georgians of robbery and murder; they had twice raided Bowlegs' town, killing three Indians, wounding a number, and driving off cattle. The Seminoles would defend themselves, Nicholls stated. He had sent them arms and ammunition for that purpose, but they would not cross the Georgia line. Maverick Indians who crossed the border, who robbed Georgians, had been and would continue to be punished by their own tribe. One such Indian had been executed for stealing cattle above the Florida line.[13]

By what right, Early asked Kindelan, did a British officer living in Spanish territory assume a superintendency over the Indians and represent them in communications? On whose authority did British troops occupy a post on the Apalachicola within Spanish domain when neither Spain nor Great Britain was at war with the United States? These were embarrassing questions. Early knew it but assured Kindelan of Georgia's desire for peace and described his efforts to restrain the lawlessness.[14]

From camps below the St. Marys River robber bands operated freely, and supplied by friends in St. Marys, they plundered East Florida plantations. White, mulatto, black – no one was secure. Mounted raiders swept within eight miles of St. Augustine where they captured the free Negro Charles and his family. Negroes were salable. Colored deserters from Spanish companies were offered a haven in Georgia; free Negroes were enticed across the St. Marys by promises of good wages, and slaves were kidnapped. Once in Georgia they were sold as slaves.[15]

THE REVIVAL OF ANARCHY — AND PEACE

Former Patriot John H. McIntosh blamed the United States Senate for the anarchy in Florida. From the safety of his Refuge Plantation near Jefferson, Georgia, he wrote William H. Crawford: "Had the wishes of our old and worthy friend, Geo. Mathews been carried into effect . . ., had your advice and that of the President been followed a few years ago, that unhappy province would now have been a flourishing country under the Government of the U. States; and probably his Catholic Majesty, his ministers and allies [would be] perfectly reconciled to the measure."

As McIntosh reflected on his personal losses and the "unfortunate policy of the Senate of the U. States on the subject of possessing the Floridas" he shook with anger. But he held dear his memories of George Mathews, never doubting that "the good old general, acted from the fairest and most patriotic motives. . . . Could I live in St. Augustine under the Government of the U. States," McIntosh declared, "I believe that many years would be added to my life, by obtaining what I have so long been wishing for. And those years would be yet increased by that delightful and healthy climate."[16]

The people of East Florida, even the Spaniards, might have agreed with McIntosh. They were sick of anarchy and longed for the protection of a strong government. Southerners demanded action from their government and an end to lawlessness below the St. Marys.

The United States needed little pushing. Great Britain abandoned the military post on the Apalachicola and Negroes established a fort there. From that point of vantage they welcomed escaped slaves and attacked American trade on the river. On July 27, 1816, an American expeditionary force bombarded the Negro fort. A cannon ball penetrated the fort's magazine and the resulting explosion instantly killed almost 300 Negroes. Sixty others were so badly burned that death alone gave them relief.

That incident brought momentary peace on the frontier. Then the adventurer Gregor MacGregor captured Fernandina, and others followed him until the United States brought peace by occupying the Spanish town. In 1818 Andrew Jackson led his militia through northern Florida killing Indians and executing two British subjects. Spain could neither control nor hold the Floridas. In 1821 after ratification of a treaty of cession the United States had at last won the Floridas.

For McIntosh, Archibald Clark, and other aggressive Georgians, the final acquisition was an empty victory. In 1812 they had sought power and land in East Florida but these were denied them. Nine years later the former Patriots received the same treatment as other citizens who moved into Florida. McIntosh and Clark remained in Georgia where they passed their remaining years in comfort. Wilson Connor, the "diplomatic agent" of the Patriots, found a church in Georgia where he preached and died in the middle of a sentence as he stood before his Baptist congregation. William Cone bought land in northern Florida and left descendants who attained distinction in the state. George Clarke prospered at Fernandina as did Zephaniah Kingsley further down the east coast. Both men continued to sire mulatto children. In contrast, Philip Fatio and Francis Sanchez observed the conventional mores and their progeny became leaders in Florida.

These and tens of other men had suffered financial losses during the East Florida revolution for which they held the United States responsible. American judges agreed with them. In 1851 United States District Judge Isaac H. Bronson concluded: "A detail of some of the more revolting instances of robbery and plunder and wanton destruction on the one hand, that occurred during this period, or of individual cases of hardship, ruin and beggary on the other, is hardly called for, and perhaps not proper in this general statement, though they might tend much to illustrate the general character of the injuries of that period. Suffice it to say, that before or when the United States troops finally evacuated the country, the whole inhabited part of the province was in a state of utter desolation and ruin. Almost every building outside of the walls of St. Augustine was burned or destroyed; farms and plantations laid waste; cattle, horses, and hogs driven off or killed, movable property plundered or destroyed, and in many instances slaves dispersed or abducted. So far as the destruction of property of every kind was concerned, the desolation of the Carnatic by Hyder Ali was not more terrible and complete."[17]

For more than half a century claims for losses cluttered courts of the United States. McIntosh and Kingsley sued for more than $100,000 each. Other claimants presented demands which ranged from a few to many thousands of dollars. The actual payments made by the United States were only a part of the total expense resulting from the East Florida revolution. Counsel fees, court costs, printing bills, and the time given to the cases by interested individuals, treasury agents, and the Congress swelled the total monetary and human expenditure.

Judge Bronson characterized the revolution as "an episode in the general history of the nation, which, as an American citizen, I could wish might remain unwritten."[18] The story of aggression, of repudiation, of executive double-dealing, of inhumanity is not a pleasant one. "It is melancholy," one American stated, "to the lover of honest dealing to discover in the first document [the instructions to Mathews and McKee] the commencement of all American aggressions against the provinces of the Floridas: to see the Secretary of State dictating to his agent the quibbles to which he should have recourse, and recommending the first of those baseless promises so to be worded as to deceive ... without being binding upon him who made them."[19]

For more than a quarter-century the United States used diplomacy, intrigue, chicanery, force, and war in its march on the Floridas. Most interesting and most indefensible of these was the revolution of 1812, fomented by George Mathews and supported by the administration. Though they officially denied the revolution, Madison and Monroe retained the territory ceded by the revolutionists. Against the will of Congress they used American military forces to sustain the Patriots.

The reputations of Madison and Monroe were tarnished by their part in the East Florida revolution. They inherited a policy and were pushed further by the aggressive nationalism of the War Hawks. By 1812 their desire for the Floridas became a mania; their acts implied a belief that "the end justifies the means." It was not an American doctrine. Yet Madison and Monroe were encouraged in it by Jefferson, many congressmen, and a host of Southerners.

Territorial expansion and the acquisition of the Floridas were natural policies for the United States. History condemns not the policies but the methods of achievement. The encouragement and consequent repudiation of eager, patriotic George Mathews was indefensible. In their cavalier treatment of him the president and secretary acted as autocrats casting aside and denouncing a faithful servant to save themselves embarrassment. By invading the territory of and making war on a friendly power without the consent of Congress, President Madison followed in the steps of old-world dictators. The ideals of the young American republic were forgotten as his desire for the Floridas overcame his sense of justice.

Strange yet marvelous was the American government. A few senators motivated more by personal dislike than honest conviction twice joined with sincere men to vote down the administration's unethical proposal. It was democracy in action. Numbers of men with their free votes, and despite their individual faults, reached a just conclusion, whereas one all-powerful dictator would have supported error. Democracy would not always attain this happy result, but more often than not it would in the United States. In 1812 and 1813 rational and irrational senators combined to prevent the perpetuation of an injustice against Spain.

Eventually the United States acquired the Floridas by fair negotiation. Title to the provinces resulted from a negotiated treaty and not from trickery and force. Yet this did not erase the stain or right the wrong which had been done the peaceable and unoffending subjects of a nation with which the United States was at peace. But by checking Madison and Monroe in their planned conquest, the Senate rejected a national policy of territorial acquisition by aggression. The lesson of 1812 was to be forgotten in a few instances, but Americans can take pride in their country's record of expansion by negotiation and treaty rather than by force and war.

Notes

CHAPTER I

1. *American State Papers* (Washington, 1832-1861), *Foreign Relations*, III, 397-398.
2. Smith to Crawford, October 2, 1810, in Domestic Letters, State Department, National Archives.
3. Folch to Robert Smith, December 2, 1810, *ibid.*, 398.
4. Madison to the Congress, January 3, 1811, *ibid.*, 394-395.
5. "Claims of Citizens of Florida," *House of Representatives Report 99*, 20th Congress, 2nd Session (Washington, 1832), 9-10. The text of the January 15 act and other secret acts are given in David Hunter Miller, *Secret Statutes of the United States* (Washington, 1918).
6. The account of George Mathews is based on Isaac J. Cox, "George Mathews," in the *Dictionary of American Biography* (New York, 1933), XII, 403-404; William F. Northern (ed.), *Men of Mark in Georgia* (Atlanta, 1907), I, 226-229; and on the following letters: Timothy Pickering to Mathews, April 18, May 8, 1798, Mathews to Pickering, October 4, 1798, Mathews to Madison, September 20, 1805, in Clarence Edwin Carter (comp. and ed.), *The Territorial Papers of the United States, The Territory of Mississippi, 1798-1817* (Washington, 1937), V, 27n, 31, 48-50, 420-421.
7. Northern, *Men of Mark in Georgia*, I, 333-334.
8. Mathews to Pickering, October 14, 1798, in Carter, *Territorial Papers of the United States, Mississippi*, V, 38-80.
9. *Ibid.*, 420-421, 421n.
10. References to Mathews' employment are made in Crawford to Smith, September 20, November 2, 1810, in Miscellaneous Letters, State Department, National Archives; Smith to Crawford, September 4, October 2, 1810, in Domestic Letters; Benjamin Hawkins to Madison, March 11, 1811, in Madison Papers, Manuscripts Division, Library of Congress.
11. For descriptions and characterization of Madison, see Sidney Howard Gay, *James Madison* (Boston, 1884), 117; Gaillard Hunt, *The Life of James Madison* (New York, 1902), 5, 137, 273; Henry Adams, *History of the United States During the Administrations of Thomas Jefferson and James Madison* (New York, 1889-1891), III, 120. Cited hereafter as Adams, *History*.
12. In 1810 most of present-day Alabama was a part of the Mississippi Territory. When Mississippi was admitted to the Union as a state in 1817, Alabama became a territory.
13. Herbert Bruce Fuller, *The Purchase of Florida* (Cleveland, 1906), 182-183.
14. Holmes to Smith, June 20, 1810, in Isaac J. Cox, *The West Florida Controversy, 1798-1813: A Study in American Diplomacy* (Baltimore, 1918), 329.
15. Smith to Holmes, July 12, 1810, in Domestic Letters.
16. Madison to Smith, July 17, 1810, in *The Writings of James Madison, Comprising His Papers and Private Correspondence*, edited by Gaillard Hunt (New York, 1900-1910), VIII, 105-106. Cited hereafter as Hunt, *Writings of Madison*.
17. Smith to Holmes, July 21, 1810, in Domestic Letters.

18. Claiborne to Wykoff, June 14, 1810, in Cox, *West Florida Controversy*, 330.
19. Philemon Thomas to John Rhea, September 24, 1810, in *Nashville Democratic Clarion and Tennessee Gazette*, October 19, 1810. Cited hereafter as *Clarion*.
20. *Ibid*.
21. Adams, *History*, V, 306-307.
22. "Declaration of the People of West Florida," in *Clarion*, October 19, 1810.
23. Rhea to Smith, October 10, 1810, in *Savannah Republican*, December 20, 1810.
24. Smith to Claiborne, October 27, 1810, in *American State Papers, Foreign Relations*, III, 396-397.
25. Smith later stated that President Madison had ordered him to prohibit the use of force in taking a Spanish held position. "Mr. Smith's address to the People of the United States," in *Savannah Republican*, July 16, 1811.
26. Folch to E. P. Gaines, November 25, 1810, in *Savannah Republican*, January 3, 1811.
27. Onís to Alexander James Dallas, December 4, 1810, in Miscellaneous Letters.
28. Turreau to Champagny [French Foreign Minister], November 1, 1810, quoted in Adams, *History*, V, 313.
29. Morier to Smith, December 15, 1810, in *American State Papers, Foreign Relations*, III, 399.
30. The statements attributed to Mathews in this interview are based on Crawford's account of Mathews' mission. Crawford to Smith, November 1, 1810, in Miscellaneous Letters.
31. Jefferson to John Wayles Eppes, January 5, 1811, in *The Works of Thomas Jefferson*, edited by Paul Leicester Ford (New York, 1904-1905), XI, 159-161. Cited hereafter as Ford, *Works of Jefferson*.
32. Smith to Mathews and McKee, January 26, 1811, in Domestic Letters.
33. *Ibid*.

CHAPTER 2

1. Isaacs to Mathews and McKee, March 31, 1811, in Miscellaneous Letters.
2. Mathews to Smith, February 25, 1811, in Territorial Papers of Florida, I, National Archives. Cited hereafter as Territorial Papers.
3. *Ibid*.
4. *Ibid*. William Eustis was secretary of war and Paul Hamilton was secretary of the navy.
5. Hawkins to Madison, March 11, 1811, in Madison Papers, Manuscripts Division, Library of Congress. This letter and the letters cited in footnotes 1 and 6 of this chapter give the itinerary of Mathews. There are definite citations to support the facts that he traveled by way of Charleston, that he was in St. Marys from February 23 to 26, that he visited Hawkins at the Creek Agency on March 9, 10, and 11, and that he reached Fort Stoddert on March 21, Isaac J. Cox in "The Border Missions of George Mathews," *Mississippi Valley Historical Review* (December, 1925), XII, 316, errs in giving March 23 as the date of Mathews' arrival at Stoddert.

McKee evidently accompanied Mathews on the trip to Charleston, St. Marys, Creek Agency, and Fort Stoddert. Hawkins referred to "Mathews and the gentleman with him," and on March 22 Mathews and McKee stated that they had arrived at Stoddert "last evening."
6. Mathews and McKee to Wade Hampton, March 22, 1811, in Territorial Papers, I.
7. Northern, *Men of Mark in Georgia*, I, 226-227.
8. As he served for money rather than honor, McKee respected a man who demonstrated financial acumen. In describing his experiences in Washington, McKee stated: "My reception here has been flattering and might lead a man of more ambition and credulity to expect great things — but money is *the subject of my*

NOTES

story and if they will, God bless them, give me but enough of that they may keep their honors for those who are more ambitious of them. . . ." McKee to James Inneraity, January 17, 1811, in Greenslade Papers, Florida Historical Society, University of Florida.

9. Northern, *Men of Mark in Georgia*, I, 227.
10. Jeanette Thurber Connor (trans.), *Pedro Menedez de Aviles*, by Gonzalo Solis de Meras (DeLand, Florida, 1923), 115, 122.
11. Marranos or "Marranos Espanoles" were Spaniards of Jewish blood who were professing Christianity.
12. Woodbury Lowery, *The Spanish Settlements within the Present Limits of the United States: Florida, 1566-1574* (New York, 1905), 333.
13. Charles Francis Jenkins, *Button Gwinnett: Signer of the Declaration of Independence* (New York, 1926), 133.
14. European alliances changed frequently after 1789. Spain declared war on France in 1793 but made peace in 1795 much to the annoyance of Great Britain. Although an ally of Spain between 1793 and 1795, Great Britain treated Spain badly and after Spain came to terms with France, England provoked the Spaniards by insult and attack. Spain was thrown toward France and the two countries became allies in 1796. For the changing picture in Spain, see Charles E. Chapman, *A History of Spain* (New York, 1931), 403.
15. Liston to William Grenville, May 2, 1798, in *Instructions to the British Ministers to the United States, 1791-1812*, edited by Bernard Mayo (Washington, 1941), 158n.
16. Liston to Grenville, June 12, 1798, *ibid.*, 158n.
17. Not all of these vessels were condemned. The records of the American legation in Madrid show that 124 of the 168 ships captured by France were condemned or unaccounted for; 29 of the vessels seized by Spain were condemned, while 24 were unaccounted for and 51 released. The recorded seizures by France and Spain began on October 1, 1796, and Secretary of State Monroe believed the records were incomplete. Monroe to Madison, January 14, 1813, in Messages of the President, Territorial Papers of Florida, Legislative Reference and Records Office, National Archives.
18. *Ibid.*
19. David Hunter Miller, *Treaties and Other International Acts of the United States of America* (Washington, 1931), II, 492-497.
20. Jefferson to Livingston, April 18, 1802, in *The Writings of Thomas Jefferson*, edited by Albert Ellery Bergh (Washington, 1903), X, 311-316. Cited hereafter as Bergh, *Writings of Jefferson*.
21. *Id.* to William Dunbar, March 3, 1803, in *Life and Letters of William Dunbar*, edited by Mrs. Dunbar Rowland (Jackson, Mississippi, 1930), 158-159.
22. Actually Napoleon had not obtained the Floridas from Spain in 1800, and continued his efforts to secure them after the retrocession of Louisiana. In 1802 Robert Livingston worked to prevent French acquisition of the Floridas and to gain them for the United States. Talleyrand suggested that the eastern boundary of Louisiana extended to the Apalachicola River, but Livingston insisted that West Florida was not a part of Louisiana. (Later when it was to the advantage of the United States, Livingston accepted Talleyrand's idea). See Cox, *West Florida Controversy*, 71-75; Madison to Livingston, January 18, 1803, in Hunt, *Writings of Madison*, VII, 5-7.
23. Madison to Livingston, January 18, 1803, *id.* to Pinckney, January 18, 1803, *id.* to Livingston and Monroe, March 2, 1803, in Hunt, *Writings of Madison*, VII, 2-7, 9-30; *State Papers and Publick Documents of the United States, From the Accession of George Washington*, etc. (Boston, 1819), II, 540. Cited hereafter as *State Papers*.

24. Adams, *History*, II, 43-44.
25. Livingston to Madison, May 12, 1803, in Adams, *History*, II, 69. Monroe to Madison, May 18, 1803, in *Writings of James Monroe*, edited by Stanislaus Murray Hamilton (New York, 1898-1903), IV, 24-27. Cited hereafter as Hamilton, *Writings of Monroe*.
26. Livingston to Madison, May 12, 20, 1803, quoted in Adams, *History*, II, 69-70.
27. Monroe to Madison, June 19, 1803, in Hamilton, *Writings of Monroe*, IV, 36-39.
28. Monroe to Livingston [no date, *c.* July 1, 1803], *ibid.*, 40-43.
29. Adams, *History*, II, 71.
30. Jefferson to Dunbar, September 21, 1803, in Ford, *Works of Jefferson*, X, 20-21; *id.* to Madison, August 25, 1803, in Bergh, *Writings of Jefferson*, X, 412-415; *id.* to Gallatin, August 23, 1803, in *Writings of Albert Gallatin*, edited by Henry Adams (Philadelphia, 1879), III, 144-145. Cited hereafter as Adams, *Writings of Gallatin*.
31. *Id.* to John Breckinridge, August 12, 1803, in Bergh, *Writings of Jefferson*, X, 407-411.
32. *Ibid.*
33. Adams, *History*, II, 246-247.
34. Charles E. Hill, "James Madison," in *American Secretaries of State and Their Diplomacy*, edited by Samuel Flagg Bemis (New York, 1927-1929), III, 44.
35. Adams, *History*, II, 261.
36. At his own request Yrujo was transferred to Milan, Italy. Hill, "James Madison," *loc. cit.*, 69-70.
37. Monroe to Madison, May 18, 1803, in Hamilton, *Writings of Monroe*, IV, 24-27.
38. In reply to a letter in which Pinckney demanded the ratification of the Claims Convention of 1802, Cevallos stated: ". . . it appears extraordinary enough that you should consider any delay in the ratification of said convention on the part of the Spanish Government, as a wrong done your Government, when that of the United States had taken up almost two years in the examination before ratification on her part. . . ." Cevallos to Pinckney, July 2, 1804, in *Annals of Congress*, 2nd Session, 1804-1805, appendix, 1313-1315. For letters of Madison, Pinckney, and Cevallos relating to Pinckney's negotiations in 1804, see *ibid.*, 1300-1327.
39. Madison to Monroe, April 15, 1804, in Hunt, *Writings of Madison*, VII, 141-153.
40. Adams, *History*, II, 310-311.
41. Adams, *History*, III, 23-37; Hill, "James Madison," *loc. cit.*, 53-56; *Annals of Congress*, 8th Congress, 2nd Session, appendix, 1364-1461. Monroe later stated: "The Spanish gov't was willing to make the cession but asked more for the territory than our Commiss'rs were willing to give." Monroe to [Madison], June 22, 1812, in Monroe Letter, P. K. Yonge Memorial Library of Florida History, University of Florida; Rembert W. Patrick, "A New Letter of James Monroe on the Cession of Florida," *Florida Historical Quarterly* (April, 1945), XXIII, 197-201.
42. Erving to Madison, December 7, 1805, quoted in Adams, *History*, III, 37-38.
43. Gallatin to Madison, August 6, 1805, in Adams, *Writings of Gallatin*, I, 237-239.
44. Jefferson to Dunbar, March 13, 1804, in Bergh, *Writings of Jefferson*, XI, 17-23.
45. Ford, *Works of Jefferson*, I, *The Anas*, 386-388.
46. Adams, *History*, III, 134.
47. Anthony Merry to Charles Fox, April 6, May 14, 1806, in Mayo (ed.), *Instructions to British Ministers*, 224n. Madison's instructions to Armstrong and James Bowdoin, who was to replace Erving as minister to Spain, were to use not more than two million dollars as an advance payment against the total price of five million for the Floridas (Hunt, *Writings of Madison*, VIII, 50).
48. Jefferson to Armstrong, July 17, 1807, in Bergh, *Writings of Jefferson*, XI, 283-284.

NOTES

49. Gallatin to Jefferson, August 5, 1808, in Adams, *Writings of Gallatin*, I, 399-400.
50. Jefferson to Secretary of War; *id.* to Madison, both letters dated August 12, 1808, in Ford, *Works of Jefferson*, XI, 42-45.
51. *Id.* to Madison, April 19, 27, 1809 in Bergh, *Writings of Jefferson*, XII, 106-107, 274-277.
52. Jackson to Canning, October 18, 1809, quoted in Cox, *West Florida Controversy*, 310.
53. Jefferson to P. S. DuPont de Nemours, February 1, 1803, in Ford, *Works of Jefferson*, IX, 436-441.
54. *Ibid.*
55. *Annals of Congress*, 7th Congress, 2nd Session, 374.
56. Julius W. Pratt, *Expansionists of 1812* (New York, 1925), 67.
57. Jefferson believed Cuba could be defended without a navy. He favored American acquisition of the island, but warned: "Nothing should ever be accepted which would require a navy to defend it." Jefferson to Madison, April 27, 1809, in Bergh, *Writings of Jefferson*, XII, 274-277.

CHAPTER 3

1. Fort Stoddert is described in Peter J. Hamilton, *Colonial Mobile* (Boston, 1898), 341, 349, 353, 363n. Although it is often spelled "Stoddard" and "Stodart," the correct spelling is Stoddert.
2. Mathews and McKee to Hampton, March 22, 1811, in Territorial Papers, I. Mathews knew Wade Hampton personally and urged his friend and fellow officer of the American Revolution to come to Stoddert. Mathews planned to leave the fort on or before April 7, 1811. Actually he remained much later but his letter to Hampton indicated the general's conception of his duties. In his opinion West Florida was incidental to his chief work in East Florida.
3. Hampton to Mathews and McKee, April 9, 1811; McKee to Smith, May 1, 1811, *ibid.*
4. McKee to Folch, January 17, 1811, in Papeles de Cuba, Legajo 1569, film copy, Yonge Library; Cox, *West Florida Controversy*, 524.
5. The conversation between Isaacs and Folch was reported in Isaacs to Mathews and McKee, March 31, 1811, in Miscellaneous Letters.
6. Folch to McKee, February 27, 1811, in Papeles de Cuba, Legajo 1569; Cox, *West Florida Controversy*, 525.
7. *Id.* to Someruelos, February 4, 1811, in Papeles de Cuba, Legajo 1569; Cox, *West Florida Controversy*, 526.
8. Mathews gave the details of his interview with Folch in Mathews and McKee to Smith, April 24, 1811, in Territorial Papers, I. The reader should keep in mind that the well-written letters of Mathews were the work of his secretary or of some friend. The general was never polished in speech, but rather than attempting to reproduce the probable utterances of Mathews, the author has based the conversations of the general on the extant reports.
9. Mathews to Eustis, May 13, 1811, in Register of Letters Received, War Records Office, National Archives.
10. Mathews and McKee to Covington, May 9, 1811, in Territorial Papers, I.
11. Covington to Mathews and McKee, May 10, 1811, *ibid.*
12. *Savannah Republican*, July 16, 1811, quoting the *Louisiana Gazette*, May 27, 1811.
13. *Georgia Journal*, July 31, 1811.
14. *Ibid.*, July 10, 1811.
15. Mathews to Monroe, May 14, 1811, in Territorial Papers, I.
16. This statement contradicts the authorities: Cox, *West Florida Controversy*, 528; Pratt, *Expansionists of 1812*, 82; Rufus Kay Wyllys, "The East Florida Revolution

FLORIDA FIASCO

of 1812-1814," in the *Hispanic American Historical Review* (November, 1929), IX, 422. The three letters cited above (Monroe to Mathews and McKee, *id.* to Claiborne, and *id.* to Mathews, June 29, 1811), are in Domestic Letters.

Notwithstanding this evidence the letters were not forwarded. In the file of Domestic Letters (State Department, National Archives), there are rough, unsigned drafts of the letters. Of them the cataloguer wrote: "Among the loose papers of the department put into my hands to arrange there are a considerable number of rough drafts of letters of old date which do not appear to have been recorded. This to Gen'l Mathews and McKee is the first belonging to this book."

17. McKee to Monroe, May 22, 1811, in Territorial Papers, I.
18. *Id.* to *id.*, June 5, 1811, *ibid.*
19. *Georgia Journal,* October 16, 1811.
20. Monroe to McKee, January 2, 1812; McKee to Monroe, May 20, 1812, in Territorial Papers, II. The letter of January 2 is also in Domestic Letters. The reports of McKee to Monroe in 1811 and 1812 are in the Territorial Papers, I and II.
21. Quoted in Adams, *History,* V, 325.

CHAPTER 4

1. Mathews to Monroe, June 28, 1811, in Territorial Papers, I.
2. *Ibid.*
3. "Statement of George Clarke," *United States vs. Ferriera,* in *Senate Miscellaneous Document 55,* 36th Congress, 1st Session (Washington, 1860), 17-18. Cited hereafter as *U. S. vs. Ferriera.*
4. Estrada to Someruelos, March 18, 1811, in Selected Papers, box 411; *id.* to Mariano, March 18, 1811, in To and from War Department, box 47H4, East Florida Papers, Manuscripts Division, Library of Congress; *Savannah Republican,* April 23, 1811.
5. Point Petre File, Judge Advocate General's Office, War Records Office, National Archives; Smith to Ridgeway, June 20, 1812, in Thomas Adam Smith Letters, Originals in Missouri Historical Society Library, typewritten copies in the T. Frederick Davis Papers, Yonge Library. Cited hereafter as Smith Letters.
6. John Melish, *A Description of East and West Florida and the Bahama Islands* (Philadelphia, 1813), 10.
7. The population of Washington, Georgia, was 596. At this time the population of Savannah was 5,215, Augusta 2,476, and Milledgeville 1,256. *Aggregate Amount of Persons Within the United States in the Year 1810* (Washington, 1811), photographic facsimile of the 1810 census; *Savannah Republican,* March 9, 1811.
8. W. B. Burroughs, "Camden County History: Dates and Events of Early Times Marking the County's Growth," in *Historical Sketch of Old St. Marys* (n.p., n.d.). Fairly complete records of the founding of St. Marys are in the Judge of Probate's Office, Camden County, Woodbine, Georgia.
9. Sources for the history of St. Marys are: James T. Vocelle, *Reminiscences of Old St. Marys* (n.p., n.d.); James T. Vocelle, *History of Camden County, Georgia* (n.p., 1914); Alexander McQueen, *Three Dead Towns of Georgia* (n.p., n.d.); George Gillman Smith, *The Story of Georgia and the Georgia People, 1732-1860* (Macon, 1900); *Georgia: A Guide to Its Towns and Countryside,* W.P.A., Federal Writers Project (Athens, 1940).
10. "Minutes of the Grand Jury of Camden County, November 1, 1811," quoted in the *Savannah Republican,* December 7, 1811.
11. *Aggregate Amount of Persons Within the United States in 1810,* photographic facsimile of the 1810 census.
12. Records of prostitution, especially as practiced by slaves who rented themselves from their masters, are scarce. During the summer of 1814 the *Augusta Herald* and the *Augusta Chronicle* carried a series of articles and editorials on Negro

310

NOTES

prostitution. Evidently the editor of the *Herald* condoned the practice. (The issues of the *Herald* which carried the editorials are not extant.) The editor of the *Chronicle* condemned a master who received $10 a month in rental for the "wages of sin." The editor estimated the expenses of the slave girl at: $120 for rental paid to the master (as long as the slave girl paid this $10 monthly fee she was free to engage in her "profession"), $50 for house rent, $50 for furniture, $100 for clothing, $100 for household expenses, and $20 for doctor bills. Although the total estimated yearly expense was $480, the slaves had an income far in excess of expenses. These were tremendous sums. In contrast, a private in the army received $60 a year and a colonel $720. *Augusta Chronicle,* July 18, 1814.

13. "Testimony of Winslow Foster" in *Petition of Joseph M. Hernandez* (n.p., n.d.), 18, 22; "Statement of Z. Kingsley," "Statement of George Clarke," "Statement of Jose Papy," "Statement of F. P. Ferriera," in *U. S. vs. Ferriera,* 24, 20, 7, 3.
14. W. B. Burroughs, "Major Archibald Clark and a Sketch of St. Marys in His Time," in *Historical Sketch of Old St. Marys.*
15. Campbell to Hamilton, January 4, 1812, in Captain's Letters, 1812, I, Navy Department, War Records Office, National Archives.
16. The Fernandina of 1812 was situated about one mile north of the present city of Fernandina. In the early 1800's it was seven miles by boat from St. Marys to Fernandina. W. W. Hunt to Frances Hunt, October 27, 1817, in Historical Records Project Papers, W.P.A., Yonge Library.
17. *Fernandina: A Guide to the City and Its Industries* (W.P.A., Florida Writer's Project, 1940), 20.
18. The description of Fernandina is based on the buildings, houses, lots, streets, and individuals given in the re-zoning order of 1811. Copies of this order and a map are in the Territorial Papers, I; David L. Yulee Papers, Yonge Library; and in *Fernandina: A Guide to the City and Its Industries,* 67-76.
19. *Niles Register* (November 15, 1817), XIII, 191.
20. In 1803 McIntosh bought the land of John McQueen on Fort George Island and McGirths Creek for $28,000. McQueen to McQueen, Jr., January 5, 1804, in *The Letters of Don Juan McQueen to His Family: Written from Spanish East Florida, 1791-1807,* edited by Walter Charlton Hartridge (Columbia, 1943), 62-63.
21. "Statement of F. P. Ferriera," in *U. S. vs. Ferriera,* 3.
22. The yields from land, commodity prices, cost of slaves, and wages are given in *U. S. vs. Ferriera,* 3, 9, 16, 21, 24.
23. Quesada to Conde de Lerena, November 15, 1791, in *Documents Relating to the Commercial Policy of Spain in the Floridas,* translated and edited by Arthur Preston Whitaker (DeLand, 1931), 155-161; Cox, *West Florida Controversy,* 22-24; Fuller, *Purchase of Florida,* 38.
24. Cespedes to Marques de Sonora, May 12, 1787, in Whitaker (ed.), *Documents Relating to the Commercial Policy of Spain,* 49-61.
25. Jefferson to Washington, April 2, 1791, in Ford, *Works of Jefferson,* VI, 235-239.
26. Whitaker (ed.), *Documents Relating to the Commercial Policy of Spain,* 161.
27. *Ibid.,* 195-197.
28. During the American Revolution George McIntosh was arrested by Georgia authorities and accused of trading with the enemy. He was eventually released without punishment. Gwinnett to Hancock, March 28, 1777, in Jenkins, *Button Gwinnett,* 215-221.
29. This incident of McIntosh's life in Charleston is given in George White, *Historical Collections of Georgia* (New York, 1854), 547-548; Thomas Gamble, *Savannah Duels and Duelists, 1733-1877* (Savannah, 1923), 20-21.
30. E. Merton Coulter, *Georgia: A Short History* (Chapel Hill, 1947), 137-138.
31. Scrapbook of T. Frederick Davis, in Yonge Library.

FLORIDA FIASCO

32. "Instructions and Authorization from Citizen Consul Mangorit," in Loose Papers, Georgia Department of Archives and History, Atlanta.
33. Some of the letters of Sara McIntosh are in White, *Historical Collections of Georgia*, 551-554.
34. Northern, *Men of Mark in Georgia*, I, 244.
35. "Proclamation of March 5, 1794," in Loose Papers, Georgia Department of Archives and History.
36. Mathews to Justices of the Inferior Court of Camden, August 24, 1795, in Letterbook of Governor George Mathews, Georgia Department of Archives and History.
37. Mathews formed a high opinion of Kindelan, the man who later defied the Americans in their attempt to grab the Floridas. "The character, deportment, and conduct of the Col. [Kindelan]," Mathews stated, "has made an impression on my mind, which operates much in his favor and is also an expression of his great merit." Mathews to L. de las Casas, November 11, 1795, *ibid*.
38. Garvin to Lopez, June 1, 1808, in Notes from the Spanish Legation, State Department, National Archives.
39. James Seagrove and others to Jared Irwin, July 8, 1808, *ibid*.
40. Hamilton to Campbell, January 22, November 18, 1811, in Letters to Officers, Ships of War, IX (December 20, 1809 - March 28, 1812), Navy Department, War Records Office, National Archives; Mitchell to Floyd, March 14, 1811, in Letterbook of Governor Mitchell, Georgia Department of Archives and History.

CHAPTER 5

1. The sources for the life of McIntosh are: gravestones in the family cemetery on the bank of the Marianna River near St. Marys, Georgia; McIntosh File, in Georgia Department of Archives and History; Gamble, *Savannah Duels and Duelists*, 101-102; Hartridge (ed.), *Letters of Don Juan McQueen to His Family*, 23, 23n, 62, 63n, 64-65, 69; Edith Duncan Johnston, *The Houstouns of Georgia* (Athens, Georgia, 1950), 366-390.
2. McIntosh was a wealthy man of good education, "but not influential with the [Spanish] government or people." "Statement of George Clarke," in *U. S. vs. Ferriera*, 18.
3. Mathews to Madison, April 16, 1812, in Madison Papers. See also Mathews to Monroe, April 16, 1812, in Territorial Papers, II.
4. Mathews to Monroe, June 28, 1811, in Territorial Papers, I.
5. *Id.* to *id.*, August 3, 1811, *ibid*.
6. *Ibid*.
7. Mathews to Monroe, October 14, 1811, *ibid*.
8. Crawford to Madison, November 5, 1811, in Miscellaneous Letters.
9. Mathews to Monroe, October 14, 1811, in Territorial Papers, I.
    President Madison evidently read this letter for he later referred to the activities of Keene (Madison to Barlow, November 17, 1811, in Hunt, *Writings of Madison*, VIII, 168-172). The activities of Keene are also described in Estrada to Someruelos, September 3, 1811, in Papeles de Cuba, Legajo 1570, and in a letter dated September 21, 1811, and signed THEMTSTOCLESATMAQNESTA, in Loose Papers, Florida Historical Society Library.
10. Mathews to Monroe, October 14, 1811, in Territorial Papers, I.
11. *Id.* to *id.*, January 23, 1812, in Register of Letters Received.
12. *Ibid*.
13. Mail for St. Marys left Savannah every Tuesday at 2:00 P.M. and arrived in St. Marys at 2:00 P.M. on Friday; mail left St. Marys at 2:00 P.M. Friday and reached Savannah at 10:00 A.M. on Monday. *Georgia Argus*, January 16, 1811.

NOTES

14. Onís to Smith, November 20, 1809, and a number of letters written by Bernaben in 1810 and 1811, in Notes from the Spanish Legation.
15. Bernaben to Monroe, June 7, 1811, *ibid.*
16. Meade to Smith, February 20, 1811, in Miscellaneous Letters.
17. Wellesley to Foster, April 10, 1811, in Mayo (ed.), *Instructions to British Ministers*, 319-321.
18. Foster to Monroe, July 2, 1811, in *American State Papers, Foreign Relations*, III, 542-543.
19. Monroe to Foster, July 8, 1811, *ibid.*, 543.
20. Foster to Monroe, September 5, 1811, *ibid.*, 543-544.
21. *Ibid.*
22. Monroe to Foster, September 5, 1811, *ibid.*, 544-545.
23. McIntosh to Monroe, July 30, 1812, in Miscellaneous Letters; Address of the Legislative Council of East Florida to Thomas Pinckney, March 30, 1813, in Territorial Papers, III.
24. McIntosh to Monroe, July 30, 1812, in Miscellaneous Letters; *Savannah Republican*, May 14, 1812.
25. The possibility of error in the list of Mathews' first recruits, or of omissions, is considerable. George Clarke later testified (*U. S. vs. Ferriera*, 18) that the general recruited seven or eight men from St. Marys and named Archibald Clark, Bogue (probably John Boog), and the overseer of McIntosh's plantation. Clarke also stated that about five men came from Florida, but he could not recall their names. He knew McIntosh and may have classified him as a citizen of St. Marys. Isaac J. Cox ("The Border Missions of General George Mathews," *loc. cit.*, 319) gives eight as the number of first recruits and names McIntosh, Ashley, Craig, and a Spaniard called Haddock. William Craig, however, did not join the Patriots until after the capture of Fernandina.

    Perhaps the most accurate list of revolutionists was made by the Spanish officials. Their list included: Mathews, Isaacs, the three American commanders (Campbell, Laval, and Smith), John Floyd of the Georgia militia, McIntosh, Ashley, Seagrove, Clark, Boog, Kelley, Young, and Sands (Papers of the Revolution, East Florida Papers, Manuscripts Division, Library of Congress).

    Laval and Campbell could not be classified as revolutionists; and although Colonel Smith did support the Patriots, he did not reach Point Petre until after the capture of Fernandina. John Floyd did not favor Mathews' plan of conquest, but he may have signified his willingness to allow the Georgia militia to volunteer in the Patriot army.
26. *Charleston Courier*, April 1, 1812.
27. "Statement of Z. Kingsley" and "Conclusion of the Court," in *U. S. vs. Ferriera*, 22, 36.
28. Onís to Monroe, September 5, 1811, in Notes from the Spanish Legation; *U. S. vs. Ferriera*, 17, 18, 36, 37.
29. Mitchell to Floyd, March 18, 1812, in Letterbook of Governor Mitchell.
30. *Ibid.* Although the March 18 letter was from Mitchell to Floyd, Mitchell summarized Floyd's letter of March 9 and proceeded to answer the questions raised by the militia general.
31. Cox, "The Border Missions of General George Mathews," *loc. cit.*, 321, based on Ellicott to Pickering, May 17, 1812, Pickering Papers, XXX, 43, Massachusetts Historical Society.
32. Campbell to Hamilton, February 29, in Captain's Letters, 1812, I.
33. War Department to Laval, January 26, 1811, in Bureau of Index and Archives, 1064, typewritten copy, T. Frederick Davis Papers.
34. Floyd to Crawford, March 21, 1812, in Miscellaneous Letters.

FLORIDA FIASCO

35. Wyllys to McIntosh, March 10, 1812, in Territorial Papers, II.
36. Mathews to Monroe, March 14, 1812, in *Secret Acts, Resolutions, and Instructions, under which East Florida Was Invaded by the United States Troops, Naval Forces, and Volunteers, in 1812 and 1813, together with the Official Correspondence of the Agents and Officers of the Government,* etc. (Washington, 1860), 9-10. Cited hereafter as *Secret Acts.*
37. That Mathews in collusion with Wyllys fabricated the threat of British aid for St. Augustine to justify his acts to Madison and Monroe is a possible but not probable interpretation. By March Mathews was confident that the administration approved his plan for seizing East Florida. Therefore it was not necessary to "frighten" Washington. Evidently the general believed there was immediate danger of British action and this forced him to act before he was ready. Mathews had taken the first step in securing aid from Governor Mitchell. Time was required to win the governor and the Georgia troops, but the danger from British aggression forced Mathews to act at once.
38. Mathews to Campbell, March 11, 1812, in Captain's Letters, 1812, I.
39. Since there was no accurate count of the men involved, the numbers are an estimate. The most reliable witness of the eventual march on Fernandina estimated the number of men at 180, approximately 110 of whom were Georgians and 70 were East Floridians. See footnote 41, chapter VII.
40. McIntosh to Troup, March 12, 1812, in Territorial Papers, II. Troup sent the letters to Monroe and added: "Since I left you it has occurred to me a new aspect may be given to the Subject of the letter received this morning. J. H. M. having long resided in the Province and bound himself in the prescribed forms of allegiance may be considered a subject of the King of Spain. If his party be made up up of Spanish subjects as is by no means improbable at least in part, to a revolution of the government by Spanish Subjects nothing can be objected. But will it be possible to keep out of sight the agency of [Mathews]?" Troup to Monroe, March 12 [sic], 1812, *ibid.*

CHAPTER 6

1. Laval to Adjutant General, March 16, 1812, in Personal Papers of Major Jacint Laval, Adjutant General's Office, War Records Office, National Archives. Mathews had been at the cottage with Laval for almost ten months since the date of his arrival at Point Petre. From time to time during this period he had been away either investigating the situation in East Florida or conferring with officials in Georgia.
2. Campbell to Hamilton, December 28, 1811, in Captain's Letters, 1811, II.
3. Hamilton to Robert Greenleaf, quoted in Edwin N. McClellan, History of the United States Marine Corps, unpublished MS., Yonge Library.
4. War Department to Laval, January 26, 1811, in Bureau of Index and Archives, 1064, typewritten copy, T. Frederick Davis Papers.
5. Laval to Adjutant General, March 16, 1812, in Personal Papers of Major Jacint Laval. The conversation between Laval and Mathews is based on this letter. Often the conversation is in the exact words of Laval's written report.
6. At this point Mathews' letters begin to describe his relations with Laval. Mathews to Laval, March 11, 13, 1812, in Territorial Papers, II.
7. Mathews to Laval, March 11, 1812, in Miscellaneous Letters.
8. The exchange between Isaacs and Laval was reported in detail in Isaacs and Appling to Mathews [March 12, 1812], *ibid.*
9. Statements of Massias, Isaacs, Stallings, and Appling [March 12, 1812], in Territorial Papers, II.

NOTES

10. Massias, Isaacs, Stallings, and Appling in their statement (*ibid.*) accused Laval of permitting two sergeants the privilege of sleeping off the post grounds.
11. Charges of Lt. Appling against Laval, in Personal Papers of Major Jacint Laval.
12. Mathews to Monroe, March 14, 1812, in Territorial Papers, II.
13. *Id.* to Laval, March 13, 1812, *ibid.*
14. Laval to Mathews, March 14, 1812, in Miscellaneous Letters.
15. Mathews to Monroe, March 14, 1812, in Territorial Papers, II.
16. *Ibid.*
17. The clash between Massias and Laval was outlined in Laval's charges against Massias of March 16, 1812, in Personal Papers of Captain Abraham Massias, Adjutant General's Office.
18. Evidently Colonel Smith arrived in camp just before midnight on April 16. Mathews stated that Smith reached Point Petre the day before the Patriots took Fernandina (Mathews to Sec'y of State, March 21, 1812, in Miscellaneous Letters). Laval reported (see letters cited in footnotes 20 and 21) that Smith arrived on March 16, and since the affair with Massias occurred in the evening of that day, Smith must have appeared sometime between nightfall and midnight. Smith stated that he reached Point Petre on March 16 shortly after Laval had ordered the arrest of Massias (Smith to Hampton, March 27, 1812, in Smith Letters).
19. Laval to Adjutant General, March 16, 1813, Personal Papers of Major Jacint Laval.
20. *Id.* to Secretary of War, May 2, 1812, *ibid.*
21. *Ibid.*
22. Colonel Smith explained the release of Massias on the following grounds: Massias was arrested by Laval, but for eight days the major preferred no formal charges against the captain. After Massias was ordered to duty, Laval preferred charges and Massias requested a court of inquiry. As Lieutenant William Laval was on leave, Lieutenant Elias Stallings under arrest (also by Laval's order), and Captain Fielder Ridgeway was waiting trial, Smith had only four officers to direct the detachment. He could not spare them for a court of inquiry. Rather he was forced to employ Massias as a commander. (Smith to Hampton, March 27, 1812; *id.* to Adjutant and Inspector General, March 27, 1812, in Smith Letters.) Smith's refusal to arrest Massias stemmed from the need for officers and "not from any disposition to retard an investigation into the conduct of the accused." (Smith to Laval, March 26, 1812, *ibid.*) Smith ordered Major Laval's arrest after the major failed to call for a court of inquiry. (Smith to Hampton, March 27, 1812, *ibid.*)
23. Smith to Laval, June 13, 1812, in Smith Letters.
24. Laval's promotion came on June 7, 1813. On August 1, 1813, he was promoted to colonel. Francis Bernard Heitman, *Historical Register and Dictionary of the United States Army, From Its Organization, September 29, 1789, to March 2, 1903.* (Washington, 1903), I, 618.
25. Charges of Captain George Haig; Haig to Lewis, July 6, 1813, in Personal Papers of Major Jacint Laval.
26. Worth (aide to General Lewis) to Haig, July 7, 1813, *ibid.* The charge of taking the twenty dollars was disregarded because it was of too old a date.
27. Laval to Sec. of War, April 24, 1816; to President, October 7, 1817, *ibid.*

CHAPTER 7

1. McIntosh to Troup, March 12, 1812, in Territorial Papers, II. The date of the planned conquest of St. Augustine given by Pratt (*Expansionist of 1812*, 91) is Monday, March 18. In 1812 March 16 fell on Monday, and McIntosh stated on March 12: "Our plan is all arranged to take the Fort of St. Augustine and the

Governor on Monday night next by surprise. . . ." The "Monday night" was probably pre-dawn of Monday morning.

2. Floyd to Crawford, March 21, 1812, in Miscellaneous Letters. The date of the Patriot manifesto has been given as March 13, 14, and 15. In this account the statements of General John Floyd are followed. He was near the actual scene of action and described events shortly after their occurrence. Other accounts which give March 14 or 15 as the date were written years after the actual event. Cox ("Border Missions of General George Mathews," *loc. cit.*, 324) accepts March 13 as the date of the manifesto, but cites no source of authority. Mathews wrote to Monroe on March 14 and enclosed the manifesto of the Patriots (Territorial Papers, II). The general's letter indicates that the manifesto was promulgated on March 13 or at the latest the morning of the following day.

There is no agreement as to the number of men involved in the revolution. On March 16 Laval informed the adjutant general that 60 to 70 Georgians and 8 to 10 residents of Florida were in the revolutionary party (Personal Papers of Major Jacint Laval). George Clarke stated there were "Some seven or eight who came from St. Marys, among them Archibald Clark, a man whose name was Bogue [John Boog], and McIntosh's overseer. About five Floridians, whose names witness does not remember, joined them at Rose's Bluff. . . ." "Statement of George Clarke," *U. S. vs. Ferriera*, 18.

3. Robert Thompson to Stephen Girard, March 21, 1812, in Territorial Papers, II.
4. Mathews to Campbell, March 14, 1812, in Captain's Letters, 1812, I.
5. Endorsement of Campbell on Mathews to Campbell, *ibid.*
6. McIntosh to Lopez, March 15, 1812, in Patriot War Papers, Office of the Clerk of Court, St. Johns County, St. Augustine, Florida.
7. Mathews to Campbell, March 15, 1812, in Captain's Letters, 1812, I.
8. Ashley to Lopez, March 16, 1812, in Patriot War Papers.
9. Lodowick Ashley could do no more than trace his name. Lopez stated that the letter signed by Ashley was written by McIntosh. Lopez to Laval, March 16, 1812, *ibid.*

A clear account of the events of March 16 and 17 is in G. I. F. Clarke to O'Reilley, March 19, 1812, in "The Surrender of Amelia Island," *Florida Historical Quarterly* (October, 1925), IV, 90-95. In this letter the name G. I. F. Clarke is used although the correct initials were G. J. F. Clarke. See Louise Bates Hill, "George J. F. Clarke, 1774-1836," *Florida Historical Quarterly* (January, 1943), XXI, 199.

10. In reporting this "treaty" Hibberson and Arredondo stated: "General Mathews directed his Secretary to read us a treaty which he had made with McIntosh, the chief of the insurgents, which appeared to us contained nothing more than a detail of the articles mentioned in Ashley's letter which you received yesterday." Hibberson and Arredondo to Lopez, March 17, 1812, in Patriot War Papers.
11. Lopez to Magistrates of St. Marys, March 10, 1812, and their reply [undated], *ibid.*
12. Clarke to O'Reilley, March 19, 1812, "The Surrender of Amelia Island," *loc. cit.*, 90-95.
13. *Ibid.*
14. Hill, "George J. F. Clarke, 1774-1836," *loc. cit.*, 211.
15. *Ibid.*, 212.
16. *Ibid.*, 200.
17. *Ibid.*
18. The description of defensive preparations in Fernandina is given in Clarke to O'Reilley, March 19, 1812, "The Surrender of Amelia Island," *loc. cit.*, 90-95.
19. Lopez to Campbell, March 16, 1812, in Patriot War Papers.

NOTES

20. In a letter dated April 11, 1812, Campbell informed Secretary of Navy Hamilton (Captain's Letters, 1812, I) that George Atkinson had been in St. Marys on March 15 seeking information as to the American support of the Patriots. The civil officials had referred him to Mathews, Laval, and Campbell. As Mathews was at Rose's Bluff and Laval at Point Petre, Atkinson had called on Campbell.
21. Campbell to Hamilton, April 11, 1812, in Captain's Letters, 1812, I.
22. *Id.* to *id.*, April 16, 1812, *ibid.*
23. Clarke to Lopez, March 16, 1812, in Patriot War Papers.
24. Lopez to Laval, March 16, 1812, *ibid.*
25. *Id.* to Ashley, March 16, 1812, *ibid.*
26. The course, conversation, and result of the Arredondo-Hibberson mission are based on their report to Lopez. Arredondo and Hibberson to Lopez, March 17, 1812, *ibid.*
27. Laval to Lopez, March 16, 1812, *ibid.*
28. Campbell to Lopez, March 17, 1812, *ibid.*
29. The description and conversation of the Atkinson-Yonge mission are based on their report to Lopez. Atkinson and Yonge to Lopez, March 17, 1812, *ibid.*
30. Ashley to Atkinson and Yonge, March 17, 1812, *ibid.*
31. Atkinson and Yonge to Lopez, March 17, 1812, *ibid.*
32. "Testimony of Captain Winslow Foster," in *Petition of Joseph M. Hernandez*, 16. Foster commanded gunboat 62 during the invasion.
33. Report of an unnamed eyewitness, in *Charleston Courier*, March 27, 1812.
34. Accounts of the movement of the gunboats are given in: "Testimony of Captain Winslow Foster," *loc. cit., passim; Charleston Courier*, March 27, 1812; "Statement of George Clarke," in *U. S. vs. Ferriera*, 18; "Statement of Z. Kingsley," *ibid.*, 22; *Niles Register* (April 11, 1812), II, 93; Campbell to Hamilton, April 16, 1812, in Captain's Letters, 1812, I; Floyd to Crawford, March 21, 1812, in Miscellaneous Letters.
35. Campbell to Hamilton, April 16, 1812, in Captain's Letters, 1812, I.
36. "Testimony of Captain Winslow Foster," *loc. cit.*, 17. Foster delivered the message to Campbell. The exact words of Laval, as reported by Foster, were: "[Laval] thought it a d--d rascally business, and advised witness to tell his commander to get his neck out of the halter as soon as possible."
37. This paragraph is based on "Testimony of Captain Winslow Foster," *loc. cit.*, 17-18.
38. "Statement of George Clarke," in *U. S. vs. Ferriera*, 18.
39. "Testimony of Captain Winslow Foster," *loc. cit.*, 17. In addition to Foster's testimony and the sources cited in preceding footnotes, the story of the capture of Fernandina was based on: *U. S. vs. Ferriera*, 37, and Lopez to Estrada, March 18, 20, 1812, in Patriot War Papers.
40. Campbell to Hamilton, March 21, 1812, in Captain's Letters, 1812, I.
41. The number of men in the Patriot force is not known. General Floyd, who was a man trained to be exact, gave the number as 180 (Floyd to Crawford, March 21, 1812, in Miscellaneous Letters), and a long account in the *Charleston Courier* (March 27, 1812) by an eyewitness reported the same number.
42. Whatever plundering the Patriots may have been guilty of later, the evidence substantiates their excellent order immediately after the capture of Fernandina. Not only do Mathews, Floyd, and McIntosh testify to this but also Lopez and Clark, two of the leaders on the other side.
43. The terms of surrender are given in *Niles Register* (April 11, 1812), II, 93. Cox ("Border Missions of General George Mathews," *loc. cit.*, 329n) states that the capitulation was signed by McIntosh for the insurgents and Lopez, Atkinson, George Clarke, Charles W. Clark [Clarke], and Archibald Clark for the Spanish Loyalists. The inclusion of Archibald Clark is an error for he was on the Patriot

FLORIDA FIASCO

side. Archibald Clark was not related to the brothers George J. F. and Charles W. Clarke.

CHAPTER 8

1. This biographical sketch of Smith is based on Francis L. Berkeley, Jr., "Thomas Adam Smith," in *Dictionary of American Biography*, XXI, 667-668, and the Smith Letters.
2. Reported in Mathews to Monroe, March 21, 1812, in Miscellaneous Letters.
3. Smith to Appling, March 18, 1812, in Smith Letters.
4. Mathews to Monroe, March 21, 1812, in Miscellaneous Letters. Other accounts of the transfer are in *U. S. vs. Ferriera*, 19, 38; Floyd to Crawford, March 21, 1812, in Miscellaneous Letters; and Lopez to Estrada, March 18, 1812, in Patriot War Papers.
5. *Charleston Courier*, March 30, 1812.
6. Floyd to Crawford, March 21, 1812, in Miscellaneous Letters.
7. Census return of May 29, 1811, in Selected Papers, II, East Florida Papers.
8. *U. S. vs. Ferriera*, 23.
9. Lopez to Estrada, March 18, 1812, in Patriot War Papers.
10. Mathews to Monroe, March 21, 28, 1812, in Territorial Papers, II; *id.* to Mitchell reported in Mitchell to Eustis, April 20, 1812, in Letterbook of Governor Mitchell; Mathews to Campbell, March 29, 1812, in Captain's Letters, 1812, I.
11. *Charleston Courier*, March 27, 1812.
12. Smith to Eustis, April 14, 1812, in Smith Letters.
13. *U. S. vs. Ferriera*, 23.
14. *Savannah Columbian Museum*, April 13, 1812; *Georgia Argus*, April 15, 1812; *Richmond Virginia Argus*, April 13, 1812.
15. Census report, in Papers of the Revolution, East Florida Papers.
16. Mathews to Monroe, March 28, 1812, in Territorial Papers, II. Pratt (*Expansionists of 1812*, 106) follows Mathews in listing Craig as president of the Patriot government.
17. McIntosh and Delany to Governor of St. Augustine, March 26, 1812, and signature attached thereto, in Papers of the Revolution, East Florida Papers.
18. Delany to Board of Officers, April 3, 1812, in Papers of the Revolution, East Florida Papers.
19. "Resolution by the Constituted Authority," dated May 2, 1812, in the *Savannah Columbian Museum*, May 28, 1812.
20. McIntosh and Delany to Governor of St. Augustine, March 26, 1812, in Papers of the Revolution, East Flordia Papers.
21. General Floyd estimated the number of Estrada's men at 300. Floyd to Crawford, March 26, 1812, in Miscellaneous Letters.
22. The trip of McIntosh and Delany is described in Delany's report to the Board of Officers on April 3, 1812, in Papers of the Revolution, East Florida Papers. Mathews informed Madison that the cession papers were signed on March 31. Mathews to Madison, April 16, 1812, in Madison Papers.
23. Mathews to Monroe, March 21, 1812, in Miscellaneous Letters. Although this letter was written ten days before the formal cession of East Florida, Mathews knew what the terms would be, for he had composed the document.
24. *Ibid.*
25. Cession agreement of March 31, 1812, in Miscellaneous Letters.
26. Delany to Board of Officers, April 3, 1812, in Papers of the Revolution, East Florida Papers.
27. Undated order [*c.* April 1, 1812] of Campbell to B. G. Hopkins, commander of gunboat 63, in Captain's Letters, 1812, I. Winslow Foster, commander of gunboat

NOTES

62, was ill and his boat was placed under the general command of Hopkins ("Testimony of Foster," in *Petition of Joseph M. Hernandez*, 18). Campbell ordered the boats to St. Augustine in compliance with Mathews' request of March 29, 1812, but did not direct Hopkins to blockade St. Augustine. The commander was to explore the waters in and near the port and to remain there from ten to twelve days.

28. Campbell to Hamilton, April 24, 1812, in Captain's Letters, 1812, I.
29. The sources for this paragraph are: Smith to Eustis, March 18, 1812; *id.* to *id.*, March 27, 1812; *id.* to Mathews, March 31, 1812; *id.* to Williams, April 3, 1812, in Smith Letters; and Mathews to Smith, March 27, 1812, in Smith File, Letters Received, Adjutant General's Office.
30. Reported by Campbell in Campbell to Hamilton, April 16, 1812, in Captain's Letters, 1812, I.
31. Smith to Eustis, April 14, 1812, in Smith Letters.
32. Laval to Eustis, May 2, 1812, in Personal Papers of Major Jacint Laval.
33. Mathews to Madison, April 16, 1812, in Madison Papers.
34. At first Mathews promised each volunteer fifty acres of land, but as the revolution progressed he increased the land bounty to 500 acres. Leaders were to receive more than the maximum allowed volunteers.
35. Mathews to Monroe, April 16, 1812, in Territorial Papers, II.
36. Editorial, in the *Charleston Courier*, March 27, 1812.
37. *Georgia Argus*, April 15, 1812.
38. Floyd to Crawford, March 21, 1812, in Miscellaneous Letters.
39. *Id.* to *id.*, March 26, 1812, *ibid.*
40. Proclamation of April 4, 1812, in *Charleston Courier*, April 20, 1812. The *Courier* left a blank space rather than print the reference to arming Negroes. An asterisk informed the reader that the omission was necessary for "local reasons." The other Southern newspapers followed this practice of deleting all references to arming Negroes and the use of Negro militiamen.
41. Campbell to Hamilton, April 15, 1812, in Captain's Letters, 1812, I.
42. *Richmond Virginia Argus*, April 30, 1812.
43. Smith to Adjutant and Inspector, April 26, 1812, in Smith Letters.
44. McIntosh and Delany to Juan Blas Entralgo, April 18, 1812; *id.* to *id.*, April 18, 1812, in Papers of the Revolution, East Florida Papers. Both letters were signed by Ashley as colonel, Craig as colonel, Cook as major, and Hogan as major of the two Patriot companies. Although addressed to Entralgo, the letters were for Governor Estrada.
45. General McIntosh to Mitchell, April 27, May 1, 1812, in Letters of General John McIntosh, Yonge Library.
46. Reported by Smith, in Smith to Adjutant and Inspector, April 26, 1812, in Smith Letters.
47. "Resolution of the Constituted Authority of East Florida," signed by William Craig, chairman, quoted in the *Savannah Columbian Museum*, May 28, 1812.

CHAPTER 9

1. Adams, *History*, VI, 154.
2. The account of Crillon's activities is given in Adams, *History*, VI, 176-182.
3. Madison to Senate and House, March 9, 1812, in *American State Papers, Foreign Relations*, III, 545.
4. Craig to Henry, February 6, 1809, *ibid.*, 546-547.
5. The series of Henry Letters, written from February 14 to June 12, 1809, are printed in *ibid.*, 547-552. For a complete account of the Henry episode see Ernest Alexander Cruikshank, *The Political Adventures of John Henry: The Record of an International Imbroglio* (Toronto, 1936).

FLORIDA FIASCO

6. Troup to Monroe [April 12, 1812], in Territorial Papers, II.
7. Crawford to Monroe, April 19, 1812, in Bureau of Rolls and Archives, State Department, typewritten copy in T. Frederick Davis Papers.
8. Monroe to Mathews, April 4. 1812, in *State Papers*, IX, 44-46.
9. Madison to Jefferson, April 24, 1812, in Hunt, *Writings of Madison*, VIII, 187-190.
10. Hamilton to Campbell, April 8, 1812, in Letters to Officers, Ships of War, Navy Department, War Records Office, National Archives. That the Madison administration was thinking only of supporting Mathews as late as March 28 is shown by a letter (Hamilton to Campbell, March 28, 1812, *ibid.*) in which Campbell was relieved of his command at Charleston and Wilmington so he could concentrate on the important duties at St. Marys, where an officer of great skill and experience was needed as it was to become the scene of active operations.
11. Smith to Campbell, May 1, 1812, in Smith Letters. Definite orders for the evacuation of East Florida were dictated by the secretary of war on April 9, but they were not forwarded to Smith. Orders dated April 10 were substituted which placed Smith under the over-all command of Governor Mitchell. Adjutant General to Smith, April 9, 10, 1812, in Register of Letters Sent, Adjutant General's office.
12. *Charleston Courier*, March 11, 1812.
13. *Ibid.*, March 19, 1812.
14. *Ibid.*, April 1, 1812.
15. *Ibid.*, March 28, 1812.
16. *National Intelligencer*, April 7, 1812.
17. *Niles Register* (April 11, 1812), II, 102.
18. *Augusta Chronicle*, May 15 ,1812.
19. *Savannah Republican*, April 30, 1812.
20. Campbell to Hamilton, April 25, 1812, in Captain's Letters, 1812, II.
21. Smith to Campbell, May 1, 1812, in Smith Letters.
22. General McIntosh to Mitchell, May 1, 1812, in Letters of General John McIntosh. A number of conflicting reports about General McIntosh appeared in Georgia newspapers. On May 5 the *Savannah Republican* stated that he had refused the post of commander-in-chief of the Patriots, but the *Athens Express* of May 22 published an interview with a man who had been in the Patriot camp when Ashley resigned and McIntosh took military command. On May 26 the *Republican* reported McIntosh still with the Patriot forces. McIntosh himself stated (to Mitchell, April 27, 1812) that he had accepted command of the Patriots.
23. *Savannah Republican*, May 26, 1812.
24. The Patriot statement was published on May 14, 1812, in the *Savannah Republican* under the heading: "Extract from a letter of a revolutionist who early took a part there."
25. General McIntosh to Mitchell, May 1, 1812, in Letters of General John McIntosh.
26. Mathews to Monroe, June 22, 1812, in *Secret Acts*, 18.

CHAPTER 10

1. Hamilton to Campbell, March 28, 1812, in Letters to Officers, Ships of War; Pratt, *Expansionists of 1812*, 109. For a reference to the guns requested by Mathews, see the source cited in footnote 5, chapter 10.
2. [Secretary of War] to Smith, April 9, 1812, in Register of Letters Sent.
3. *Id.* to *id.*, April 10, 1812, *ibid.*
4. Monroe to Mitchell, April 10, 1812, in *State Papers*, IX, 47-48.
5. The description and conversation of the Monroe-Isaacs meeting are given in Isaacs to Monroe, January 3, 1814, in Miscellaneous Letters.
6. *Milledgeville Journal*, April 22, 1812.

NOTES

7. Mitchell to Floyd, March 29, 1812, in Letterbook of Governor Mitchell. Mitchell received Floyd's letter of March 21 (which had a brief account of the capture of Fernandina) on March 28.
8. *Id.* to *id.*, April 16, 1812, *ibid.*
9. Mitchell to Eustis, April 20, 1812, *ibid.*
10. *Milledgeville Journal,* April 29, May 6, 1812; *Savannah Republican,* April 28, 1812; *Charleston Courier,* May 1, 1812; *Augusta Chronicle,* May 1, 1812.
11. Mitchell to Monroe, May 2, September 19, 1812, in Territorial Papers, II.
12. *Id.* to *id.*, May 2, 1812, *ibid.*
13. Sources for the life of Mitchell are: Northern, *Men of Mark in Georgia,* II, 183-186; Gamble, *Savannah Duels and Duelists,* 109-113; John H. T. McPherson, "David Byrdie Mitchell," in the *Dictionary of American Biography,* XIII, 40-41.
14. Mitchell to Smith, May 4, 1812, in Smith Letters; *Charleston Courier,* May 13, 1812.
15. Campbell to Hamilton, May 1, 9, 14, 1812, in Captain's Letters, 1812, II; Hamilton to Campbell, May 27, 1812, in Letters to Officers, Ships of War.
16. Smith to John Williams, May 5, 1812, in Smith Letters.
17. Mitchell to Estrada, May 4, 1812, in Patriot War Papers.
18. Estrada to Mitchell, May 9, 1812, *ibid.*
19. Mitchell to Monroe, May 16, 1812, in Territorial Papers, II.
20. *Ibid.*
21. The Spanish sortie is described in Smith to Mitchell, May 16, 1812; and *id.* to Adjutant and Inspector General, May 21, 1812, in Smith Letters.
22. Isaacs to Smith, June 10, 1812, *ibid.*
23. *Savannah Republican,* June 16, 1812.
24. *Ibid.,* June 23, 1812.
25. Mitchell to Smith, May 25, 1812, in Smith Letters.
26. *Savannah Republican,* June 16, 1812; *Augusta Chronicle,* June 19, July 3, 1812; *Charleston Courier,* June 23, 1812.
27. *Milledgeville Argus,* July 8, 1812.
28. Smith to Adjutant and Inspector General, June 15, 1812, in Smith Letters.
29. Kindelan to Smith, June 11, 1812, in Patriot War Papers.
30. *Id.* to Mitchell, June 11, 1812, *ibid.*
31. Smith to Kindelan, June 12, 1812, *ibid.*
32. Kindelan to Smith, June 12, 1812, *ibid.*
33. Smith to Kindelan, June 13, 1812, *ibid.*
34. Kindelan to Smith, June 13, 1812, *ibid.*
35. Smith to Doctor Dandridge, June 15, 1812; Smith to Mitchell, June 17, 1812, in Smith Letters.
36. Mitchell to Kindelan, June 16, 1812, in Patriot War Papers.
37. Kindelan to Mitchell, June 23, 1812, *ibid.*
38. Mitchell to Kindelan, July 6, 1812, *ibid.*
39. Garzia to Mitchell, December 12, 1812, in *Niles Register* (January 16, 1813), III, 311; Garzia to the Editor, January 10, 1813, in *Charleston Courier,* February 3, 1813.
40. Estrada had first appealed to the Indians in March, 1812. The governor reported his efforts to secure allies in letters dated March 17 and 26. Estrada to Someruelos, in To the Captain General, June 1811 - June 1812, East Florida Papers.
41. Mitchell to Monroe, September 19, 1812, [letter no. 1] in Territorial Papers, II.
42. *Id.* to *id.*, September 19, 1812, [letter no. 2] *ibid.*
43. *Ibid.*

FLORIDA FIASCO
CHAPTER 11

1. Technically there have been no aggressive wars, for there has been no international authority with power to label war as defensive or aggressive. As long as the sovereign state remains supreme and a law unto itself, war will always be defensive or offensive according to the definition of the individual state. Nevertheless, by a careful examination of the motives and reasons for a particular war, the historian may draw a conclusion as to the nature of that war. In a moral sense, though not legally, the United States was guilty of aggression in 1812.
2. Madison to Senate and House, June 1, 1812, in *Annals of Congress,* 12th Congress, 1st Session, 1624-1629.
3. *Ibid.,* 1632.
4. *Ibid.,* 1637.
5. *Ibid.,* 271-283.
6. *Ibid.,* 290.
7. *Ibid.,* 297, 298.
8. The statements in this and the preceding paragraph are based on an analysis of the votes of senators and representatives as recorded in *Annals of Congress* and on Pratt, *Expansionists of 1812.*
9. *Annals of Congress,* 12th Congress, 1st Session, 1683; *Niles Register* (September 26, 1812), III, 49.
10. *Annals of Congress,* 12th Congress, 1st Session, 1683, 1684-1685.
11. Jefferson to Madison, June 6, 1812, in Ford, *Works of Jefferson,* XI, 249-250. On March 8, 1812, Jefferson had expressed the hope that the Congress was in secret session for the purpose of authorizing the seizure of East Florida, and he stated: "It would give no more offense any where than taking the Western province." Jefferson to Madison, March 8, 1812, in Madison Papers.
12. *Augusta Chronicle,* May 15, 1812.
13. *Ibid.,* May 8, 1812.
14. A number of these petitions, dated in June, July, and August, 1812, are in Miscellaneous Letters.
15. Monroe to Doctor Robinson, July 1, 1812, in Domestic Letters.
16. *Annals of Congress,* 12th Congress, 1st Session, 324.
17. *Ibid.,* 326.
18. *Ibid.*
19. Only one senator from each of the states of New Hampshire, Pennsylvania, and Maryland voted. The senators who did not cast a ballot were Reid of Maryland, Cutts of New Hampshire, and Gregg of Pennsylvania. Senator Reid had voted against the declaration of war with Great Britain, while Cutts and Gregg had voted for it.
20. Julius W. Pratt, "James Monroe," in *The American Secretaries of State,* III, 215.
21. Pratt, *Expansionists of 1812,* 129-130.
22. Monroe to Mitchell, July 6, 1812, in *State Papers,* IX, 161-164.
23. *Ibid.*
24. Onis to Monroe, July 18, 1812, in Notes from the Spanish Legation.
25. *Id.* to *id.,* August 5, 1812, *ibid.*
26. *Id.* to *id.,* August 29, 1812, *ibid.*
27. Crawford to Monroe, August 6, 1812, in Monroe Papers, Manuscripts Division, Library of Congress.
28. *Id.* to *id.,* September 9, 1812, *ibid.*
29. Madison to Monroe, August 8, 1812, *ibid.*
30. John A. Harper to William Plumer, December 1, 1812, quoted in Pratt, *Expansionists of 1812,* 215-216n.
31. Mitchell to Monroe, July 17, 1812, in *State Papers,* IX, 164-165.

NOTES

32. *Ibid.*
33. "Petition of the Citizens of Greene County, Georgia," dated August 13, 1812, in Miscellaneous Letters.
34. McIntosh to Monroe, July 30, 1812, in "Claims of Citizens of Florida," *House of Representatives Report 99*, 19-21.
35. *Id.* to *id.*, October 3, 1812, in Territorial Papers, II.
36. Mitchell to Monroe, September 19, 1812, in *State Papers*, IX, 168-172.
37. *Id.* to *id.*, October 13, 1812, *ibid.*, 174-175.
38. Monroe to Mitchell, October 12, 1812, *ibid.*, 172-174.

CHAPTER 12

1. Mitchell to Monroe, May 16, 1812, in Territorial Papers, II.
2. An account of the work of Williams is given in Edwin N. McClellan, History of the Marine Corps, unpublished MS., in Yonge Library.
3. Smith to Williams, April 28, 1812, [letter no. 1], in Smith Letters.
4. *Ibid.*
5. Smith to Williams, April 28, 1812, [letter no. 2], in Smith Letters.
6. *Savannah Columbian Museum*, May 28, 1812.
7. Hulburd to Hamilton, May 16, 1812; Campbell to Hamilton, May 22, 1812, in Captain's Letters, 1812, II.
8. *Charleston Courier*, May 29, 1812, quoting the *Savannah Columbian Museum*, May 25, 1812.
9. Mitchell to Monroe, May 16, 1812, in Territorial Papers, II.
10. *Ibid.*
11. Mitchell to Massias, July 1, 1828, in *House of Representatives Report, no. 176*, 22nd Congress, 1st Session, 6-7. Mitchell wrote this letter to support the claims being made by Massias in 1828 for losses incurred in 1812.
12. Smith to Williams, July 5, 1812, in Smith Letters.
13. Smith's order was dated June 20, 1812 (Smith to Ridgeway, in Smith Letters) and Ridgeway probably assumed command at Fernandina about July 1.
14. "Minutes" [written by George Clarke], in Patriot War Papers.
15. Smith to Massias, July 12, 1812, in Smith Letters; "Minutes," in Patriot War Papers.
16. Mitchell to Massias, July 12, 1812, in *House of Representatives Report, no. 176*, 5-6.
17. The regulations, orders, and public notices of Massias, dated July 14 and 26, 1812, and February 1 and 10, 1813, are given in *ibid.*, 9-12.
18. *Ibid.*, 1-2; John Forbes to John Graham, February 3, 1813, in Miscellaneous Letters.
19. Smith to Thomas Flournoy, November 13, 1812, in Smith Letters.
20. *Id.* to Massias, September 22, 1812, *ibid.*
21. The *Augusta Chronicle* of August 7, 1812, reported that Captain Cheveleer, a Patriot, prevented a British ship with $20,000 in specie from escaping while the American naval officers were celebrating the Fourth of July. With the aid of the Patriots seventeen British vessels were seized at Fernandina.
22. *Niles Register* (July 18, 1812), II, 335; Smith to Mitchell, July 10, 1812, in Smith Letters.
23. Rowland H. Rerick, *Memoirs of Florida*, edited by Francis P. Fleming (Atlanta, 1902), I, 118-119.
24. McIntosh to Monroe, July 30, 1812, in "Claims of Citizens of Florida," *loc. cit.*, 20.
25. *Augusta Chronicle*, August 7, 1812.
26. The other delegates were: T. Hollingsworth, Nathaniel Hale, Zephaniah Kingsley, D. S. H. Miller, John C. Houstoun, Nathaniel Mason, William and John Brad-

dock, William G. Christopher, and Hugh Stellings.
27. A copy of the original document is in the Florida Historical Society Library.
28. *Niles Register* (September 5, 1812), III, 16; *Savannah Republican*, August 11, 1812, quoting the *Georgia Journal*.
29. Massias to Campbell, September 27, 1812; Campbell to Foster, September 28, 1812, in Captain's Letters, 1812, III.
30. McIntosh to Campbell, October 1, 1812, in Territorial Papers, II.
31. *Id.* to Monroe, October 3, 1812, *ibid.*
32. Campbell to McIntosh, October 3, 1812, in Captain's Letters, 1812, III.
33. Postscript attached to Campbell to McIntosh, October 3, 1812, *ibid.*
34. Order of General Flournoy, dated December 23, 1812, in Patriot War Papers; endorsement by McIntosh on General Flournoy's order of December 23, 1812, *ibid.*
35. Smith to John Tate, June 25, 1812, in Smith Letters.
36. *Savannah Republican*, July 14, 16, 1812.
37. *Savannah Republican*, July 28, August 4, 1812.
38. Smith to Newnan, August 26, 1812, in Smith Letters.
39. *Id.* to Thomas Bourke, August 21, 1812, *ibid.*
40. Ridgeway to his brother, September 11, 1812, in Papers of the Revolution, East Florida Papers.
41. *Id.* to Tally, September 11, 1812, *ibid.*
42. Kinnear to his mother and brother, September 11, 1812, *ibid.*
43. *Ibid.*
44. *Georgia Journal*, June 3, 1812.
45. Smith to William R. Boote, September 4, 1812; *id.* to Mitchell, September 7, 1812; *id.* to Flournoy, January 31, 1813, in Smith Letters.

CHAPTER 13

1. Isaacs to Monroe, July 3, 1814, in Miscellaneous Letters.
2. Isaacs left St. Marys on June 7 and probably reached the Patriot camp near St. Augustine about the middle of June. Isaacs to Smith, June 10, 1812, in Smith Letters.
3. *Id.* to Monroe, July 3, 1814, in Miscellaneous Letters.
4. *Ibid.*
5. *Ibid.*
6. *Ibid.* Crawford wrote to Mathews before the Senate rejected the bill for occupation of the Floridas. Isaacs refers to the letter of Crawford in describing the attitude of Mathews.
7. Isaacs was acting as liaison officer between Smith and Mitchell. After reaching St. Marys and making his reports, Isaacs fell ill and could not continue his work. Mitchell to Smith, July 1, 1812, in Smith Letters.
8. Crawford to Monroe, August 6, 1812, in Monroe Papers, Library of Congress.
9. *Ibid.*
10. *Augusta Chronicle*, September 11, 1812. Mathews had been expected in Augusta as early as July 24 (*Savannah Republican*, July 30, 1812; *Niles Register* [August 15, 1812], II, 399) but the general's conferences with Crawford and Hawkins delayed his arrival.
11. Northern, *Men of Mark in Georgia*, I, 234; Pratt, *Expansionists of 1812*, 115.
12. Accounts of the death of Mathews are in the *Augusta Chronicle*, September 4, 11, 1812, and *Athens Express*, October 2, 1812.
13. *Augusta Chronicle*, September 11, 1812.
14. *Ibid.*, September 4, 1812; General Orders, Georgia Headquarters, September 14, 1812, quoted in the *Athens Express*, October 2, 1812.

NOTES

15. *Athens Express*, October 2, 1812.
16. *Augusta Chronicle*, September 11, 1812, quoting the *Augusta Herald*.
17. Cox, "The Border Missions of General George Mathews," *loc. cit.*, 333.

CHAPTER 14

1. John T. Sprague, *The Origin, Progress, and Conclusion of the Florida War* (New York, 1848), 19.
2. McClellan, History of the Marine Corps, unpublished MS. in Yonge Library.
3. Proclamation of May 11, 1812, quoted in the *Savannah Republican*, May 21, 1812. Campbell reported that the Seminoles returned home "apparently satisfied." Campbell to Hamilton, May 14, 1812, in Captain's Letters, 1812, II.
4. Mitchell to Campbell, June 23, 1812; Campbell to Hamilton, June 27, August 1, 1812; *id.* to *id.*, March 6, 1813, in Captain's Letters, 1813, II; Pratt, *Expansionists of 1812*, 201; Rerick, *Memoirs of Florida*, I, 119; Kenneth W. Porter, "Negroes and the East Florida Annexation Plot, 1811-1813," in *Journal of Negro History* (January, 1945), XXX, 18-19.
5. Report of Tuskegee Tustumugee to Hawkins, September 18, 1812, in *State Papers*, IX, 181-187.
6. *Savannah Republican*, September 3, 1812, Louis de Onís denied that Spain had encouraged the Indians (Onís to Monroe, September 3, December 30, 1812, in Notes from the Spanish Legation). Kindelan, however, took pride in acknowledging his success in rousing the Indians (Kindelan to Apodaca, July 29, August 9, 1812, in Papers of the Captain General, East Florida Papers; Kindelan to William Vesey Munnings, August 9, 1812, in Donnan (ed.), *Papers of J. A. Bayard*, 223-226).
7. Alexander Cornells to Hawkins, September 19, 1812, in Miscellaneous Letters. Cornells was an interpreter.
8. Tuskegee Tustumugee to Hawkins, September 18, 1812, in *State Papers*, IX, 181-187.
9. For an excellent account of the life, ambition, and activity of the Negro, see Porter, "Negroes and the East Florida Annexation Plot, 1811-1813," *loc. cit.*, 9-29.
10. *Ibid.*, 17.
11. Garzia to Mitchell, December 12, 1812, in *Niles Register* (January 16, 1813), III, 311-312. This conference was evidently held in July just before Mathews left East Florida. From the sources available, it appears that the general talked with the Indians three times: first, in May at Picolatti when Isaacs found him and delivered the letters from Monroe; second, at the general conference at Picolatti in June; and, third, in July at Payne's town in the Alachua country.
12. Cornells to Hawkins, September 19, 1812, in Miscellaneous Letters.
13. *Ibid*.
14. Hawkins to Mitchell, September 20, 1812, in Loose Papers, Georgia Department of Archives and History.
15. Smith to Adjutant and Inspector General, July 30, 1812, in Smith Letters.
16. *Id.* to Pinckney, July 30, 1812, *ibid*.
17. Kindelan to Apodaca, July 29, August 9, 1812, in To the Captain General, East Florida Papers; Kindelan to Munnings, August 9, 1812, in Donnan (ed.), *Papers of J. A. Bayard*, 223-226.
18. Smith to Burke, July 30, 1812, in Smith Letters.
19. *Id.* to Mitchell, August 11, 1812, *ibid*.
20. Abraham Bessent to Mitchell, August 15, 1812, in Creek Indians: Letters Talks and Treaties, 1705-1839, unpublished letters compiled under the direction of Mrs. J. E. Hays, Georgia Department of Archives and History. Indians did not purposely

kill slaves unless the Negroes resisted or refused to go with the Indians. In attacks, however, Negroes were inadvertently shot.
21. *Savannah Republican,* August 6, 1812; *Georgia Argus,* August 26, 1812.
22. Smith to Mitchell, August 21, 1812, in Smith Letters.
23. *Ibid.*
24. Susan L'Engle, *Notes of My Family and Recollections of My Early Life* (New York, 1888), 29-30.
25. "Letter from a Volunteer," in *Milledgeville Journal,* September 2, 1812.
26. Floyd to Editor, September 26, 1812, in *Augusta Chronicle,* October 16, 1812; Hawkins to Mitchell, September 20, 1812, in Loose Papers, Georgia Department of Archives and History.
27. *Milledgeville Journal,* August 5, 1812.
28. Smith to Pinckney, July 30, 1812, in Smith Letters.
29. *Id.* to Armstrong, August 17, 1812, *ibid.*
30. *Id.* to Officer Commanding the Georgia Volunteers at Davis Creek [Captain Fort], August 21, 1812, *ibid.* Smith had ordered Fort to Davis Creek (Smith to Mitchell, August 21, 1812, *ibid.*), while Newnan, the commander of the volunteers remained at Camp New Hope.
31. *Id.* to Newnan, August 23, 1812, *ibid.*
32. *Id.* to Newnan, August 26, 1812, *ibid.*
33. *Id.* to Newnan, August 26, 1812; Smith to Fort, August 23, 1812, *ibid.*
34. *Id.* to McIntosh, August 26, 1812, *ibid.*
35. Newnan to Smith, August 31, 1812, *ibid.*
36. *Id.* to *id.,* September 6, 1812, *ibid.*
37. Smith to Mitchell, September 7, 1812, *ibid.*
38. *Id.* to *id.,* September 7, 1812; *id.* to Flournoy, September 7, 1812, *ibid.*
39. *Id.* to Newnan, September 9, 1812, *ibid.*
40. Ryan to Barton, September 11, 1812, in Papers of the Revolution, East Florida Papers.
41. The account of the engagement is based on: Smith to Massias, *id.* to Pinckney, *id.* to Cushing, *id.* to Flournoy, and *id.* to Mitchell, all dated September 22, 1812, in Smith Letters; Floyd to Editor, September 26, 1812, in *Augusta Chronicle,* October 16, 1812; a correspondent's report of September 19, 1812, in *Charleston Courier,* September 28, 1812; "Letter from St. Marys," in *Savannah Republican,* September 24, 1812; Porter, "Negroes and the East Florida Annexation Plot, 1811-1813," *loc. cit.,* 20-21; McClellan, History of the United States Marine Corps, unpublished MS., Yonge Library; Pratt, *Expansionists of 1812,* 207-208.

The total number of Negroes and Indians in the attacking party is not known. Smith estimated the number at 50 to 60, Floyd at 70 Negroes and 6 Indians, and the newspaper accounts at over 70.
42. Smith to Newnan, September 12, 1812, in Smith Letters. A scouting party informed Smith of the skirmish which began about 9 P.M. on September 12.
43. Newnan to Smith, September 16, 1812; Smith to Newnan, September 21, 1812; Smith to Mitchell, September 22, 1812, in Smith Letters.

CHAPTER 15

1. Smith to Massias, September 22, 1812, in Smith Letters.
2. *Id.* to Mitchell, September 22, 1812, *ibid.*
3. Mitchell to Smith, September 21, 1812, *ibid.*
4. Smith to Mitchell, September 24, 1812, *ibid.*
5. Newnan to Smith, September 16, 1812, *ibid.*
6. *Id.* to Smith, September 23, 1812, *ibid.*
7. Smith to Mitchell, September 24, 1812, *ibid.*

NOTES

8. "Letter from one of the Volunteers," in *Milledgeville Journal*, August 12, 1812.
9. Copy of a letter of September 21, 1811, signed THEMTSTOCLESATMAQNESTA, in Loose Papers, Florida Historical Society Library.
10. Archibald Clark to Mitchell, August 12, 1812, in Hays (comp.), Creek Indians: Letters, Talks and Treaties, 1705-1839, Georgia Department of Archives and History.
11. "Letter from Newnan's Volunteers," dated August 10, 1812, in *Milledgeville Journal*, September 2, 1812.
12. *Ibid.*
13. Smith to Burke, August 21, 1812, in Smith Letters.
14. Newnan to Smith, September 22, 1812, *ibid.*
15. "Letter from East Florida," dated September 2, 1812, in *Savannah Republican*, September 22, 1812, and *Charleston Courier*, September 25, 1812.
16. "Letter from an Early Adventurer to his Friend" [n. d.], in *Savannah Republican*, September 22, 1812, and *Charleston Courier*, September 25, 1812.
17. Newnan to Smith, August 31, 1812, in Smith Letters; *Savannah Republican*, September 22, 1812.
18. Unless otherwise indicated the source for the description of the Newnan expedition is: Newnan to Smith, October 19, 1812, in *Niles Register* (December 12, 1812), III, 335-337.
19. Pratt, *Expansionists of 1812*, 208.
20. Newnan to Smith, October 2, 1812, in Smith Letters.
21. Smith to Floyd, September 30, 1812, *ibid.*
22. *Id.* to Whitticer [Whitaker], October 2, 1812, *ibid.*
    In his letter Smith did not give a reason for Whitaker's failure to cross the St. Johns. A hurricane hit central Florida during the first week of October, and in another letter (Smith to Wyman, October 12) Smith mentions the high winds.
23. In addition to Newnan's account (footnote 18, chapter 15), the failure of the relief party to reach Newnan is told in Smith to Flournoy, October 7, 1812, in Smith Letters.
24. *Id.* to Wyman, October 2, 1812, *ibid.*
25. *Id.* to *id.*, October 7, 1812, *ibid.*
26. Both Smith and Newnan testify to the saving of the scalped man. Smith to Mitchell, postscript of October 13, on a letter of October 10, 1812; Newnan to Smith, October 11, 1812, *ibid.*
27. Smith to Flournoy; *id.* to Mitchell; *id.* to Cushing, October 7, 1812, *ibid.*
28. Newnan to Smith, October 11, 1812, *ibid.*
29. *Charleston Courier*, October 28, 1812.
30. *Ibid.*, November 3, 1812; *Savannah Republican*, October 20, 1812; *Milledgeville Journal*, December 2, 1812.
31. *Milledgeville Journal*, December 2, 1812.
32. Mitchell to Floyd, April 12, 1813, in Letterbook of Governor Mitchell. This letter refutes the generally accepted idea that Payne had been killed in battle. Actually, months after his reported death, Payne sent a delegation to Benjamin Hawkins with a request for peace.
33. Smith to Floyd, September 30, 1812, in Smith Letters.
34. *Id.* to Newnan, October 12, 1812, *ibid.*
35. Newnan to Smith, October 12, 1812, *ibid.*
36. Smith to Newnan, October 13, 1812; Smith to Mitchell, October 20, 1812, *ibid.*
37. This conference and its results are described in Mitchell to Floyd, April 12, 1813, in Letterbook of Governor Mitchell.
38. Although there is no evidence to support this incident, the words attributed to

FLORIDA FIASCO

Bowlegs are an authentic reproduction of those used in the funeral of an Indian chief as reported in the *Augusta Chronicle* of October 20, 1815.

CHAPTER 16

1. Smith to Mitchell, October 20, 1812, in Smith Letters.
2. *Id.* to Burke, October 25, 1812, *ibid.*
3. *Ibid.*
4. Smith to Joseph Chambers, October 25, 1812, *ibid.*
5. Pinckney to Smith, November 3, 1812, *ibid.*
6. Flournoy's letter is summarized in Smith to Mitchell, November 7, 1812, *ibid.*
7. Pinckney to Smith, November 25, 28, 1812, *ibid.*
8. Campbell to Hamilton, August 1, 1812, in Captain's Letters, 1812, II.
9. Mitchell to Floyd, September 26, 1812, in Letterbook of Governor Mitchell.
10. *Id.* to Smith, October 13, 1812, quoted in Pratt, *Expansionists of 1812*, 210.
11. *Id.* to Floyd, October 13, 1812, in Letterbook of Governor Mitchell; Minutes of the Executive Department, October 1, 1812 - April 30, 1814, in Georgia Department of Archives and History.
12. Floyd to Mitchell, November 7, 1812; *id.* to *id.*, same date, in Floyd Papers, Georgia Department of Archives and History.
13. Governor's Message of November 2, 1812, in Minutes of the Executive Department, October 1, 1812 - April 30, 1814.
14. *Augusta Chronicle*, October 16, 1812; *Savannah Republican*, October 10, 1812.
15. *Savannah Republican*, October 20, 1812.
16. *Augusta Chronicle*, October 23, 1812.
17. *Charleston Courier*, November 20, 1812. The information was forwarded to the *Courier* in a letter of November 10, which began: "A bill yesterday reported in the Senate by Dr. Porter of Savannah...." Pratt (*Expansionists of 1812*, 213-214) refers to a bill which was introduced after the joint committee reported in November. It appears that the bill was introduced on November 9 and was then studied by the joint committee which eventually reported, and on the basis of the committee report, resolutions were drawn calling for federal action and authorizing Governor Mitchell to establish a border patrol.
18. "Committee Report of November 20, 1812," in *Niles Register* (December 12, 1812), III, 259-260.
19. *Acts of the General Assembly of the State of Georgia, November and December, 1812* (Milledgeville, 1812), 133-137, 142-143.
20. *Ibid.*, 133-137.
21. Garzia to Mitchell, December 12, 1812, in *Columbian Sentinel*, January 20, 1813.
22. Mitchell to Smith, November 7, 1812, in Smith Letters.
23. Pinckney to Flournoy, September 24, 1812; *id.* to Secretary of War, October 1, 16, 1812, in Register of Letters Received.
24. Monroe to Pinckney, November 3, 1812, in *State Papers*, IX, 188.
25. Pinckney to Monroe, November 14, 1812, in Territorial Papers, II.
26. *Id.* to *id.*, November 14, 1812, *ibid.* This letter was marked "Private."
27. *National Intelligencer*, November 21, 1812, quoted in Pratt, *Expansionists of 1812*, 215.
28. Jefferson to Madison, November 5, 1812, in Ford, *Works of Jefferson*, IX, 369.
29. Harper to Plumer, December 1, 1812, in William Plumer Letters, 1809-1815, quoted in Pratt, *Expansionists of 1812*, 215-216n.
30. Monroe to Pinckney, December 8, 1812, in *State Papers*, IX, 188-191.
31. *Annals of Congress*, 12th Congress, 2nd Session, 124.
32. Onis to Warren, December 28, 1812, in Notes from the Spanish Legation.
33. On October 12, 1812, Commodore Campbell was directed to obey the order of

NOTES

Pinckney. Secretary of the Navy Hamilton stated this order did not reflect a lack of confidence in Campbell, but arose from the indispensable necessity of having one head to direct operations in the St. Marys area. Hamilton to Campbell, October 12, 1812, in Letters to Officers, Ships of War, X, March 28, 1812 - June 30, 1813.

34. Monroe to Chairmen Campbell and Williams, December 23, 1812, in Reports to Congress, February 3, 1803 - April 13, 1818, pp. 245-254, War Records Office, National Archives.
35. *Augusta Chronicle*, December 18, 1812.
36. Pinckney to Monroe, December 29, 1812, in Territorial Papers, II.
37. Id. to id., December 24, 1812, *ibid*.
38. Id. to id., December 29, 1812, *ibid*.
39. Secretary of War to Pinckney, November 27, 1812, in Military Book VI, July 1, 1812 - June 29, 1813.
40. Id. to id., December 2, 1812, *ibid*.
41. Pinckney to Secretary of War, December 10, 1812, in Register of Letters Received.
42. Monroe to Pinckney, January 13, 1813, in Military Book, VI, July 1, 1812 - June 29, 1813.
43. Smith to Flournoy, January 3, 1813, in Smith Letters.

CHAPTER 17

1. *Clarion*, November 23, 1812.
2. Williams to Madison, December 3, 1812, in Messages of the President, Territorial Papers of Florida, Legislative Reference and Records Office, National Archives.
3. *Niles Register* (January 9, 1813), III, 240.
4. *Augusta Chronicle*, January 1, 1813.
5. *Clarion*, January 5, 1813.
6. Williams to Madison, December 3, 1812, in Messages of the President, Territorial Papers of Florida.
7. Blount to Eustis, December 12, 1812, *ibid*.
8. *Clarion*, January 5, 1813.
9. In addition to the *Clarion*, accounts of the march from Knoxville were reported in the following: *Washington Monitor*, December 21, 1812; *Niles Register* (January 9, 1813), III, 300.
10. *Washington Monitor*, December 21, 1812.
11. Flournoy to Williams, January 2, 1813, in *Clarion*, July 13, 1813. The *Savannah Republican* on January 21, 1813, reported that the volunteers had arrived in Coleraine on Sunday, January 6, and had immediately crossed the St. Marys River. In its March 2 issue the *Republican* corrected the error and stated that the volunteers had remained at Coleraine for almost a month.
12. Williams to Mitchell, December 11, 1812, in *Clarion*, February 9, 1813.
13. Mitchell to Williams, December 24, 1812, *ibid*.
14. *Clarion*, February 9, 1813, quoting the *Milledgeville Journal*, December 30, 1812.
15. *Charleston Courier*, March 3, 1813, quoting the *Georgia Journal*. *Niles Register* (January 9, 1813), III, 300, carried the reports of Hawkins' negotiations with the Indians.
16. Pinckney to Hawkins, January 4, 1813, in Creek Indians: Letters Talks and Treaties, 1705-1839.
17. Pinckney to Secretary of War, January 12, 1813, in Register of Letters Received.
18. Reported in the *Clarion*, March 2, 1813.
19. *Charleston Courier*, January 6, 1813, quoting the *Georgia Argus*.
20. [Secretary of War] to Pinckney, February 9, 1813, in Military Book, VI, July 1, 1812 - June 29, 1813.

FLORIDA FIASCO

21. Smith to Kingsley, February 2, 1813, in Smith Letters.
22. Flournoy to Smith, February 2, 1813, in *Clarion*, July 13, 1813; *Nashville Whig*, July 30, 1813.
23. Smith to Flournoy, February 24, 1813, in Smith Letters.
24. The account of the joint expedition of Smith and Williams is taken from: Williams to Flournoy, February 23, 1813, in Register of Letters Received; Smith to Flournoy, February 24 (two letters of the same date), 1813; *id.* to Massias, February 24, 1813, in Smith Letters; William Cocke to ...., February 24, 1813, in Miscellaneous Letters.
25. Smith to Flournoy, February 24, 1813, in Smith Letters. Other accounts of the property destroyed and captured differ slightly from that of Smith. Williams estimated the destruction at 336 houses, 250 horses, and 300 to 400 cattle. Cocke listed 380 houses, 500 horses and cattle, 1,500 bushels of corn, and 2,000 deerskins.
26. Smith, Cocke, and Williams estimated that 20 Indians had been killed, but they did not list the number wounded. *Niles Register* (March 20, 1813), IV, 49, reported that 50 to 60 Indians had been killed, but one week later reduced the number to 38.
27. *Savannah Republican*, March 4, 1813; *Nashville Whig*, March 31, 1813.
28. Flournoy to Williams, February 25, 1813, in *Clarion*, July 13, 1813.
29. Smith to Flournoy, February 24, 1813, in Smith Letters.
30. *Id.* to Massias, February 24, 1813, *ibid.*
31. *Id.* to Flournoy, March 2, 1813, *ibid.*
32. Pinckney to Smith, March 10, 1813; Smith to Manning, March 27, 1813; *id.* to Floyd, March 27, 1813, *ibid.* Smith planned to leave Coleraine and Camp Pinckney on April 4, 1813.
33. Mitchell to Pinckney, March 2, 1813, in Letterbook of Governor Mitchell.
34. Pinckney to Mitchell, March 10, 1813, Creek Indians: Letters Talks and Treaties, 1705-1839.

CHAPTER 18

1. James Parton, *Life of Andrew Jackson* (New York, 1861), I, 361.
2. Eustis to Blount, October 21, 1812, in Military Book, VI, July 1, 1812 - June 29, 1813.
3. *Id.* to *id.*, October 23, 1812, *ibid.*
4. Jackson to Blount, November 11, 1812, in *The Correspondence of Andrew Jackson*, edited by John Spencer Bassett (Washington, 1926), I, 238-239. Cited hereafter as Bassett, *Correspondence of Jackson*.
5. Announcement of November 14, 1812, and general orders of November 23, 1812, *ibid.*, 241-243.
6. *Clarion*, December 1, 1812.
7. Albert Campbell Holt, *The Economic and Social Beginnings of Tennessee* (Nashville, 1923), 148.
8. *Clarion*, December 28, 1812.
9. *Ibid.*, December 15, 1812.
10. The *Clarion* (December 15, 1812) carried a long account of the events of December 10 in Nashville.
11. Parton, *Jackson*, I, 368.
12. *Ibid.;* Marquis James, *The Life of Andrew Jackson* (New York, 1940), 146.
13. *Clarion*, December 15, 1812.
14. *Ibid.*, January 19, 1813.
15. *Ibid.*, January 5, 1813.

NOTES

16. "General Orders on Martial Law," December 31, 1812, in Bassett, *Correspondence of Jackson*, I, 253-254.
17. Parton, *Jackson*, I, 372.
18. "A Journal of the trip down the Mississippi," in Bassett, *Correspondence of Jackson*, I, 257. This journal gives a day by day account of the expedition from January 10 to March 5, 1813. *Ibid.*, 256-271.
19. Parton, *Jackson*, I, 373.
20. Jackson to Wilkinson, February 16, 1813, in Bassett, *Correspondence of Jackson*, I, 276-277.
21. *Id.* to *id.*, February 20, 1813, *ibid.*, I, 277-278.
22. Coffee to Donelson, March 1, 1813, in Parton, *Jackson*, I, 375-376.
23. Jackson to Armstrong, March 1, 1813, in Bassett, *Correspondence of Jackson*, I. 283-285.
24. Armstrong to Jackson, February 6, 1813, in Parton, *Jackson*, I, 377-378.
25. Jackson to Armstrong, March 15, 1813, in Bassett, *Correspondence of Jackson*, I, 291-292.

CHAPTER 19

1. *Annals of Congress*, 12th Congress, 2nd Session, 124.
2. *Ibid.*
3. *Ibid.*, 124-125.
4. *Ibid.*, 125-126.
5. Monroe to Madison, January 14, 1813, in Messages of the President, Territorial Papers of Florida.
6. *Annals of Congress*, 12th Congress, 2nd Session, 127.
7. *Ibid.*, 128.
8. "Speech of William Hunter, February 2, 1813," *ibid.*, 13th Congress, 1st Session, 504-535. This speech was also published in a pamphlet as: William Hunter, *Speech of the Hon. William Hunter, In Secret Session of the Senate of the United States, Feb. 2d, 1813. On the Proposition for Seizing and Occupying the Province of East Florida, By the Troops of the U. States* (Newport, 1813).
9. *Annals of Congress*, 12th Congress, 2nd Session, 130.
10. *Ibid.*, 132.
11. *Ibid.*, 133.

CHAPTER 20

1. [Armstrong] to Pinckney, February 9, 1813, in Military Book, VI, July 1, 1812 - June 29, 1813.
2. *Id.* to *id.*, February 15, 1813, *ibid.*
3. Pinckney to Secretary of War, February 26, 1813, in Register of Letters Received. One day later Pinckney requested additional instructions from Monroe. Should he communicate with St. Augustine, what protection should he give the Patriots, and what were the intentions of President Madison? Pinckney to Secretary of State, February 27, 1813, in Monroe Papers, New York Public Library, film copy in Yonge Library.
4. [Armstrong] to Pinckney, March 6, 1813, in Military Book, VI, July 1, 1812 - June 29, 1813.
5. *Id.* to *id.*, March 7, 1813, *ibid.*
6. Adams, *History*, VII, 28-29.
7. Monroe to Gallatin, Adams, and Bayard, in Donnan (ed.), *Papers of James A. Bayard, 1795-1815*, 214-215.
8. Gallatin to Monroe, May 2, 1813, in Monroe Papers, Library of Congress.
9. Monroe to Gallatin, May 5, 1813, *ibid.*

FLORIDA FIASCO

10. Gallatin to Monroe, May 8, 1813, *ibid.*
11. Pinckney to Armstrong, March 18, 1813, in Register of Letters Received.
12. *Id.* to Kindelan, March 20, 1813, in Patriot War Papers; also in Territorial Papers, III.
13. Kindelan to Pinckney, March 31, 1813, *ibid.*
14. The *Savannah Republican* of April 10, 1813, and *Niles Register* (April 24, 1813), IV, 127, printed Kindelan's proclamation in full.
15. Pinckney to Kindelan, April 7, 1813, in Patriot War Papers.
16. *Id.* to Secretary of War, March 13, 1813, in Register of Letters Received.
17. Fragment of a letter dated March 4, 1813, *ibid.*
18. Kindelan to Pinckney, April 16, 1813, in Patriot War Papers.
19. Pinckney to Kindelan, April 16, 18, 1813; Kindelan to Pinckney, April 26, 1813, *ibid.*
20. Harris to Mitchell, March 6, 1813, in Loose Papers, Georgia Department of Archives and History.
21. *Id.* to *id.*, March 14, 1813, *ibid.*
22. Address of the Legislative Council to Pinckney, March 30, 1813, *ibid.*
23. Resolution of the Legislative Council, March 30, 1813, *ibid.*
24. Proclamation of March 30, 1813, in Papers of the Revolution, East Florida Papers; *Niles Register* (April 24, 1813), IV, 127.
25. Pinckney to Monroe, April 23, 1813, in Territorial Papers, III.
26. Address to Pinckney, April 9, 1813, *ibid.*
27. Pinckney to Miller and other Inhabitants of the St. Johns, April 18, 1813, *ibid.*
28. Details of this conference are given in McIntosh to Pinckney, April 13, 1813, and *id,* to [Monroe], April 16, 1813, *ibid.*
29. Pinckney to McIntosh, April 14, 15, 1813, *ibid.*
30. McIntosh to [Monroe], April 16, 1813, *ibid.* This copy of the original letter was addressed to General Pinckney, but it is evidently a mistake of the copyist, for the letter was for Monroe.
31. Pinckney to Monroe, April 17, 1813, *ibid.*
32. *Id.* to Kindelan, April 18, 1813, in Patriot War Papers.
33. Kindelan to Pinckney, April 26, 1812, *ibid.*
34. Proclamations of Alvarez and Kindelan (n. d.), in the *Charleston Courier,* April 23, 1813. It is questionable whether these proclamations were issued by the Spanish officials or by the Patriots as propaganda.
35. Pinckney to Manning, April 16, 1813, in Territorial Papers, III.
36. Pinckney to Monroe, April 8 [May 8], 1813, *ibid;* Kindelan to Pinckney, April 28, 1813, in Patriot War Papers.
37. *Niles Register* (May 29, 1813), IV, 216; Pinckney to Monroe, April 8 [May 8], 1813, in Territorial Papers, III.
38. The restoration of Spanish authority is described in Corbitt, "The Return of Spanish Rule to the St. Marys and St. Johns, 1813-21," *loc. cit.,* 47-68.
39. Pinckney to Monroe, April 29, 1813, marked "Private," in Territorial Papers, III.
40. *Ibid.*
41. Pinckney to Monroe, July 2, 1813, in Monroe Papers, New York Public Library.
42. *Id.* to *id.*, July 3, 1813, *ibid.*
43. *Id.* to *id.*, July 2, 1813, *ibid.*
44. *Id.* to Secretary of War, July 1, 1813, in Register of Letters Received.

CHAPTER 21

1. McIntosh to Mitchell, September 11, 1813, in Georgia, East Florida, West Florida and Yazoo Land Sales, 1764-1850, Georgia Department of Archives and History.

NOTES

2. G. J. Pacot to Kindelan, May 2, 1813, in Patriot War Papers.
3. Harris to Mitchell, May 24, 1813, in Loose Papers, Georgia Department of Archives and History.
4. Hawkins to Mitchell, May 31, 1813, *ibid.*
5. Harris to Mitchell, June 9, 1813, *ibid.*
6. Pinckney to Monroe, June 10, 1813, in Territorial Papers, III.
7. Ashley to Pinckney, June 11, 1813, *ibid.* The affidavit of Black was signed with an "X," but Hall and Broodway signed their names. Hall had given a similar affidavit on May 5, 1813.
8. Pinckney to Monroe, July 22, 1813, in Monroe Papers, New York Public Library.
9. Mitchell to Major General John McIntosh, June 13, 1813, in Letterbook of Governor Mitchell.
10. Pinckney to Monroe, July 29, 1813, in Monroe Papers, New York Public Library. Pinckney enclosed a copy of a statement by William Fitzpatrick, sworn to before William Ashley on July 12, 1813, complaining of his treatment by Negro troops after he had received a pardon. Pinckney had sent a copy of the affidavit to Kindelan, who ordered an investigation and also pointed out that Fitzpatrick, if really a loyal citizen of East Florida, would have appealed to a Spanish court rather than running into St. Marys and making a statement before a judge who was known to be a propagandist of the Patriots. (Kindelan to Pinckney, July 20, 1813, *ibid.*) Pinckney believed Kindelan's argument was logical and the statement of Fitzpatrick false.
11. Kindelan to Pinckney, August 3, 1813, enclosed is Onis to Monroe, December 19, 1813, in Notes from the Spanish Legation.
12. Pinckney to Monroe, July 31, 1813, in Monroe Papers, New York Public Library.
13. Accounts of the expedition and the ensuing skirmishes are in: Harris to Mitchell, August 18, 1813, in Harris Papers, Georgia Department of Archives and History; "Report from St. Marys," in *Savannah Republican,* August 17, 1813; *Niles Register* (August 28, 1813), IV, 24; Apodaca to Minister of War, November 18, 1813, in Papeles de Cuba, Legajo 1856, letter 278; L'Engle, *Notes of My Family and Recollections of My Early Life,* 31-33.
14. Harris to Mitchell, August 18, 1813, in Harris Papers.
15. The details of the Monroe-McIntosh conference are given in: McIntosh to Monroe, August 14, 1813, in Territorial Papers, III; *id.* to Mitchell, September 11, 1813, in Georgia, East Florida, West Florida and Yazoo Land Sales, 1764-1850; *id.* to Adams, May 5, 1818, in Miscellaneous Letters; Madison to Monroe, August 19, 1813, in Monroe Papers, Library of Congress.
16. Madison to Monroe, August 19, 1813, in Monroe Papers, Library of Congress.
17. *Clarion,* May 3, 1814. Similar reports were published in the *Savannah Republican, Savannah Columbian Museum, Augusta Herald, Georgia Argus,* and *Charleston Courier.*
18. *Augusta Chronicle,* October 22, 1813.
19. *Ibid.,* December 10, 1813.
20. Scott to Mitchell, November 11, 1813, in Creek Indians: Letters Talks and Treaties, 1705-1839.
21. Hibberson to Harris, November 19, 1813, in Loose Papers, Georgia Department of Archives and History; "East Florida Documents" in *Georgia Historical Quarterly* (June, 1929), XIII, 156-158.
22. Fatio to Early, December 11, 1813, in Loose Papers, Georgia Department of Archives and History.
23. Hopkins to Mitchell (with enclosed affidavits), December 14, 1813, in Georgia, East Florida, West Florida and Yazoo Land Sales, 1764-1850.
24. Cone to Fatio, August 24, 1813, in Papers of the Revolution, East Florida Papers.

FLORIDA FIASCO

25. Harris and Dell to Kindelan, September 7, 1813 (enclosed in Harris and Dell to Young [Yonge], September 7, 1813), *ibid.*
26. Betts to Yonge, September 13, 1813, in Various Subjects, East Florida Papers.
27. Harris to Kindelan, October 23, 1813, in Papers of the Revolution, East Florida Papers; Harris and Dell to Yonge and Arredondo, December 11, 1813, enclosed in Kimball to Pickering, January 22, 1814, in Pickering Papers, XXX, 200, quoted in Pratt, *Expansionists of 1812*, 242.
28. Monroe to David R. Williams, October 16, 1813, in Monroe Papers, New York Public Library.
29. Jefferson to DuPont de Nemours, November 29, 1813, in Bergh, *Writings of Jefferson*, XIX, 195-200.
30. *Georgia Journal*, September 29, 1813.
31. *Savannah Republican*, March 1, 1814.
32. Harris to Pinckney, February 2, 1814, in Miscellaneous Letters.
33. *Ibid.*; Hawkins to Pinckney, February 16, 1814, in *Niles Register* (March 12, 1814), VI, 37.
34. Address of Harris to Legislative Council, January 25, 1814, in Territorial Letters, III.
35. Resolution of January 25, 1814 (signed by Sanchez and Harris); Petition to Congress, January 25, 1814 (signed by James Dell, Colonel Commanding), *ibid.* An excellent account of the settlement of Alachua is in T. Frederick Davis, "Elotchaway, East Florida, 1814," *Florida Historical Quarterly* (October, 1929), VIII, 143-155.
36. Harris to Pinckney, February 2, 1814, in Miscellaneous Letters.
37. Kindelan to Early, January 27, 1814, in Georgia, East Florida, West Florida and Yazoo Land Sales, 1764-1850.
38. Early to Kindelan, February 23, 1814, in Letterbook of Governor Early, Georgia Department of Archives and History.
39. *Id.* to Hawkins, April 27, 1814, *ibid.*
40. Harris to Pinckney, February 2, 1814, in Miscellaneous Letters.
41. Conner to Monroe, March 15, 1814, in Territorial Papers, III.
42. *Id* to *id.*, April 7, 1814, in Miscellaneous Letters.
43. Monroe to Conner, April 19, 1814, in Domestic Letters.
44. *Savannah Republican*, May 26, 1814; Apodaca to Minister of War, July 14, 1814, in Papeles de Cuba, Legajo 1856, letter 345. By the American account Negroes killed Harris, but the Spanish attributed his death to the Indians. Probably it was a force of Indians and Negroes.
45. "Extract from an Officer in Lotchway," May 23, 1814, in *Savannah Republican*, May 26, 1814.

CHAPTER 22

1. Early to Hawkins, May 18, 1814, in Loose Papers, Georgia Departmnet of Archives and History.
2. Cochrane to The Indian Chief, July 1, 1814, in Public Records Office, F.O., 5, CXXXIX, photostat in Joseph B. Lockey Papers, Yonge Library.
3. John Francis and Peter McQuin to Cochrane, September 1, 1814, *ibid.*
4. Cochrane to Bathurst, July 14, 1814, in Public Records Office, W.O., 1, CXLI, Lockey Papers.
5. Postscript dated July 15, 1814, *ibid.*
6. Early to Armstrong, September 2, 1814, in Loose Papers, Georgia Department of Archives and History.
7. Address to the Chiefs of Creek and other Indian Nations, December 5, 1814, in Public Records Office, W.O., 1, CXLI, Lockey Papers.

NOTES

8. Kindelan to Woodbine, December 30, 1814, in Notes from the Spanish Legation.
9. Rerick, *Memoirs of Florida*, I, 125.
10. Massias to Floyd, January 11, 1815, in *Niles Register* (February 11, 1815), VII, 361-362; Early to Monroe, January 20, 1815, in Loose Papers, Georgia Department of Archives and History.
11. *Id.* to *id.*, January 20, 1815, *ibid.*
12. References to British activities in and near St. Marys are given in: Massias to Floyd, January 11, 1815, in *Niles Register* (February 11, 1815), VII, 361-362; *Savannah Republican*, January 17, 1815; Massias to Floyd, January 13, 1815, in *Augusta Chronicle*, January 20, 1815; John Sawyer to David Blackshear, January 27, 1815, and Floyd to Blackshear, January 31, 1815, in Miller, *Bench and Bar of Georgia*, I, 455-457.
13. Swainson to Douglass, February 9, 1815, in *Niles Register* (April 8, 1815), VIII, 102.
14. J. R. Glover to Captain Westfall, February 1, 1815, *ibid.*
15. Cochrane to Thomas Troubridge, February 12, 1815, *ibid.*
16. John Miller to Thomas Miller, February 12, 1815, *ibid.*, 102-103.
17. *Niles Register* (February 11, 1815), VII, 364; *Savannah Republican*, January 19, 1815.
18. Floyd to Blackshear, January 31, 1815, in Miller, *Bench and Bar of Georgia*, I, 456-457; *Niles Register* (February 11, 1815), VII, 382.
19. Cochrane to Troubridge, February 12, 1815, in *Niles Register* (April 8, 1815), VIII, 102.
20. Cockburn to Kindelan, February 13, 1815, in Selected Papers, II, East Florida Papers.
21. Accounts of the river expedition of the British are given in: Scott to Early, February 28, 29, 1815, in *Niles Register* (March 25, 1815), VIII, 59; *Savannah Republican*, March 2, 14, 1815; McIntosh to Blackshear, April 2, 1815, in Miller, *Bench and Bar of Georgia*, 465-466; Northern, *Men of Mark in Georgia*, II, 198.

    Northern states that William Cone commanded the Patriots on the Florida shore, but the other and more reliable sources place James Dell in command.
22. The Hulburd-Bartholomew incident is based on: Campbell to Crowninshield (Secretary of the Navy), March 29, 1815; Hulburd to Campbell, March 18, 1815, in *Niles Register* (April 15, 1815), VIII, 118-119; *Savannah Republican*, March 23, 1815.

CHAPTER 23

1. *Charleston Courier*, April 24, 1813; *Savannah Republican*, April 29, 1813.
2. *Niles Register* (March 25, 1815), VIII, 56, quoting the *Charleston Courier*, March 13, 1815.
3. *Niles Register* (July 15, 1815), VIII, 347.
4. *Augusta Chronicle*, December 1, 1815.
5. Monroe to Adams, December 10, 1815, in Hamilton, *Writings of Monroe*, V, 380-382.
6. *Niles Register* (December 9, 1815), IX, 252-253, quoting the *London Morning Chronicle*, September 21, 1815.
7. Onis to Monroe, December 30, 1815, in Notes from the Spanish Legation.
8. Monroe to Onis, January 19, 1816, in *Niles Register* (February 3, 1816), IX, 395-397.
9. Onis to Monroe, February 22, 1816, in Notes from the Spanish Legation.
10. Kindelan to Early, December 2, 1814, in Georgia, East Florida, West Florida and Yazoo Land Sales, 1764-1850.
11. Early to Scott, January 11, 1815, in Letterbook of Governor Early.

12. Early to Kindelan, January 12, 1815, *ibid.*
13. Nicholls to Hawkins, April 22, May 12, 1815, in Public Records Office, F.O., 5, CXXXIX, Lockey Papers.
14. Early to Kindelan, May 24, 1815, in Letterbook of Governor Early.
15. The Georgia, East Florida, West Florida and Yazoo Land Sales, 1764-1850 contain numbers of letters with reports on border raids, slave stealing, robberies, and kidnappings.
16. McIntosh to Crawford, October 30, 1817, in Dispatches from Consuls, State Department, National Archives.
17. *Decision of Hon. Isaac H. Bronson, Judge of the District Court of the United States for the Northern District of Florida, in the Matter of the Claim of Francis P. Ferriera, Administrator of Francis Pass, Dec'd, Vs. the United States, under the Ninth Article of the Florida Treaty. Delivered August 30, 1851* (Washington, 1851), 10.
18. *Ibid.*, 12.
19. Joseph M. White [Territorial Delegate from Florida] to P. P. Barbour, January 2, 1827, in "Claims of the Citizens of Florida," *House of Representatives Report 99.*

Bibliography

Physical Survivals

The nonliterary remains along the Georgia-Florida line and in East Florida are essential to an understanding of the "Patriot War." Near the site of the former frontier town of Coleraine, Georgia, are the rotting timbers of the old ferry abutments; in St. Marys are a few frame houses, tree-lined streets, and the old cemetery with its spreading, moss-covered oaks which date back to the first decade of the eighteenth century; and near the town are the McIntosh family graveyard on the Marianna River, the ruins of Point Petre, and Cumberland Sound, which lies between the island of the same name and the mainland.

St. Marys has remained somnolent for almost one hundred and fifty years, but Fernandina below the border has developed into a thriving industrial town with irritating odors from pulp and fertilizer factories. The old Fernandina of 1812 is almost gone. Only the reconstructed outline of the fort is there and on the streets where Arredondo, Clarke, and Yonge walked are weeds, scrub trees, and dilapidated frame buildings. The modern industrial Fernandina, situated only a mile south of old Fernandina, has little in common with the historic town of 1812.

From Amelia Island south to the St. Johns and down that river there are few survivals. Switzerland marks the former site of the Fatio Plantation and Picolata is almost as dead as its predecessor, Picolatti. East of these stands the barrier of Twelve Mile Swamp, the ruins of Moosa Old Fort, and the most impressive of all ancient forts in North America, the Castillo de San Marcos. Southwest of Picolata at Newnan's Lake near Gainesville, Florida, where Newnan's Georgians suffered defeat, are sand embankments; but there is nothing to show where Williams' Tennesseans marched or Harris' empire-builders erected Fort Mitchell.

The rivers and creeks, sounds and inlets, islands and mainland, bluffs and lowlands offer the historian means of research which are as interesting as they are necessary to a knowledge of the plotting and revolution in East Florida.

Manuscripts

More than one-half of the footnote citations in this study are taken from letters and reports in original manuscript collections.

FLORIDA FIASCO

The National Archives of Washington has the most voluminous and most important material. In the State Department Archives are the Domestic Letters, Miscellaneous Letters, Notes from the Spanish Legation, and Dispatches from Consuls. Source collections in the War Records Office include: the Personal Papers of Major Jacint Laval, Personal Papers of Captain Abraham Massias, Military Book, VI, July 1, 1812 - June 29, 1813, Point Petre File, Register of Letters Received, Register of Letters Sent, Reports to Congress, February 3, 1803 - April 13, 1813, and the Personal Papers of Colonel Thomas Adam Smith in the War Department files; and Captain's Letters and Letters to Officers, Ships of War in the Navy Department records. The Messages of the President, Territorial Papers of Florida, in the Legislative Reference and Records Office, contain some important letters in addition to valuable reports. The Territorial Papers of Florida is a special bound collection of letters, the first three volumes of which were the most important single collection in English for this study of East Florida.

Second only to the National Archives are the materials in the Georgia Department of Archives and History in Atlanta. The official archives contain the letterbooks of governors Mathews, Mitchell, and Early, and the Minutes of the Executive Department of Georgia, October 1, 1812 - April 30, 1814. The Personal Papers of John Floyd, the McIntosh File (Personal Papers of John Houstoun McIntosh), and the Buckner Harris Papers are valuable sources of important letters. Collected and bound papers relating to East Florida are scattered throughout the Georgia, East Florida, West Florida and Yazoo Land Sales, 1764-1850, and the Creek Indians: Letters Talks and Treaties, 1705-1839 (unpublished letters compiled under the direction of Mrs. J. E. Hays). Instructions, proclamations, and letters relating to East Florida in the 1790's and from 1810 to 1815 are to be found here and there in the Georgia Department of Archives and are identified for the purpose of this study as Loose Papers rather than under the individual title of each letter, proclamation, and instruction.

In the P. K. Yonge Memorial Library of Florida History at the University of Florida are a number of valuable letters, but of more importance are the microfilm and photostatic copies of materials. The Joseph B. Lockey Papers have useful photostats from the Public Records Office of London which include transcripts from the British Foreign Office and War Office. Microfilm copies of the Papeles de Cuba, Legajos 1569, 1570, and 1856 contain illuminating material on the Spanish reaction to the invasion of East Florida, and film copies of the Monroe Papers in the New York Public Library have a few essential letters. The Thomas Adam Smith Letters give a detailed account of activities in East Florida in 1812 and 1813. The originals of these letters are in the Missouri Historical Society Library, and without access to the Smith Letters no study of the Patriot War would be complete. One original letter of Monroe, two of General John McIntosh, and the David L. Yulee

BIBLIOGRAPHY

Papers offer some valuable information. The T. Frederick Davis Papers include a scrapbook as well as copies of sources in the Library of Congress. In the Historical Records Project Papers, copies of which are on deposit in the Yonge Library, is descriptive material on Fernandina and the St. Johns area.

The most valuable source in Spanish are the East Florida Papers of the Library of Congress. Although the story of the Patriot War is told from the American point of view and not the Spanish, an account of the revolution would not be complete without the information in the Selected Papers, Various Subjects, Papers of the Captain General, To the Captain General, To and From the War Department, and To and From the Captain General, all of which are in the East Florida Papers. In the same collection are the essential Papers of the Revolution, ninety per cent of which are in English, and pertain in every detail to the Patriot War. Also in the Library of Congress is the large collection of Madison Papers and Monroe Papers with their few key letters.

County records were both disappointing and excitingly productive. A fire of the 1870's destroyed whatever there was in the Courthouse of Nassau County at Fernandina, but the letters and documents of 1812 are preserved in the county records of St. Johns County in St. Augustine. Among these are the essential Patriot War Papers and the Patriot War Claims in the Office of the Clerk of Court of the county. At Woodbine, Georgia, the deed books, wills, and court records in the Judge of Probate's Office are filled with material on individuals and events of 1812.

The Florida Historical Society Library at the University of Florida has a number of letters, a copy of the Patriot Constitution, and newspaper clippings, all of which have been classified as Loose Papers. The Greenslade Papers in the same library contain a few letters of Colonel McKee. The collections in the University of Georgia Library at Athens, the Georgia Historical Society at Savannah, and the Georgia State Library at Atlanta are valuable for Georgia newspapers.

COLLECTED PRINTED SOURCES

Official Collections include the *Acts of the General Assembly of the State of Georgia, November and December, 1812* (Milledgeville, 1813); *American State Papers: Documents, Legislative and Executive of the Congress of the United States,* 38 vols. (Washington, 1832-1861), Class I, 6 vols., *Foreign Relations; Annals of Congress: The Debates and Proceedings in the Congress of the United States . . . March 3, 1789 to May 27, 1824,* 42 vols. (Washington, 1834-1856); Clarence Edwin Carter (comp. and ed.), *The Territorial Papers of the United States: The Territory of Mississippi, 1798-1817,* 2 vols. (Washington, 1934); David Hunter Miller (ed.), *Treaties and Other International Acts of the United States of America,* 8 vols. (Washington, 1931-1948); *id., Secret Statutes of the United States* (Washington, 1918);

FLORIDA FIASCO

State Papers and Publick Documents of the Untied States, From the Accession of George Washington the Presidency, Exhibiting a Complete View of Our Foreign Relations Since That Time, 11 vols. (Boston, 1819); and *United States Versus Ferriera,* Senate Miscellaneous Documents 55, 36th Congress, 1st Session (Washington, 1860).

Excellent edited collections for a study of the Patriot War are in Henry Adams, *The Writings of Albert Gallatin,* 4 vols. (Philadelphia, 1879); John Spencer Bassett, *The Correspondence of Andrew Jackson,* 7 vols. (Washington, 1926-1935); Albert Ellery Bergh, *The Writings of Thomas Jefferson,* 20 vols. (Washington, 1903); Elizabeth Donnan, *Papers of James A. Bayard, 1796-1815; Annual Report,* American Historical Association (Washington, 1915); Paul Leicester Ford, *The Works of Thomas Jefferson,* 12 vols. (New York, 1904-1905); Worthington Chauncey Ford, *The Writings of George Washington,* 14 vols. (New York, 1889-1893); Stanislaus Murray Hamilton, *The Writings of James Monroe, Including a Collection of His Public and Private Papers and Correspondence,* 7 vols. (New York, 1898-1903); Walter Charlton Hartridge, *The Letters of Don Juan McQueen to His Family: Written from Spanish East Florida, 1791-1807* (Columbia, 1943); Gaillard Hunt, *The Writings of James Madison, Comprising His Papers and Private Correspondence,* 9 vols. (New York, 1900-1910); Bernard Mayo, *Instructions to the British Ministers to the United States, 1791-1812* (Washington, 1941); Mrs. Dunbar Rowland, *Life and Letters of William Dunbar* (Jackson, Mississippi, 1930); and Arthur Preston Whitaker, *Documents Relating to the Commercial Policy of Spain in the Floridas* (DeLand, Florida, 1931).

Although brief the photographic facsimile entitled *Aggregate Amount of Persons Within the United States in the Year 1810* (Washington, 1811) gives the population of St. Marys and other places in Georgia.

NEWSPAPERS

Second only to the manuscript collections are the extant newspapers of Georgia, South Carolina, Tennessee, Virginia, and the District of Columbia. Letters of participants in the Patriot War, and of eyewitnesses of the events, official proclamations, acts, and reports were reproduced in the newspapers and often commented on by editors. Every newspaper in the list below which was available for the years from 1810 until 1815 in the Library of Congress, Georgia State Library, University of Georgia Library, Georgia Historical Society, Florida Historical Society, and the Yonge Library was studied with care. Microfilm copies of rare newspapers were secured and these are now in the Yonge Library at Gainesville.

The best newspapers for the revolution in East Florida are in the order of their importance: *Savannah Republican, Charleston Courier, Augusta Chronicle, Nashville Democratic Clarion and Tennessee Gazette (Clarion), Mil-*

BIBLIOGRAPHY

ledgeville Journal, Georgia Journal, Milledgeville Argus, Savannah Columbian Museum, Athens Express, Washington (Georgia) Monitor, Nashville Whig, National Intelligencer, Augusta Herald, and Richmond Argus.

Niles Register which carried reports from the nation's newspapers was more useful than any paper other than the Savannah Republican.

PAMPHLETS

There are literally hundreds of pamphlets which were written about the time of the Patriot War and in the decades following that conflict. Most of them contain copies of contemporary letters, but these letters are available elsewhere in their originals. Most of the pamphlets were printed to substantiate claims against the United States for individual losses sustained in 1812 and 1813. From this mass of pamphlet material only the following gave additional material which was not found in primary sources, or presented plausible interpretations of events: "Claims of the Citizens of Florida," *House of Representatives Report 99* (Washington, 1832); *Secret Acts, Resolutions, and Instructions, Under Which East Florida Was Invaded by the United States Troops, Naval Forces, and Volunteers, in 1812 and 1813, together with the Official Correspondence of the Agents and Officers of the Government*, etc. (Washington, 1860); *Petition of Joseph M. Hernandez* (Copy in Yonge Library); William Hunter, *Speech of the Hon. William Hunter, In Secret Session of the United States, Feb. 2d., 1813. On the Proposition for Seizing and Occupying the Province of East Florida, By the Troops of the U. States* (Newport, 1813); *House of Representatives Report 176*, 22nd Congress, 1st Session (copy in Yonge Library); *Decision of Hon. Isaac H. Bronson, Judge of the District Court of the United States for the Northern District of Florida, in the Matter of the Claim of Francis P. Fierriera, Administrator of Francis Pass, Dec'd, vs. the United States, under the Ninth Article of the Florida Treaty. Delivered August 30, 1851* (Washington, 1851); John Melish, *A Description of East and West Florida and the Bahama Islands: With An Account of the Most Important Places in the United States, Bordering Upon Florida and the Gulf of Mexico. To Which Is Added, A Short View of the Recent Transactions Relative to the Taking Possession of the Floridas* (Philadelphia, 1813).

ARTICLES

The *Florida Historical Quarterly* is a prime source of material on the Patriot War. Articles on the subject are scattered throughout the *Quarterly* for the more than twenty-five years of its publication. Citations were made of the following: T. Frederick Davis, "Elotchaway, East Florida, 1814" (October, 1929), VIII, 143-155; D. C. Corbitt, "The Return of Spanish Rule to the St. Marys and the St. Johns, 1813-1821" (July, 1941), XX, 47-68; Louise Bates Hill, "George J. F. Clarke, 1774-1836" (January, 1943), XXI, 197-253; Rembert W. Patrick, "A New Letter of James Monroe on the Cession of Florida" (April, 1945), XXIII, 197-201; *id.*, "Letters of the Invaders of East Florida, 1812" (July, 1949), XXVIII, 54-65; and [Julien C. Yonge, ed.], "The Surrender of Amelia Island" (October, 1925), IV, 90-95.

Four articles which discuss the activities of Mathews, the course of the revolution, and the Negro in East Florida are: Isaac J. Cox, "The Border Missions of George Mathews," *Mississippi Valley Historical Review* (December, 1925), XII, 309-333; Rufus Kay Wyllys, "The East Florida Revolution of 1812-1814"; *Hispanic American Historical Review* (November, 1929), IX, 416-445; and Kenneth W. Porter, "Negroes and the East Florida Annexation Plot, 1811-1813," *Journal of Negro History* (January, 1945), XXX, 9-29; Paul Kruse, "A Secret Agent in East Florida: General George Mathews and the Patriot War," *Journal of Southern History* (May, 1952), XVIII, 193-217.

Other articles which were cited in footnotes are: W. B. Burroughs, "Camden County: Dates and Events of Early Times Marking the County's Growth" and "Major Archibald Clark," *Historical Sketch of Old St. Marys* (n.p., n.d.); Marmaduke Floyd, "Certain Tabby Ruins on the Georgia Coast," *Georgia's Disputed Ruins* (Chapel Hill, 1949); Charles E. Hill, "James Madison" and Julius W. Pratt, "James Monroe," *The American Secretaries of State and Their Diplomacy*, edited by Samuel Flagg Bemis, 10 vols. (New York, 1927-1929), III, 3-148, 201-277; "Testimony of Captain Winslow Foster," *Petition of Joseph M. Hernandez* (copy in Yonge Library); Thomas Jefferson, "The Limits and Bounds of Louisiana," American Philosophical Society (New York, 1904), 5-45; and "East Florida Documents," *Georgia Historical Quarterly* (June, 1929), XIII, 154-158.

Books

Biographical references include the *Dictionary of American Biography*, edited by Allen Johnson and Dumas Malone, 20 vols. (New York, 1928-1936); *Biographical Dictionary of the American Congress, 1774-1927* (Washington, 1928); Francis Bernard Heitman, *Historical Register and Dictionary of the United States Army, from Its Organization, September 29, 1789, to March 2, 1903*, 2 vols. (Washington, 1903); Lucian L. Knight, *Georgia's Landmarks, Memorials and Legends*, 2 vols. (Atlanta, 1913); Stephen Frank Miller, *The Bench and Bar of Georgia*, 2 vols. (Philadelphia, 1858); William F. Northern (ed.), *Men of Mark in Georgia*, 2 vols. (Atlanta, 1907); and George White, *Historical Collections of Georgia* (New York, 1854).

General background material and excellent reference to other works were found in the volumes by Samuel Flagg Bemis, *Jay's Treaty: A Study in Commerce and Diplomacy* (New York, 1923) and *Pinckney's Treaty* (Baltimore, 1926). Philip Coolidge Brooks, *Diplomacy and the Borderlands: The Adams-Onís Treaty of 1819* (Berkeley, 1939) has an excellent summary of the Florida problem and a useful bibliography.

BIBLIOGRAPHY

Most valuable of all accounts is Julius William Pratt, *Expansionists of 1812* (New York, 1925). Though not as good as Pratt, Herbert Bruce Fuller, *The Purchase of Florida: Its History and Diplomacy* (Cleveland, 1906) and Isaac Joslin Cox, *The West Florida Controversy, 1798-1813: A Study in American Diplomacy* (Baltimore, 1918) are still useful. Scattered throughout the nine volumes of Henry Adams, *History of the United States During the Administrations of Thomas Jefferson and James Madison* (New York, 1889-1891) are excellent accounts of the diplomacy relating to the Floridas.

Pertinent material on national figures is found in: Henry Adams, *The Life of Albert Gallatin* (Philadelphia, 1879); Gilbert Chinard, *Thomas Jefferson, The Apostle of Americanism* (Boston, 1929); William Penn Cresson, *James Monroe* (Chapel Hill, 1946); Sidney Howard Gay, *James Madison* (Boston, 1884); Gaillard Hunt, *The Life of James Madison* (New York, 1902); Marquis James, *The Life of Andrew Jackson* (New York, 1940); Charles Francis Jenkins, *Button Gwinnett: Signer of the Declaration of Independence* (New York, 1926); and James Parton, *Life of Andrew Jackson*, 4 vols. (New York, 1861).

Useful histories of Florida are: Caroline Mays Brevard, *A History of Florida: From the Treaty of 1763 to Our Own Times*, edited by James Alexander Robertson, 2 vols. (DeLand, Florida, 1930); William Thomas Cash, *The Story of Florida*, 4 vols. (New York, 1938); Jeanette Thurber Connor (trans.), *Pedro Menéndez de Aviles*, by Gonzalo Solis de Meras (DeLand, 1923); Carita Doggett Corse, *The Key to the Golden Islands* (Chapel Hill, 1931); Frederick Dau, *Florida: Old and New* (New York, 1934); George Rainsford Fairbanks, *History of Florida* (Jacksonville, 1904); *Fernandina: A Guide to the City and Its Industries*, W.P.A., Federal Writers Project (Fernandina, 1940); Katherine Abbey Hanna, *Florida: Land of Change* (Chapel Hill, 1947); Rowland R. Rerick, *Memoirs of Florida: Embracing a General History of the Province and State*, edited by Francis P. Fleming, 2 vols. (Atlanta, 1902); and John Titcomb Sprague, *The Origin, Progress, and Conclusion of the Florida War* (New York, 1848).

Accounts of Georgia or of Camden County which throw light on American activities in Florida are: Ellis Merton Coulter, *Georgia: A Short History* (Chapel Hill, 1947); id. (ed.), *Georgia's Disputed Ruins* (Chapel Hill, 1947); Thomas Gamble, *Savannah Duels and Duelists, 1733-1811* (Savannah, 1923); *Georgia: A Guide to Its Towns and Countryside*, W.P.A., Federal Writers Project (Athens 1940); Edith Duncan Johnston, *The Houstouns of Georgia* (Athens, 1950); Alexander McQueen, *Three Dead Towns of Georgia* (n.p., n.d.); George Gillman Smith, *The Story of Georgia and the Georgia People, 1732 to 1860* (Macon, 1900); James T. Vocelle, *Reminiscences of Old St. Marys* (n.p., n.d.); and *id., History of Camden County, Georgia* (n.p., 1914).

Books on special topics include Henry M. Brackenridge, *Views of Louisiana*

(Pittsburg, 1814); Henry E. Chambers, *West Florida and Its Relation to the Historical Cartography of the United States* (Baltimore, 1898); Charles E. Chapman, *A History of Spain* (New York, 1931); Ernest Alexander Cruikshank, *The Political Adventures of John Henry: The Record of an International Imbroglio* (Toronto, 1936); Peter Joseph Hamilton, *Colonial Mobile* (Boston, 1898); Albert Campbell Holt, *The Economic and Social Beginnings of Tennessee* (Nashville, 1923); Louis Houck, *The Boundaries of the Louisiana Purchase* (St. Louis, 1901); Susan L'Engle, *Notes of My Family and Recollections of My Early Life* (New York, 1888); Woodbury Lowery, *The Spanish Settlements within the Present Limits of the United States: Florida, 1566-1574* (New York, 1905); and Edwin N. McClellan, History of the United States Marine Corps (unpublished MS., Yonge Library).

Index

Abbeville, South Carolina, 275
Abraham, heights of, 246
Adams, John, policies of, 4, 7, 20
Adams, John Quincy, in Russia, 256; negotiates treaty, 295-296, 297
Adams, William, 296
Africans, 58
Aggression, U. S., 61-62, 144-146, 251-252; plans for, 116; Kindelan condemns, 139
Alabama, river, 32; state, 19
Alachua, 142, 231; country of, 278; Indians of, 185, 211, 232; Patriot settlement in, 269, 272, 275, 279-282, 284; towns of, 197, 199
Albany, New York, 237
Alexander, Samuel, raid of, 275
Alliances, European, 20, 307
Alligator, Indians, 185, 211, 232
Alpha, burned, 215
Altamaha River, 288, 291
Alvarez, Jose, tavern of, 47
Amelia, harbor of, 95; island of, 45, 46, 80, 92, 98, 123, 128, 248, 250, 255, 259, 265, 271, 276, 278, 285; river of, 45, 89, 93, 95, 163, 272
America, ideals of, 70-71, 74
American Revolution, 4, 5, 260
Amherst, New Hampshire, 118
Amite River, 9
Amnesty, for Patriots, 151, 255, 260-263, 268, 271, 273-274
Anarchy, in Florida, 12, 135, 266, 299-301
Anastasia Island, 111
Anderson, Joseph, 221, 248-250
Anglo-Saxon, 9
Anglo-Spaniards, 265
Anna, wife of Clarke, 88
Apalachicola River, 9, 30, 73
Appalachian Mountains, 30
Appling, Daniel, 75,76; charges of against Laval, 76-78; in Fernandina, 101, 102
Armstrong, John, 27, 286; dismisses Jackson, 254; letters of, 245, 246, 255
Armstrong, Patriot killed by Indians, 191

Army, U. S., 72, 238
Arredondo, Joseph de la M., 87, 90, 91, 139, 159
Asheville, North Carolina, 227
Ashley, Lodowick, 43, 45, 48, 90, 92, 93, 97, 102, 103, 112, 120, 165, 279; joins Patriots, 65; military leader, 68, 84, 86; plantation of, 113, 271; proclamation of, 110; terms offered to Lopez, 94-95
Ashley, William, 43, 45, 52, 279; propaganda of, 270, 271, 276
Atkinson, George, 99; advises Lopez, 87; confers with Mathews, 41, 93, 94; emissary of Lopez, 89-90; signs treaty, 98
Atrocities, 186, 187
Augusta, Georgia, 16, 17, 177; theater at, 172
Augusta Chronicle, editorials of, 123, 148, 215-216, 222, 275-276, 297-298

Bahamas, 164
Baldwin, Abraham, first representative of Georgia, 6
Baltimore, Maryland, 42
Banditti, 139, 140, 217
Barbé-Marbois, Francois, French minister, 26
Barrington, Georgia, 287
Bartholomew, Captain, engagement with Hulburd, 291-294
Bartlet, raid of, 275
Baton Rouge, Louisiana, 9, 10, 34, 35; capture of, 11
Battles, of Yorktown and Germantown, 5
Bayard, James A., opposes war, 146-147, 149; negotiations of, 256, 258, 295, 296
Belgium, U. S. ministers in, 288, 295
Bell's River, 86, 93, 223; Patriot camp at, 90, 92
Bernaben, Juan B., protests of, 61
Bethune, Farquahar, office of, 265; plantation of raided, 275
Betts, Samuel, Loyalist, 163, 277
Bibb, George M., Georgia representative, 39, 149

345

Big Hammock, Florida, 197
Black, James, report of, 270
Blackburn, Gideon, speech of, 239-240
Blackman, Chaplain with Jackson, 243
Blockade, of St. Augustine, 111, 112, 221; British, 145
Blount, Willie, praises volunteers, 227, 240-241, 243; confers with Jackson, 238
Bonaparte, Joseph, 8
Bonaparte, Napoleon, see Napoleon
Boog, John, joins revolutionists, 65
Boston, Massachusetts, 39; Henry in, 118
Boundaries, of Floridas, 19, 26, 27, 28
Bourke, Thomas, commissary agent, 131, 197
Bowlegs, rebuffed and threatened, 180, 184; favors war, 185, 223; raids by, 188; reported wounded, 207; delivers funeral oration, 209-210; town of, 231, 232, 233; plans of, 276
Bradley, Stephen R., opposes Florida bill, 149-150
Bravo River, 24
Bribery, of Spanish official, 51-52
British, forces of, 51, 67, 244, 288; plans of, 87, 249; colonies, 104; defeated, 283; invade Georgia, 287-291
Broad River, 5
Broadnax, John H., company of, 200
Broadway, Abner, treatment of, 270
Bronson, Isaac H., criticizes U. S. policy, 302, 303
Brown's Ferry, 16, 43
Buena Vista, Florida, 189
Burlington, Vermont, 118
Burr, Aaron, comments on Jackson, 237
Bush, Oliver, dismissed from service, 242
Buttermilk Bluff, Georgia, 42

Calhoun, John C., favors war, 2, 115, 146
Calibri, British warship, 111
Camden County, Georgia, 43, 51, 56, 66, 276; commissioners of, 44, 87
Campbell, Hugh, 60, 74, 78, 79, 89, 127, 221, 291; orders to, 54, 95-96, 128, 134; cooperates with Mathews, 67, 73-74, 106; refuses Mathews, 84, 85, 87; hesitancy of, 92-93; recalls orders, 97; relief of, 123; aids Massias, 167; relations with McIntosh, 168; leaves St. Marys, 267
Camp New Hope, 185, 186, 190, 193, 219, 221, 233; Smith at, 213, 231; Floyd at, 211, 212, 214; prisoners at, 234; medical services at, 235; destroyed, 265
Camp Pinckney, 228, 290
Canada, possible annexation, 2, 3, 7, 23, 115, 116, 144, 147; governor of, 117; U. S. failure in, 238, 245, 248
Capitan de Pardido, 265
Capitol Hill, 1
Caribbean, islands of, 20
Carolinas, 16, 18
Caroline, U. S. warship, 287
Carroll, William, company of, 242
Casas de Puntas, 47
Cashen, James, Loyalist, 47, 159; plantation of raided, 275, 276
Castillo de San Marcos, 18, 19, 67, 68, 83, 102, 103, 104, 134, 170; description and strength of, 142, 223; plans to conquer, 213
Castlereagh, Lord, proposals of, 295
Catholic Church, 49
Census, Spanish of 1812, 103
Centerville, Georgia, 42
Cespedes, Manuel de, governor of St. Augustine, 50
Cevallos, Pedro de, Spanish minister, 21, 26, 27; comment of, 308
Ceylon, British warship, 294
Charles, free Negro, 300
Charleston, South Carolina, 16, 42, 81, 218
Charleston Courier, editorials of, 109, 122, 229
Chatham Artillery, 138
Chattahoochee River, 9, 16, 19, 32, 284, 286
Cheves, Langdon, favors war, 115
Claiborne, William, 10, 11, 12, 38, 49; occupies West Florida, 3
Claims, of Patriots for damages, 275, 283, 302-303
Claims Convention, 21, 308
Clark, Archibald, 53, 55, 56, 65, 74, 279, 302; captive, 288, 289; sawmill of, 290
Clark, William B., joins revolutionists, 43, 45
Clark's Creek, 45, 46
Clarke, Charles W., Loyalist, 87, 98
Clarke, George, Methodist minister, 43
Clarke, George J. F., 47, 87, 98, 101, 163; children of, 88; with Lopez, 89; carries surrender flag, 96-97; property of, 302
Clarke, Honoria, 87, 88
Clarke, Thomas, 87

INDEX

Clarksville, Tennessee, 243
Clay, Henry, in House, 2, 115
Climate, Florida, 158, 170, 173, 197
Cochrane, Alexander, appeals to Indians, 285, 286
Cochrane, Thomas, at St. Marys, 288
Cockburn, George, British admiral, 284, 287, 289, 291, 293, 294
Coffee, John, with Jackson, 245
Cole, Richard, 43
Coleman, Thomas, company of, 200
Coleraine, Georgia, 17, 42, 228, 231, 279, 290, 300; volunteers at, 233; prisoners at, 234; Smith at, 235; ferry near, 267
Colorado River, 26
Columbus, Georgia, 16
Commerce, importance of in Florida, 17, 27, 30, 36, 58, 253; in St. Marys, 42; in Fernandina, 46, 47
Cone, William, 43, 56, 190, 200, 208; wounded, 205; demands of, 277; settles in Florida, 302
Congress, U. S., 1, 2, 4, 6, 13, 39, 114, 125, 144; debate in, 146-147; 250-252; Continental, 4
Connecticut, senators from, 150, 253
Connor, William, mission of, 280-281; death of, 302
Constitution, of East Florida, 165-166; U. S., 215; Spain, 265
Continental system, 28
Cook, George, Patriot leader, 65, 86, 92, 93, 112
Cooper, John, 81
Copenhagen, Denmark, 109, 122
Cornstalk, Indian leader, 4
Cornwallis, Lord, 5
Cortes, Spanish, 21, 34, 35, 39, 255, 258, 262, 263, 264
Cossacks, 285
Cotton, trade in, 42
Covington, Leonard, refuses request of Mathews, 36
Cow Ford, Florida, 52, 54, 84, 102, 169
Cowkeeper, Indian chief, 179-180
Craig, James, governor of Canada, 117, 118; acts compared to Madison's, 120
Craig, William, Patriot leader, 48, 54, 65, 101, 103, 112, 113, 165, 279
Crawford, William H., recommends Mathews, 3, 7; conference with Mathews, 59; mentioned, 100, 120, 131, 252, 301; comment on Mathews, 121; report to Mitchell, 132; favors occupation of

Florida, 152; optimism of, 175; reassures Monroe, 176-177
Creek Agency, 16, 17, 177
Creek, Confederation, 66, 225; Indians, 30, 177, 231, 235
Crillon, Edward de, promotes Henry, 116, 117, 119
Criticism, of U. S., 37, 109, 122, 229; of Jackson, 241
Cuba, 29, 54, 59, 258; acquisition of, 31; aid from, 104, 224
Cumberland, Island of, 44, 72, 101, 161, 288, 289, 291; river, 240, 243; sound, 45, 60, 95, 97, 287
Customs, U. S., 15; West Florida, 11-12, 25; Spanish, 31; enforcement of, 54; Fernandina, 98, 134, 158, 159; McIntosh claims income from, 166, 260, 274
Cuthbert, emissary of Mitchell, 134, 135, 141

Darien, Georgia, 17, 80
Daschkoff, André, 256
Davis Creek, 186, 191
Day, punishment of, 172
Dearborn, Henry, failure of, 237
Delany, Daniel, as Patriot leader, 103, 104, 105, 106, 269, 270, 277
Delaware, senators from, 150, 253
Delaware River, 24
Dell, James, as Patriot leader, 277, 279
Delyon, Isaac, death of, 215
Deposit, right of at New Orleans, 19, 20, 22, 62, 63, 105, 218
Deserters, 9, 58, 110, 170, 172, 173, 203
Diamond, raid of, 275
Diplomacy, to secure Florida by, 61-63, 250; results of aid Mathews, 59, 64-65
Donahue, Daniel, tavern of, 47
Downs, William, raid of, 52
Dublin, slave, 187
Dublin, Georgia, 138, 196
Dudley, Miss, 242
Duprée, Sterling, army of, 33
Dusenberry, Dr., criticized, 235

Early, Peter, governor of Georgia, 100, 276, 290; condemns Patriots, 281; fears of, 287, 288; declares martial law, 288; communicates with Kindelan, 300
East Florida, occupation of, 4, 14, 33, 63-64, 73, 78, 92, 94, 157, 248; area of, 8-9; conditions in, 17, 60, 158ff, 266; U. S. claims on, 21, 63-64, 256, 289; no independent state planned for,

347

37; descriptions of, 40, 41, 171, 234; resources and prosperity of, 48, 108; cession, 57, 105-106; desire for, 71, 254; restoration provided for, 105-106; possession of repudiated, 121; evacuation of, 129, 133, 140, 258, 261, 264-265, 268; territory of, 166, 259; revolution, 260; governmental costs of, 266; Patriot raids in, 275-276; republic of, 279-280, 282

Egmont, Florida, 46

Elba, Napoleon on, 284

Elections, of 1810, 2

Elholm, Captain, duel of, 51

Elotchaway, district of, 279, 281, 282, 290

Embargo, effect of, 28, 42, 46

England, see Great Britain

Erebus, British warship, 291, 292, 293

Erving, George W., U. S. minister, 27

Erwin, Mrs., aids volunteers, 227

Estrada, Juan de, opposes cession, 41, 103-104; describes plans of Mathews, 62; orders of, 102; mentioned, 107, 110, 142; proposals sent to, 111-112; patriotism of, 113; letters to Mitchell, 134-135; seeks Indian aid, 180

Europe, war in, 2

Eustis, William, secretary of war, 7, 17, 132-133; resigns, 220; dislikes Jackson, 238

Evacuation, plans for, 129, 133, 140, 258, 259, 261, 264-265, 268

Expansion, U. S. demands for, 21, 144-145

Expenses, of U. S. agents, 15, 109; of revolutionists, 268

Fairfield Plantation, 66

Fannin, Abram B., company of, 199, 200

Farmers, 9, 44, 48, 53, 147

Fatio, Francis P., Loyalist, 48, 187, 276, 277, 302

Fatio, Francisco, office of, 265-266

Federal Road, 16, 17

Federalists, decline of, 114; fear Henry disclosures, 118, 119; oppose war, 147; senators, 251, 253

Felicia, the fortune teller, 47

Felipa, the witch, 47

Fenwick, Joseph, property of, 48

Ferdinand VII, of Spain, 139, 297

Fernandina, Florida, 9, 45, 60, 83, 88, 99, 100, 106, 254, 271, 272; description of, 45-48; defense of, 54, 85-86, 89; capture of, 83ff; conditions in, 97-98, 101-102, 158-159; trade in, 105; harbor of, 160; evacuation of, 264-265; Spanish authority in, 299

Fernando, escape of, 160

Fishers Island, 111

Flag, Patriot, 84, 92, 97; Spanish, 97; U. S., 107, 239

Flint River, 9

Flora, wife of Clarke, 88

Floridas, acquisition of, 1, 2, 7, 13, 20, 249; desire for, 3, 8, 25, 29ff, 175, 297-298; population of, 9; history of, 18, 19; title to, 19-20; boundaries of, 20, 307; negotiations for, 25-27; occupation of, 28, 36, 147-149, 151, 250, 253; description and resources of, 29, 30, 197; commercial importance of, 31, 58; destined for U. S., 82; plans to conquer, 115, 220-223, 224, 236, 245; cession of, 123, 152, 153, 212, 249, 257, 296-298; Monroe's report on, 249-250; evacuation of, 255; instructions regarding, 258; cost of government in, 298

Flournoy, Thomas, letters of, 168, 213, 222, 231, 234; Williams tenders services to, 228

Floyd, John, character of, 38; mentioned, 45, 57, 66, 77, 108; ordered to St. Marys, 54; with Mathews, 73; signs charges, 78; criticizes U. S. policy, 109; militia of, 138, 208, 211, 212; preparations of, 214

Folch, Vincente, suggests cession of Floridas, 3, 4; problems of, 11-12; and Mathews, 13, 35-36; strategy and loyalty of, 34, 35; and Isaacs, 33-35; praised, 37; mentioned, 175

Forbes and Company, 47, 87, 88, 181

Fort, Tomlinson, forces of in Florida, 187, 188, 189, 191, 197, 199; wounded, 192

Fort Charlotte, 39

Fort George, 188

Fort Hawkins, 16

Fort Mims, 16

Fort Mitchell, Alabama, 16

Fort Mitchell, Florida, 279, 282

Fort San Carlos, 46

Fort Stallings, 187, 189, 191, 193, 195

Fort St. Augustine, 243

Fort Stoddert, 16, 17, 25, 32, 36, 38, 40, 58

Foster, Augustus, protests U. S. policy, 61-63, 67, 120, 128

Foster-Monroe letters, 64, 124, 155

INDEX

Foster, Winslow, commands gunboat, 96, 167
Forsyth, John, attends funeral of Mathews, 177
Fourth of July, plans to celebrate, 162
France, 71, 115, 289; quasi war of, 20; Louisiana ceded to, 21; negotiations with, 28; to control Spain, 250
Franklin County, Tennessee, 239
French, in Florida, 18; revolution, 20

Gaddy, Mrs., complaint of, 177
Galatin, Albert, opposes Florida acquisition, 7, 27, 28, 150; U. S. minister, 256, 296; objects to occupation of Mobile, 257-258
Gambier, Lord, appointed British commissioner, 296
Garambouville, L. M. Turreau de, French minister, 12
Garcia, Jose, business of, 47
Garvin, David, property raided, 55
Garzia, Benigno, replies to Mitchell, 141-142; accuses Georgians, 217
Genêt, Edmond C. E. (Citizen), agents of in Florida, 52
George III, British king, 180, 286
Georgia, 5, 16, 18, 30, 32, 43, 44, 56, 59, 65, 150, 233, 234, 235, 249, 251, 252, 258, 259, 281, 289; militia of, 6, 19, 66, 67, 138, 143, 270, 276, 277; Loyalists, 19; population pressure in, 53; volunteers, 54, 83, 94; fear of Negroes, 89; dangers facing, 109-110, 135, 271; raids in, 188; legislature, 215-216; welfare of, 250; defenses of, 267, 285-286; Patriots in, 268, 278
Georgia Argus, editorial of, 109
Georgia Journal, editorial of, 229
German, settlers in Florida, 46, 48
German, Obadiah, opposes Madison administration, 146, 150
Germantown, battle of, 5
Ghent, Belgium, negotiations in, 288, 295, 296
Giles, William B., opposes Madison administration, 149, 150, 253
Gilman, Nicholas, opposes acquisition of Florida, 150
Glynn County, Georgia, 43
Godoy, Manuel, warns U. S., 26, 27
Gonzales, Mateo, blacksmith shop of, 47
Good Hope, Cape of, 293
Goodrich, Chauncy, requests information on Florida, 249

Goose Pond, plantation, 5
Goulburn, Henry, British commissioner, 296
Gracia Real de Santa Teresa de Mosé, 183
Grandpré, Louis, death of, 11
Grayson, John, commands gunboat, 96
Great Britain, policies of, 2, 13, 256, 264, 286; settlers of, 9; possible occupation of Floridas, 14, 19, 91, 112, 221, 224, 238, 249; diplomatic protests of, 28, 59, 60-62; U. S. fears of, 54, 196, 296-298; ships of, 60; accused of aiding Spanish, 94; part in Henry episode, 119-120; Patriots' fear of, 165; period of in Floridas, 179-180; to control Spain, 250; invasions by, 284; tired of war, 289; triumph of, 299; citizens of killed by Jackson, 301
Great White Father, 180, 181
Green County, Georgia, 154
Greene, Nathanael, Revolutionary general, 5
Grenville, William, British minister, 20
Griffin, Andrew, death of, 215
Grundy, Felix, favors war, 2, 115
Guards, to prevent volunteering at Point Petre, 77-79
Gulf of Mexico, 9, 25, 30, 244, 286, 287
Gunboats, U. S., 84, 85, 87, 90, 93, 95, 97, 104, 106, 111, 127, 134, 142, 167, 291-294; Spanish, 107, 136, 137

Haig, George, army officer, 81, 139
Halifax, Nova Scotia, 249
Hall, James, reports treatment by Spaniards, 270
Hamilton, British sea captain, 294
Hamilton, Joshua, U. S. lieutenant, 33
Hamilton, Paul, secretary of war, 8, 17; orders to Campbell, 122
Hamilton, William, Patriot leader, 165
Hammond, Samuel, invades Florida, 52
Hampton, marine, 195
Hampton, Wade, relations with Mathews, 33, 37
Hanna, wife of Clarke, 88
Harper's Ferry, 81
Harpeth River, 243
Harris, Buckner, Patriot, 43, 56, 113, 165; confers with Mathews, 177; acts as judge, 223; seeks aid from Mitchell, 259-260; leads Patriot settlement, 268, 270, 275-280, 282; raid of, 275; death of, 282, 284

349

Harris, Charles, Mathews recommends appointment of, 108; report of, 276
Hartly, settler in Florida, 48
Havana, Cuba, 4, 215
Hawkins, Benjamin, relations with Mathews, 17, 66; desires peace for Indians, 209, 229, 255, 269, 281; criticized, 230
Hendrix, settler in Florida, 48
Henry, John, letters of, 116-120, 176
Hibberson, Joseph, prepares defenses of Fernandina, 89; emissary to Mathews, 90, 91-92; appeals to Harris, 276
Hibberson, and Yonge, business of, 47
Hogan, settler in Florida, 48
Holder, private, shot, 172
Holland, 122
Hollingsworth, James, death of, 186
Hollingsworth's, camp at, 185
Holmes, David, governor of Mississippi Territory, 9, 10, 39
Holy Charter, of Spain, 265
Hopkins, Francis, report of, 276-277
Howell, Jeremiah B., opposes occupation of Florida, 149
Hulburd, John, engagement with *Sappho*, 160; incident with Bartholomew, 291-294; desires revenge, 295
Hull, William, Jefferson's criticism of, 220
Humphries, John, agitates against Newman, 198, 203-205; company of, 199, 200, 201
Hunter, William, speech of opposing Florida invasion, 251-252
Hunter, William, killed in duel with Mitchell, 133
Hurricanes, 204, 205, 208

Iberville River, 39
Independence, wars of in Latin America, 2
Independent Blues, of Augusta, 177
Indian Agent, 55, 66
Indians, Shawnee, 4; problem of, 16, 18, 31, 103, 132; in Fernandina, 46; mentioned, 71, 115, 232; hated by Americans, 48, 99; fear of, 52, 179; conference with, 125; Kindelan plans to use, 142; fear white aggression, 181-182; numbers of, 185, 211; attack Newnan, 201, 202; captured, 232; desire peace, 235, 255; prisoners, 266-267; towns of, 269; raids of reported, 272; Harris seeks conference with, 275, 278; kill Harris, 282; Great Britain appeals to, 285-286, 300

Instructions, to Mathews and McKee, 14-15
Invaders, retreat of, 254-267
Irish, 5; in Fernandina, 46, 48
Isaacs, slave of Newman, 199; killed, 206
Isaacs, Ralph, secretary of Mathews, 16, 91, 93, 108, 127; negotiates with Folch, 33-35; in St. Marys, 40; delivers message to Laval, 75-76; signs charges against Laval, 78; Laval's comment on, 81; designs Patriot flag, 84; conference with Monroe, 130-132; defends Mathews, 131; reports to Mitchell, 137; describes feelings of Mathews, 174-175; with Mathews, 176
Island of Orleans, 23, 31
Italy, 122

Jackson, Andrew, administration's plans for, 221, 237; forces and volunteers of, 224, 225, 230, 236, 237-247; expedition of, 237-247; letter to Armstrong, 246; dismissal of, 254; defeats British, 287; invades Florida, 301
Jackson, James, representative from Georgia, 6
Jackson, Rachel, 239
Jacksonville, Florida, 186
Jacobin, of France, 251
Jamaica, troops from, 58
James, Miss, 242
Jefferson, Thomas, 2, 7, 21, 43, 54, 116, 121, 133, 301; supports plans to occupy Floridas, 13, 148, 220, 278, 303; policies of, 21, 22, 23, 27, 50; proclamation of, 25; successor to, 237
Jefferson, Georgia, 287
Jewish Cemetery, duel in, 133
Jews, 75, 80
John, Dago, raids of, 270
Johnson, Richard M., representative from Kentucky, 115
Johnston, William, resident of St. Marys, 45

Kanawha River, 4
Keene, Richard R., reported land grant to, 59
Kelley, William, joins Patriots, 65
Kempler, Reuben, army of, 33
Kentucky, senators from, 150, 253
Kindelan, Sebastian, Mathews' opinion of, 53, 63, 312; mentioned, 135, 207, 213, 214, 222, 266, 268, 281; negotiations of, 139-141; offensive plans of, 142-

INDEX

143; seeks Indian aid, 176, 180, 182; attitude toward Negroes, 184, 189; success of, 194; promulgates amnesty for Patriots, 258-259, 265, 273; Patriot opinion of, 261; arranges for evacuation, 263-265; problems of, 266; sincerity of, 270, 271; ignores Patriots, 277-278; neutrality of, 286, 289; requests suppression of raiders, 300

Kinderick, James, raid of, 275
King, Thomas, of St. Marys, 45
Kingsley, Zephaniah, 48, 113, 207; joins Patriots, 101; Indian attacks on, 186, 272; plantation of, 190, 231; appeals to Pinckney, 261; prospers in Florida, 302
Kinnear, William, describes Florida, 171
Knoxville, Tennessee, 100, 213, 226, 227

Lafayette, General, 70
Lake Ontario, 81
Lambert, John, opposes occupation of Florida, 150
Land, American desire for, 2, 11, 30, 45, 53, 71, 92, 145; titles to, 14; Spanish policy regarding, 50; grants of, 59, 105, 279; promise of induces volunteering, 62, 65, 124, 197; Patriots seek and demand, 269, 277; of Seminoles, 278
Lassus, Carlos Dehault de, loses power to rebels, 10
Laurel Grove, plantation, 186, 207
Laval, Jacint, shares cottage with Mathews, 41; mentioned, 68, 83, 99; relations with Mathews, 69ff; early life of, 70-71; orders to on Florida, 73; charges against, 76-78, 81; incident with Massias, 79-80; arrested, 80; reports of, 80, 81; later life and death, 81; evaluation of, 81-82; reassures Lopez, 90-91; condemns Mathews, 91; influences Campbell, 95-96; condemned by Mathews, 108
Laval, William, son of Jacint, 77
Laws, Spanish, 14
Legislative Council, of Patriots, 166, 259-260, 279-280
Legislature, Georgia, 216-217, 250
Leslie, John, Clarke lives in home of, 88
Leon, Juan Ponce de, discovers Florida, 18
Lewis, collector of customs at Fernandina, 101, 158
Lewis, Andrew, Indians attack forces of, 4
Lewis, Miss, 242
Lewis, William B., with Jackson, 241

Lexington, Georgia, 176
Lieb, Michael, opposes occupation of Florida, 149, 150, 248-249, 253
Liston, Robert, British minister, 20
Little Belt, British warship, 115
Livingston, Robert, negotiations of and ideas on Louisiana boundary, 22ff, 307
Loans, to be repaid by U. S., 56, 112; Patriots seek, 269
Local Authorities, meaning of, 49, 73, 75, 91; to be created in Florida, 57; cede territory to U. S., 78, 100-101
London, 61, 295, 296
London Chronicle, editorial of on Florida, 298
Lopez, Justo, urged to join Patriots, 85; surrender of demanded, 86; calls council, 87; asks intentions of U. S., 87, 89; refuses to surrender, 90, 92; surrenders, 96, 97, 100; opinion of Patriots, 102
Lotchaway Hammock, Florida, 197
Louisburg, North Carolina, 281
Louisiana, purchase and boundaries of, 3, 11, 22, 23, 26, 27, 29, 35, 39, 60, 62, 157, 253, 256; title to, 24; state of, 31, 39, 248, 253
Louisiana, U. S. warship, 287
Louisiana, Gazette, criticizes U. S. policy, 37
Lower Bluff, Patriots at, 86
Lowndes, William, favors war, 2, 115
Low's Plantation, Patriots at, 92, 93, 97
Loyalists, of American Revolution, 19; of East Florida, 159-160, 168, 271, 272; of Spain, 158, 159
Lutherans, in Florida, 18

MacGregor, Gregor, captures Fernandina, 301
Madison, James, problems of, 1; policies of, 2, 3, 10, 24, 28, 29, 220-223, 238, 255-256; proclamation of, 3, 11, 35; relations with Mathews, 6, 8, 58, 107-108, 121-122, 131; mentioned, 41, 49, 50, 54, 56, 57, 59, 72, 73, 101, 113, 150, 166, 175, 218, 246, 247, 262, 264, 273, 280; administration of, 54, 210, 245, 256, 273; silence of, 60, 230; orders of, 72; position of, 114; follows expansionists, 116; sends Henry letters to Congress, 117; vacillation of, 128-129; war message, 145-146; signs declaration of war, 147; lacks faith in Onís, 152-153; hesitation of, 213; letters to, 227, 263; ideas of Jackson, 237;

351

confidence of, 248; transmits Monroe's report on Floridas, 249; supporters of, 250; plans of defeated, 253; comments on McIntosh, 274-275; evaluation of, 282, 303-304
Madrid, Spain, 21, 26, 152, 218
Magrith's Ferry, 228
Mail, U. S., schedules of, 312
Manning, Lawrence, replaces Smith, 235; evacuates Florida, 264-265
Marianna River, 43
Marine Corps, 72
Marines, U. S., 44, 101, 159, 161, 193
Martin, Brice, rescues men, 244
Martinez, Antonio, tavern of, 47
Maryland, senators from, 150, 249, 253
Maryville, Tennessee, 239
Massachusetts, 39; Henry in, 117, 118; senators from, 150, 249, 253
Massias, Abraham, 73, 75, 107, 223; charges against Laval, 76-78; encounter with Laval, 79-80; work of in Fernandina, 162-163, 166, 167; evacuates forces from Fernandina, 265; duties collected by, 274; defense of St. Marys, 287
Matanzas, origin of name, 18
Matanzas Inlet, 111, 112
Matanzas River, 110, 111
Matériel, needs in Florida, 55, 58, 67-68, 128, 131, 138; for volunteers, 68; of war, 73, 89; for defense of Fernandina, 89
Mathews, Charles, attends funeral of Mathews, 177
Mathews, George (General), in Washington, 1; life of, 4ff; wives of, 6; conference with Madison, 6, 8ff; description of, 8; opinions of, 12-13; instructions to, 14-15; character of, 17-18; at Fort Stoddert, 33ff; conference with Folch, 35, 36; plans to annex West Florida, 36; leaves West Florida, 37, 38; congratulates Monroe, 37; illness of, 40; relations with Laval, 41, 69ff, 78; enters East Florida, 45; plans of, 49-50; governor of Georgia, 52; optimism of, 54; organizes revolution, 55ff; relations with McIntosh, 56-57, 69, 263-264; reports of, 58, 79; confers with Crawford, 59, 176; action protested by Foster, 62-63; confers with Mitchell, 66; conferences and requests of Campbell, 66-67, 84, 85, 86; recommends appointment of friends, 72; schemes of, 83ff; conferences with Atkinson and Yonge, 90, 93-94; describes Patriot plans, 91-92; waits for news, 99; accepts cession, 100-101; informs Monroe of needs, 102; moves to St. Augustine, 106-107; reports mission accomplished, 107-108; acts compared with Henry's, 120, 122; reaction to repudiation, 125-126; realizes his work continues, 127; praised by Monroe, 129; mentioned, 135, 151, 245, 246, 249, 267, 275, 297, 301, 303; influence of his promises, 155; orders concerning Fernandina, 158-159; conferences with Indians, 174, 176, 180, 181, 184, 325; plans revenge, 175; starts trip to Washington, 177; death and burial, 177-178; praised, 178, 273-274; Hunter expresses sympathy for, 251-252; acts of never recognized, 261; treatment of, 303; route of to west, 306; writing of, 309; opinion of Kindelan, 312
Mathews, George, son of General Mathews, 7
Mathews, John, father of General Mathews, 4
Mathews, John, son of General Mathews, 7
Maxey's Creek, 106
McHenry, James, secretary of war, 7
McIntosh County, Georgia, 276
McIntosh, Eliza, wife of J. H. McIntosh, 68, 69
McIntosh, George, 43, 50, 56, 311
McIntosh, John (General), life of, 50-52; arrest and imprisonment of, 52; confused with John H., 56n; elected leader of Patriots, 112-113, 320; criticizes repudiation of Mathews, 123-124; comment of on Mathews, 125; militia of, 138
McIntosh, John H., 45, 54, 67, 74, 78, 90, 92, 97, 102, 108, 113, 120, 279; plantation of, 43, 48, 56, 65, 275; early life of, 56; commissioner of East Florida, 57; questions powers of Mathews, 58; convinced of Mathews' powers, 64-65; letter to Troup, 69; children of, 69; aids in Patriot declaration of independence, 83-84; urges Lopez to surrender, 84-85, 86; signs treaty with Mathews, 98; cedes Amelia Island to U. S., 101; demands surrender of St. Augustine, 103-104; cedes part of East Florida to U. S., 105; calls for volun-

INDEX

teers, 124, 125; appeals to Madison, 155-156; offices of, 165, 166; appeals to Monroe, 168, 263-264; controversy with Massias, 167-168; conferences with Seminoles, 181, 184; plans to aid Newnan, 198; hopes of, 223; powers of as Patriot leader, 260; protests proposed evacuation of East Florida, 259-264; dislikes Pinckney, 268; property losses of, 268; confers with Monroe, 273-275; reports defeat of British, 290; comment on revolution, 301; later life of, 302

McIntosh, John M., son of John Mohr, 50

McIntosh, John Mohr, prisoner of Spanish, 19

McIntosh, Lachlan, son of John Mohr, 50

McKee, John, instructions to, 14-15; accompanies Mathews, 16, 306; proposals of to Folch, 33; aids Mathews, 36, 37; terminates work, 38, 39; Mathews requests information from, 59; appointment of, 72; experiences in Washington, 306-307; mentioned, 303

McQueen, John, sells property to McIntosh, 56

Medical service, 235

Merchants, 9, 32, 47

Methodists, in St. Marys, 43

Mickausee Indians, 209

Militia, of Georgia, 6, 19, 52, 66, 67, 80, 103, 134, 138, 143, 214, 270, 276, 290; Negro, 141, 154, 215, 270; of Newnan, 169, 170; of Augusta, 177-178; refuse to cross boundary, 220; of Tennessee, 225, 259; criticism of, 227; praised by Jackson, 246; of Spain, 251; of Jackson, 287

Milledgeville, Georgia, 16, 132, 138, 148, 196, 269, 270

Milledgeville Artillery, 138

Milledgeville Journal, editorial of, 228-229

Miller, Pleasant A., carries dispatch to Mitchell, 228

Minorcans, 48; lure soldiers, 171

Missions, Spanish, 18

Mississippi, territory of, 6, 7, 9, 16, 30, 32, 148; river, 9, 19, 23, 71, 148, 238, 240, 243-244; state, 19; defense of valley of, 238

Mitchell, David, conference with Mathews, 66; receives General McIntosh's reports, 112, 113; replaces Mathews, 129; mentioned, 130, 175, 245, 246, 272, 297; studies East Florida problem, 132, early life of, 133-134; ideas and comments relating to Mathews, 134, 178; negotiations with Estrada, 134-135, 137; negotiations with Kindelan, 140-141; considers offensive, 142, 214; instructions to, 151; ideas and plans of, 153-154; illness of, 154, 214; sends report to Monroe, 156; replaced by Pinckney, 157; orders relating to Fernandina, 160-161; fear of Indians and Negroes, 184; needs Georgia troops, 196, 213; receives report on Newnan, 209; message to legislature, 215; reasons for dismissal, 218; replies to Williams, 228; requests peace for Indians, 229, 255; protests attack on Indians, 235; Patriots appeal to, 259-260, 269-270; not fooled by Patriot propaganda, 271; fort named for, 279

Mobile, Alabama, 9, 12, 32, 34, 35, 38, 66, 105, 107, 221, 222, 238, 240, 243, 256, 258, 287; district of, 11; river, 30, 32, 33; bay, 32, 36, 66, 73

Mobile Act, 25

Monroe, James, negotiations of, 22-26; letters written by but not sent, 37, 38, 310; appointed secretary of state, 37; views on West Florida, 37; mentioned 54, 59, 73, 150, 166, 175, 218, 246, 247, 254, 271, 280; Mathews seeks ideas of and reports to, 58-60, 79, 108-109; silence of, 60, 143, 156, 230; receives and answers protests, 61-64; Monroe-Foster letters, 65; buys Henry letters, 117; repudiates Mathews, 120-122; letters to Mathews, 125-126; answers Foster and Onís, 128; instructions of to Mitchell, 129, 151; conference with Isaacs, 130-132; confidence of, 148-149, 248; dealings with Onís, 151-153; praises Mitchell, 156-157; instructions of to Pinckney, 218, 230; acting secretary of war, 220; plans conquest of Florida, 220-223; report on Florida, 249-250; favored by Jackson, 237; plans of defeated, 253; to secure Florida by diplomacy, 255-256; instructions of to Gallatin, 257-258; interview with McIntosh, 273-275; hopes of, 278; repudiates Patriots, 281-282; evaluation of, 282, 303-304; on importance of Florida, 297-298

Montpelier, Madison at, 10

Moore, James, invades Florida, 18

353

Moosa Creek, fort on, 136
Moosa Old Fort, 104, 107, 127, 136, 138, 140, 183, 186, 196, 197, 213, 219, 252
Morales, Juan V., suspends right of deposit, 22
Morier, John P., questions U. S. motives, 12
Moro Castle, Cuba, 41
Morrison, George, raid of, 275

Napoleon, 2, 8, 29, 116, 122, 256, 284; controls Spain, 25; schemes of, 28; ambition of, 34; dictatorship of, 71; imprisonment of, 285
Nashville, Tennessee, volunteers in, 238, 240-243, 246
Natchez, Miss., 24, 32, 244, 245
National Intelligencer, comments on Florida, 123
Nationalism, 2, 115
Navy, department of, 67, 72, 122
Negro, prostitutes, 44, 47, 310-311; free, 47; as slaves, allies and advisors of Seminoles, 58, 104, 109, 180, 182-184, 185, 202, 269, 284; troops, 89, 91, 94, 139, 141, 155, 184, 189, 260, 276, 277, 278, 287; slaves, 96, 231; at Moosa, 136; American fear of, 154, 159, 179, 214; lawlessness of, 160, 287; attack Smith's supply line, 192-193; work of in Florida, 194; kill Harris, 202; militia, 251, 270; prisoners, 267; organize for defense, 271; stolen in raids, 275; Spanish return, 277; British appeal to, 285; fighting qualities of, 285, 288; enslavement of, 300; fort of destroyed, 301; references to deleted, 319
Neuse River, 275
Neutral Rights, 20, 115, 145-146
Neutrality, 20
New England, relative decline of, 39; Henry in, 117, 118
New England Mississippi Land Company, 7
New Feliciana, rebellion in, 9
New Hampshire, Henry in, 118; senators from, 150, 253
New Jersey, senators from, 150, 253
Newlin, Harry, refuses aid, 244
Newnan, Daniel, volunteers of, 26, 169, 170, 196, 199, 234; gains recruits, 138, 197, 199; arrives in Florida, 187, 188; difficulties of, 190, 198; expedition of, 195ff, 228, 235; dispatches to, 191; aids Smith, 193; character of, 198-199; results of expedition, 206-207; amazed by Smith's criticism, 208; mentioned, 239, 269
New Orleans, Louisiana, 7, 15, 19, 30, 33, 213, 221, 222, 237, 240, 245; right of deposit at, 22, 27, 62, 63, 105; Wilkinson at, 238; British at, 287; Jackson's victory at, 295
New Smyrna, colony at, 171
Newton, Georgia, 53
New York, harbor of, 5; senators from, 150, 253; troops in, 150, 237
Nicholls, Edward, British Indian agent, 285, 297, 300
Niles Register, comments of on Indians, 48; on Florida, 123, 229
None Such, capture of, 164
North Carolina, 43, 169, 275; senators from, 150, 253
North River, 136, 171

Oglethorpe County, Georgia, 59
Oglethorpe, James, invades Florida, 19
Ohio, river, 4, 240, 243; senators from, 150, 253
Okefenokee Swamp, 17
Onis, Louis de, protests U. S. action in Florida, 12, 60-61, 128, 151-152; mentioned, 62, 120, 213; fears U. S. to occupy Florida, 221; arranges amnesty for Patriots, 255, 262, 273; suggests restoration of Florida, 298; denies Spanish responsibility, 299
Orleans Territory, 3, 7, 10, 11, 39
Overseers, of plantations, 65

Palmyra, Tennessee, 243
Panton, Leslie and Company, 88
Pardons, for Patriots, 124
Paris, France, 26, 284
Parron, Mary, Ridgeway inquires about, 171
Parsons, Enoch, delivers letter to Mitchell, 228
Pascagoula, river, 9, 30, 34; district of, 11
Pass, Francis, wealth of, 48
Patch, Ezra, shop of, 47
Patriots, of East Florida, mentioned, 57, 76, 80, 88, 169, 287; cause of, 79; flag of, 84; numbers of, 85, 97, 103, 316; declare independence, 83-84; military organization of, 86; plans to capture Fernandina, 90; camps of, 90, 106; movements of, 92, 96, 102; negotiations

INDEX

of, 93-94; in Fernandina, 100-101, 159, 160; organization and government of, 103, 154-155, 164-166; relations with Indians, 104; proposals and promises of, 110-112; seek recruits, 112-113; discouragement of, 113; propaganda of, 124-125, 159, 223, 264, 270, 276, 278, 280; reaction to repudiation, 124; protection for, 129, 130, 137, 151, 219, 261; Mitchell's ideas of, 132; protests of, 133; Mitchell's actions reassure, 134; attacked at Moosa, 136; demands of, 158, 277, 278; dislike Massias, 163-164; work of, 164, 185, 198; Mathews to lobby for, 176; Indians fear activities of, 182; skirmishes of, 188; volunteers opinion of, 198; join Newnan, 199; elation of, 223; amnesty for, 255, 258-259; protest evacuation, 259-264; raids by, 266, 271, 276; confusion in ranks of, 268; settlement in Alachua, 272, 275, 279-282; defeat Loyalists, 272; treatment of, 273; atrocities of, 275; criticized, 275-276, 281; dispersement of, 282-283; defeat British, 290-291; claims of for losses, 302-303
Patriots, of Spain, 122
Patterson, Daniel, at New Orleans, 287
Payne, King, neutrality of, 104, 176, 180, 181, 185; country of, 197; supplies of, 199, 207; leads in war, 201; forces of, 202, 326; wounded, 202; falsely reported killed, 207; plans general war, 209; death and burial, 209-210; towns of, 191, 231, 232, 233, 279; people of, 232
Pearl River, 3, 9, 10, 12, 253
Peck, Mrs., tavern of, 43
Pennsylvania, senators from, 150, 248, 253
Pensacola, Florida, 9, 13, 16, 33, 35, 36, 38, 238, 239, 240, 243; plans to capture, 66, 105, 107, 221
Perdido River, 3, 4, 9, 11, 12, 23, 24, 29, 36, 72, 78, 252, 253, 256, 298
Philadelphia, Pennsylvania, 221
Philis, daughter of Clarke, 88
Picolata, Florida, 54, 102, 104, 106
Picolatti, Florida, 181, 186, 189, 191, 195, 197, 205, 206
Pierce, raid of, 275
Pinckney, Charles, negotiations of in Spain, 21, 25, 26
Pinckney, Thomas, replaces Mitchell, 157, 218; issues orders to Smith, 212-213; life and description of, 218-219; requests instructions, 219, 230; opinions on Florida policy, 219-220; plans of, 222-223; forces of, 223, 225, 236; no power to stop war on Indians, 229, 255; answers Mitchell, 235; powers of, 254-255; plans evacuation of East Florida, 258-259, 263, 264, 265; relations with Patriots, 261-264; 268, 281; urges purchase of Florida, 266; reports of, 267, 271; affirms faith in Kindelan, 271; McIntosh condemns, 273
Pinckney Treaty, 218
Pirates, 9
Plantations, 43, 45, 48, 56, 65, 66, 201; destruction of, 185-186; Bowlegs raids, 188
Plumer, Daniel, robbed by Georgians, 52-53
Point Petre, Georgia, military post at, 41, 44, 57, 60, 68, 73, 75, 76, 79, 90, 99, 106, 115, 128-129, 161, 212, 254, 259, 290; garden of, 70; Mathews ordered from, 74; Laval places guards at, 77, 78; Smith in, 80, 213; troops to mobilize at, 221, 224; condition of, 267; defense of, 287; burnt by British, 288
Point Pleasant, battle of, 4
Politics, of Georgia, 5
Pope, John, opposes occupation of Florida, 150
Population, of Florida, 13; of St. Marys, 43, 44; of Mobile area, 36; of East Florida, 48
Portugal, 58
Potomac River, 24, 252
Preoccupation of Florida, 94, 151, 221
Presbyterians, in St. Marys, 43
President, U. S. warship, 115
Prices, in 1811, 45; of slaves, 48-49; of food, 171
Primrose, British ship, 288
Prisoners, Indian and Negro, 232, 233, 234, 266-267
Pritchard, Daniel, killed by Indians, 186
Privateers, 20, 164
Proclamations, of 1810, 3, 11, 34; of Patriots, 110-111, 261; of Kindelan, 262, 265
Propaganda, for annexation of Florida, 148; of Patriots, 124-125, 159, 223, 264, 270, 271, 276, 278, 280
Property, rights in guaranteed, 65, 86, 98; in Fernandina, 101; Estrada orders destroyed, 102; of Patriots, 124, 273;

355

confiscation of, 167; protection of, 250
Prosperity, of East Florida, 49
Prostitution, 44, 47, 310-311

Quebec, fortress at, 237
Quesada, Juan, governor of St. Augustine, 50 52
Quincy, Josiah, speech of, 39

Raids, along Georgia-Florida border, 18, 31, 43, 46, 52-53, 55, 269, 270, 271, 275, 276
Randolph, John, criticizes Spain and Florida projects, 24-25, 28, 29; opposes war, 146
Rangers, of Georgia, 138; of Augusta, 177
Rape, charge of, 77
Rearmament, U. S., 115-116
Rebellion, U. S. fosters in Florida, 10, 29
Rebels, rampaging on frontier, 268-283
Recruiting, 84, 101, 102, 112-113
Reese, John C., rides for aid, 204, 205, 206
Refuge Plantation, 43, 48, 56, 65
Regency, of Spain, 258
Religion, freedom of in Florida, 62, 65, 86, 250
Rensselaer, Stephen Van, Jefferson's criticism of, 220
Republic, of East Florida, 279-280, 282
Republicans, fear of Henry disclosures, 118; party, 114, 133, 146-147, 150, 248, 253
Republican Blues, volunteer for duty, 137, 138
Repudiation, of Mathews, 120-122
Resources, of Florida, 48, 197
Revolution, in Spanish colonies, 10; in Florida, 13, 19, 49-50, 54, 55ff, 59, 65, 128ff, 260; French, 20
Revolutionary War, 50, 70, 73, 238
Rhea, John, activities in West Florida, 10, 11; comment on boundaries, 39
Rhode Island, senators from, 150, 250, 253
Ridgeway, Fielder, character and acts of, 161-162; letters of, 170-171; illness and drunkenness, 172
Right of deposit, 22, 27, 62, 63, 105
Rivera, Francisco, represents Kindelan, 139; occupies Fernandina, 265
Roads, 16, 17, 32, 43
Roman Catholics, in Florida, 88
Rose's Bluff, Patriots at, 75, 76, 86, 87; ceded to U. S., 84, 93

Ross, Doctor, imprisoned by British, 288
Rumanzoff, Nicholas, offers mediation, 256
Rushing, John, house of in Fernandina, 48
Russia, 116; offers mediation, 256, 295; army of, 285

Sackett's Harbor, 81
St. Augustine, Florida, 9, 13, 19, 40, 41, 45, 50, 59, 60, 88, 155, 215, 230, 238, 239, 240, 249, 258, 259, 260, 261, 265, 271, 273; defenses of, 57, 104; capture of planned, 66, 67, 68, 82, 83-84, 101-102, 138, 169, 195-213, 221; U. S. gunboats at, 106; impossible to blockade, 111, 164; Patriot camp near, 125; stalemate at, 143; siege of, 174, 179; Negroes defend, 184, 189; siege of broken, 185, 194; joy in, 193; dismay in, 224; fortress of, 252; former Patriots in, 268; people of, 270; Spanish authority in, 278, 299
St. James, Court of, 218
St. Johns Plains, 10
St. Johns River, 13, 18, 19, 30, 40, 51, 84, 87, 188, 195, 204, 233; U. S. gunboats on, 106, 127, 134; Indian warfare along, 187, 191; area and district of, 255, 265, 278; evacuation of, 259, 264
St. Marys, Georgia, 16, 40, 55, 57, 59, 74, 89, 99, 111, 259, 261, 267, 273, 283, 291; description of, 42, 267; people of, 43-45; center for revolution, 49; Mitchell in, 133, 160; citizens of act to stop trade, 215; Harris in, 270; plans to invade, 276; plundered, 287-288
St. Marys River, 8, 13, 18, 19, 30, 41, 50, 83, 84, 155, 188, 279; British on, 284, 289, 290, 295
St. Patricks, Georgia, 42
St. Pauls Church, Mathews buried at, 177
St. Petersburg, Russia, 256, 257, 295, 296
Salas, Francisco de, hotel of, 47
San Ildefonso, treaty of, 21, 24
San Lorenzo el Real, treaty of, 218
San Nicholas, 51; destroyed, 52; Patriots capture, 102
San Sebastian River, 102, 136
Sanchez, Francis, with Patriots, 269, 270, 279; remains in Florida, 302
Sands, Benjamin, joins Patriots, 65
Santage, Karl, hospital of, 47

INDEX

Santo Domingo, island of, 20
Sappho, aids Spanish, 160
Satilla River, 17, 43, 287
Savannah, Georgia, 15, 16, 17, 42, 133, 137, 259, 291; Blues, 137, 138, 169-170, 196; Volunteer Guards, 137, 138, 169-170, 196; citizens of, 148, 215; troops needed to defend, 222; martial law in, 288
Savannah Republican, editorial of, 123
Sawpit Bluff, 19
Sawpit Creek, 19
Scipio, slave of Fatio, 187
Scotland, 133, 265
Scott, William, defends Georgia against British, 276, 287, 290-291, 300
Seagrove, James, aids Mathews, 45, 55, 56, 65, 73, 74, 108
Seas, freedom of, 115, 145
Segregation, not in Fernandina, 47
Seminoles, 31, 142, 235; trade of, 42; promise neutrality, 104, 177, 179; description of, 181-182; warfare of, 185-187; fail to destroy Newnan, 207, 208; desire peace, 209, 229; expedition against, 255; prisoners, 266; Harris negotiates with, 269-270; Hawkins fears reaction of, 281, 284; policy of, 300
Senate, U. S., 21; defeats occupation bill, 149, 248, 253; McIntosh condemns action of, 301
Senators, recalcitrant, 248-253
Serurier, Louis, accepts Crillon, 117
Settlers, in Florida, 9, 46, 48, 279-282
Seventy-Six, men of, 73, 74, 126, 218, 238
Shawnee Indians, 4
Ships, British, 86, 94, 111, 112
Shipworth, Fulwar, sails for France, 28
Sibbald and Bethune, firm of, 47
Sickness, in Florida, 171, 172
Six Mile Creek, 195
"Slaughters," 18
Slaves, in Florida, 30, 46; raids, 31, 53, 275; trade and traders, 43, 47, 49, 54, 155, 158, 266, 299-300; prices of, 48-49; incited to rebellion, 155; runaway, 183; of Seminoles, 183-184; British protect, 289
Smith, Cynthia, wife of Thomas Adam, 100
Smith, George, son of Thomas Adam, 100
Smith, George William, cousin of Thomas Adam, 100
Smith, Francis, father of Thomas Adam, 99

Smith, John, raid of in Florida, 275
Smith, John, lieutenant, killed in Florida, 233
Smith, John, senator, 150
Smith-Lieb-Giles, faction of, 150
Smith, Meriwether, cousin of Thomas Adam, 100
Smith, Robert, secretary of state, 73, 150, 175; instructions of, 9; statements on Florida, 12, 29; dismissed, 37
Smith, Samuel, opposes occupation of Florida, 149, 150, 249, 250, 252
Smith, Thomas Adam, delayed in reaching Point Petre, 24; life and character, 71-72, 99-100, 208-209; assumes command at Point Petre, 80, 315; instructions to Laval, 81; agrees with and aids Mathews, 100, 107; opinion of Patriots, 103, 164; praised by Mathews, 108; position of, 113, 143, 169; forces of, 111, 233, 234, 254, 260; criticizes Madison, 122; orders to, 122, 128-129; reaction to repudiation of Mathews, 123; Spanish attack, 136-137; ordered to hold ground, 137, 212, 223; camp of, 138; answers Kindelan, 139; need for troops, 154, 222; supply line of, 159, 161; supports Massias, 163; dislikes Florida, 170, 171, 172; punishes deserters, 172-173; plans of, 186-187, 195, 211; difficulties of, 189; opinion of militia, 190, 191; retreat of, 193-194; opinion of Newnan, 197-198, 199, 208, 209; sends aid to Newnan, 203, 204; mentioned, 219, 239, 246, 267; expedition against Indians, 231; dissatisfaction of, 234; critical of medical service, 235; replaced, 235; explains release of Massias, 315
Smith, William, son of Thomas Adam, 100
Smuggling, 43, 44, 46, 49, 58, 123, 155, 158, 266, 299-300
South America, revolutions in, 10
South Carolina, 70, 218, 251, 275, 281; senators from, 150, 253
Spain, 3, 66, 71, 115, 218; king of, 10; title of to Florida, 19; cedes Louisiana to France, 21; U. S. diplomats in, 25, 26; policies of, 50-51, 56, 278, 296-298; plots against colonies of, 56, 66, 70-71; victories of in Europe, 58; control of, 61, 250; protests U. S. acts, 60-62; indebtedness to U. S., 63; guarantees to, 105; ally of Russia, 256, 257;

weakness of in Florida, 279, 298; colonial losses of, 299; cedes Florida to U. S., 301; Cortes of, see Cortes
Spanish, provinces, 1, 9, 249; rebellion, 2; U. S. occupies territory, 12; missions, 18; authority in Florida, 40, 41, 53-54; in Florida, 48, 103; American opinion of, 99, 234; offensive of, 136; Patriot opinion of, 260; veracity of, 262, 276-277; rule of restored, 265
Spanish Creek, 290
Spoliation claims, 21, 26, 105, 151, 256, 261, 307
Speculators, 9, 32
Stagecoaches, 16
Stallings, Elias, signs charges against Laval, 76-78; in Florida, 186
Stephens, Henry, wounded, 233
Stephens, William, of Georgia, 133
Stoddert, Benjamin, fort named for, 32
Sunbury, Georgia, 57
Suwannee River, 30
Swinton, Sara, wife of General McIntosh, 50-51
Swiss, in Florida, 48, 265
Switzerland, 122

Tait, Charles, favors occupation of Florida, 149, 249, 250
Talbot Island, 188
Tally, John, asked to secure food, 171
Tallyrand, French minister, 23, 26
Tampa Bay, 108, 197, 269
Tennessee, 30, 32, 100, 150, 221, 224, 237, 248; volunteers of, 225ff, 231-233, 235, 255, 259, 260; senators from, 253
Tensaw River, 33, 38
"Territory of East Florida," Mathews proposes officers for, 108; plans for, 166, 259
Texas, 35
Thomas, Phileman, forces of, 34
Three Chopped Way, 16
Tippecanoe, battle of, 115
Tombigbee River, 32
Trade, in southern Georgia, 42; of Fernandina, 46-47, 51-52, 88, 98, 105, 158; illegal, 135, 266; of Indians, 185
Traders Hill, Georgia, 42, 214, 215, 269
Treaties, of San Ildefonso, 21, 24; of 1783, 19; proposed, 92; with Lopez, 97-98; with Patriots, 104; of San Lorenzo, 218; of Ghent, 299
Troops, U. S., 32, 57, 68, 152, 254, 256, 259, 261, 273

Troup, George, senator, 7, 39; friend of Smith, 100; McIntosh writes to, 69; on repudiation of Mathews, 120; resolution of, 147
Turnbull, Andrew, colony of, 171
Twelve Mile Swamp, 192, 195
Tybee Bar, 291

Underwoods Mile, 269, 270
Union, dissolution of, 39
United States, neutrality of, 1; policies of, 2, 3, 10, 19-20, 21, 54, 62-64, 90, 115; occupies West Florida, 11, 12, 22, 37; Quasi war of, 20; fears Great Britain, 28, 289; reasons for desiring Floridas, 29ff; settlers of, 50; troops of in East Florida, 72, 79, 91, 100-101; responsibility and obligations of, 57, 83, 105, 155-156, 274, 275; claims of, 151, 249-250; failure of on Canadian front, 220; military needs in 1813, 222; acquires Floridas by treaty, 301, 304; Patriot claims against, 302-303

Van Buren, Martin, 237
Varnum, Joseph, vote of, 249
Vattel, Emerich de, definition of war, 251
Venezuela, Mathews plans to conquer, 107
Vera Cruz, Mexico, 4, 38
Vermont, Henry in, 118; senators from, 150, 253
Virginia, 4, 6, 16, 71, 99; senators from, 150, 253
Volunteers, 57, 68, 84, 85, 109, 260, 279; Georgia, 49, 54, 68, 83, 137, 194; inducements offered to, 65, 66, 105, 113, 124, 197; from U. S. Army, 74, 75, 76, 78, 79, 100; of Newnan, 187, 189; of Jackson, 224, 236, 237-247, 287; unreliability of, 190; opinion of Patriots, 198-199; Tennessee, 225-236, 240, 241, 255, 259; secured by Mathews, 313

Wagner, John P., Mathews suggests office for, 108
Walker, Freeman, attends funeral of Mathews, 177
Walker, John, theft of, 172
Wallace, John, boat of, 244
Washington, D. C., 1, 5, 58, 61, 125, 238, 244, 245, 246, 255
Washington, Georgia, 228
Washington, George, 2, 50, 52, 218
War, in Europe, 1, 2, 42; possibility of,

INDEX

1, 27, 28, 70; U. S. prepares for, 3; demands for, 115, 144-145; declared in 1812, 147; does not affect Florida, 169; aggressive, 251; last scene of, 294; Napoleonic, 299

War Department, U. S., orders of, 67, 122, 128-129, 213

War Hawks, 2, 114-115, 144, 147

Warren, John, British admiral, 221

Watermans Bluff, skirmish at, 272

Weems, Elizabeth, Ridgeway inquires about, 171

Western Hemisphere, 249

West Florida, conditions in, 3, 9, 10, 11; mentioned, 7, 31, 73; area of, 8-9; U. S. occupies, 11, 248; boundaries of, 23; U. S. claims on, 23, 29, 39, 60, 62, 63, 256ff; conditions of U. S. occupation, 33; authority to occupy, 253; U. S. retains, 298-299

West Indies, islands of, 20, 30, 249; militia from, 154

Whitaker, John, rides for aid, 203, 204

White, Henry (Enrique), governor of St. Augustine, 13, 40, 41, 47

White House, 6, 114

White, Hugh L., prominent in Tennessee, 100

White, James, of Knoxville, 100

White prostitutes, 44, 47

Wildear, finds son's scalp, 234

Wilkes County, Georgia, 99

Wilkinson, James, commands at New Orleans, 237, 238, 244; Jackson sends report to, 245

Williams, David R., senator, 115

Williams, John, marine captain, 72, 239; commands at Fernandina, 101, 159; guards wagons, 191; wounded in battle, 191, 192; dies, 193

Williams, John, of Tennessee volunteers, calls volunteers, 226; offers forces to president, 227; expedition of against Indians, 228-234; praised, 234; expenses of, 259

Williamson County, Tennessee, muster in, 239-240

Windsor, Vermont, 118

Winn, Thomas M., Jackson dines with, 244

Wolf Warrior, 209

Woodbine, George, British agent, 286, 288, 297

Woodruff, Joseph, favors Mathews, 78; serves in Florida, 139

Wykoff, William, to create revolution in West Florida, 10

Wyllys, undercover agent, 67, 314

Wyman, T. W., stationed at Picolata, 205

Yamassee War, 18

Yazoo, land frauds, 126, 133

Yonge, Philip R., Loyalist, 48, 99, 159; advises Lopez, 87; confers with Mathews, 93-94; to care for poor, 163; office of, 265

Yorktown, battle of, 5

Young, Francis, joins Patriots, 65

Yrujo, Martinez de Casa, protests of, 22, 24, 25

www.ingramcontent.com/pod-product-compliance
Lightning Source LLC
Chambersburg PA
CBHW032000220426
43664CB00005B/82